The Psychology
of
Interpersonal
Relations

NEW YORK · JOHN WILEY & SONS, INC.

London · Chapman & Hall, Limited

# The Psychology

# of

# Interpersonal

# Relations

**FRITZ HEIDER**

University of Kansas

SECOND PRINTING, SEPTEMBER, 1959

Library of Congress Catalog Card Number: 58–10801

Printed in the United States of America

# Acknowledgments

As I offer this book in its present form I want to express my gratitude to the people and groups who have helped to make its appearance possible. It is a book that has been germinating over a long period of years. Some of its basic ideas go back to my doctor's dissertation, others have worked their way into print in a number of shorter papers. The integrated approach to this work began about fifteen years ago and at first received only the time that could be given to it during summer vacations and scattered intervals, and the effort of picking up the thread absorbed some of the energies that should have gone into the work itself. As I began to realize how difficult it would be to finish it under these conditions, the question of securing a grant to give myself a longer period of uninterrupted time arose. But because it involved conceptual research rather than a project with a staff of investigators, the question of finding support was not an easy one. Nevertheless, my own feeling was that if the workers in a field do not occasionally take time to sit back and consider the meaning of the concepts they use, the work in that field will lack the direction and the depth that it might have. On this account I am especially grateful for the support I have received.

First, I want to thank the John Simon Guggenheim Memorial Foundation which twice, in 1947–48 and in 1951–52, gave me grants that enabled me to free myself for unbroken periods of time to work on the book.

*v*

Then, during the year 1956–57 the Behavioral Sciences Division of the Ford Foundation gave the help that brought the book to its present form. Their grant-in-aid supplemented my sabbatical salary from the University of Kansas and made it possible for me to devote another year to the book, and a second grant, also from the Ford Foundation, made available the aid of Dr. Beatrice A. Wright, who worked with me for fifteen months as a collaborator, helping both by criticising and reorganizing the ideas that were contained in the work as it then stood, and by rewriting large parts of it in a way that brings it much closer to the reader. I was extremely fortunate to secure the assistance of someone whose point of view was so sympathetic to that of the book and who possesses a rare combination of power in abstract thinking and psychological understanding. Without this assistance the book would not have been completed for several more years.

It is impossible to express fully my sense of obligation and gratitude to the Guggenheim Memorial Foundation and the Ford Foundation for their generous help with these grants.

In addition I want to express my thanks to the Administration of the University of Kansas, especially to Dr. John H. Nelson, Dean of the Graduate School, for continued support and encouragement, and for help with the incidental expenses of putting the manuscript into its final form. I am also grateful to the Psychology Advancement Fund of the Department of Psychology of the University of Kansas which provided for having the first draft of the manuscript dittoed in 1953 so that it could be read by colleagues here and elsewhere. Their comments did much to make me feel that it was worthwhile to go on with the work.

I am also greatly indebted to the group of colleagues in the Department of Psychology at the University of Kansas who have participated over the years in our staff seminars. These seminars have served as forums where some of the ideas of this book have been among the topics of discussion, and from which the book has greatly benefited. I would like to mention Roger G. Barker, who brought the Department into being, along with Alfred Baldwin, now at Cornell; Milton Horowitz, now at Queens College; Martin Scheerer, Anthony Smith, Erik M. Wright, and Herbert F. Wright.

I also owe a large debt to my students, both at Smith College and at the University of Kansas, who have been involved in discussions on interpersonal relations, especially to those who have gone on to research of their own in which they developed and tested some of the concept of the book. Among them are Nehemiah Jordan, Aaron Hershkowitz, and Ronald Shor.

A summer seminar under the leadership of Renato Tagiuri and supported by the Social Science Research Council was very valuable to me in giving me a wider understanding of the issues involved in the perception of persons.

A special note of thanks is due to Professor Wolfgang Köhler, who although he has not yet seen the work as it has developed, gave me the encouragement in its first stages without which it might never have taken shape as a completed book.

And, like the many who were associated with Kurt Lewin during his working years, I want to pay tribute to his stimulating influence, which has affected much of my thinking and which is still strong even in this book, although it does not derive directly from his work.

To my wife, Grace M. Heider, I owe a special word of gratitude. She gave help and advice at innumerable points in the slow growth of the manuscript and her interest in the book was a constant stimulus.

Finally, I wish to express my appreciation to the following publishers and journals who have generously granted permission to reproduce copyrighted material: Harvard University Press, McGraw-Hill Book Company, Inc., Prentice-Hall, Inc., and The American Journal of Psychology.

FRITZ HEIDER

*Lawrence, Kansas*
*April, 1958*

# Contents

# CHAPTER 1

# Introduction

IN THE CONTEXT OF THIS BOOK, the term "interpersonal relations" denotes relations between a few, usually between two, people. How one person thinks and feels about another person, how he perceives him and what he does to him, what he expects him to do or think, how he reacts to the actions of the other—these are some of the phenomena that will be treated. Our concern will be with "surface" matters, the events that occur in everyday life on a conscious level, rather than with the unconscious processes studied by psychoanalysis in "depth" psychology. These intuitively understood and "obvious" human relations can, as we shall see, be just as challenging and psychologically significant as the deeper and stranger phenomena.

The discussion will center on the *person* as the basic unit to be investigated. That is to say, the two-person group and its properties as a superindividual unit will not be the focus of attention. Of course, in dealing with the person as a member of a dyad, he cannot be described as a lone subject in an impersonal environment, but must be represented as standing in relation to and interacting with another person. Moreover, the fact that the interrelation is with another person and not an object means that the psychological world of the other person as seen by the subject must enter into the analysis. Generally, a person reacts to what he thinks the other person is perceiving, feeling, and thinking, in addition to what the other person may be doing. In other words, the presumed events inside the other person's skin usually enter as essential features of the relation.

## The Lag of Scientific Psychology

Interpersonal relations have commanded man's attention from early times and he has recorded his beliefs about the ways of people in innumerable myths, folk tales, novels, poems, plays, and popular or philosophical essays. That man is curious about human relations, that he has an affinity for such matters and is able to assimilate them, is seen in the fact that his attention is often caught by even an ordinary view of two people talking together or of one person doing something to another. Writers and popularizers have made use of this quality of human nature; the human-interest angle of stories is played up and even atoms are described as if they were people.

Though the full significance of man's relations to man may not be directly evident, the complexity of feelings and actions that can be understood at a glance is surprisingly great. It is for this reason that psychology holds a unique position among the sciences. "Intuitive" knowledge may be remarkably penetrating and can go a long way toward the understanding of human behavior, whereas in the physical sciences such common-sense knowledge is relatively primitive. If we erased all knowledge of scientific physics from our world, not only would we not have cars and television sets and atom bombs, we might even find that the ordinary person was unable to cope with the fundamental mechanical problems of pulleys and levers. On the other hand, if we removed all knowledge of scientific psychology from our world, problems in interpersonal relations might easily be coped with and solved much as before. Man would still "know" how to avoid doing something asked of him, and how to get someone to agree with him; he would still "know" when someone was angry and when someone was pleased. He could even offer sensible explanations for the "whys" of much of his behavior and feelings. In other words, the ordinary person has a great and profound understanding of himself and of other people which, though unformulated or only vaguely conceived, enables him to interact with others in more or less adaptive ways. Köhler (1940), in referring to the lack of great discoveries in psychology as compared with physics, accounts for this by the fact that "man was acquainted with practically all territories of mental life a long time before the founding of scientific psychology" (p. 3).

Paradoxically, with all this natural, intuitive, common-sense capacity to grasp human relations, the science of human relations has been one of the last to develop. Different explanations of this paradox have been suggested. One is that science would destroy the vain and pleasing illusions man has about himself (Krech and Crutchfield, 1948,

p. 6); but one might ask why people have always loved to read the pessimistic, debunking writers from Ecclesiastes to Freud. It has also been proposed that just because we know so much about people intuitively, there has been less incentive for studying them scientifically; why should one develop a theory, carry out systematic observation, or make predictions about the obvious? In any case, the field of human relations with its vast literary documentation but meager scientific treatment is in great contrast to the field of physics in which there are relatively few nonscientific books.

The study of interpersonal relations has been treated only tangentially in the field of personality and social psychology. Personality investigators have been largely concerned with the isolation of personality traits and their patterning in personality structure. Though many personality traits, for example, introversion or extroversion, imply certain characteristic behavior toward other people, the interpersonal behavior itself has not often been a focus of study.

The scientific study of interpersonal relations may be thought of as belonging to social psychology. However, social psychologists have been mainly interested in the relations between people when larger groups play a role. In these cases problems arise that are more conspicuous and of more obvious importance than those that characterize the relations between two people. What determined John's attitude to Jim has not been investigated as thoroughly as John's attitude toward a group or the attitude of the group toward John; persuading another person has been neglected in favor of propaganda directed toward a wider public; and we hear little about conflicts between two people but much about industrial or international conflict. One might ask whether a study of the relations between two people might not throw new light on group problems.

To be sure, in recent times interpersonal relations in the two- or three-person group have more and more engaged the attention of workers in different fields. H. S. Sullivan and the Neo-Freudians in clinical psychology; Mayo, Roethlisberger and Homans in industrial psychology; Cartwright, Festinger, Lippitt, and Newcomb in social psychology; Moreno and Jennings in sociometry—all these and many others treat problems belonging to the psychology of interpersonal relations.

## The Approach Used in the Present Study

This book is neither meant to provide an exhaustive survey of the literature and findings in the field of interpersonal relations, nor is it meant to be complete in the treatment of the problems selected. Its main purpose is to present some considerations that may be helpful in building a conceptual framework suitable to some of the problems in this field.

We could go about this in the Baconian way, that is, by seeking further empirical and experimental facts. We side, however, with those who think that we shall not attain a conceptual framework by collecting more experimental results. Rather, conceptual clarification is a prerequisite for efficient experimentation. Northrop presents a concrete case for this point of view by illustrating what Galilei would have done and achieved had he followed the Baconian way:

> . . . Galilei would have thrown and shot off all kinds of projectiles, carefully observing and describing what happened, gathering more and more detailed empirical information until this information added up to a generalization which was the answer. It is likely that had Galilei done this, he or his successors would still be observing, with the problem unsolved. . . . [Instead Galilei analyzed his problem by] noting the traditional assumptions which generated it. Once this was done, it became evident that his problem centered not in the projectile but in the Aristotelian definition of force, a definition which applied not merely to projectiles but to any motion whatever. (Northrop, 1947, p. 22.)

This discussion must not be construed to mean that experimentation could be dispensed with. Our point is rather that each definite advance in science requires a theoretical analysis and conceptual clarification of the problem. It is our belief that in the field of interpersonal relations we have a great deal of empirical knowledge already, and that we can arrive at systematic understanding and crucial experiments more rapidly by attempting to clarify the theory.

The task of conceptual clarification will be approached from two bases or starting points: We shall make use of the unformulated or half-formulated knowledge of interpersonal relations as it is expressed in our everyday language and experience—this source will be referred to as common-sense or naive psychology; we shall also draw upon the knowledge and insights of scientific investigation and theory in order to make possible a conceptual systematization of the phenomena under study. Such systematization is an important feature of any science and reveals relationships among highly diverse events. Lewin's field-theoretical approach known as topology (Lewin, 1936, 1938) has been in the background of much of the thinking in the present theory of interpersonal relations. Though not many of the specific concepts of topology have been taken over, they have helped in the construction of new ones with which we have tried to represent some of the basic facts of human relations.

## Common-Sense Psychology

The study of common-sense psychology is of value for the scientific understanding of interpersonal relations in two ways. First, since common-sense psychology guides our behavior toward other people, it is an essential part of the phenomena in which we are interested. In everyday life we form ideas about other people and about social situations. We interpret other people's actions and we predict what they will do under certain circumstances. Though these ideas are usually not formulated, they often function adequately. They achieve in some measure what a science is supposed to achieve: an adequate description of the subject matter which makes prediction possible. In the same way one talks about a naive physics which consists of the unformulated ways we take account of simple mechanical laws in our adapted actions, one can talk about a "naive psychology" which gives us the principles we use to build up our picture of the social environment and which guides our reactions to it. An explanation of this behavior, therefore, must deal with common-sense psychology regardless of whether its assumptions and principles prove valid under scientific scrutiny. If a person believes that the lines in his palm foretell his future, this belief must be taken into account in explaining certain of his expectations and actions.

Second, the study of common-sense psychology may be of value because of the truths it contains, notwithstanding the fact that many psychologists have mistrusted and even looked down on such unschooled understanding of human behavior. For these psychologists, what one knows intuitively, what one understands through untrained reflection, offers little—at best a superficial and chaotic view of things, at worst a distortion of psychological events. They point, for example, to the many contradictions that are to be found in this body of material, such as antithetical proverbs or contradictions in a person's interpretation of even simple events. But can a scientist accept such contradictions as proof of the worthlessness of common-sense psychology? If we were to do so, then we would also have to reject the scientific approach, for its history is fraught with contradictions among theories, and even among experimental findings. We would have to concur with Skinner who actually draws this conclusion in regard to theory-making in the psychology of learning (Skinner, 1950).

This book defends the opposite point of view, namely, that scientific psychology has a good deal to learn from common-sense psychology. In interpersonal relations, perhaps more than in any other field of knowledge, fruitful concepts and hunches for hypotheses lie dormant and unformulated in what we know intuitively.  Homans (1950) in sociology and Ryle (1949) in philosophy have also given a central place in their disciplines to everyday practice and knowledge concerning human relations.  Whitehead, writing as a philosopher, mathematician, and educator, has still further elevated the status of common-sense ideas by according to them an essential place in *all* sciences.  He has stated

> . . . science is rooted in what I have just called the whole apparatus of common sense thought.  That is the *datum* from which it starts, and to which it must recur. . . . You may polish up common sense, you may contradict it in detail, you may surprise it.  But ultimately your whole task is to satisfy it.  (Whitehead, 1929, p. 110.)

Oppenheimer, the physicist, has also stated this view with equal firmness:

> . . . all sciences arise as refinement, corrections, and adaptations of common sense.  (Oppenheimer, 1956, p. 128.)
> . . . we may well say that all ideas that occur in common sense are fair as starting points, not guaranteed to work but perfectly valid as the material of the analogies with which we start.  (p. 134)

Actually, all psychologists use common-sense ideas in their scientific thinking; but they usually do so without analyzing them and making them explicit.

It is also our belief that the insights concerning interpersonal relations embodied in fables, novels, and other literary forms, provide a fertile source of understanding.  This belief has been shared by many psychologists.  Lewin has said,

> The most complete and concrete descriptions of situations are those which writers such as Dostoevski have given us.  These descriptions have attained what the statistical characterizations have most notably lacked, namely, a picture that shows in a definite way how the different facts in an individual's environment are related to each other and to the individual himself. . . . If psychology is to make predictions about behavior, it must try to accomplish this same task by conceptual means.  (Lewin, 1936, p. 13.)

Allport (1937), too, thinks that a "still greater treasure for the psychologist lies in the world's store of drama, biographies, poetry, and fiction" (p. 60).  Of course, it is clear that the job of the psychologist does not stop with the insights of the creative writer.  Allport points out that

> The psychologist . . . has an inescapable interest in the discovery of general principles, of laws of human behavior . . . the literary writer cares primarily for the individual case, leaving to the reader the task of generalizing the insight he gains.  (Allport, 1937, p. 61.)

Though this is doubtless true for many writers, one might add that there are also a great number who are interested in revealing the laws of human nature through their characterizations. If we scan any collection of quotations we find a great many general statements concerning human behavior. Many writers would agree with Proust, who says

... it is the feeling for the general which in the future writer automatically selects what is general and can therefore enter into a work of art. For he has listened to the others only when, however mad or foolish they were, by repeating parrot-like what people of like character say, they had thereby become the prophet-birds, the spokesmen for a psychological law. (Proust, 1926, pp. 230–231.)

However, as Allport says, these generalizations are usually debatable. We cannot simply classify them and expect to get a psychology of interpersonal relations.

But if it is true that novelists are able to give descriptions of human behavior that are often more complete and concrete than those of a psychologist, we must assume that there are some valid features in these representations. Though the ultimate evidence on which we base our theories should be gained by scientific methods, we might use common-sense psychology to advantage in the development of hunches and concepts. The veil of obviousness that makes so many insights of intuitive psychology invisible to our scientific eye has to be pierced. The psychologist must first, however, translate the basic outlines of the nonscientific propositions into a language of more use to scientific investigations.

## Language as a Conceptual Tool

The fact that we are able to describe ourselves and other people in everyday language means that it embodies much of what we have called naive psychology. This language serves us well, for it has an infinite flexibility and contains a great number of general concepts that symbolize experiences with the physical and social environment. After all, it is ordinary, nonscientific language that has served as the tool for writers in their representations of human behavior. However, this instrument lacks one important feature—a systematic representation —which is ultimately required by science. Ernst Cassirer, who was greatly concerned with the way in which reality is represented in myths, art, literature, and science, writes as follows about language:

In language we find the first efforts of classification, but these are still un-coordinated. They cannot lead to a true systematization. For the symbols of language themselves have no definite systematic order. Every single linguistic term has a special "area of meaning." It is, as Gardiner says, "a beam of light, illumining first this portion and then that portion of the field within which the thing, or rather the complex concatenation of things signified by a sentence lies." But all these different beams of light do not have a common focus. They are dispersed and isolated. (Cassirer, 1944, p. 211.)

In other words, though nonscientific language in the hands of a master is unsurpassed for the description of even the most subtle relationships, it lacks the features of a real system. It is true that philology, whose purpose is to ascertain the elements and laws of language, has brought some order into the concepts that language expresses. Relations among words and phrases are indicated by etymological derivations, syntactical groupings and rules, and lists of antonyms and synonyms. But still the relations between terms are only crudely defined and understood. Though we know the meanings of words like "promise," "permit," or "pride" we do not know them in the same way we know the meaning of words like "two" and "four," or of words like "speed" and "acceleration." The words referring to interpersonal relations are like islands separated from each other by impassable channels. We do not know how to reach one from the other, we do not know whether they contain a certain number of basic principles of variation, or basic elements, different combinations of which produce the manifold of qualitative differences. These words have a tantalizing quality; they seem to present important concepts in their full meaning, and yet we cannot quite get hold of these concepts, because so much is hidden.

We can better appreciate this lack of systematic order if we confront representation by language with representation by numbers.

We cannot speak of single or isolated numbers. The essence of number is always relative, not absolute. A single number is only a single place in a general systematic order . . . Its meaning is defined by the position it occupies in the whole numerical system. . . . We conceive it as a new and powerful symbolism which, for all scientific purposes, is infinitely superior to the symbolism of speech. For what we find here are no longer detached words but terms that proceed according to one and the same fundamental plan and that, therefore, show us a clear and definite structural law. (Cassirer 1944, p. 212.)

Lewin, influenced by Cassirer in this respect, has emphasized again and again the importance of clarifying the systematic relations among the concepts used in scientific discourse. Operational definitions are not sufficient. In an operational definition, the concept is given meaning by the method used in arriving at it, as, for example, defining intelligence as that which is measured by an intelligence test. In addition, Lewin proposes that a "method of construction" should be used,

> which has been first developed in mathematics itself. To consider qualitatively different geometrical entities (such as, circle, ellipse, parabola) as the product of a certain combination of certain "elements of construction" (such as, points and movements) has since the time of the Greeks been the secret of this method . . . It is able, at the same time, to link and to separate; it does not minimize qualitative differences and still lays open their relation to general quantitative variables. Cassirer (1910) shows how the same method proved to be fruitful in empirical sciences where the "elements of construction" are mathematically described empirical entities (such as, forces, ions, atoms). (Lewin, 1944, pp. 5–6.)

Though the words of conventional language do not reveal their interrelations, this does not mean that there are none. It will be our task to make them manifest through a conceptual analysis. In doing so, we have to be aware of Skinner's warning:

> The important objection to the vernacular in the description of behavior is that many of its terms imply conceptual schemes. I do not mean that a science of behavior is to dispense with a conceptual scheme but that it must not take over without careful consideration the schemes which underly popular speech. The vernacular is clumsy and obese; its terms overlap each other, draw unnecessary or unreal distinction, and are far from being the most convenient in dealing with the data. (Skinner, 1938, p. 7.)

One can agree with Skinner that an uncritical use of the concepts of the vernacular is not advantageous, and still be of the opinion that psychology can learn a great deal from a critical analysis of these concepts and the underlying conceptual schemes.

This, then, will be the purpose of this book: to offer suggestions for the construction of a language that will allow us to represent, if not all, at least a great number of interpersonal relations, discriminated by conventional language in such a way that their place in a general system will become clearer. This task will require identifying and defining some of the underlying concepts and their patterns of combination that characterize interpersonal relations.

We shall find that drawing upon the knowledge and concepts of psychological science will help sharpen and relate these common-sense concepts to each other. Carnap (1953) has referred to this task of redefining old concepts as the problem of *explication;* he points out that making more exact a concept that is used "in a more or less vague way either in every-day language or in an earlier stage of scientific language" is often important in the development of science and mathematics (p. 438).

We do not pretend that the scientific language that we gained in this way is as systematic as the language of physics and mathematics or, in psychology, as the language of topology or of some of the stimulus-response theorists. But we do believe that it is broader and more flexible than these other psychological languages, and at the same time, in spite of its crudeness, sufficiently exact to permit analysis of a wide variety of commonly experienced human interactions, an analysis which will at the same time "link and separate" them.

On the following pages we shall give two examples of this explication of common-sense concepts, one concerning the meaning of words, and one concerning the meaning of situations.

## Word Analysis

For reasons already discussed, our search for concepts crucial to the understanding of interpersonal relations will begin with common-sense psychology as expressed by everyday language. The words of the vernacular, to say nothing of combinations of words in sentences and longer units, present such an endless variety of concepts that it is hopeless to study the nature of interpersonal relations by simply classifying them. By careful analysis of language expressions, however, we can attempt to arrive at concepts that will enable us to clarify the implicit relations among words referring to psychological phenomena.

Let us illustrate this thesis by an example of word explication. Consider the following words: *give, take, receive,* and *keep.* Grammar has prescribed one relationship—they are all transitive verbs, words that refer to some action. A thesaurus of antonyms may note that *take, receive,* and *keep* are all opposites of *give.* The dictionary, calling upon such disciplines as etymology and semantics, records their qualitative meaning. But in spite of all this information, their relationships to each other remain quite obscure. Examine the simplest definitions of these terms:

Give—to hand over to another
Take—to gain possession of by putting forth exertion
Receive—to get as a result of delivery
Keep—to retain in one's possession

These words have something to do with the transaction of property. But explicitly what are their interlocking relationships? Just how is it, for example, that *take, receive,* and *keep* are all antonyms of *give* without being equivalent to each other? The following chart records the essential underlying concepts that bring these common-sense concepts into an ordered, systematic relationship. These basic concepts

## Patterning of Concepts Underlying
### *Give, Take, Receive, Keep*

| Common Sense Concept | Causal Source of Action | Direction of Action (Movement of $x$) |
|---|---|---|
| $p$ gives $x$ to $o$ | $p$ | $p \rightarrow o$ |
| $p$ takes $x$ from $o$ | $p$ | $p \leftarrow o$ |
| $p$ receives $x$ from $o$ | $o$ | $p \leftarrow o$ |
| $p$ keeps $x$ from $o$ | $p$ | no movement |

$p$ = reference person; $o$ = other person; $x$ = a thing

are: (1) Reference person, i.e., the person who is the subject of the verb considered. He is designated as $p$, and the other person as $o$. (2) Source of action. (3) Direction of the movement of a thing from one region of ownership to another.

The following systematic statements emerge from an examination of the chart: (1) We notice immediately that the four terms are distinguishable by the different combinations of the basic concepts. No two patterns are alike. (2) *Take* is the opposite of *give* in regard to the direction of movement of $x$. With *take* the direction is from $o$ to $p$, and with *give* it is from $p$ to $o$. (3) The same statements hold for the connections between *receive* and *give*. In addition, the source of action in *receive* and *give* differ: In the former, $o$ is the source. In the latter, $p$ is the source. (4) *Keep* is an opposite of *give* because with *give* there is a movement of $x$ away from $p$ and with *keep* no movement occurs.

The system also allows us to construct other combinations that are missing from the chart. For instance, we might think of a case in which $x$ is kept by $p$ through $o$'s efforts. Again, as with "$p$ keeps $x$ from $o$," there is no movement of $x$, and $p$ owns $x$; but the source, in this case, lies in $o$, not in $p$.

This analytical procedure encompasses a variety of interpersonal relations in yet another way. There are some kinds of human interaction that may fit the system as far as it goes, but require the addition of other basic concepts for their precise delimitation. For example, the pattern of *to take from* may also be seen to apply to the concept *to steal from*. In order to distinguish these two everyday concepts, it becomes necessary to introduce a fourth underlying concept, that of *ought*. To steal expresses an ethical violation, whereas to take from need not. Now the horizons extend still further and we can begin to search for everyday ideas that fit the patterns of four underlying concepts in combination. Such transactional concepts as *lend, borrow, barter, lose, beg, relinquish,* and *find*, can be placed within the framework. By dropping out one or another of the underlying concepts and by adding others as the analysis proceeds, it gradually becomes possible to incorporate a wide variety of human relations within the system of underlying concepts.

Note the steps that were involved in this type of analysis: We began with four words that had a vague relationship to each other. They were antonyms and had to do with the transaction of property. We then searched for basic underlying concepts that could represent these interpersonal relations. The patterning of these constitutive elements suggested other interpersonal relations that could be systematically represented by them. In turn, some of these new interpersonal relations required additional underlying concepts for their adequate representation. And so the basic underlying concepts may be gradually uncovered and a host of interpersonal relations conveyed by their combinations.

Ryle's book *The concept of mind* (1949) contains many similar analyses of the concepts of naive psychology and we will be able to refer to it in more than one place. However, his discussion, though it contains many stimulating ideas of great value, is not always immediately applicable to the work of the psychologist. In contrast to the present approach, he is mainly concerned with the actual meaning of words in ordinary usage with all their ambiguities, whereas our main purpose is to make explicit the system of concepts that underlies interpersonal behavior, and the analysis of words and situations is considered only a means to this end. We want to find a reality that lies beyond this rough sketch language gives us, and are not so much concerned with the sketch as such.

## Situation Analysis

In addition to word explication as a method of discovering underlying concepts, one may use conceptual analysis of descriptions of social situations narrated in stories, plays, and novels. Let us begin with the fable of the fox and the crow:

A fox once saw a crow fly off with a piece of cheese in its beak and settle on a branch of a tree. "That's for me, as I am a Fox," said Master Renard, and he walked up to the foot of the tree. "Good-day, Mistress Crow," he cried. "How well you are looking today; how glossy your feathers; how bright your eye. I feel sure your voice must surpass that of other birds, just as your figure does; let me hear but one song from you that I may greet you as the Queen of Birds." The Crow lifted up her head and began to caw her best, but the moment she opened her mouth the piece of cheese fell to the ground, only to be snapped up by Master Fox. "That will do," said he. "That was all I wanted. In exchange for your cheese I will give you a piece of advice for the future—Do not trust flatterers."

Let us analyze the significant parts of this fable one by one:

A fox once saw a crow fly off with a piece of cheese in its beak and settle on the branch of a tree. "That's for me," said Master Renard, and he walked up to the foot of the tree.

The important underlying concepts are:

Perceiving—this refers to the fact that events in the outside world have entered the awareness of the fox.

Belong to—the cheese is seen as belonging to the crow.

Want—the fox wants the cheese.

Cause—this refers to the source of a change. Here the fox cannot cause or bring about climbing the tree.

Can—the fox cannot get the cheese directly.

In terms of our abstracted concepts, the story thus far means: The fox sees something that belongs to someone else, and that he wants, but that he cannot have because he cannot execute the necessary locomotions.

"Good-day, Mistress Crow," he cried. "How well you are looking today; how glossy your feathers; how bright your eye . . . let me hear but one song from you that I may greet you as the Queen of Birds."

In the following statements, the concepts that have already appeared are italicized. The fox believes that flattery, which he *can cause*, will *cause* the bird to trust him and to *want* to show off, which in turn will *cause* the bird to *want* to sing. This will *cause* the crow to open his beak, which will *cause* the cheese to belong no longer to the crow. The fox *can* then *cause* the cheese to *belong* to him. A new concept which enters is that of:

Sentiment—that the fox likes and admires the crow is the substance of the belief he wishes, through flattery, to impart to the crow.

Here we shall not take time to analyze such concepts as flattery, trust, and showing off into their constitutive elements, but merely wish to point out that the kind of flattery the fox uses in this case is quite different from the more usual kind designed to incur favor from another. The fox did not believe that the crow would wish to bestow a favor upon him, but he did expect the crow to be flattered into displaying her wonderful self. The meaning of opening the beak, therefore was very different for the two. To the crow, opening the beak was required by the physical mechanisms of vocalization, and releasing the cheese was not even in her awareness. To the fox, on the other hand, the song was completely incidental to the release of the cheese.

The Crow lifted up her head and began to caw her best, but the moment she opened her mouth the piece of cheese fell to the ground, only to be snapped up by Master Fox.

The events ensue as planned.

"That will do," said he. "That was all I wanted. In exchange for your cheese I will give you a piece of advice for the future—Do not trust flatterers."

This is retribution: you gave me something good and so I'll give you something good.

In this analysis of the old story of the fox and the crow, we have not specified all the concepts important to its meaning. Our purpose, as with the preceding word analysis, was to show how the concepts of naive psychology may be fashioned into a language of underlying concepts that coordinates a great number of ordinary human relations in a systematic way. Many varied kinds of human interactions can then be pinned down. Because their conceptual definitions have become more explicit, questions that are more precise, and we believe more sensible, can be raised for experimental investigation.

This book does not claim to present a complete program for describing interpersonal relations in terms of underlying concepts. But it should serve as the beginning of such a task and will include an attempt to clarify some of the basic concepts that are most frequently encountered in an analysis of naive descriptions of behavior.

It would be an impossible task to describe in detail how these concepts were arrived at. Long years of analyses of word meanings of short stories or daily experiences contributed to the belief in the fruitfulness of working with them. The attitude that underlay these analyses was a feeling that there is a system hidden in our thinking about interpersonal relations, and that this system can be uncovered.

When Lewin developed topological psychology, I had at first great hopes that it would furnish the tools for the representation and analysis of interpersonal phenomena. However, though the concepts of topology were of great help in disentangling the underlying means-end structures in the actions of a person, they were rather cumbersome and in many cases inadequate in dealing with two-person situations. It is difficult or impossible to describe in topological terms how one person's life space is represented in another person's life space—how, for instance, the sentiment of $A$ can be a goal for $B$, or how $A$ reacts to what $B$ does to him. I once discussed with Lewin attempts to analyze social situations and pointed out some examples that were difficult to represent in topological terms. He recognized the difficulties, and it is illuminating that the last sentence of his treatise on forces reads as follows:

An adequate treatment of social problems, especially social conflicts, however, makes certain distinctions necessary, particularly that between "own" and "foreign" forces, which we have merely mentioned. (Lewin, 1938, p. 210.)

In groping for a language that would allow the representation of a great variety of social interactions there was developed this list of basic concepts which seemed to occur again and again in the analyses and which could not be reduced further to expressions of still greater generality.

A sort of shorthand description of social situations was arrived at in which these concepts played the role of a word list of basic English. This symbolic representation uses some of the features of symbolic logic without pretending to be as exact and systematic. It was employed a great deal in the actual analyses and was of great help because it forces one to think in general terms. A brief description of it is given in the Appendix. It did not seem wise to burden the text of the book with these expressions, which are rather difficult to read for one who is not used to them.

In the following section we shall describe the basic concepts briefly. Further specification, through whatever knowledge can be brought to bear on them from naive and scientific psychology, will be given in the succeeding chapters.

## The Underlying Concepts

**Subjective environment or life space.** According to naive psychology, both ourselves and other people have an awareness of the environment and the events in it. This awareness is what is referred to as the subjective environment of a person, or life space. In a general way, the expression "he thinks thus and so" is used to state the conscious contents of the life space, which consists of different kinds of relations characterizing people, objects, and events. Examples of contents of life space are: spatial relations, as when the person believes that the gas station is on the northeast corner of Main Street; functional relations, as when the person recognizes that a gas station is for servicing cars; and evaluations, as when the person thinks that the attendant is dishonest.

**Perceiving.** Perceiving is experienced as a direct contact with the environment; it is a means whereby objective facts enter the life space.

That is why we react in a special way when we notice someone observing our behavior. He has obtained certain information through perceiving and may now act on it. A fact can also enter a life space by way of language transmission, as when we read something or when somebody tells us something. Then there is the process of inference through which we arrive at conclusions on the basis of the existing contents of the life space.

**Suffering, experiencing, or being affected by.** Man, as we know, is affected by events in his environment. He is the recipient of acts of others and of impersonal presses. This is expressed to some extent by the passive form of verbs as in "I am hit," "He is pushed." The most important characteristics of events that affect us are, first whether or not they are positive, pleasant, and satisfying, and second their causal sources.

**Causing.** Of great importance for our picture of the social environment is the attribution of events to causal sources. It makes a real difference, for example, whether a person discovers that the stick that struck him fell from a rotting tree or was hurled by an enemy. Attribution in terms of impersonal and personal causes, and with the latter, in terms of intent, are everyday occurrences that determine much of our understanding of and reaction to our surroundings. An additional fact of importance is that personal causation not only effects changes in the physical environment, as when a man winds his watch; it also has social implications. Thus, "benefiting" means that a person has caused a change that is agreeable or positive to another person. Also, one person can cause another person to cause a change by asking him to do something, or commanding him, etc.

**Can.** A fundamental concept that is linked with causation, and that refers in some way to the possibility of the change or action being performed by a specific person, may be expressed in the most general way by the auxiliary verb "can." Whether a person can do something or not is a very important consideration which affects our attitude toward him and our predictions of his future behavior. The concepts of power and ability are related to this concept.

**Trying.** A second fundamental concept related to causation is that of trying to cause a change. When we notice someone trying very hard but not succeeding it implies several things: First, that the person does not really cause the change; second, that the person is doing something more than just wishing to cause the change; and finally, that the situation represents something different from being able to cause the change but not trying.

**Wanting.** Want is also connected with causation in the sense that when one wants something, one wants to bring about a certain state of affairs. Motivational factors in ourselves and others are often spontaneously recognized. For example, by observing the behavior of another person or by listening to what he says and how he says it, we discover that he wants to do something but cannot do it, or does not dare to do it. Or we discover that the change he produced in the environment is exactly what he wanted to bring about; he intended it.

**Sentiments.** The positive or negative valuation attached to persons and objects, namely our sentiments toward them, enormously influence our behavior. When we observe or sense that person $A$ likes or dislikes person $B$, we also sense that $B$ plays a certain role in $A$'s life space; the representation of $B$ in $A$'s life space has a certain functional significance. Of special importance is the awareness we have of the positive or negative character of the representation of ourselves in another person's life space.

**Belonging.** Another concept that also plays an important role in the so-called perception of forms or movement is the concept of belonging. This concept is applied when separate entities are seen to form a unit. Things can "belong" to people either as property or in some other sense, as, for instance, when one talks of one's alma mater. Two people can belong together because they are related, or because they are similar in some respect, for instance, in their likes or dislikes.

**Ought and may.** Finally, that a person ought or ought not to do something can also be a very vivid and direct experience. The relations of "ought" to "can" and "want" will be treated later. The meaning of "he may do it" is really based on the negation of the "ought" concept and is equivalent to: "it is not true, that he ought not do it."

To sum up: According to naive psychology people have an awareness of their surroundings and the events in it (the *life space*), they attain this awareness through *perception* and other processes, they are *affected* by their personal and impersonal environment, they *cause* changes in the environment, they are able to (*can*) and *try* to cause these changes, they have wishes (*want*) and *sentiments,* they stand in unit relations to other entities (*belonging*), and they are accountable according to certain standards (*ought*). All these characteristics determine what role the other person plays in our own life space and how we react to him.

Some of these concepts might rate as "dimensions." Just as color, form, space, or motion are basic components of a more peripherally oriented perception, these concepts are the basic components, or some of the basic components, of our direct experiences of the social environment.

This cursory survey is meant only to present a preliminary approach to an analysis of basic components of our naive ideas about other people and social situations. These fundamental concepts give rise to intriguing problems as one tries to understand the conditions and effects of the psychological phenomena they represent. They will be discussed in the following order:

| Concept | Chapter |
|---------|---------|
| Life space | 2 |
| Perceiving | 2, 3 |
| Causing | 4, 9, 10 |
| Can | 4 |
| Trying | 4 |
| Wanting | 5 |
| Suffering | 6, 11 |
| Sentiments | 7 |
| Belonging | 7 |
| Ought | 8 |

It may be useful to describe briefly the contents of the chapters that follow.

Chapter 2. This chapter deals with the problem of how *p*, the person whose psychological processes form the topic of the discussion, perceives *o*, the other person; how *p* experiences this perceptual contact with *o*, and how it is made possible by the mediation between person and environment, i.e., the processes that furnish the cues for perception.

Chapter 3. In this chapter the discussion of "naive" psychology begins with a study of the implicit theory of perception. The common-sense ideas about the conditions and effects of perception are analyzed. It is necessary to understand these ideas if we are to understand how we perceive that *o* perceives something, or how we go about making *o* perceive something.

Chapter 4. This chapter deals with the naive psychology of action, with the effects of action and with its conditions in the person and in the environment. The factors of ability, exertion, and environmental difficulty are described. They play an important role in our assessment of *o*'s actions and in our attempts to influence them.

Chapter 5. This chapter contains an exploration of the naive psychology of motivation and affect. Our ideas about the connection between desire, pleasure, and success are considered, and the question of the source of positive and negative experiences is studied. The purpose of these considerations is to find clues to the relevant variables that determine under what circumstances we perceive, or believe we perceive, that *o* wants or enjoys something, and that decide what means we choose when we try to produce or prevent *o*'s wishes and pleasures.

Chapter 6. The subject under discussion is what happens to the person undergoing or suffering the effect of environmental changes, and in what way these events are interpreted by the person.

Chapter 7. This chapter deals with how one person feels about another person—how *o* is represented in the life space of *p*—and especially the positive or negative character of this representation, that is, *p*'s liking or disliking *o*; it also considers the problem of how this liking or disliking is influenced by things or other persons to which *o* is related in some way, or which in some way belong to him.

Chapter 8. Questions of the role of values and norms in interpersonal relations are approached—how we come to feel that another person ought to do something, and what effects this feeling has.

Chapters 9 and 10. Specific actions that are of great importance for interpersonal relations are considered. Systematically, they belong with Chapter 4; however, it was decided to put them here since it is helpful in dealing with these problems if we first become familiar with the concepts discussed in Chapters 5 through 8. In Chapter 9 the actions of inducing *o* to do something and the ways in which *o* reacts to such impositions are studied. In Chapter 10 the actions by which *p* causes *o* to undergo positive or negative experiences are examined; the relations of benefiting or harming another person to ability, sentiments, ought, etc., are touched upon. Also, the problem of retribution is dealt with as one of the reactions to being benefited or harmed by another person.

Chapter 11. The reactions to the positive or negative experiences of another person, like sympathy or envy, are studied in their relation to other factors.

Chapter 12. A short review of the contents of the book.

# CHAPTER 2

# Perceiving the
# other person

THROUGH PERCEPTION we come to cognize the
world around us, a world made up of things and people and events.
Obviously, the existence of the other person, $o$, as an object with not
only physical and spatial particulars, but also with complex psychological properties, must be mediated in some way to the subject, that is
perceived by $p$, if $o$ is to feature in $p$'s thinking, feelings, and actions.
Likewise, if $p$ is to influence $o$, he must create changes that in some
way can be perceived by $o$, barring, of course, internal reactions such
as those instigated by drugs that affect $o$. The nature of this perception, in particular the principles that underly the coordination between
the stimulus conditions outside the person and his experience or phenomenal representation of them, is the topic to which we shall address
ourselves here.

Bruner and Tagiuri, to whom we can refer for a discerning integration of representative studies concerning the perception of people, have
grouped the studies into three categories: the recognition of emotions
in others, the accuracy of appraisals of other personalities, and the
process by which personality impressions are formed. They conclude
that the current trend in research

... appears to be in the direction of investigating what kinds of organized
impressions are formed under varying conditions of cue, role, set, and prior
information. There appears to be a deemphasis of interest in the nature of
judgmental accuracy, and a renewed emphasis in the judging process. ...
(Bruner and Tagiuri, 1954, p. 648.)

Our orientation is directed toward explicating some of the naive, implicit principles that underlie perception, principles that connect the stimulus configurations presented to the person with his apprehension of them. During the course of this explication, we shall leave the realm of naive psychology and make use of knowledge gained from the scientific, causal analysis of the perceptual process. Moreover, because many of the principles underlying social perception have parallels in the field of nonsocial or thing perception, and because in many instances their significance has first been recognized in this field, we shall frequently have recourse to knowledge about the perception of things. We shall speak of "thing perception" or "nonsocial perception" when we mean the perception of inanimate objects, and of "person perception" or "social perception" when we mean the perception of another person. The term "object perception" which has been traditionally used in discussions of the perception of things is avoided in this chapter, since the word "object" is also used in its more general sense—"the object of perception" or "the distal object"—which includes persons as well as things. Brunswik's (1934) conclusion, that the objects of social and nonsocial perception are similar in regard to their formal characteristics as well as in regard to the processes by which they are perceived, is in general a valid framework for discussion (p. 211).

This is not to say, of course, that there are no differences between the perception of things and people. It is a commonplace that inanimate objects differ from persons in important ways. In discussing thing perception, we assume that there are real, solid objects with properties of shape and color, things placed in particular positions in real space, having functional properties making them fit or interfere with our purposes, and in general defining their place in the space of means-end relations. There is a chair on which one can sit; there is an object with which one can cut paper, tie a package, or write a note.

In discussing person perception, we also assume that these "objects" have color and occupy certain positions in the environment. They are, however, rarely mere manipulanda; rather they are usually perceived as action centers and as such can do something to us. They can benefit or harm us intentionally, and we can benefit or harm them. Persons have abilities, wishes and sentiments; they can act purposefully, and can perceive or watch us. They are systems having an awareness of their surroundings and their conduct refers to this environment, an environment that sometimes includes ourselves. And yet, just as the contents of the nonsocial environment are interrelated by certain lawful connections, causal or otherwise, which define what can or will happen, we assume that there are connections of a similar character between the contents of the social environment.

At the outset we should like to distinguish two roles of perception in interpersonal relations.  In the first, the concern of this chapter, the emphasis is on the conditions that lead $p$ to perceive his environment and the people in it as he does.  In the second, the topic of the following chapter, $p$'s attention is directed toward $o$ as a perceiver; there the main problems concern the conditions that lead $p$ to realize that $o$ is perceiving something, the effects of $o$'s perceptions on himself as understood by $p$, and how all this affects $p$'s feelings and behavior.  One might say the first role deals with perceiving the other person, whereas the second deals with the other person as perceiver.

## Phenomenal and Causal Description in Perception

By phenomenal description is meant the nature of the contact between the person and his environment as directly experienced by the person. By causal description is meant the analysis of the underlying conditions that give rise to perceptual experience.  There is no a priori reason why the causal description should be the same as the phenomenal description, though, of course, the former should adequately account for the latter.  We shall see, however, that though there are differences between the two, the parallels are marked.

It has often been stressed, especially by phenomenologists, that the person feels that he is in direct contact with things and persons in his environment.  He sees objects directly, just by focusing his eyes upon them.  He acts on objects directly by touching them and lifting them. The same is true of person perception.  He not only perceives people as having certain spatial and physical properties, but also can grasp even such intangibles as their wishes, needs, and emotions by some form of immediate apprehension.  Asch has made the point that the

. . . attitude, which has been aptly described as naive realism, . . . sees no problem in the fact of perception or knowledge of the surroundings.  Things are what they appear to be; they have just the qualities that they reveal to sight and touch.  The surroundings open themselves to us directly and almost without deviation, as if we were face to face with objective reality. (Asch, 1952, p. 46.)

Duncker, who describes the direct presence of the objects of perception as "participation," has urged that the phenomenal "self-givenness" of the object must be recognized as an important characteristic of perception:

Seeing has the phenomenal characteristics of "*being open to*," more generally, of "*participating in*."  "I see the tree" is equivalent to: "I participate (in a definite manner) in the tree"; or, "The tree is given to me in a definite manner." . . . We must not fail to mention the phenomenal *self-givenness* of the object in which I participate by seeing. The tree appears "in person," not by any chance "as image." (Duncker, 1947, 506–507.)

For Scheler (1913, trans. 1954, Part III) the immediate awareness of other people's minds is of central importance. Asch presents a vivid description of the experience of direct contact with other people's thoughts, wishes, and emotions:

To naive experience the fact of being "in touch with" other persons is most direct and unmediated by intervening events. We experience direct communication with others: emotion clashing with emotion, desire meeting desire, thought speaking to thought. Often there is virtually no lag between the psychological event in one person and its grasp in the other. We may even anticipate the thought and feelings of those we know, and it would appear that we are as directly connected with others as with our own psychological processes. It seems sufficient for the actions and purposes of others to be there to make them visible and comprehensible; the process appears entirely translucent. (Asch, 1952, p. 142.)

In contrast to phenomenal description is the causal analysis which, instead of revealing the person as being in direct contact with the objects of perception, distinguishes a number of steps. A somewhat technical vocabulary has been built up to describe these steps. According to causal analysis, the perceptual process may be conceived of as a perceptual arc (Brunswik, 1952) encompassing two end points—the object, i.e., the part of the environment toward which perception is directed; and the percept, i.e., the way the object appears to us. The former has been referred to by Brunswik (1952) as the *initial focus* inasmuch as it is the starting point of the perceptual arc. It has also been referred to as the *distal stimulus* since it pertains to something "outside the person's skin," at a distance from the person. It is the chair "out there" that is seen or the melody coming from the violin that is heard. Whatever its designation, it refers to the environmental reality, an objective stimulus defined by properties perceivable by everyone.

The distal stimulus, however, does not directly affect the person. Rather it is mediated, for example, by light or sound-wave patterns that excite his sensory organs. This stimulus pattern, impinging as it does directly upon the sense organs, has been designated the *proximal stimulus;* it is the stimulus that is physically in direct proximity to the person. With touch or taste the object must come in direct contact with the sensory receptors, and the starting point of the perceptual process is the proximal rather than the distal stimulus; nonetheless the distinction between the two is still meaningful inasmuch as the sensory quality is attributed to the distal object—the object as separate from the person. Should the sensory quality be "looked at" for itself, stripped of its object reference, as when the taste of cool water is savored, or when one basks in the warmth of sunlight, or feels the texture of silkiness, then the proximal stimuli appear in the life space as sensation.

The perceptual process thus far involves distal stimuli, and mediation ending in the proximal stimuli. Within the organism there is, then, the constructive process of perception which leads to some event corresponding to the awareness of the object, the reality as perceived. The terms, *representation* or *image* of the object have been used to describe this awareness. It has also been referred to as the percept, the phenomena, and the terminal focus, the latter pointing to the fact that it is the end point of the perceptual arc, completing its function of providing an awareness of the "environmental reality." The constructive part of the perceptual process within the person is sometimes spoken of as involving central or higher phenomena, processes, or layers, whereas the proximal stimuli entering the organism, the so-called raw material, involve more peripheral or lower layers. The proximal stimuli, being unorganized and uninterpreted are also described as being more superficial.

With person perception, causal analysis also divides the phenomenally given immediate presence of the other person into steps. The other person, with his psychological processes such as needs and intentions, functions as the distal stimulus. He is the "object" toward which $p$'s perception is directed. The mediation consists of the manifestations of the personality of the other, as they determine the proximal stimulus pattern. Often the manifestations of $o$'s inner psychological processes are behavioral though they may be data gained from other sources, such as verbal communication from a third person. Finally, there is the perceptual construction within the person that leads from this raw material to the awareness of the other.

However, the process does not proceed in a one-way fashion from peripheral to central excitation. There is an interaction between the central processes in the brain and the more peripheral data, the "raw material" from the outside, so that the former determine, in some cases more, in some cases less, how the raw material is organized. What is of primary importance is that the central processes provide the "terms" in which the lower layers are interpreted, making it possible, for instance, for a movement to be perceived as a personal action. Often only the contents of the higher levels are directly present, and the lower levels—the raw material of peripheral data—are either not given at all, or are already in terms of the higher levels.

Other features of the phenomenal and causal description of perception will be discussed later. But here we wish to stress that the two descriptions should not be confused. The different analytic parts of the perceptual process are not always apparent in direct experience. We usually do not perceive any of the mediating processes, for instance, nor do we see images. Rather, the distal objects are given to us directly. We see them through the mediation, as it were. In spite of these differences, however, further considerations make us realize that the disparity between the phenomenal and causal descriptions is not as complete as it seems at first.

For one thing, the mediation does not always completely disappear phenomenally in the service of presenting the object. When we see the object through the mediation, not only what we see may be given, but also the cues upon which our perception rests. For comparative purposes, let us first note instances in which the mediation is clearly not a phenomenal fact. Though the pattern of visual stimuli informs us about the shape, color, location, and size of an object, phenomenally we do not know what the raw material is on the basis of which we learn of these important properties. We just see them, and to identify the raw material is often a problem for science. When, however, our concern is with the function or causal possibilities of objects, then we often do become aware of the perceptual cues which mediate this information.

Many visual properties, for example, imply certain causal possibilities. The location tells me how to move in order to put my hand on the object. The shape tells me something about the way the object would interact mechanically with other solid bodies. A spherical object can be rolled around; if I put it on the table it might roll off. I will be able to put that object into this box because of their size relations, etc. The visual pattern can also give me an idea about the pliability of the object because of the common-sense fact that the shape of an object is determined by its support according to its flexibility. That we see certain objects as pliable cannot always be explained by the fact that we have experienced them as such in the past; the point of Dali's well-known picture of watches is that objects we know from experience to be solid present a visual pattern of pliability. Another example in which the mediation is clearly accessible to the person's awareness is that of reading. The terminal focus or the meaning of what is read rarely appears without our being able to say on what raw materials it is based. We see the words and sentences, and we can even pay attention to the figural properties of the letters. The same is true when we "see" the direction of the wind from the movement of a flag, or when we see an object by way of its shadow.

In social perception, too, there are some instances in which the mediating factors are very obscure, and others in which we are or can become quite cognizant of the cues for the perception of *o*. For instance, we may see that a person is displeased, without being able to say just what about his appearance or behavior gave us that impression. This very often is true when the cues involve the interpretation of physiognomies, gestures, the tone of voice, and similar expressive features. They often mediate personality traits, wishes, or attitudes of persons without our being able to say what the material is upon which we base our perceptions. On the other hand, there are many occasions when we can quite precisely elucidate the mediating conditions for our perceptions of other people. Often the raw material consists of actions and reactions of the person that can be perceived in their own right and can be separated from the terminal focus. We can say, "I believe he is displeased because he said so and so or did thus and thus." Throughout this book, our attention will be drawn to just this problem, namely the conditions that permit us to become aware of such distal objects as the perceptions, intentions, desires, pleasures, abilities, and sentiments of another person.

Perhaps in cases in which the raw material and the percept are so clearly separated, the more inconclusive term "cognition" might be preferred to "perception." The problem of defining perception, especially as it differs from cognition, has bothered psychologists over the years. Floyd Allport has presented a trenchant statement of the issues involved:

As a first approximation, let us say that it [perception] has something to do with our awareness of the objects or conditions about us. It is dependent to a large extent upon the impressions these objects make upon our senses. It is the way things look to us, or the way they sound, feel, taste, or smell. But perception also involves, to some degree, an understanding awareness, a "meaning" or a "recognition" of these objects. . . . Thus we can include all the senses and can interpret perception as covering the awareness of complex environmental situations as well as of single objects. Though some psychologists tend to assign this last consideration to cognition rather than to perception the two processes are so closely intertwined that it would scarcely be feasible, especially from the standpoint of theory, to consider one of them in isolation from the other. (F. H. Allport, 1955, p. 14.)

In line with Allport's position, it seems that the distinction between perception and cognition is currently being drawn less and less sharply, doubtless because there are so many gradual transitions between the extreme cases of the most direct and immediate forms of perception on the one hand and the most indirect interpretations on the other. That the extremes and the degrees within them can all be handled in terms of the same concepts is perhaps even more important in the obliteration of the distinction. In ordinary discourse one is likely to speak of inference or diagnosis rather than of perception when the construction of the percept on the basis of the raw material is itself given to awareness; yet upon analysis, a data pattern may be found in both rational inference and direct perception which is used in the construction of the apparent reality.

The similarities between perception and inference are stressed, for instance, by Brunswik, Nuttin, and Helmholtz, though to be sure, these men are also aware of the differences. Brunswik describes his view of perception as a "ratiomorphic" model, at the same time cautioning that ratiomorphism is

not to be confused with rationalism or with intellectualism . . . it even helps us to nail down more concretely the rather important secondary differences between "perception" and "thinking." (Brunswik, 1956, p. 141.)

Nuttin (1955) reminds us that the fact that consciousness is an exposure of the self to the outside world "does not contradict the theory of perception as a selective and constructive process" (p. 351). In short, for purposes of understanding the perceptual process, we agree at least partly with Brunswik (1934) that it does not very much matter "whether a part of the mediation goes on in awareness or whether the whole process is in the preconsciousness" (p. 211). For our purposes, then, we shall designate by the term perception all the different ways we have of getting to know the environment, from direct perception to explicit inference.

Summarizing, we can say that in many cases of both thing and person perception the raw material remains phenomenally unidentifiable, the only fact that appears ready-made in our life space being the percept, the end product of the organizing process. In other cases the raw material is phenomenally given, or at least can become so as we concentrate on the "visual field" instead of the "visual world," to use Gibson's (1950) expression. It is then that the whole process of perception seems more visible, more spread out for our inspection. It is probably fair to say that the less one depends on direct visual properties such as size and shape, and the more on events or behavior, the more the mediation becomes accessible to awareness.

## Coordination Between Distal Object and Percept

**Constancy phenomena.** In perception, the percepts (or impressions or representations) of the environment largely furnish an adequate picture of the surroundings. That is to say, there is a high degree of coordination between the percept and the distal object. According to a phenomenal description of naive psychology this is to be expected, for if the person is in direct contact with his environment, a true correspondence is naturally expected.

But the causal analyst quickly realizes that the object as perceived is not equal to the stimuli that are actually in direct contact with the person, namely the proximal stimuli mediated, for example, by light waves. Thus, even though the light waves from the surface of a table form varying patterns on my retina depending on my position with respect to the table—sometimes a trapezoid, sometimes a parallelogram, sometimes a large retinal image, sometimes a tiny one—I still perceive the table as rectangular and do quite well at approximating its size. Or, even though the stimuli on the retina are affected by illumination, the color of an object appears surprisingly little influenced. In other words, perception of the object remains fairly constant in spite of the enormous variation in the proximal stimuli which mediate it through the excitation of sensory organs. This phenomenon is referred to as the problem of perceptual constancy. It should be noted, however, that constancy does not hold completely.

The term constancy phenomenon is usually applied to the perception of color, brightness, size, and shape, but it is also applicable in the social perception of such crucial distal stimuli as wishes, needs, beliefs, abilities, affects, and personality traits. If we assert that a "wish constancy" is possible just as there is a size, shape, or color constancy, that means we recognize a wish as being the same in spite of its being mediated by different cues. The same wish may be conveyed, for example, by an innumerable variety of word combinations, ranging from "I want that" to the lengthy and complicated reflections transmitted to the therapist in a psychoanalytic session. Or, the same wish may be conveyed by a colorful array of actions, as when a child, wanting a red wagon above all else, goes up and takes it, pushes a competing child from it, and even angrily kicks it in a fit of frustration. Brunswik's generalization of constancy phenomena to person perception holds:

Indeed we can, exactly as in thing perception, talk of a "constancy" of the apparent personality in the variety of its actions. This is the case, for instance, if we, in spite of changing conditions—the instigations from the environment—, always perceive the same personality in another person, in spite of the fact that he produces in each case different behavior, which corresponds to the reaction laws of his personality, and which stands merely in the same relation to the conditions. (Brunswik, 1934, p. 217.)

It is just because manifestations (the mediation) of personal characteristics are vicarious that, as pointed out by Hammond, it is often difficult for the clinician to indicate with confidence exactly what the evidence is on which his judgment is based:

> Observers of the state of anger may agree that such a state exists (i.e., high reliability may be achieved), *but* they may not be able to communicate the basis for their decision. . . . (Hammond, 1955, p. 257.) The clinician is attempting to discover the patient's motive. The patient substitutes one form of behavior for another as he attempts to achieve his goal (equifinality). The clinician perceives these behaviors, as they substitute for one another, as cues which also substitute for one another (equipotentiality). Because of vicarious functioning, then, the clinician is hard-pressed to point at, to communicate, the basis for a decision. . . . *Vicarious functioning, then, lies at the heart of the private, quasi-rational nature of the clinical decision.* (Hammond, 1955, p. 258.)

Thus, again we see that the interaction between the person and his environment, in this case between a person and someone he is observing, can best be described as going on between two foci separated by the mediation which can, to some extent, be neglected in the description. Later we shall examine the conditions that impede veridical perception, but in a first approach we will assume that the significant features of the other person (distal objects) are more or less invariantly connected with the perception of them, while neither object nor phenomenon show invariant relations to the mediation.

Probably the constancy in social perception, however, is less perfect than the constancy in thing perception. It is not easy to decide this matter since we do not have simple methods to define psychological processes objectively. We are able to measure the actual size of an object and correlate the perceived size with it much more easily than we can measure the actual strength of a wish and its perceived strength. Nevertheless, it is very likely that the correlation between the distal stimulus in social perception and the impression of it is much greater than the correlation between either of these foci and the mediation. Therefore, we can say of the phenomenal and causal descriptions of perception, that both recognize the correlation between the foci, but the latter is also cognizant of the relatively chaotic mediation.

***Coordination with dispositional properties.*** A further point, closely related to the constancy phenomenon, also concerns the comparison between the way we experience the environment and the way a causal analysis presents it: The parts or characteristics of the environment that are directly given phenomenally and towards which perception (or action) is directed, are those parts that either themselves show an invariance (i.e., do not change very much in their properties), or which, when they change, change mostly in ways that follow macroscopically visible laws. Such properties have been referred to as *dispositional properties* and are discussed more fully in Chapter 4, which deals with the naive analysis of action. Here we should like to emphasize that the object as we perceive it is not coupled with just any arbitrarily selected part of the environment; rather it is coupled with such properties as shape, color, and size, properties that are relatively invariant features of the object and show consistent relations with other events. The shape of a solid object, for instance, is relatively enduring. It is something one can rely upon finding again. It is connected with important and lasting possibilities of the object. It allows us to predict to a certain degree how the object will behave when we handle it; for instance, if I see an object is spherical, I predict it can be rolled. This prediction is possible because shape is connected in an invariant way with a possible event, namely all spherical solid objects can be rolled. It is because these intrinsically invariant properties belong so often to distant objects, that is, objects separated in space from the person, that distal perception plays such an important role in interaction with the environment.

It is interesting that in social perception, also, the direct impressions we form of another person, even if they are not correct, refer to dispositional characteristics. At least, relative to the events that mediate these impressions, the characteristics show a high degree of intrinsic invariance. For instance, the impression that a person is friendly, which may be conveyed in any number of ways, points to a relatively enduring characteristic of the person. In fact, any personality trait refers to something that characterizes the person, that is, holds over time in spite of irregularities of circumstance and behavior. As a dispositional property, a personality characteristic enables one to grasp an unlimited variety of behavioral manifestations by a single concept, e.g., friendliness. A description of a manifold of interpersonal relations becomes far more systematically simple by reference to such enduring characteristics. Furthermore, insofar as personal dispositions are connected in lawful ways with other features, predictions about behavior of the other person become possible. Just as one can predict the rolling behavior of the ball because its spherical shape is a persisting property, so one can predict (albeit with less confidence) that $o$ will help $p$ because of his friendly nature, an enduring personality trait.

Two kinds of invariant relations that characterize the coordination between the distal object and the percept may now be distinguished. As we have just seen, the percept is coordinated to dispositional properties of environmental contents, properties that show invariant relations with possible events and are in themselves relatively enduring. Then there are the constancies, the more or less invariant relations between the percept and the distal object in spite of variability of the mediation. Boring has called attention to these two kinds of invariant relations. Using size as an example, he refers to the first as the invariance of physical size, and to the second as the invariance of perceptual size:

> Objects do not shrink or expand as you move them around, and neither do our perceptions of them when you have those conditions . . . under which size-constancy occurs. We have under these circumstances, the correlation of two similar invariancies, the invariance for physical size and for perceptual size. . . . (Boring, 1952, p. 145.)

***Psychological dispositional properties in social perception.*** The dispositional properties that are the important distal stimuli in social perception frequently refer to psychological or mental entities, to concepts that are not defined in a physical sense. The preceding example of friendliness is a case in point. Without the aid of such psychological, dispositional properties, the behavior of persons mediated by the proximal stimuli would remain largely unintelligible.

Experimentally, this has been demonstrated by the use of a film in which, physically speaking, only an enclosure with a moveable part in the upper right-hand corner plus the movements of three geometrical figures are seen (Heider and Simmel, 1944). A still of this film is presented in Fig. 1. As long as the pattern of events shown in the film is perceived in terms of movements as such, it presents a chaos of juxtaposed items. When, however, the geometrical figures assume

*Figure 1. Geometrical figures in apparent behavior (Heider and Simmel, 1944, p. 244).*

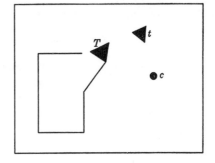

personal characteristics so that their movements are perceived in terms of motives and sentiments, a unified structure appears:

... the movements are organized in terms of acts of persons. It is obvious that this organization has many advantages from the point of view of ... the adaptation of the organism to the environment. The changes, when identified with a constant figural unit, no longer follow each other in an arbitrary and unconnected way. They are connected with invariable characteristics of the environment, they are meaningfully embedded in our picture of reality ... the interpretation of movements is intimately connected with the interpretation of invariancies. ...

A description of movements in terms of motives again taps environmental layers of greater invariancy. Just as the successive perspective views of a landscape seen through the window of a moving train can only be "resolved," or made to yield a meaningful unit, by reference to distant objects laid out in space, so acts of persons have to be viewed in terms of motives in order that the succession of changes becomes a connected sequence. (Heider and Simmel, 1944, pp. 256–258.)

But motives and sentiments are psychological entities. They cannot be measured by a ruler, weighed by a scale, nor examined by a light meter. They are "mentalistic concepts," so-called intervening variables that bring order into the array of behavior mediating them.

Another example is given by Hebb's highly relevant analysis of the unrewarding efforts of scientists to be "objective" by attending only to the physical or space-time descriptions of animal behavior:

A thoroughgoing attempt to avoid anthropomorphic description in the study of temperament was made over a two-year period at the Yerkes Laboratories. . . . All that resulted was an almost endless series of specific acts in which no order or meaning could be found. On the other hand, by the use of frankly anthropomorphic concepts of emotion and attitude one could quickly and easily describe the peculiarities of the individual animals, and with this information a newcomer to the staff could handle the animals as he could not safely otherwise. Whatever the anthropomorphic terminology may seem to imply about conscious states in the chimpanzee, it provides an *intelligible and practical guide to behavior.* The objective categorization therefore missed something in the behavior of the chimpanzee that the ill-defined categories of emotion and the like did not—some order, or relationship between isolated acts that is essential to comprehension of the behavior. (Hebb, 1946, p. 88.)

For social perception on the human level, the uses of "mental" dispositional concepts in the understanding and even description of interactions between persons are legion. Let us suppose that person *A* likes person *B* and that he wants to do him a favor. He takes into account *B*'s wishes, and also what *B* can do: perhaps there is something *B* desires very much but cannot get by himself. *A* also has to consider the possibility that the benefit might embarrass *B*, or that *B* might feel that it implies a lack of respect. Finally, *A*, deciding on a particular action, goes through with it. *B* is overjoyed. He concludes that *A*, about whose attitudes he had been in doubt, really likes him; he appreciates especially the tactful way in which *A* handled the matter.

Descriptions of this kind seem to capture the essential features of an interpersonal event. One might go even further and try to discover the reasons why *A* likes *B*, or why *B* was questioning *A*'s sentiments; or one might try to assess the personality characteristics that played a role in this event. Though the description as it stands does not go far back into the history of the relation between *A* and *B*, nor into deep psychological motivations, within its limits it is a meaningful episode.

If we examine the concepts that are used in making this episode intelligible, we find sentiments, wishes, abilities, and emotions. The particular behavioral data on which the judgments or perceptions of the other person's wishes, abilities, or traits are based are not mentioned. One may even feel that the description of the essential interpersonal process would not gain very much in exactitude if they were specified. Neither would a more detailed report of *A*'s particular actions change very much our understanding of the main features of the event. The particular action by which *A* benefited *B* is of importance only insofar as it is judged by *B* and is related by him to his self-evaluation. To be sure, we might describe the event by concentrating on the surface, on the overt behavior, on what can be seen from the outside. But even then the reader would certainly translate the overt syndromes into concepts very much like the ones used in the description given above. These concepts provide the nodal points in terms of which the event can be described most economically, which allow for extrapolation to other possible events and which allow for prediction.

Social perception in general can best be described as a process between the center of one person and the center of another person, from life space to life space. When *A* observes *B*'s behavior, he "reads" it in terms of psychological entities (and his reactions, being guided by his own sentiments, expectations, and wishes, can again be understood only in terms of psychological concepts). *A*, through psychological processes in himself, perceives psychological processes in *B*. Asch has clearly expounded this view in the following:

The paramount fact about human interactions is that they are happenings that are *psychologically represented* in *each* of the participants. In our relation to an object, perceiving, thinking, and feeling take place on one side, whereas in relations between persons these processes take place on both sides and in dependence upon one another. . . . We interact with each other not as the paramecium does by altering the surrounding medium chemically, nor as the ants do by smell, but via emotions and thoughts that are capable of taking into account the emotions and thoughts of others. (Asch, 1952, p. 142.)

One might say psychological processes such as motives, intentions, sentiments, etc., are the core processes which manifest themselves in overt behavior and expression in many variable ways. The manifestations are then directly grasped by $p$, the observer, in terms of these psychological core processes; they would otherwise remain undecipherable. By looking through the mediation, $p$ perceives the distal object, the psychological entities that bring consistency and meaning to the behavior; $p$'s reaction is then to this meaning, not to the overt behavior directly, and this reaction is then carried back by the mediation to $o$, etc.

Of course, such an analysis of the separate processes involved in perceiving the other person has ignored the usual interplay between $p$ and $o$ in which $p$'s perception of $o$ are constantly modified by what he believes are $o$'s perceptions of $p$ and of other matters. This interdependent give and take in interpersonal relations is nicely described by Merleau-Ponty. The topic, the nature of conversation, is a propos since it implies the cognition on the part of $p$ of $o$'s thoughts, wishes, intentions, etc:

In the experience of a conversation, a common ground constitutes itself between the other one and myself, my thought and his make up a single tissue, my words and his are called out by the phase of the discussion, they insert themselves in a common operation of which neither one of us is the sole creator. A double being comes about, and neither is the other one for me a simple behavior in my transcendental field, nor am I that for him, we are, one for the other, collaborators in a perfect reciprocity, our perspectives glide one into the other, we coexist within the same world. (Merleau-Ponty, 1945, p. 407.)

As a beginning, however, a simplified analysis in which the interpersonal relation is divided into steps, such as the behavior of $o$, the reaction of $p$ to $o$, then the reaction of $o$ to the reaction of $p$, etc., allows the detection of important perceptual processes, though we must bear in mind that these processes arise within one encompassing situation. Thus far, our stepwise analysis has brought out that the perceptual process in person perception goes on essentially between two core regions, the persons $p$ and $o$, and that they are separated by a mediation that causally has a function different from that of the core regions. Generally $p$'s perceptions of $o$ are coordinated to psychological dispositional properties of *o*, and not to the cues mediating those properties. True enough, the perception of *o* in these terms must have been mediated by some characteristics of overt behavior or by some features of the situation, but it seems that the interpretation of behavior in terms of "mentalistic" or psychological concepts often enhances understanding and prediction.

However, though the main process of social perception goes on between person and person spanning the mediation, and though often a first over-all description can catch the essentials without considering the mediation, we also want to know how the mediation carries the process. After all, the perceiving person gets information about the environment only through the proximal stimuli. This, then, poses the important problem of relating the proximal stimuli to two end points (the foci of the perceptual arc), namely the contents of the environment on the one hand and the phenomena, the way these contents appear to us, on the other. Only then will we also be able to explain cases in which one person misunderstands another, or in which an action (a primary medium for the transmission of psychological characteristics) does not correspond to the intention of the agent.

In later chapters we shall attempt to analyze the mediating processes of such psychological referents as intention, ability, and desire, by making explicit the raw material upon which the perceptual construction takes place. Here we should like to explore further certain general principles that aid the person in utilizing the ambiguous mediation in the service of veridical perception.

## The Mediation

It has already been pointed out that the contents of the environment toward which perception is directed, be they things or persons, are mediated to the person by vicarious manifestations. Other terms such as "manifold of offshoots" or "event patterns" can also be used to refer to this mediation. Though the mediation is vicarious, in order to give information about the environmental contents (the distal stimuli of perception) it must to some degree be coordinated to them. Our job now is to define certain of the principles of this coordination.

**Its grammatical structure.** The simplest model for the coordination of mediation to distal stimuli would be one in which a specific offshoot is coordinated to each content or property. The organism would then only have to learn the specific connections between offshoots and contents. He would, so to speak, have to memorize a vocabulary of mediation consisting only of nouns. If the organism perceived one of the offshoots, he would react to it as if he were

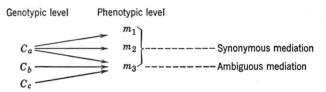

**Figure 2.**  *Ambiguous  and  synonymous  mediation.*

perceiving the content, the offshoot being an unambiguous sign of
the content.  This would be the case, if, for example, a raised eyebrow
were the necessary and sufficient indication that *o* was dubious.

However, the language of nature is more complicated.  It offers
its contents to us not merely through patterns comparable to univocal
nouns but also through patterns that are in some way analogous to
ambiguous words and synonyms, or to adjectives and verbs, and which
even contain something of a grammatical structure.  A parallel to
ambiguous messages is seen when an offshoot is coordinated to two
or more different contents.  Then, of course, the manifestation taken
by itself can be a sign of any one of these contents.  In Fig. 2 $m_3$ is
represented as an ambiguous mediation, since it can be caused by
$C_a$, $C_b$, or $C_c$.  The mediation language is analogous to synonyms
when two or more offshoots are coordinated to the same content, any
one of them then being a sign of the content.  In Fig. 2 $m_1$, $m_2$, and $m_3$,
equivalently or synonymously reflect cause $C_a$.  Thus, the coordination
between the layer of mediation events and the layer of contents toward
which perception is directed is not a simple one.

Tolman and Brunswik in discussing the ambiguity and synonymity
of mediation events point out that though the presence of more or
less constant causal couplings in the environment leads the organism to
accept one event as a representative for another event, the organism
also adjusts to the fact

. . . that such causal connections are probably always to some degree
*equivocal.* . . . Types of local representatives are, that is, not connected in
simple one-one, *univocal* . . . fashion, with the types of entities represented.
Any one type of local representative is found to be causally connected with
differing frequencies with more than one kind of entity represented and
vice-versa. (Tolman and Brunswik, 1935, p. 44.)

Science in general has had to deal with the problems presented by
the fact that observable manifestations or data refer to one level of
discourse, whereas the conditions underlying the manifestations refer

to another, namely the level of concepts, or, to use a more technical term, the level of constructs. The terms "phenotype" and "genotype" respectively have been employed to distinguish these levels. As stressed by Lewin (1935b, p. 11) their coordination is complicated. The distinction is easily exemplified in the biological field from which the term originated. The same phenotype, that of brown eye color, for instance, may be similar in appearance only, for with one person offspring with blue eyes may occur and with another this is precluded. Genotypically, that is, there is a difference. In Fig. 2, $m_3$ represents the phenotype that may be genotypically differentiated according to whether the dynamic properties stem from $C_a$, or $C_b$, or $C_c$. Likewise, as pointed out by Frenkel-Brunswik, the distinction between overt behavior and underlying motivational tendencies

. . . is necessitated by the facts that one and the same phenomenon [behavior as observed] may have different kinds of "causes," and one and the same "cause" may lead to a diversity of phenomena, depending on other conditions. A statement about a phenotype (e.g. a behavioral technique) does not permit unequivocal conclusions about the genotype (e.g., motivation) and vice versa. (Frenkel-Brunswik, 1942, pp. 127–128.)

Figure 2 may again be used to represent the distinction between overt behavior (the phenotypic $m$'s) and underlying motives or other causes (the genotypic $C$'s), that is, between perceptual appearance and dynamic properties.

**Embeddedness.** Carrying the analogy of grammatical structure further, we can say that, just as ambiguous words become more specifically defined when they are placed in sentences that give them a contextual setting the ambiguity of mediation events is reduced when the stimuli or manifestations referring to the distal stimulus are *embedded* in the total situation. In discussions of embeddedness, the term "local stimulus" is sometimes used to refer to a part of the stimulus pattern as distinct from the total stimulus which includes the surroundings as well. The distinction between local and total stimulus is consistent with that between local and total relevance discussed in connection with benefit and harm (cf. p. 253).

The term embeddedness refers to the fact that in many cases the appearance of the local stimulus is determined, or at least co-determined, by its environment—the setting in which it appears, the stimuli which surround it. To use the phrasing of Krech and Crutchfield:

The perceptual and cognitive properties of a substructure are determined in large measure by the properties of the structure of which it is a part. (Krech and Crutchfield, 1948, p. 94.)

Embeddedness may be applied to the part of the perceptual arc belonging to the organism, that is, to the relation between the proximal stimuli and the percept. In regard to this part of the perceptual arc, Koffka has remarked that

. . . no local stimulation can determine the corresponding excitation by itself . . . but only in connection with the totality of stimulation. . . . Only when we know the kind of organization in which a local process occurs can we predict what it will be like. . . . (Koffka, 1935, p. 97.)

But embeddedness has its counterpart in the environmental section, that part including the distal and proximal stimuli. Thus,

. . . to the statement "the meaning of a sensation is determined by the whole in which it is placed" corresponds another statement which refers to the physical environment: "an offshoot can be caused by different core events, and usually only a manifold of offshoots is coordinated univocally to the core." (Heider, 1930, p. 378.)

Since the local proximal stimulus, not being uniquely coordinated to a certain distal stimulus, is ambiguous, its meaning in a concrete case will be determined by the surrounding stimuli. Only the surrounding can determine to which content of several possible ones the local stimulus refers in the specific case (Heider, 1926, pp. 152 ff.). It therefore becomes necessary, in the words of Koffka,

. . . to replace laws of local correspondence . . . by laws of a much more comprehensive correspondence between the total perceptual field and the total stimulation. (Koffka, 1935, p. 97.)

Numerous examples demonstrating the influence of the surrounding on the appearance of a part have been published, especially in visual perception. We remind the reader of the picture of the three men who are of equal size on paper, but who appear to be of different size because the surrounding lines suggest a long hallway in which the men stand at different distances from the observer. Even in a scientific description of the causally relevant direction of a motion we usually have to consider additional data and not merely the concrete movement as such. (Heider, 1939, p. 385; Brunswik, 1955, p. 194.)

Very often in social perception, what a person says and does provide important cues for such distal properties as motivations, intentions, abilities, etc. But this raw material is also not univocally coordinated to these important properties of the person. Corresponding to the surrounding in thing perception is the situation in social perception, with the consequence that the ambiguity of behavior as a local stimulus is reduced when it is seen in a situational context. As Brunswik has said:

. . . for the perception . . . of the other person behavior alone does not suffice as stimulus, also the conditions of this behavior have to be a stimulus for the perceiver. (Brunswik, 1934, p. 213.)

The total stimulus contributing to adequate cognition may or may not be presented by a single incident, or exposure. In the picture of the three men phenomenally varying in size, the necessary information is perceived at a glance, the total stimulus field being given all at once. Sometimes, however, the total stimulus field relevant for adequate cognition requires extension in time so that a sequence of events can occur. For instance, I often have to watch the object taking part in events, interacting with other objects, or I have to handle it to perceive its causal possibilities. I may have to bend a wire in order to cognize its pliability, or to scratch a stone to cognize its hardness. In examining a machine I may move some parts to see with what other parts they are connected, and in testing a car I must at least drive it. Then the causal possibilities are mediated to me through *events*. As we have seen, however, a look at the static object often tells us much about the way it would perform.

It is probably fair to say that the stimulus fields basic for person perception are usually *more extended in time* than those relevant to thing perception. Let us assume that we enter an unfamiliar room for the first time, and that in it we find a few people we have never met before. A glance around the room will suffice to get an approximately correct idea of the shape of the room and of the objects in it. We shall be much more insecure in our judgments of the people. We may get a global first impression of them but we do not perceive the relevant properties of the social situation as quickly. We do not know whether $A$ likes or dislikes $B$, whether $C$ intends to thwart $D$, and so on. Many more data, a much wider manifold of stimuli, are needed to give us this information. We have to get acquainted with these people. We have to interact with them and observe how they interact with each other. We might say that person perception will be like reduction screen vision (familiar in experiments on color constancy) if we exclude the perception of events and actions. Although we believe that we get to know something about a person from the shape of his face, or even the color of his hair, these physiognomic properties are far outweighed by his actions as cues to his personality. In most cases we cognize a person's traits, and especially his wishes, sentiments, or intentions from what he does and says, and we know considerably less when we are limited to what we can see of him as a static object.

That the meaning of even relatively simple personal acts often requires data provided by a wide stimulus field extended in time, has been demonstrated in the experiment with the film mentioned on p. 31 (Heider and Simmel, 1944) in which geometrical figures seem to behave as persons (see Fig. 2). There are three such figures in the picture: a large triangle $T$, a small triangle $t$, and a circle or disk $c$. There is also an outline rectangle with a moveable part which is typically seen as a one-room house with a door. During the film, the figures move in contact with this "door." In itself, this movement is ambiguous; it can mean that the figure pushes the door, or it can mean that the door pushes the figure. The local stimulus, this movement alone, does not give any information about the origin of the movement. Nevertheless, the figures are always seen as pushing the door!

The reason for the fact that $T$, $t$ or $c$, rather than the door, is always seen as origin must lie in the larger field in which the local event door-actor-movement is embedded. The door never moves of itself, *i.e.* without another moving unit in contact with it. $T$, $t$ and $c$ continually move around by themselves. These units are therefore described as "persons," as potential origins of movement. If the door had been shown in other parts of the picture as moving independently, and $T$ (for instance) as never moving alone, then a combined movement of the door and $T$ would be ascribed to the door as origin, the door would push $T$.

The interesting question of why $T$ is seen in one of the scenes as chasing $t$ and $c$ rather than as following them is also resolved by the fact that the meaning of a local stimulus is affected by the surrounding data:

The film order is as follows: $T$, $t$, and $c$ move together, but not in contact with each other, twice around the house. $T$ moves behind $t$ and $c$. We can safely say that the reason for this uniform interpretation of $T$ as the origin [of the movement, i.e., as chasing rather than following] lies in the interpretation of the previous parts of the picture. The event "$T$ chases $t$ and $c$" is coordinated to two facts; $T$ is stronger than $t$ and $c$, and there is an antagonism between $T$ and the pair $t$ and $c$. These two features are contained in almost all interpretations of the . . . picture. Therefore, the event has to be interpreted as "$T$ chases $t$ and $c$" if it is to conform to what has happened before. (Heider and Simmel, 1944, p. 254.)

Throughout this volume we shall examine different interpersonal relations in which single events or acts are ambiguous and in which only further information, often coming from the surrounding stimuli, help to specify their meaning. But now we shall explore some features of the total stimulus field that contribute to adequate perception.

***Stimulus configurations.*** At first glance it seems difficult to arrive at scientific generalizations concerning the stimulus field mediating perception, for if we have to consider the total field in order to achieve good coordination between distal stimulus and percept, the task seems complex indeed.

One possibility of reducing the infinite variety of total stimulus fields is to focus on stimulus patterns or arrangements that can be geometrically or figurally defined, and that then can be coordinated to the percept. One type of stimulus pattern has been suggested by Koffka (1935) in his proposition that "the qualities of perceived objects depend upon *gradients* of stimulation" (p. 248). Gibson (1950), to whom we owe many studies and interesting theoretical discussions in the field of perception, makes a similar point with his concept of "ordinal stimulation," a concept referring to the "*simultaneous* variation over the set of receptors, or a differential excitation of different receptors, and the order of such a variation" resulting from a stimulus (p. 63). "Ordinal" simply connotes order or succession. Gibson describes, for instance, the ordinal stimuli that give rise to the impression of depth.

Though a fair amount of work has been done in investigating stimulus patterns as cues in thing perception, little has been done in regard to social perception. Gibson stresses this lack when he asks:

> How do we perceive, for instance, that one person is being kind to another, bearing in mind that we do this with some accuracy? How do we perceive the intentions and abilities of a political candidate, taking it for granted that he does not fool *all* of us all the time? In other words, what do we discriminate and identify in these complex stimulus-situations which, when conditions are favorable, yields a correct perception? This ought to be the primary line of inquiry, but instead it is almost completely neglected. (Gibson, 1951, pp. 95–96.)

Some significant laboratory research, however, has been carried out on spatial patterns responsible for physiognomic perception. The experiments utilized schematized, facial drawings whose spatial arrangements could be clearly defined. Brunswik reports that variation of

> . . . "mouth" elicits the most extreme responses, high mouth (chin) appearing as gay and young, low chin as sad, old, and bad. . . . Wide eyes and short nose exert influences somewhat similar to those of high mouth even though to a lesser extent. The longest noses are unfavorable throughout. (Brunswik, 1956, p. 105.)

Similar experiments by Hochberg (1956), using profile faces instead of en face, dealt with spatial cues producing the impression of "cuteness." Cline (1956), extending the visual patterns to include pairs of faces in social interaction, found that certain psychological properties of the faces appear to inhere in the drawings independently of their perceived social matrix, while others are clearly a function of the nature of the interaction. For instance, the face labeled "Smiling" for purposes of identification was never reported as "Frowning" or "Glum," but always characteristically deriving pleasure of some sort, no matter with what other face it was having commerce. On the other hand, when paired with the Glum face, Smiling is perceived as a taunting bully, but when paired with the Frowning face this vicious gloating is displaced by pleasure in being friendly and helping.

There is good reason to believe that often, in person perception, changing stimulus patterns, rather than static ones, are necessary for the univocal coordination between stimuli and percepts. This has already been implied by the previous discussion in which the significance of events over time as part of the total stimulus field was stressed. There is yet another reason, advanced by Köhler (1929), Koffka (1935), and others, that has to do with the fact that inner states, particularly emotions, are dynamic, their very nature involving development and change. If we assume that such temporal sequences are mapped in overt behavior, then stimulus patterns with corresponding temporal changes are necessary in order to apprehend the feelings or emotions of *o* correctly. Köhler has vividly expressed this idea, pointing out that

. . . the inner processes . . . show types of development which may be given names, usually applied to musical events, such as: *crescendo* and *diminuendo, accelerando* and *ritardando.* As these qualities occur in the world of acoustical experiences, they are found in the visual world too, and so they can express *similar* dynamical traits of inner life in directly observable activity. (Köhler, 1929, p. 248.)

That temporal gradients of inner experience are isomorphically reflected in overt behavior has also been proposed by Koffka:

If an emotional stress steers action, then the ensuing movements will, to some extent, mirror the emotions; characteristics of overt behavior will map characteristics of the field in which this behavior is started. The slow dragging movements of the depressed, the jerky, discontinuous movements of the irritable, correspond indeed to the leaden state of depression or the disrupted state of irritability. (Koffka, 1935, p. 658.)

A great wealth of observations concerning the way in which the dynamics of inner states is mapped in the temporal sequences of overt behavior has been recorded by Klages (1942). According to Klages, the eighteenth century writer, J. J. Engel, was one of the first to call attention to these relations. Following is a translation of a quotation from Engel:

When a man develops his ideas easily and without obstruction, his gait is free and fast; . . . when the succession of ideas is beset with difficulties, the gait is more slow and impeded; when suddenly a serious doubt arises, it will be completely interrupted and the man will stand still; when he wavers between different ideas, his gait will be disorderly and uneven. . . . (Engel, 1785, p. 125.)

If it is assumed that overt behavior maps inner states to a certain degree then the fact that psychological processes often have reference to objects in the environment leads us to a further specification of the stimulus pattern mediating those psychological processes: the stimulus pattern may include overt behavior *in relation* to the surrounding environment. Michotte has remarked that

. . . emotion toward a thing, animal, or person establishes some form of liaison between the object and the subject whom it affects. Emotion is a modification of the subject *in regard to* these objects. (Michotte, 1950, p. 123.)

It is understandable, therefore, that ". . . the motor reactions of men and animals, *when related in certain ways with other objects,* are of great importance as *expressive behavior*" (p. 122; cf. also Buijtendijk and Plessner, 1925, p. 80; also Asch, 1952, pp. 150 ff.). Even the direction of a glance may provide a strong hint as to what the person is thinking, feeling, and wishing.

During his investigations of phenomenal causality, Michotte (1946, 1950) observed that certain combinations of visual stimuli, usually movements of two dots, produced impressions of one object chasing another, fleeing from another, attacking, etc. The production of such phenomena is dependent upon a dynamic pattern of stimulation, or ordinal stimuli to use Gibson's term, involving the approach and withdrawal of one object *in regard to another in its environment.* The Heider-Simmel movie previously described (p. 31) can also be drawn upon for a clarification of specific subject-environment relations significant in the cognition of "aggressive and angry hitting." $T$ refers to the big triangle, $t$ to the little triangle:

The stimulus consists of coordinated movements of $T$ and $t$. $T$ rapidly approaches $t$ until it comes into contact with it. Then $T$ stands still while, at the moment of contact, $t$ starts moving in the direction of $T$'s previous movement. S has the strong impression of a transfer of kinetic energy from $T$ to $t$. $T$'s movement is clearly the cause and $t$'s movement ("reeling back under the impact of $T$'s blows") is the effect. (Heider and Simmel, 1944, p. 253.)

Visual patterns representing behavioral withdrawal, as pointed out by Michotte (1950), are also seen in such segregative relationships as antipathy or disgust; stimulus patterns of approach are pictured in integrative relationships—sympathy or friendship, for instance.

Thus, there is no doubt that correlations between geometrically defined features of the ordinal stimuli and impressions in social perception can also be found. The discussion thus far has dealt with such features as gradients, static and dynamic relations of the stimulus pattern, and patterns in which behavior is related to the environment. However, even if we were to pursue the attempt to discover further distinguishable space-time configurations of the mediating stimuli, it is unlikely that we would arrive at such infallible coordinations that we could say: whenever this ordinal stimulus is given a certain impression will be produced. To be sure, as we have seen, such unique coordinations are approached when one extends the stimulus pattern in time so that the local stimulus, being embedded in additional data, loses some of its ambiguity.

It is well to remember that even the gradients that have been so carefully isolated and analyzed by Gibson (1950) do not always produce the same visual experiences. Consider the perspective gradient represented by converging contours. An object may have converging sides, like a gable or a ladder, or poles may be stacked in a pyramid, but whether the impression of depth will be produced depends on embeddedness in the environment. Brunswik (1955), after investigating the "ecological validity" of stimulus patterns that give the impression of depth, concludes that "it is easily seen that not even the so-called primary depth cues, such as binocular disparity, are foolproof in our ecology" (pp. 199-200). Nevertheless, it is certainly true that the coordination between these gradients and the impression of depth is highly, if not completely, univocal.

But in social perception, the influence of additional data that resist geometrical definition is often essential, and it seems that the most fruitful way to treat the process of perception is to assume stages that intervene between the proximal stimulus and the percept. This would lead to the notion of a hierarchical process, in which the proximal stimulus gives rise to more peripheral meanings, which in turn play the role of data for the higher levels of construction.

## Constructive Processes Within the Observer

**Meanings as data.** Let us begin with the "chasing versus following" problem presented earlier (Heider and Simmel, 1944). In the film two geometrical figures are moving in the same direction, one a short distance behind the other. In this case the ordinal stimulus can be seen as $T$ chasing $t$ or $T$ following $t$.

What are the conditions that determine whether chasing or following will be seen? Knowing that information from the environment must be mediated to the person through proximal stimuli, we first search for spatial-temporal properties of the mediation which distinguish those ordinal stimuli that produce the impression of chasing from those that do not. But our search keeps ending in blind alleys. No matter how much we attempt to take into account ever more inclusive stimulus patterns, we cannot find definite *spatial-temporal* features that are univocally related to the phenomena in mind. This of course does not imply that we have to give up looking for figural relations in the stimulus pattern that produce a particular impression. But it does suggest that the proximal stimulus pattern as geometrically defined, even in its widest sense of the local proximal stimulus plus its surroundings, is not sufficient to account for perception, that nonspatial-temporal conditions, namely, meanings as data, are part and parcel of the perceptual process.

The plausibility of this hypothesis can be shown in countless ways. In the case of the ambiguous stimuli pointing either to chasing or following, the more or less unequivocal impression of $T$ chasing $t$ is produced if the observer considers $T$ the more powerful person (Heider and Simmel, 1944, p. 255). Conversely, if $T$ is seen as inferior, the impression will be that $T$ is following $t$. But this bit of "surrounding data," the information concerning $T$'s power, is a condition lying in the sphere of meaning. It does not refer to a particular arrangement of stimuli. It can be produced by any number of previous perceptions. For instance, $T$ may have been seen to win in a fight with $t$, or both may have been seen to interact with a third person. Perhaps one might interject at this point that winning itself is, after all, a conclusion based on the stimulus patterns presented during the fight, to which one may answer affirmatively, but still point out that the winning itself may be presented by many different spatial-temporal patterns. Besides, the power of $T$ may be transmitted by verbal information, through innumerable soundwave patterns, all of which may be reduced to a single fact by the meaning ascribed to such vicarious mediation.

Or even knowledge about a third person may serve as important data for the cognition of a particular individual, though again such data are not coordinated to specific stimulus patterns. This has been demonstrated in an experiment by Shor (1957) in which S's were given preinformation about one of the animated geometric figures in the Heider-Simmel movie. Some of the S's were told that the big triangle $T$ represented an aggressive, unlikeable person, others that it was a fair-minded person liked by most people. The two remaining and undescribed figures, after being seen interacting with the former in the movie, took on very definite characteristics depending on the prior information, suggesting that "the impressions formed of an individual may be a function of the characteristics ascribed to another person seen to interact with him" (Shor, 1957, p. 126). But these characteristics themselves were not coordinated to any unique stimulus patterns. They were data, to be sure, but meanings as data, not behavior "spatially defined" as data.

The proposition that meanings as "intervening variables" are necessary in order that stimulus patterns may be coordinated with phenomena is significant enough to warrant further explications. Let us suppose that *o* is perceived as being "courageous." This impression can be produced by many different concrete stimulus configurations. We can conceive of all these stimulus configurations as making up a manifold which is defined by the fact that each member of it produces the impression "*o* acts courageously." Then each configuration has the position of a synonym. Yet it is impossible to find a geometrical pattern, an ordinal stimulus definable by a figural feature, which would distinguish the members of this manifold from, let us say, stimulus patterns producing the impression "*o* acts in a cowardly way." It is even unlikely that one can point to a limited number of figurally identifiable subgroups of this manifold, as is possible to a certain extent, with the ordinal stimuli producing the impression "this surface is slanting." This, of course, does not preclude the possibility of finding a figural parameter coordinated to the impression "courageous" in a particular situation. Thus, if one presents different motion picture scenes in which an obviously dangerous animal is shown with different persons, the impression that person *A* is more courageous than *B* might be produced by simple motions of approachment or withdrawal. But one cannot say that motions of approachment or withdrawal, defined in a temporal and spatial way, are *generally* coordinated with these impressions. Only when the level of meaning is included can a feature common to all the cases producing the impression "courageous" be found. The meaning might be something like: going ahead or not withdrawing in spite of danger ahead. Bear also in mind that in this case "going ahead" does not have to be defined spatially in the physical sense; it can be defined "hodologically," as doing something that is a condition for coming into contact. The actions can be in social space. Also "danger" cannot be defined figurally.

Perception through speech provides another area where the crucial data are meanings, and not simply stimulus patterns reduced to spatial coordinates. This is even clear in cases in which a person reports his thoughts and feelings literally, as when he says, "I am angry" or "I think thus and so." But it is even more sharply brought out when we infer his thoughts and feelings indirectly from what he says and how he says it. In either case we immediately are in the realm of meaning, but in the latter the direct or concrete meaning of the sentence is only one factor in understanding. Many other factors are taken into account, such as knowledge about the person uttering the sentence, to whom it is said, the relation between speaker and the one spoken to, the situation that provoked to utterance, etc. Again there is no simple coordination between a particular utterance and the impression produced by it: a particular utterance can have many different meanings in different situations and one and the same impression can be produced by many different utterances. Nevertheless, the hearer has the feeling of being directly in the presence of anger or other feelings of *o*, and it would be hard to find a difference between this feeling of presence and the feeling of being in the presence of directly, visually seen objects. There certainly does not have to intervene a "judgment" or an "inference" just because meanings are essential data in the perceptual process.

Lest one erroneously assume that the intervention of meanings is important only for person perception, we should like to point out that even in such cases of visual perception as the perception of size, meanings in the end make their appearance. For instance, consider the picture of three men, drawn in equal size, who stand one behind the other in a hallway leading away from the observer. True enough, the lines surrounding the men create the impression that they are of different size, but this impression requires that the men be seen in different apparent distances, which is already a requirement of meaning. In this connection one ought to mention that the correlation between apparent size and apparent distance does not hold without exception, as, for instance, Kilpatrick and Ittelson (1953) and Gruber (1954) have shown.

. . . the basic reason of the illusion is the fact that the three men are, by means of surrounding lines, put into different apparent distances; and that could have been achieved by many different line structures which have nothing in common figurally. Thus, if one would consider only the figural region, one would make an error, which could be called a neglect of meaning. One would overlook the fact that the effect from figure to figure does not occur within the figural region, but in a region of meaning. (Heider, 1930, p. 384.)

***Meanings as integrating factors.*** The role of meanings in perception becomes even more central because the consistent representation of the world towards which perception tends depends upon meanings (or beliefs or interpretations or evaluations, to indicate a wider scope

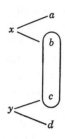

of connotations) as organizing factors. The integrative phenomenon may be expressed in general as follows: Let us assume that a certain stimulus, $x$, is ambiguous. It can be seen as $a$ or $b$. Whether $a$ or $b$ is seen depends upon the *meaning* to which any additional stimuli give rise and how these meanings fit with $a$ or $b$. We can even assume that the additional stimulus, $y$, is also ambiguous, that is, it can be seen as $c$ or $d$. If meaning $b$ fits with meaning $c$, while neither fits with $a$ or $d$, nor $d$ with $a$ or $b$, then the first stimulus will be seen as $b$, the second as $c$. The world we perceive has to be consistent, and the equivocal stimuli, even ordinal stimuli, will give rise to percepts that fit together and produce an integrated picture.

In this connection, Michotte (1950) stresses the "difference that exists between the system of stimuli and the structural organization of the perceptual field" (p. 120), an organization that depends upon meanings. As an example, he discusses approach as a manifestation of friendliness:

Let us suppose there are three objects (three persons, for example) all in sight of each other—$A$, $B$, and $C$. $B$ feels attracted by $A$ and goes gently toward him, but remains indifferent to $C$. . . . As far as the retinal images are concerned, there is a diminution of the distance between $A$ and $B$ and an increase in the distance between $B$ and $C$. If the impressions were the literal translation of the stimuli the situation would be absolutely ambiguous —$B$ approaching $A$ could be a manifestation of friendship, $B$ moving away from $C$ could be a sign of antipathy or fear (which emotions, ex hypothesi, do not exist). But in point of fact, because the structural organization is determined by various factors . . . only the approach and union come into the perceptual field of the observer, and the impressions he receives actually correspond to the sentiments of the agent. (Michotte, 1950, p. 121.)*

As applied to thing perception, examples of the integrative process exist at every turn. Such variables of the visual world as distance, the size, color, and shape of objects, shadows, the relations of objects to each other and their manipulative properties, are all interrelated so that if the values of some are given, the values of the others are required—required, that is, if an orderly world is to result. If the surface relations are given by the contours, and if the light source is at a certain place, the shadows thrown by the objects are implied. If the shape of a solid object is given and a pliable cloth lies on the object, the shape of the cloth is determined within certain limits; and also the reverse holds, the shape of a pliable cloth requires an object

* By permission from *Feelings and emotions* by M. I. Reymert (ed.). Copyright 1950 by McGraw-Hill.

of a certain shape on which it lies. Solid objects usually require a solid ground to lie on, they do not float; if the distance of the ground is given, the distance of the object is given with it, and vice versa.

Similar considerations can also be applied to the ordinary constancies. Retinal size is an equivocal stimulus; it is coordinated to a certain relation between object size and distance, two variables belonging to the visual world. The information given by retinal size can be compared to an equation with two unknowns. If we get more information about the value of one of the unknowns through additional data, we will also know the value of the other one. For instance, if there are data defining the distance, the object size is thereby defined too. But, again, let us not forget that there are an infinite number of patterns that could lead to a definite impression of the distance of the object without our being able to find any general feature that would distinguish these patterns from other patterns.

Once again we can draw upon the animated geometrical figures for demonstrations of the integrative process in social perception. A simple example is the now familiar chasing-following problem: If a person is seen once as the more powerful one, chasing fits his personality better than following does. If a more powerful person is seen as being chased by a less powerful person, one has to make additional assumptions to make this event plausible.

Another example is the work of Shor (1957) already referred to. His experiment suggests that the perception of one person can be influenced by the way in which another person with whom he is interacting is seen, because a consistent picture of the whole is thereby achieved. The movie, you may recall, was given to two groups of subjects: the first group was told that the person represented by the big triangle is fairminded and popular, the other group that he is aggressive and unpopular. In the movie the big triangle $T$ is seen as fighting with the small triangle $t$. When $T$ is perceived as a "good person" this opposition is consistent with the impression that $t$ is a "bad person" and vice versa. In general, when two people $A$ and $B$ fight, we are inclined to put the blame on one of them; if in our judgment $A$ has positive traits, we will tend to ascribe negative traits to $B$. In this way, the relation between their personalities fits the fact that they are opposed to each other in the fight. Of course, our assumptions about how environmental facts and personalities fit together may sometimes be too simple if not totally incorrect; our judgments may be led astray. We do not wish to imply that the tendency to construct a consistent world always leads to veridical cognition.

In discussing the integrative process which led to a coherence in the

movements of the animated figures, it was pointed out that the movements were organized in terms of *actions of persons*, i.e., personality
invariancies which brought order out of chaos (Heider and Simmel,
1944, p. 256). The interpretations of the subjects reminds us of
Bartlett's (1932) observations in the serial retelling of a story: he
talks about the tendency "which gives to what is presented a setting
and an explanation" (p. 84) which he calls rationalization:

> The general function of rationalization is in all instances the same. It is
> to render material acceptable, understandable, comfortable, straightforward;
> to rob it of all puzzling elements. As such it is a powerful factor in all
> perceptual and in all reproductive processes. (Bartlett, 1932, p. 89.)

That the valuations of different parts of the stimulus manifold are
put together in such a way as to form an integrated impression leads
to the assumption of a hierarchy of structures interposed between the
stimulus manifold and the resulting impressions, of stages of intervening
variables that help us to analyze in a fruitful manner the correlations
between the total stimulus field and the total phenomenal field. The
parts of the stimulus manifold are evaluated, and these evaluations
combine to produce still more encompassing evaluations, and so on—
though in considering this process we must never forget that its direction is not all one way, from stimuli to impressions, but that the
evaluations or meanings of the higher levels in turn influence the
meanings of the lower levels. We are aware of the fact that this
description is still very inexact; however one can trust that it can be
made more objective. A promising beginning in this direction has
been made by Hayek with his ideas about a hierarchy of evaluations.
It would lead us too far afield to present Hayek's theories in detail but
we cannot refrain from giving at least one quotation from his book
to indicate the direction of his thinking:

> This process by which the relations on which the classification of primary
> impulses is based, become in turn the object of classificatory processes, can
> evidently be repeated on many levels. Not only relations between im-
> pulses, but relations between relations between impulses, and so forth, may
> all acquire their distinct following and in consequence become capable of
> forming the starting point for distinct further processes. . . . The com-
> plexity of the order which can be built up by means of this variety of
> relations is for all practical purposes unlimited. (Hayek, 1952, p. 74.)

Within the hierarchy of required relations, conflicts arise when
relations that hold between parts of the visual world are incompatible
with relations required by other parts or by the total visual field. Such
conflict is in evidence, for example, when I can see through an object
which casts a shadow, or when Object *A* seems nearer than *B*, and *B*

nearer than *C*, but also *C* nearer than *A*. Merleau-Ponty, believing that

. . . there exists a complete logic of the picture or the scene, an experienced coherence of the colors, the spatial forms and the meaning of the object,

calls attention to Katz's concept of a "logic of illumination":

. . . our whole perception is pervaded by a logic which assigns to each object all its properties in relation to those of the others, and which excludes as unreal any non-fitting information. (Merleau-Ponty, 1945, p. 361.)

Thus, the world as we perceive it has certain systematic features; its parts imply each other to a certain degree. It is not a manifold where just anything can happen, but one with restrictions. Therefore, the parts can fit or can be in conflict with each other, or, if one part is given other parts can be extrapolated. The requirement of fitting together in a consistent world puts limits on the possible effects of stimulus patterns. It is in a certain sense an internal limitation of the cognitive system—however, when these limitations correspond to actual limitations of the objective world they will make cognition more veridical.

***Economy of interpretation—redundancy.*** We have seen that a stimulus which is ambiguous as long as it is given singly, may become unequivocal with the addition of further data. It is important to stress that this specificity is established through the meaningfulness of the integrated perceptual field. But of two equally meaningful integrations, the one that is less complex, the one that requires fewer assumptions, fewer data in general, seems in general to be preferred. This is sometimes referred to as the principle of parsimony, a principle well known in the philosophy of science, and which may have its analogue in perception.

It is sometimes said that the objective of science is to describe nature economically. We have reason to believe, however, that some such process of parsimonious description has its beginnings on a fairly naive perceptual level. . . . It appears likely that a major function of the perceptual machinery is to strip away some of the redundancy of stimulation, to describe or encode incoming information in a form more economical than that in which it impinges on the receptors. (Attneave, 1954, p. 189.)

Now to illustrate economy in perception. Let us assume that stimulus *x* is ambiguous, that it could be interpreted as mediating either *a* or *b*, two different features belonging to the distal sphere, i.e., the environmental world. In the same way stimulus *y* could be seen as *b* or *c*. If *x* and *y* are given together, they can be "explained" by the hypothesis "*b* is there," or by the hypothesis "*a* and *c* are there." The first hypothesis is "cheaper"; it refers the stimuli to only one underlying entity, whereas the second hypothesis assumes two entities

The same principle can be applied if two of several meanings underlying ambiguous data imply each other. For instance, suppose that *x* means *a* or *b*, that *y* means *c* or *d*, and that *b* and *c* imply each other mutually. Then, if *x* is interpreted as *b*, it also transmits the information that *c* is there, since *b* implies *c*. Or, it is a simpler hypothesis to interpret *xy* as *bc* than as *ad*, since *a* and *d* are two independent facts and *bc* makes an integrated group and contributes only one fact according to the restrictions of the system. It will be seen that the first example above in which two meanings are identical is really just a special case of this one.

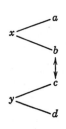

Moreover, if one knows the system of implications of one fact in regard to another, then this knowledge is important in extrapolating from one bit of information to the whole. For example, from one bone sticking out of the rock one can reconstruct the whole animal, provided that the bone is not an ambiguous stimulus or sign and the structure of the animal is sufficiently defined. As a matter of fact, knowledge of the structure of the whole makes additional data redundant, for if the rest of the animal were also given, we do not gain any new information. Of course, if the structure is not known, additional data can be most useful. (Cf. to this point, Bruner, 1957.)

Social perception also has systems of implied facts, with the possibility that certain data may be superfluous for providing additional information. If, for example, one already knows that *A* is superior in power to *B*, then the fact that *A* is chasing *B* does not add much information about the power relation between *A* and *B*. Such behavior is "just what one expected." As we have seen, the motion of *A* moving behind *B* will be seen as "chasing" and not "following" just because of the principle of economy of interpretation. If, however, the observer was told that *A*, though superior in power, is in fact following *B* (or that *B* is leading *A*) then additional information is presented, information that is not at all redundant and therefore sheds a new light on the relation between *A* and *B*. The integrative process then presses for a sensible explanation, one that brings order into the array of facts. One might conclude, for instance, that though *A* is more powerful than *B*, he is trying to teach *B* to assume qualities of leadership, or that he is engaged in a friendly game with *B*. But if the only fact at hand is the power superiority of *A*, such explanations are clearly more expensive than perceiving the notion of *A* and *B* as chasing. In these examples, the integration of only two data is required. The expense difference between the simplest and the most complicated hypothesis mounts very rapidly when examples with a greater manifold of data are considered.

In the first part of this chapter, it was pointed out that in person perception, the manifold of incoming messages (the proximal stimuli of perception) is encoded in terms of the motives, sentiments, beliefs, and personality traits of other persons. There we mentioned that these are dispositional properties, the relatively stable distal features that are relevant to us. We now should like to add that it is through the process of construction within the central layers of the observer that these dispositional features serve to integrate a bewildering mass of data in the most economical terms.

## Misperception

The coordination between the percept and the distal stimulus in spite of ambiguities of the local proximal stimulus is, of course, of vital importance for an efficient interaction on the part of the person with his environment. To say that it would be confusing if the shape of objects were transformed with every positional shift, or if persons were perceived as changing character with every action, or if what I perceive as *o*'s desires might just as easily be his antipathies, is but a great understatement of how much more disturbing the world would be. We need to perceive things and people with their invariant properties more or less as they are, even though these properties are mediated to us in a complicated way and not simply by the local proximal stimulus.

As has already been stressed, the principle of embeddedness refers to a process essential to this coordination, namely the integration between the local stimulus and its surroundings. Moreover, the meaning of the local stimulus is often, if not always, a function of the integration of the perceptual field. As examples of this kind of constructive embeddedness, we have noted the perceptual constancies in which the surrounding helps determine the properties of the object by eliminating the ambiguity of the local stimulus. For social perception, it is the surrounding situation that makes it possible to determine the motivations and intentions that lie behind a specific overt behavior.

Unfortunately (or fortunately if distortion and pretense aid and abet one's intentions), though the surrounding influences the appearance of a subpart of the perceptual field, it does not always improve cognition. It may be so misleading as to interfere with the coordination between the distal object and the perception of it. Before examining further some of the common sources of error in social perception, a few examples of distorting embeddedness will be mentioned. Optical illusions that lead to incorrect judgments of the length of lines, the size of objects, etc., are legion. In social perception one can refer to such phenomena as the halo effect, prestige suggestion, believing an act to be good when it is performed by a friend and bad when it is performed by someone disliked, or disliking a person simply because he was first encountered in a personally disagreeable situation though he had no responsibility for it.

It is Piaget's (1950) belief that constructive embeddedness is characteristic of thinking, and destructive embeddedness is characteristic of perception. He refers to these two ways in which the surrounding can affect the appearance of the part as "intellectual relativity" and "perceptual relativity":

Perceptual relativity is a distorting relativity, in the sense in which conversational language says "everything is relative" when denying the possibility of objectivity. . . . The relativity of intelligence on the other hand is the very condition of objectivity. . . . (Piaget, 1950, pp. 75–76.)

Though it may be true that instances of distorting embeddedness are more frequent in perception whereas thinking is favored by constructive embeddedness, the two kinds are certainly present in both perception and thinking.

The issues thus far discussed can illuminate certain factors that impede cognition. An essential point is brought out by the following comparison: In the perception of color, where the illumination (the surrounding conditions in this case) is completely taken into account, the color is perceived adequately. But just as the illumination may be taken into account in different degrees, so in social perception, the relevant situation may be partly or completely ignored with the result that cognition is impeded. It seems that behavior in particular has such salient properties it tends to engulf the total field rather than be confined to its proper position as a local stimulus whose interpretation requires the additional data of a surrounding field—the situation in social perception. The consequence is, as Brunswik has noted,

. . . that two people show the tendency to seem to have the same personality if their momentary actions are the same, and the instigations to their actions are not sufficiently taken into account. (Brunswik, 1934, p. 218.)

Many examples of the inadequate apprehension of the significant conditions surrounding behavior appear in Ichheiser's essay "Misunderstandings in human relations." He points out that a mother and teacher may have very different pictures of the personality of a child because they do not take into account the fact that the home situation is different from the school situation. Moreover, they tend to overestimate the unity of the child's personality because of a tendency to think that the child will behave in the same way in all situations:

This tendency blinds mother and teacher to the "obvious" fact that the boy has, as do many other people, two or more "characters," each coming to the surface, depending on the situation in which he finds himself, and also that there might exist a very complicated under-the-surface connection between these "characters" which cannot be defined in a too simple manner. (Ichheiser, 1949, p. 27.)

In many cases, a false idea of the invariance of the behavior of the other person is produced because the perceiver himself is

. . . a very important factor in the total situation which determines and evokes the type of behavior the other person is expected to play in the given relation. . . . It is our own presence which either evokes or suppresses the manifestations of certain personality aspects of other people. (pp. 28–29.)

Thus, the father always sees his son in the role of son, the employer sees the employee only as an employee behaving in front of the employer, etc. Varying somewhat an analogy of Ichheiser, we might say it is as if we always carried a flashlight with a filter of red color when examining an empty room; we would then ascribe the color to the room. We are reminded of discussions regarding the influence of the method of observation on what is observed in science.

Another case of misjudging the factor of situation occurs when the situation is perceived egocentrically, that is, if the situation of the other person is silently presupposed to be the same as the situation of the observer. Ichheiser (1949) quotes the example of Marie Antoinette who, upon being told that the people were hungry because they had no bread, asked why they did not eat cake instead.

Sometimes the raw materials of social perception are the things that belong to a person. We form an idea of a person when we see his room, his books, his pictures, etc. (Ichheiser, 1949, p. 5). If we are sure that the person himself selected the things because he likes them, then this idea may be more or less adequate. But again, in many cases other factors besides personal preference determined the ownership of the things, and we are misled by this raw material.

Misperceptions also occur when the properties of a person are mediated to us through what other people say or write about him, through gossip, newspapers, etc. Consequently, the interpretation of new behavioral data may also be in error because of its integration with false beliefs.

There is yet another basis for cognitive error, one which concerns attribution, though in principle it also can be seen as a question of insufficient or inadequate data upon which the perception is constructed. We shall have a good deal more to say about the meaning and conditions underlying attribution in later chapters, but here let it suffice to point out that behavior can be ascribed primarily to the person or to the environment; that is, behavior can be accounted for by relatively stable traits of the personality or by factors within the environment. Failure, for instance, can be attributed to lack of ability, a personal characteristic, or to the supposition that the task is very difficult, an environmental condition. Whether attribution to one or the other source will occur depends on a number of factors, for instance, on information concerning the success and failure of other people, and on the tendency to attribute the consequences of actions to the person (Ichheiser, 1949, p. 31; Brunswik, 1934, p. 220).

The problem of attribution also applies to thing perception. In the perceptual constancies, for example, the retinal color may be attributed in varying degrees to either the object or to the illumination; the retinal shape may be ascribed to the shape of the object or to the position of the object with respect to the observer. In other words, even though the stimulus pattern impinging on the organism may provide some information about the interaction between two entities—the object and its illumination, the person and the environment—additional data are required before one can determine which of the two poles of the relation is primarily responsible for the interaction. The additional data may take the form of further observations or of beliefs based upon information transmitted through previous proximal stimulus patterns.

In all of the cases discussed, the reason for the misperceptions or differences in interpretations concerning another person lies in the lack of correlation between the raw material and the intended object of perception. We take the raw material too literally without taking into account additional factors that influence it.

### Perceptual Styles

The fact that there is a lack of correspondence between the raw material of perception and the intended object of perception allows idiosyncratic approaches to the world on the part of the observer a much freer reign in the organization and interpretation of incoming proximal stimuli. The issue here does not concern errors of perception as much as it does perceptual styles—what the person extracts from his world because of his manner of perceiving.

A striking case is the calculating prodigy who was so prone to perceive the world in terms of numerical combinations that, after seeing a play, he was entirely unaffected by the scene but instead "informed his hosts of the exact number of words uttered by the various actors, and of the number of steps taken by others in their dances" (Ball, 1956, p. 469).

Physiognomic perception, the mode of perception in which things appear animate, shows interesting individual differences. From Werner's (1948) writings, the proposition that physiognomic perception "plays a greater role in the primitive world than in our own" (p. 69) has become familiar. Children, for example, show more physiognomic perception than adults. Chronic schizophrenics, in a study by Ihrig (1953) produced fewer animistic responses to the Heider-Simmel film than the control groups. Even with normal adults there seem to be differences in the tendency to interpret stimulus configurations in terms of personal behavior.

Another case in point concerns depth of personal contact with one's environment. We know that the degree of intimacy of contact between two people depends on the situation, how long the persons have known each other, and on individual differences. Some people perceive the more superficial layers of personality in interpersonal relations and act accordingly, whereas the perceptions and actions of others are more concerned with central layers, the deeper and sometimes more covert psychological aspects of the person. Karl Buehler (1929), in his interesting analysis of interactions in a dyad, discusses examples of different degrees of depth of contact. Lewin (1948) has extended individual differences concerning this dimension to differences in national character, notably to differences between the United States and Germany (especially p. 24). Interesting differences in social perception between Russian displaced persons and Americans are described by Hanfmann (1957).

Phenomenologically oriented psychologists in particular have stressed that for one person to be in contact with another and to perceive and react to the other's sentiments and wishes, it is not enough that he is exposed to certain stimulus configurations. A general readiness to perceive psychologically is necessary; this receptivity makes possible the arousal of such percepts as "he is angry," or "he wants to tell me something." As we know, people vary widely in such social-psychological perceptivity.

The inclination of the observer to perceive his world according to individual perceptual styles could also be elaborated by reference to such concepts as "levellers" versus "sharpeners" (Klein, 1951), "authoritarians" versus "nonauthoritarians" (Titus and Hollander, 1957), the optimist who sees a rosy glow to everything versus the pessimist who extracts the negative values. All these are perceptual attitudes, general ways of "being in the world" which lead to the arousal of different percepts in spite of the fact that the stimulus configurations presented are the same.

## Summary

The phenomenal description of perception attests to the value of naive psychology, the pretheoretical and implicit system which underlies interpersonal relations, by showing that direct experience centers on points that are also central causally, namely the environmental contents with which we are concerned, and that direct experience more or less adequately assesses the role of mediation. Causal analysis, in splitting up the "direct presence of the objects" into object, mediation, and percept, to some extent does violence to the phenomenal description of perception.

The following statement connecting the object of our perception and the resulting percept (the two foci) points up the theoretical problem: Invariance is in general connected with the foci, variance with the mediation. To a limited degree, one can find coordinations between ordinal patterns of stimulation, i.e., patterns defined spatially or temporally, and the resulting perceptual experience. It also seems to be approximately true that the smaller the part of the pattern taken into account, the more ambiguous it is. But in many cases, no simple coordinations between ordinal stimuli and phenomena can be found. Therefore, in order to understand the relation between stimulus patterns and phenomena theoretically, to make general statements about it, intervening variables must be assumed. These intervening variables consist of a hierarchy of meanings and evaluations which can be compared to a system of interlocking concepts or schemata. That percept will arise that best fits the stimulus conditions and at the same time this system of schemata.

The study of social perception deals with the perception of such important dispositional and psychological properties of another person as his actions, motives, affects, beliefs, etc. A great part of this book will be devoted to such topics, and in studying them we shall attempt to achieve a somewhat more differentiated picture of the matrix of schemata in terms of which the social environment is seen.

# CHAPTER 3

# The other person

# as perceiver

IT IS NOTEWORTHY that the usual treatment of perception in psychology does not include the area of problems in which $p$'s attention and behavior are directed toward $o$ as a perceiver. The following questions are pertinent in this respect: How do we perceive (know) that another person perceives something in the environment? What are our reactions to being an object of $o$'s perceptions? How do we bring about or prevent his perceiving? When do we look forward to his perceptions and when are we afraid of them? When do we believe that $o$ wants to see something or that he can or ought to see it? Certainly, the naive psychology of perception is not merely a figment of the imagination. In its way it provides an admirable analysis of perception for practical purposes.

In order to reach a better understanding of these processes, it will be helpful to study the ideas one ordinarily has about the conditions and effects of another person's perceptions. These ideas are the basis of our actions and cognitions in regard to the perception of other people, though they are seldom made explicit.

The idea that our cognitions, expectations, and actions are based on a mastery of the causal network of the environment, is, of course, the main tenet of a cognitive psychology, and it will be applied throughout this essay. For instance, in the perception of a "wish" of another person, the perceiver will rely on what he believes are the effects of a wish as cues for the cognition of it, though certainly not always in a conscious way. If he tries to produce a wish in another person he will do so by producing its conditions. If he knows that another person harbors a wish he will expect the usual consequences of this phenomenon "wish," and he will try to produce it as a means if he wants to bring about one of its consequences.

Therefore, in order to study the cognitions and actions directed toward the perceptions of another person, we have to explore our beliefs regarding the conditions and effects of perception.

### Conditions of Perception

The common-sense assumptions about the conditions that make it possible for one person to recognize what another is perceiving are for the most part implicit. If people were asked about these conditions they probably would not be able to make a complete list of them. Nevertheless, these assumptions are a necessary part of interpersonal relations; if we probe the events of everyday behavior, they can be brought to the surface and formulated in more precise terms.

To give a simple example: If you want another person not to look at something, you may ask him to close his eyes; that is, by annulling the condition, perception is prevented. Or you may have a conviction that someone has not seen $x$ because he had his eyes closed; that is, the absence of perception is inferred from the absence of the condition. Or you may attribute the fact that someone has not seen $x$ to the fact that he has his eyes closed; that is, the absence of perception is attributed to the absence of the condition. All this means that "open eyes" are recognized as one of the conditions for visual perception.

Thus, by analyzing the data through which our beliefs are revealed, particularly the conditions we set up to produce or prevent perception or from which we infer and attribute perceptual states, we shall try to obtain insight into the common-sense assumptions about the conditions of perception.

**The object as a condition of perception.** When we see a person who, after intently watching a traffic signal, starts crossing the street the moment the sign changes from red to green, then we are quite certain that he has perceived the change. However, a behavioral reaction is not always necessary for the recognition that another person is perceiving. Even when we see only that the glance of the other person is directed toward an object, we get the impression that he perceives it.

This presupposes first of all that the other person is experienced by us as living in the same world as ourselves and as perceiving approximately the same things that we would from his position. Asch says:

> We start with the bare observation that a number of persons will in a given situation perceive objects and happenings within it in a similar way and that their modes of action in the situation will also have a basic similarity. The tree that I see others see too; what I hear they hear. (Asch, 1952, p. 128.)

Asch uses the term "mutually shared environment" to refer to this fact. (Cf. Schuetz, 1945, p. 534.)

It is also obvious that the object itself is a condition for the inference that *o* has seen it. A consequence of this is that, by and large, we trust eye witnesses. If someone tells us that he has seen something, we usually assume that what he has seen was actually there, that we ourselves would have seen it if we had been there. Furthermore, recognition that the object itself plays a role in the perceptual process guides *p*'s behavior when he wishes to prevent or encourage perception of it. He may destroy the object or remove it from view, or he may direct *o*'s attention to it.

Duncker's (1947) description of how we experience our own perception of objects, namely, that "seeing a tree" means to be open to the tree, or participating in the tree (p. 506) can also be applied to how we feel other people experience objects. The meaning of "I see a tree" and "He sees a tree" both involve this phenomenal participation in the object on the part of the perceiver, the object being outside of and independent from the observer.

PERCEPTIBILITY AS AN OBJECT PROPERTY. Some objects in our mutually shared environment can be more easily perceived than others. For example, an object can be easily visible, or visible only with difficulty, or even invisible; it can be conspicuous and striking, or inconspicuous and indistinct. Sometimes the perceptibility of an object is contingent upon the mediating conditions between observer and object: something may be visible from one location but not from another; it may be momentarily concealed by another object or obliterated because of the lack of illumination. But in other cases, the perceptibility refers definitely to a property of the object itself without regard to the mediation. When we say that the writing is invisible, we mean that it cannot be seen even if one looks closely at it under good light. The invisibility is a property of the object. The science of camouflaging makes use of object properties in altering visibility.

Perceptibility, as a dispositional property of the object, is crucial in regard to matters one wishes to keep private. Such matters may be considered as "objects" more or less liable to the scrutiny of other people.

Different criteria can be used to distinguish between what is private and what is public. One is perceptibility—the concept of privacy can be restricted to what only the person himself can observe, what is cognitively accessible only to him. This criterion is used, for instance, by Lapiere and Farnsworth who say:

The whole complex of covert behaviors of an individual may be conceived of as his private self, that which he knows, however vaguely, but which others can know if at all only by influence from his overt behavior (his "social self," as it is sometimes termed). (Lapiere and Farnsworth, 1949, p. 160.)

Similarly, Ichheiser writes:

The counterpart of the collectively perceivable world is the world of our individual (private) experiences. The desk on which I am writing is an object which can be perceived by myself, by you, and by anyone else, as something which is "located" in the interpersonal, collective world. By contrast, my feeling of being happy, or my conviction of being right, is perceived and can be directly perceived, as this particular feeling or conviction, only by me. (Ichheiser, 1949, p. 12.)

However, this is not the usual sense in which we apply the words "private" and "privacy" in interpersonal relations. If it were, one could hardly ever talk about an "intrusion into privacy." Many people feel that their privacy has been invaded when strangers read letters addressed to them. The letter certainly can be perceived and read by other persons; from the point of view of cognitive accessibility it belongs to the interpersonal world. Nevertheless, it belongs in a special sense to the own person. It is felt to be a peculiarly "personal" matter not meant for the eyes of $o$; $p$ wishes that its perceptibility were restricted to himself or at least within his control. Another example is visible injury. White, Wright, and Dembo point out that

An injury, as a characteristic and inseparable part of the body, may be felt to be a personal matter which the man would like to keep private. However, the fact of its visibility makes it known to anyone whom the injured man meets, including the stranger. A visible injury differs from most other personal matters in that anyone can deal with it regardless of the wish of the injured person; anyone can stare at the injury or ask questions about it, and in both cases communicate to and impose upon the injured person his feelings and evaluations. His action is then felt as an intrusion into privacy. (White, Wright, and Dembo, 1948, p. 16.)

Nuttin (1950) also stresses the fact that some personal contents are accessible to others; he says: "The private interiority of psychological life, combined with this inherent possibility of its exposure, constitute what we may call the *functional conditions* for the origin of shame" (p. 345). Thus the region of privacy does not coincide with the region that is perceptible or accessible only to the own person.

Besides these two criteria, namely, perceptibility and belonging in an intimate way to the person, there are other distinctions that are relevant for the content of the somewhat general and vague concept of "privacy." One can differentiate between those contents that one wants others to perceive, that one does not mind having them perceive, and that one wants to keep under cover. Furthermore, there is the question of power over accessibility, of whether one can prevent others from seeing something or not.

These differences can be related to more abstract concepts. Thus, the criterion of perceptibility in the sense of accessibility is formally analogous to that of the space of free movement and is based on the fundamental concept of can (cf. Chapter 4). The space of free movement includes all the goals the person *can* reach. The space of what is accessible to perception includes all the things the person *can* notice. The inclusiveness of this space depends on the conditions taken into account in determining can. Something can be inaccessible to direct perception which is accessible through symbolic means; for instance, though $p$'s dreams are not directly detectable by $o$, $p$ can tell $o$ about them. The case in which $p$ controls the perceptibility of $x$ can also be defined by the concept, can; $p$ can cause others not to perceive $x$, that is, he can prevent others from seeing it.

In regard to the "personal" meaning of privacy, conceptualization can be furthered if we assume that the concept of privacy is based on a special kind of intimate relation between $p$ and the particular $x$. In this way, what is personal as a criterion for privacy can be connected with the concept of unit formation (see p. 176).

The underlying concept, want, also appears in the analysis of privacy, for $p$ does not *want* the particular matter to be perceived by others.

As a summary example, a visible injury may be described in the following way: it is perceptible to others, it is personal, $p$ does not have the power to prevent others from seeing it, $p$ wishes (wants that) others would not see it. Thus we have seen that perceptibility as an object property is significant in the analysis of privacy. Its significance was conceptualized in terms of the concept "can." Privacy, in addition, was related to such other fundamental concepts as "unit formation" and "want."

APPEARANCE VS. REALITY AS AN OBJECT PROPERTY. Connected in some ways with perceptibility as a property of an object is the distinction we make between appearance and reality. There are occasions when the true object (or matter under scrutiny) is less perceptible than its outward manifestations:

> Things are seldom what they seem.
> Skim milk masquerades as cream.
> (W. S. Gilbert, *H.M.S. Pinafore*)

One thing may appear to be another when its proximal stimuli are ordinarily not coordinated to it. The proximal stimuli are caused by the surface of a thing. They provide the direct cues for perception. But the functional significance of a thing, its nature as it is relevant for our behavioral reaction, is less directly given. Therefore, we may alter the surface of a thing, or the outward manifestation of a process or a property, without touching its real essence. The paint of camouflage, the mask of disguise, serve to conceal the underlying reality.

The difference between appearance and reality is utilized all the time in our dealings with other people, particularly when sentiments and emotions are involved. The range of intended pretenses that are enacted to an audience one hopes will believe them is sufficient testimony: We pretend to like something, to dislike something, to be angry, to be enthusiastic, to be gay, to be sad, to be grieved; we force a laugh in order to show that we understand a joke; we pretend agreement by nodding; we feign happiness by exaggerated good cheer; we conceal contempt by silence; we pretend to be brave when we are frightened.

Not always is the distinction between appearance and reality used to cover up, however. The possibility of their congruence is also recognized so that highlighting the appearance of a thing may highlight its reality and vice versa. For example, if we wish to emphasize the anger we feel (underlying reality) we bring into play a whole repertoire of expression and behavior (appearance). (Cf. the distinction between "open" and "enigmatic" personalities by S. G. Estes, reported in Allport, 1937, pp. 507 ff.)

Thus far we have talked about the object, the thing, the matter that is being perceived, as a necessary part of the experience that $o$ is perceiving something. We have pointed out that the object itself has properties that enhance or restrict its perceptibility and that this feature is an important variable in the problem of privacy. That appearance and reality are distinguished was also seen to have important implications for perception. However, the fact that we recognize another person as perceiving something does not only hinge on the object and its characteristics in a mutually shared environment. We also have definite ideas of the environmental conditions surrounding the person and the object which make it possible for contact between the two to be established. It is to these mediating conditions that we shall now give our attention.

***Mediating conditions for establishing contact between person and object.*** Man routinely makes use of the following propositions: We can see best when the scrutinized object is in frontal parallel position and when it is well illuminated; for good perception, the distance should be optimal, which means a greater distance for larger objects; obstacles between the viewer and the object interfere with perception; in regard to auditory perception, masking noises and distance may be mentioned as important factors. These assumptions show that naive psychology is well aware of the significance of surrounding conditions for perception. The surrounding conditions are recognized as making possible the perceptual contact between the person and the object, as mediating between them, rather than as belonging to either of them.

This is the kind of knowledge that man utilizes when he wishes to affect perception. He will hold the object straight before him (or before *o* if he wishes to help *o* perceive the object). He will look at it near the window or a lamp. He will say, "Be quiet! I want to speak." Knowing that the medium has to be clear for optimal perception, he will produce smoke to prevent the enemy from spotting the target. In short, knowledge of the mediating conditions permits him to influence perception. If he wishes to promote perception, he will establish mediating conditions that are optimal for perception, and if he wishes to prevent perception, he will attempt to eliminate them.

Man also applies his knowledge of mediating conditions when he cognizes that another person is perceiving: When he sees that *o* has his eyes open and directed toward an object in good illumination and that this object is in full view and not too far away, then he has the impression that *o* is perceiving the object. In other words, when we see that all the necessary conditions for perception are present, including the necessary mediating conditions, then we have the experience that the consequence, namely perception, will also occur. As we shall see later, the act of perceiving may also be inferred from its consequences.

Asch reminds us that the role of mediating conditions can be intelligibly applied to the other person as perceiver only because we act in terms of a mutually shared environment:

An object moves out of my field and into the field of another, and conversely. The other perceives what has eluded me and what I only later observe; similarly, I direct him toward what I already see. On the basis of the fundamental identity in our functioning we are able to derive the reasonable ground for differences based on differences in our positions and perspectives. (Asch, 1952, p. 129.)

Man's recognition of the significance of mediating conditions is also reflected in his metaphorical language. The fact that good illumination produces the clarity of a well-structured environment, whereas darkness is fraught with the dangers of the imperceptible, has extended the meaning of light and darkness in our everyday life. Light is something positive; darkness something negative. A problem may be *illuminated* or *beclouded* and *obscured*.

The difference between object conditions and mediating conditions also appear in the statements of scientific psychology. Duncker says:

. . . the sense organ exhibits the . . . astonishing ability to split in varying ways, according to circumstances, one and the same datum of stimulation—for example, one given retinal intensity of light, one kind of light, one retinal size, one retinal form, one position, the completeness and clearance of stimulation, etc., into the two phenomenal components: *property of the thing* (cf. object color, object size, object form, object position, completeness and clearness of the object) and *property of the intervening circumstances* (cf. illumination, distance, orientation, and position with regard to the eye, covering or veiling medium). This makes it possible to attribute a large class of changes not to the things themselves, but to the respective intervening factors. (Duncker, 1947, p. 540. See also Heider, 1926.)

Thus, there exists a "splitting" of the data into two parts which refer to two different groups of conditions—the object on the one hand, and the intervening circumstances on the other. One might object to characterizing this as "attribution," a term that may sound too "intellectual." However, Duncker did not mean to imply that there is a consciously rational process of analysis into factors present; he talks about an attribution that occurs "spontaneously and immediately" (p. 537). One can only say that there is a certain similarity between this perceptual "factor analysis" and cases of more conscious, rational attribution.

We know from the work of Piaget (1950), that the separation between mediational and object properties depends to some extent upon age. The gradual building up of the idea of permanent objects is a case in point. Thus, the young child will feel that the mountain is changing as he walks around it, whereas an older child knows that the mountain is the same but that his own perspective is changing. Even when the perception of object constancy occurs in the immediate action sphere, it is delayed "where distant space and reappearances at intervals are concerned" (p. 128). Piaget attributes such developmental differences to the fact that the immediate act of perception is accompanied by certain kinds of perceptual activity which increase with age and which are closely allied to intelligence. He describes these perceptual activities under the labels of decentralizations, transportations, comparisons, transpositions, etc.

It is important for us here that mediating conditions or intervening circumstances are taken into account, not only in the perceptual mechanisms that make for object constancy, but also in our behavior and expectations referring to our own and other people's perceptions. To be sure, the manner and extent to which these conditions are taken into account varies with age.

**Factors within the person as influencing perception.** Thus far two sets of conditions taken into account in perception have been examined, namely, those pertaining to the object and those pertaining to the mediation. These conditions provide the clues from which information about the object being perceived is obtained.

Common-sense psychology recognizes a third set of conditions, those that exist within the organism itself. A nearsighted person without glasses attributes the blurred outlines of objects to his poor eyesight and not to the objects themselves or to his distance from them. Recognizing the inadequacy of his sensory equipment, he may ask someone else to look up a number in the phone book for him. Likewise, poor auditory reception may be attributed to a faulty sensory organ. Our perceptual apparatus (sometimes even brain processes) is held responsible for the fact that ambiguous figures change in appearance as we gaze upon them. Illusions of all sorts, such as that of the moon wandering through the clouds, are often attributed to the nature of man's organic processes. For example, with a magician, the hand is quicker than the eye.

Knowledge about organismic factors enables the person to improve perception by affecting the functioning of the sensory tools. Thus, when he undergoes surgery for scotomas, or removes a particle of dust from his eye, he is doing nothing to the object or to the mediating conditions. Wearing glasses or a hearing aid also affects the functioning of the sensory organs, though in one sense they may also be considered as affecting the mediating conditions.

In some cases, not only the peripheral sensory organs are regarded as having something to do with perception, but also more psychological factors, such as motivation, beliefs, mental set, and judgment. The mother complains, "He hears what he wants to." The teacher advises, "He isn't bright enough to see the danger." The lover is chided for being blind. The opponent is accused of bias and prejudice.

Parenthetically we may note that when a perceptual phenomenon or the behavior based upon it is attributed to a person's sensory tools or brain functioning, he is not held responsible for it in the same way as when it is attributed to his motivations. In the former, the phenomenon is experienced as something that happens to the person, as being outside his control; therefore it is not his fault. Instead of being blamed, he is regarded with pity. But when motivation is involved, his perceptions are seen as directly connected with his ego, his behaving self. Intentions are more intimately connected with the person than are abilities and therefore we become impatient with the child who is not paying attention. If we learn that he cannot hear our attitude changes.

Attribution of perceptual phenomena to factors within the person is shown in an experiment by Asch on the modification of judgments by groups (1952, pp. 450 ff.). He presented his subjects with the perceptual task of selecting from three lines differing in length the one that matched a standard line in length. Twelve such comparisons were made and reported aloud so that all members of the group (seven to nine people) could hear. In one form of the experiment, only one member of the group was naive. All the others had previously been instructed to report unanimously an incorrect judgment on a certain seven of the twelve trials. The experiment then became one in which the critical subject was a minority of one in a situation where he not only felt that the perceptual conditions were simple and clear matters of fact (most of the unequal comparison lines were obviously longer or shorter than the standard), but where he also saw that he was being unanimously challenged on most of his estimates. How would the subject account for his strange situation? Most frequently, the reason for the discrepancy was localized by the naive subject within himself. Sometimes the more peripheral tools were blamed: he feared that something was wrong with his vision. Sometimes a subject felt that there was something more basically wrong with his judgment and he became fearful of exposing himself "as inferior in some way."

In a variation of this experiment, the majority was naive, and one subject was instructed to report incorrect judgments on seven of the twelve trials. Unlike the previous experiment, none of the majority had any doubts about the accuracy of his own estimates. Again the explanation for the discrepancy was felt to reside in the deviating subject. The majority felt that he was handicapped by some abnormality in perception, or that he was attempting some stupid joke, or that he had misunderstood the directions.

The question arises as to why, in some instances, a percept is attributed to factors within the perceiver and in other instances to properties of the object or of the mediating conditions. The *method of difference* formulated by Mill designates one important canon for such attribution (Cohen and Nagel, 1934, p. 256). In essence, the method states that the cause of a difference resides within the variant condition rather than in the conditions common to the diverse instances. For example, if an auditory stimulus is constant and several individuals perceive it: if one person cannot hear what everyone else hears well, then his impression that the speaker's voice is too low will be attributed to himself as the variant factor. Now let us consider an example in which the object is the variant condition and the person is held constant: if one type of print appears fuzzy whereas the other letter forms are sharp in outline, the blurredness will be attributed to the particular print and not to the perceiver's eyes. Duncker (1947) says that a change in a percept will be attributed to the person, or to the person-object relation (mediating conditions) if it "affects the most diverse objects in a highly uniform, non-individual way (cf. for example, their uniform disappearance when the eyes are closed)" (p. 538). Likewise, when one opens one's eyes, ". . . the emergence of this surrounding world (which conforms to the voluntary and bodily act of opening the eyes) is experienced as originating in the opening of the eyes. But the *content* of this surrounding world is experienced as *not* so originating" (p. 539).

In the Asch experiment (described on p. 68) the variant factor is quickly located in the deviant subject—everybody else sees that the two lines are equal while the subject sees one as longer than the other. Therefore the subject becomes suddenly aware that what he sees has to do with himself in an idiosyncratic way.

**The conditions behind the conditions of perception.** The preceding three sets of conditions make it possible for more or less adequate information from the environment to reach our sense organs. Very often, however, the conditions of perception with which our behavior is most concerned do not refer to this more immediately present trio, but rather to the conditions that brought them about. When we ask, for example, "How did he happen to see that?" we may want to know whether he himself searched for it, whether he accidentally stumbled upon it, or whether it was shown to him.

The person may single out for attention different sets of more remote conditions. Interest in the circumstances of object properties is seen when he asks who originated a particular recipe or why one color fades in the sunlight when another does not. Interest in the story behind mediating conditions is seen when we ask how it happened that $p$ was introduced to the special food or why altering the illumination affects color harmony. Interest in the conditions behind organismic factors is seen when we question why $p$'s vision is poor or why dogs can hear certain frequencies that man cannot.

Often we wish to discover those antecedent conditions that have to do with the behaving organism, particularly his intentions, as distinguished from those that reside in the environment. It makes a great deal of difference whether a person overheard us because he could not help hearing or because he put his ear to the door.

Knowledge of the conditions that lead up to a perceptual contact enables the person to control $o$ as a perceiver just as does knowledge of the more immediate conditions of perception themselves. If $p$ knows that his friend showed $o$ the gift intended as a surprise, $p$ is less apt to confide in his friend again. Often the mediating conditions can be manipulated more easily than can object properties or factors within the person, and on this account we turn to the former when we wish to influence perceptual contact. It may be easier for $p$ to put in a brighter bulb than to improve $o$'s eyesight or enlarge the newspaper print. Also, he knows that he can bring about clearer perception by having $o$ come closer to the object more easily than he can influence perception in this sense: when he looks at a rabbit, he cannot voluntarily produce the percept of a dog (though in certain conditions of the laboratory, those involving ambiguous figures, for example, the way a figure is seen can sometimes be influenced intentionally).

As a survey of this section on the conditions of perception, the following may be noted: In our everyday relations with other people we take the conditions of perception into account. We note the properties of objects, their visibility, appearance, and underlying reality; we are aware of mediating conditions and factors within the person that influence perception. We may be concerned with the circumstances or underlying conditions of these conditions. The knowledge of these conditions bears upon our actions: we attempt to produce or prevent perception by affecting the conditions. It bears upon our expectations: we shall expect $o$ to perceive something or not depending upon whether or not the necessary conditions are present. And finally it bears upon our attributions: we account for the perceptual experience of others in terms of existing conditions.

The effects on actions, expectations, and attributions as we have discussed them are effects on $p$ as he reacts to $o$ as a perceiver. Common-sense psychology also recognizes that $o$'s perceptions have certain effects on $o$ which in turn affects $p$ in important ways. It is to these effects that we now direct our attention.

## Effects of Perception

The meaning of the content "$o$ perceives $x$" and the way we react to this content is greatly influenced by our beliefs concerning the effects on *o* when *o* perceives *x*. We have seen that perception is experienced as a participation of the perceiver in the environment. When *o* sees *x*, his knowledge of *x* will usually be improved; he will form a more adequate representation of *x*, of its location and properties. Most of the effects of perception, as we accept them in common-sense psychology, can be interpreted as effects of the improved representation of the thing perceived. The following are some of the more important effects of perception which play a role in our behavior toward other persons as perceivers.

**Perception and control.** Perception aids control over the part of the environment that becomes clarified by it. In Lewin's (1936) terms, an unstructured region, that is, a region whose properties are not known to the person, can be considered a barrier which makes action and therefore control difficult if not impossible (pp. 130 ff.). Perception helps to structure the region and to remove this barrier. If *o* sees *p*, the knowledge gained of his location gives *o* a much greater possibility of acting on *p*. If *o* does not know where *p* is, then *p* is out of the direct range of the physical power of *o*. Therefore, if *p* is fearful lest *o* harm him, *p* may "hide" from *o* by making it difficult for *o* to perceive him. Then *p* prevents *o*'s action by placing himself in a region that is unstructured for *o*. One may likewise hide one's wishes, intentions, or attitudes from other people in order to keep them from the control of other people. In many cases the idea that knowledge is power is objectively justified. In magic thinking, however, the application of this idea is not always warranted by scientific fact, as when a person keeps his name a secret because this knowledge would give his enemies power over him.

Sartre's theory of the "look" (1943, pp. 252 ff.) can be interpreted as an emphasis on the power aspect of perception to the exclusion of everything else—though one should be aware of the danger of reading a too concrete psychological meaning into a philosophical discussion. The following quotation is from Schuetz's description of Sartre's ideas:

If another looks at me, a basic change occurs in my way of being . . . He, by merely looking at me, becomes the limit of my freedom. Formerly, the world was open to my possibilities; now it is he, the other, who defines me and my situation within the world from his point of view, thus transforming my relations to objects into factors of *his* possibilities. . . . My own possibilities are turned into probabilities beyond my control. I am no longer the master of the situation, or at least the situation has gained a dimension which escapes me. I have become a utensil with which and upon which the other may act. I realize this experience not by way of cognition, but by a sentiment of uneasiness or discomfort, which, according to Sartre, is one of the outstanding features of the human condition. (Schuetz, 1948, p. 188.)

Schuetz criticizes this extreme point of view and argues against Sartre's alternatives, "Either the Other looks at me and alienates my liberty, or I assimilate and seize the liberty of the Other" (p. 199). People can perceive each other in the freedom of their actions. If $o$ looks at $p$, it is true that $p$ becomes an "object" of $o$'s perception; but this does not mean that he necessarily becomes an "object" in the sense that he becomes a thing, an entity at the mercy of outside forces. Though perception can help produce a relationship of mastery and dependence, it does not necessarily do so.

The tendency to protect one's privacy will be the stronger the more the tendency toward autonomy is developed. It is the tendency to want a "place of one's own," some personal regions whose fate is not determined by someone else, which is expressed by the need for privacy. Either $p$ himself wants to have control over these regions or he wants them to develop according to their immanent trends undisturbed by extraneous factors. If another person knows about them, they are integrated in a transactional interpersonal process on which their fate will depend in part.

We have said that perception, at least under certain circumstances, gives the perceiver power over the object perceived. One should add that, in a sense, the reverse relation also holds. Since the life space is more or less influenced by the perceived environment, the one who is perceived is to some extent the source of what goes on in the perceiver's life space. To be recognized or to be listened to, means to be influential. The person who occupies the "center of the stage," who is the "cynosure of all eyes" plays an important role in the life spaces of the spectators. When children try to get attention they want to control the situation.

Since control over the environment depends on perception, the latter may be inferred from the former. When we observe a person driving without a collision, we are certain that he sees the cars around him.

**Perception and evaluation.** The second point that is important for the functional meaning of perception in interpersonal relations is that if $o$ gets to know something about a matter that concerns $p$, $o$ is apt to react to it positively or negatively. While the first point concerns power relations and the concept of "can" (cf. Chapter 4), this point concerns sentiments (cf. Chapter 7). In order to produce a good opinion of himself in $o$, $p$ will try to show his positive sides and will try to hide what is negative about him.

Especially significant is the fact that $p$'s awareness of $o$ as a perceiving and evaluating organism leads him to become keenly aware of himself as a separate entity that is being evaluated. He becomes, in short, self-conscious. He is not necessarily aware that he is or will become self-conscious upon being observed, though in some cases this may be the focus of his concern. In any case, the effects of self-consciousness will be discussed not so much in terms of the common-sense beliefs about them, but as real consequences that may be described by a systematic observer.

The experience of being scrutinized pulls *p* very strongly into the interpersonal process going on between *p* and *o*. Because *o*'s judgment of him is often vital to *p* in a uniquely personal way, he seeks to inform himself of this evaluation. If he believes that *o*'s reception is favorable, *p*'s action may become strengthened and more organized; but if he is insecure about *o*'s reaction, or believes it is negative, *p*'s action may go on with a conflicting and interfering content present in *p*'s life space.

The disturbance stemming from the relation of perception and evaluation is stressed by White, Wright, and Dembo (1948) in their analysis of the difficulties between persons with disabilities and the nondisabled. The person with a disability shields himself from prying eyes and curious minds when he fears that the inquisitors will look down upon him because of his disability. It is particularly disturbing to be stared at, where the analogy to a "monkey in the zoo" readily fills in the unstructured content of "*o* perceives *p*."

Also in Wapner and Alper's study of the effect of an audience on behavior, the apprizing character of perception is seen to play a significant role. The task consisted of selecting one of two words that best applied to a given phrase (e.g. "a masculine characteristic" followed by the words "strong-weak"). Forty phrase-word combinations were used. The result was:

Time to make a choice was longest in the presence of an unseen audience, next in the presence of a seen audience, and shortest when there was no audience other than the experimenter. (Wapner and Alper, 1952, p. 228.)

The authors conclude that the important factor was that

. . . an audience may serve to threaten self-status (need to be thought well of by others). The audience, after all, is a potential interpreter of the choices made by the individual . . . an audience that cannot be seen but is "out there" watching and listening to the choices being made is indeed more threatening to self-status than an audience whose composition is known. (p. 227.)

This factor influences the choice, since the more threatening the audience, the longer is the decision time. The content of "*o* perceives

$p$" was most unstructured in the case of the unseen audience, and as was pointed out in the analysis of staring (cf. above), it is this factor that gives such an uncertain range to the way in which $p$ is being evaluated.

McTeer (1953), in a paper on emotions, has stressed that experimental findings may be expected to differ depending on who is directing the experiment and recording the data since the subject perceives this person as an *evaluating observer*. He reports the divergent results of a replicated study and accounts for them by just this factor. The research used changes in grip tension following electric shock in mirror tracting. The first study reported considerable tension as measured by pressure upon a rubber bulb, but the second study found little evidence for this. The only significant difference between the two studies was the relationship of subject to experimenter. In the first, the subjects were students of the experimenter, making the supposition tenable that the tension stemmed from the interpretation of the experiment as a testing situation in which the experimenter observed and "graded." In the second, the experimenter was just another student.

The disintegrating effect of self-consciousness produced by the seeming exposure of oneself to the perception of another is familiar to naive psychology. Words like shyness and embarrassment often imply this component. J. M. Baldwin forcefully describes, on the basis of his own experiences, the disintegration that can occur:

> To people who are thus constituted, the social relation is, purely from an organic point of view, the most exhausting, nerve-trying relation which one can well imagine. It is quite impossible to keep up even the most trivial social contact, such as travelling with an acquaintance, sitting or walking with a friend, etc., without soon getting in a condition of such nervous strain that, unless one break the relation occasionally to be alone, even the "yes" and "no" of conversation becomes a task of tasks. If, however, the relation involves thought of an objective kind which does not bring the social relation itself forward, such intercourse is most exhilarating and enjoyable. . . . This "sense of other persons" may break up all the mental processes. The present writer cannot think the same thoughts, nor follow the same plan of action, nor control the muscles with the same sufficiency, nor concentrate the attention with the same directness, nor, in fact, do any blessed thing as well, when this sense of the presence of others is upon him. (Baldwin, 1902, pp. 213–214.)

Embarrassment and its expression is discussed in detail by Hellpach (1913). According to Hellpach, though almost all emotions contain a reference to other persons, embarrassment is the most social one since the actual presence of the other person is necessary. The superiority of the other person over $p$ is the strongest factor making for embarrassment of $p$, especially intellectual superiority. An adult is rarely embarrassed in front of a small child, but the child often in front of an adult. Of situations which make for embarrassment, Hellpach mentions: (1) to be found out in an insincerity or deceit, be caught in relatively harmless trespasses, lies, contradictions, malapropisms, or erotic concealments; (2) to feel oneself observed by $o$ when entering a group, meeting a person, greeting, or appearing in public; (3) when we want to get something from $o$, and we are not sure of success (for instance in sexual wooing); or (4) when we have to tell $o$ something which is disagreeable to $o$. Thus, scolding can be embarrassing for the scolder, and transmitting unpleasant messages for the messenger. Embarrassment is often mitigated when a third person is present. If $p$ has to tell $o$ bad news, he will be afraid that $o$ will react in an emotional way; but when a third person is present, there is less likelihood of this.

From these cases Hellpach deduces the features that make for embarrassment. First, embarrassment implies the presence of $o$; second, it implies an awareness that the attention of $o$ is directed toward $p$, and an apprehension that refers to the feelings of $o$ about $p$; third, embarrassment is often furthered by empathy.

It is plausible that shyness and embarrassment will be the more intense the greater the potency $o$ and $o$'s opinion of $p$ have for $p$. Lord Chesterfield writes:

How many men have I seen here, who ... when they have been presented to the king, did not know whether they stood upon their heads or their heels! If the king spoke to them, they were annihilated; they trembled, endeavored to put their hands in their pockets, and missed them; let their hats fall, and were ashamed to take them up; and in short, put themselves in every attitude but the right, that is, the easy and natural one. (Chesterfield, p. 74.)

The most primitive way of reducing the discomfort of self-consciousness is to avoid or escape from the situation producing it. A child may hide behind its mother in an attempt to block out the offending condition, namely $o$ as an evaluating perceiver. By breaking the visual contact with $o$, $p$ severs the interpersonal process and thereby weakens the intolerable self-consciousness stemming from it. Subtler ways of management become part of the resources of the more mature person for whom direct flight is but an exposure of his insecurity. Instead he may lower his eyes or shift the conversation to nonpersonal matters.

As for establishing the conditions in order to produce embarrassment, we generally apply our knowledge with another person rather than ourselves as the target. Even the school age child understands well how to create embarrassment in another in spite of the fact that he would be hard-pressed to define his techniques in terms of necessary conditions.

Not only is it true that perception leads to evaluation; evaluation can also lead to perception. People like to look at persons with high prestige, and being "noticed" or "regarded" has both cognitive and evaluative meanings. The vain man will think that everybody looks at him and listens to him because of his positive value; the guilty man will think they do so because of his negative value.

*Motivation of further action.* We have already seen that perception influences $o$'s action possibilities, what he can and cannot do, and thus influences his control over the environment. Perception also influences action by arousing motivational states in the person. This is not only true in the stock examples of "incentive" as when a child sees appetizing candy, but holds also for more complex situations. Such examples as the following are common:

When we see that something is possible, we may try to do it.

When we see that $o$ benefits or harms us or our friends, we may be motivated to reciprocate.

Evaluation on the basis of perception may lead to sentiment-derived actions: praising, damning, rewarding, punishing.

Perceiving a sign of $o$'s sentiments toward $p$ may arouse $p$'s sentiment toward $o$ and lead to sentiment-derived actions.

Seeing a situation fraught with danger may lead to avoiding and correcting actions: I see that the tire is about to blow out; I smell a leak in the gas pipe; I see a child playing in traffic; I notice termites in the foundation of my house.

In common-sense psychology, we have many beliefs on the order of "if $o$ were to see $x$, he would do $y$." Therefore, we know that in order to produce or prevent action, the most efficacious *modus operandi* may be to produce or prevent perception.

*Ability to report on the perceived.* One of the significant action possibilities with which $p$ is concerned is that of communication. He knows that when $o$ has perceived something, he can tell about it. He also may infer, when $p$ tells about something, that $p$ has seen it. Moreover, $o$'s descriptions as a firsthand witness to the situation become particularly potent. Therefore, $p$ may prevent $o$ from coming into perceptual contact with $x$ in order to prevent him from becoming such a messenger. Or, just because he wishes $o$ to become a link in the transmission of information, he may tell him about $x$, or show him $x$, or send him out as a scout to observe $x$.

**Perception and communion between persons.** Perception can also serve to establish a union between persons. Simmel says:

> Of the special sense organs, the eye has a uniquely sociological function. The union and interaction of individuals is based upon mutual glances. This is perhaps the most direct and purest reciprocity which exists anywhere. This highest psychic reaction, however, in which the glances of eye to eye unite men, crystallizes into no objective structure; the unity which momentarily arises between two persons is present in the occasion and is dissolved in the function. So tenacious and subtle is this union that it can only be maintained by the shortest and straightest line between the eyes, and the smallest deviation from it, the slightest glance aside, completely destroys the unique character of this union. . . . This mutual glance between persons, in distinction from the simple sight or observation of the other, signifies a wholly new and unique union between them. . . . By the glance which reveals the other, one discloses himself. By the same act in which the observer seeks to know the observed, he surrenders himself to be understood by the observer. The eye cannot take unless at the same time it gives. . . . What occurs in this direct mutual glance represents the most perfect reciprocity in the entire field of human relationships. (Simmel, 1921, p. 358.)

Of course, one may object that the fact that two people look at each other is no guarantee that they really understand each other, or that a real union arises. Both may have unrevealed thoughts, or they may even fight with their glances, in which case there is a struggle and one wants to outstare the other. Nevertheless, there is a peculiar functional closeness and interaction in a mutual glance. One could assume that $o$ holds a special position within $p$'s life space since the representation of $o$ includes the fact that in $o$'s life space the representation of $p$ is also potent at the moment. Each is aware that he sees the other. It is also noteworthy that in the conversational union, in what Malinowski (1928) called the "phatic communion" (p. 478) the mouth gives and the ear receives, whereas in the optic communion the same organ gives and receives.

Communion through the eyes creates such an intense interpersonal experience that usually only when a deep intimacy is sought is the mutual perception maintained. More typically, one of them breaks the connection by gazing away.

## Summary

In this presentation of the effects of $o$'s perceptions on $o$, as understood by $p$, we have again seen that $p$ in turn is affected in important ways:

1. His actions are influenced: If the effects are desirable he will try to produce perception; if not he will try to prevent it.

2. His expectations are affected: If he knows that $o$ has perceived something, he will expect the consequences of this perception to occur also.

3. His attributions are determined: If he knows that a consequence has occurred, he will infer that perception, as the necessary condition of this consequence, has also occurred.

Among the experienced effects of perception, the following were singled out for special emphasis:

1. Control over the environment as an effect of perception: When he can observe it, $o$ has more control over the environment than when he cannot. Knowing this, $p$ may try to influence $o$'s perception in order to influence $o$'s action possibilities. For instance, he may hide himself or his thoughts in order to escape $o$'s control.

2. Evaluation as an effect of perception: What is perceived is often judged favorably or unfavorably. Also, $p$ may influence $o$'s perception in order to influence $o$'s evaluation of $x$, especially of $p$ himself; or $p$ reveals himself and what belongs to him in order to produce a positive reaction; he brags and shows off. Or, he hides himself in order to prevent a negative evaluation. Furthermore, $o$ as an evaluating perceiver creates a heightened self-consciousness in $p$ which may take the form of shyness and embarrassment, and $p$ attempts to ward off this discomfiting state by avoiding the conditions that give rise to it. He may, by design, establish the conditions for embarrassment in another.

3. Motivation of further action as an effect of perception: $p$ may influence $o$'s perception in order to motivate $o$ towards an action, or prevent such motivation. For example, $p$ may hide what he has done if he thinks that $o$ would get angry and harm him if he were informed of it.

4. Ability to report as an effect of perception: $p$ may influence $o$'s perception because if $o$ were to see $x$ he would be able to report about $x$ to other people. Therefore, $p$ hides what he has done in order to prevent $o$'s telling about it, or he reveals something just to initiate gossip.

5. Communion as an effect of mutual perception: There is a peculiar functional closeness in the mutual glance; $p$ allows this communion when he seeks intimacy and avoids it by deflecting his gaze.

# CHAPTER 4

# The naive analysis
# of action

IN THIS CHAPTER we shall be concerned with
the actions of another person, in particular with the basic constituents
of an action sequence which lead us to know that another person is
trying to do something, intends to do something, has the ability to
do something, etc. The concepts also apply to one's own actions,
but our main emphasis will be on actions in interpersonal relations.
We shall also explore the consequences of such cognition—how we
utilize knowledge of the basic constituents of action in interpreting
action and in predicting and controlling it. The concepts involved
in the naive analysis of action stand, as we shall see, in systematic
relations to each other just as do the terms of a good scientific system
of concepts. Our task will be to formulate this system more explicitly.

This task requires a description of the causal nexus of an environment which contains not only the directly observable facts about the
behavior of another person, but also their connection with the more
stable structures and processes underlying that behavior. It is an
important principle of common-sense psychology, as it is of scientific
theory in general, that man grasps reality, and can predict and control
it, by referring transient and variable behavior and events to relatively
unchanging underlying conditions, the so-called dispositional properties
of his world. This principle, already discussed in this book, will
become increasingly familiar as we continue the investigation of
common-sense psychology. It is time that we examined it more fully.

## Dispositional Properties

***The nature of and search for dispositional properties.*** The term dispositional properties is applied to those properties that "dispose" objects and events to manifest themselves in certain ways under certain conditions. Dispositional properties are the invariances that make possible a more or less stable, predictable, and controllable world. They refer to the relatively unchanging structures and processes that characterize or underlie phenomena. (Cf., for instance, Ryle, 1949, Chapter 5.)

Instances of relatively unchanging structures are such object properties as color and size, such person properties as character and ability. We feel, for example, that John's good grades make sense when we refer his achievement, a relatively momentary event, to his high intelligence, a more or less permanent property, and we then believe we are safe in predicting a successful college career. But static structures are not the only ones that can serve as reference points for understanding. Processes may also provide a basis for understanding as long as they show relatively constant coordination to changes in underlying structures or to other processes. For example, "practice makes perfect" is satisfying as an explanatory principle insofar as the process of repetition is felt to be highly coordinated to skill.

The causal structure of the environment, both as the scientist describes it and as the naive person apprehends it, is such that we are usually in contact only with what may be called the offshoots or manifestations of underlying core-processes or core-structures. For example, if I find sand on my desk, I shall want to find out the underlying reason for this circumstance. I make this inquiry not because of idle curiosity, but because only if I refer this relatively insignificant offshoot event to an underlying core event will I attain a stable environment and have the possibility of controlling it. Should I find that the sand comes from a crack in the ceiling and that this crack appeared because of the weakness in one of the walls, then I have reached the layer of underlying conditions which is of vital importance for me. The sand on my desk is merely a symptom, a manifestation that remains ambiguous until it becomes anchored to dispositional properties—cracks and stresses in this case.

***The depth dimension of the invariances.*** The search for relatively enduring aspects of our world, the dispositional properties in nature, may carry us quite far from the immediate facts or they may end hardly a step from them. That is, there exists a hierarchy of cognitive awarenesses which begin with the more stimulus-bound recognition of "facts," and gradually go deeper into the underlying causes of these facts. What is called "fact" here is similar to what Ichheiser (1949) calls the "raw material" of social perception: "Let us call those data which are interpreted and misinterpreted by mechanisms of social perception the 'raw material' of social perception" (p. 12). The raw material is the stuff, so to speak, of which the organism forms a conclusion. Thus, in the hierarchy of cognitive awareness, each previous layer stands to the succeeding one in the relation of raw material to interpretation.

For a concrete illustration, let us assume that a person, $p$, is confronted with an agreeable, happy experience, $x$. This is the raw material at a level close to the peripheral stimulus. The next step of interpretation may be: What is the immediate source of $x$? Is it chance? Am I the cause of it? Or is another person, $o$, the cause? If $o$ is accepted as cause, the question of motive or intention may well arise. Did he do it in order to please me, or was the event only an accidental by-product of a different goal? Perhaps he was ordered to help me, perhaps he did it to put me under an obligation to him, or to relieve his conscience, or to please someone else. But if $p$ perceives $o$ as really wanting to please him, there are still deeper layers of interpretation possible. The need "$o$ wants to please $p$" may be caused by temporary goodwill in $o$; it may be "displaced love"; or it may come from a more permanent sentiment that $o$ feels toward $p$. Finally, the underlying attitude itself may be traced to further sources. For example, $p$ may feel that $o$'s attitude toward him is a function of $o$'s personality, that $o$ is a kind person. Or, $p$ may feel that the sentiment stems from the compatibility in their natures, etc.

Underscoring the main points of this illustration, we note first, that man is usually not content simply to register the observables that surround him; he needs to refer them as far as possible to the invariances of his environment. Second, the underlying causes of events, especially the motives of other persons, are the invariances of the environment that are relevant to him; they give meaning to what he experiences and it is these meanings that are recorded in his life space, and are precipitated as the reality of the environment to which he then reacts.

As applied to the actions of another person, the depth dimension of relevant invariances is often of the following order: There is first the raw material which provides the information that change $x$ occurs or has occurred and that $o$ causes or has caused $x$ (though this can already be a further level of interpretation). Then, further meaning is given to these facts when, relating them to certain dispositional properties of the person and of the environment, we conclude that *o* can do *x*, *o* wants to do *x*, o is trying to do *x*, *o* likes to do *x*, etc. These conclusions become the recorded reality for us, so much so that most typically they are not experienced as interpretations at all. We shall now investigate certain features surrounding the actions of another person which lead us to penetrate the depth dimension of the invariances and precipitate into reality the meaning of actions.

### Effective Forces of the Person and Environment in the Action Outcome

In common-sense psychology (as in scientific psychology) the result of an action is felt to depend on two sets of conditions, namely factors within the person and factors within the environment. Naive psychology also has different terms to express the contributions of these factors. Consider the example of a person rowing a boat across a lake. The following is but a sample of expressions used to refer to factors that are significant to the action outcome. We say, "He is *trying* to row the boat across the lake," "He has the *ability* to row the boat across the lake," "He *can* row the boat across the lake," "He *wants* to row the boat across the lake," "It is *difficult* to row the boat across the lake," "Today there is a good *opportunity* for him to row the boat across the lake," "It is sheer *luck* that he succeeded in rowing the boat across the lake." These varying descriptive statements have reference to personal factors on the one hand and to environmental factors on the other. One may speak of the effective force (*ff*) of the person or of the environment when one means the totality of forces emanating from one or the other source.

The action outcome, *x*, may then be said to be dependent upon a combination of effective personal force and effective environmental force, thus:

$$x = f \ (ff \ \text{person}, ff \ \text{environment})$$

One is tempted to formulate the underlying relation between the two independent variables as an additive one, for if the effective environmental force is zero (which would mean that the combination of environmental factors neither hinders nor furthers the result *x*), then *x* will depend only on the effective personal force. One would also have to assume that *x* would occur without any personal intervention if the effective environmental force were greater than zero (that is if those environmental factors favorable to *x* were greater than those unfavorable to *x*). This would be the case if the wind carried the boat safely to shore while the rower was asleep.

The effective personal force is also analyzed into two contributing factors: a power factor and a motivational factor. We shall have more to say about these components in the course of our discussion, but here let it suffice to point out that the power factor is often represented by ability; there are other characteristics of a person that affect his power, temperament for example, but ability is commonly felt to head the list. The motivational factor refers to what a person is trying to do (his intention) and how hard he is trying to do it (exertion). The contribution of the rower to the outcome *x*, therefore, depends on his ability to maneuver the boat and on how hard he tries to accomplish the goal.

Thus, the schema that is used is the following:

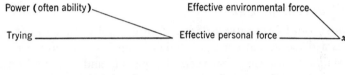

Or,

$$x = f \text{ (trying, power, environment)}$$

The personal constituents, namely power and trying, are related as a multiplicative combination, since the effective personal force is zero if either of them is zero. For instance, if a person has the ability but does not try at all he will make no progress toward the goal.

The personal and environmental contributions to action do not have the same status. The effective personal force shows the traits of personal causality (see later, pp. 100 ff.); it is truly directed toward the goal in the sense that this direction is an invariant characteristic of the force, invariant to the changing circumstances. When we talk of direction toward or away from the goal in regard to impersonal environmental forces, we are using the term in a different sense. Notice that in the above schema, "trying" was not given as a constituent of the effective environmental force. The wind has the direction of furthering or hindering the progress of the boat only accidentally. It is not "trying" or "exerting itself" to produce a certain state of affairs. Only when we think of the wind in an anthropomorphic way would we say: "It could hold up the boat if it only tried hard enough."

Whether a person tries to do something and whether he has the requisite abilities to accomplish it are so significantly different in the affairs of everyday life that naive psychology has demarcated those factors still further by regrouping the constituents of action in such a way that the power factor and the effective environmental force are combined into the concept "can," leaving the motivational factor clearly separate and distinct. The conceptual groupings may be indicated as follows:

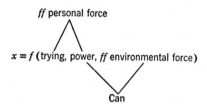

$$x = f \,(\text{trying, power, } \mathit{ff} \text{ environmental force})$$

with *ff* personal force above and Can below.

Our plan is first to examine the concept of can, to discuss the properties and conditions underlying its power and environmental components and end with an analysis of the concept of "try" in action.

## The Concept of Can

**Dispositional character of can.** Can generally, though not exclusively, is a dispositional concept, which means that it refers to a relatively stable relationship between the person and the environment. As a dispositional concept it allows the person to ask and answer such questions as, "Will I be able to do the task again?" "Will other people be able to do it as well?" Temporary factors that affect an action outcome are generally ascribed to luck or to transitory personal states such as fatigue rather than to the "can." Thus, if I accidentally hit the bull's eye, I will not feel that I can hit it in the sense of being able to hit it again should I try. I was just lucky.

Sometimes, however, can is used to represent temporary relations between person and environment. We say, "I can't do it now because I am too tired." Or we say, "He can swim the channel when the weather conditions are just right." Notice, however, that the temporary factors, fatigue in the first case and opportunity in the second, are explicitly indicated as disrupting the usual state of affairs obtaining between the powers of the person and the environmental situation.

**Can and may.** The distinction between can and may as understood by naive psychology is offered by the Webster dictionary under "may":

. . . *can* expresses ability, whether physical or mental; *may* implies permission or sanction; as he will do it if he possibly *can;* I shall call tomorrow, if I *may.*

In topological psychology, this difference is found in the source to which the limits of the space of free movement are ascribed. The totality of activities a person can perform has been designated by

Lewin (1936) as the "space of free movement." Or, the space of free movement consists of those regions (areas, particularly activities, within the person's life space) accessible to the person. The limits of the space of free movement are mainly set by (1) quasi-physical barriers—what is beyond a person's abilities and (2) quasi-social barriers—what is forbidden to a person.

Expressing the difference between can and may in terms of our basic concepts, we have:

Can: absence of imposed restraining environmental forces, or imposed restraining forces smaller than own power.

Cannot: imposed environmental restraining forces greater than own power.

May: another person who has power over me, or the objective order (moral laws, etc.) does not wish me not to do $x$; if that is true then I may do $x$.

May not: another person who has power over me, or the objective order wishes me not to do $x$. If I do it anyway (and that is possible in case I can do it but may not) then my action was counter to the wish forces of $o$, or of the objective order. If $o$ is powerful enough he will "punish" me.

As a succint statement of the difference between can and may we note:

Can: if he tries he will succeed.
May: if he tries he will not be punished.

Both may and can are sometimes used in the sense of possibility. When we say "He may do $x$" we may mean "It is possible that he will do it." To say "It can happen" is equivalent to saying "It is possible that it will happen." But it is not equivalent to "It is possible that he will do it." On occasion it makes good sense to say "He could do it but I am perfectly sure he never will."

The may and may not of permission is sometimes transformed into the can and cannot of possibility. If a person marks things with his name, he has symbolically indicated that "other people may not use these things"; if he puts them into a safe, he has transformed the may into "other people cannot use these things." The honor system of examinations relies on the may not; separating the examinees on the cannot. Markers are sufficient to indicate may and may not but it is the height of the fences that is the determining factor in the can and cannot.

*Can and try as conditions of the outcome.* It will be helpful to restate the basic constituents of can and the position of can in the action outcome:

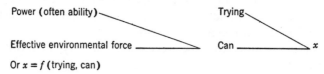

Or $x = f$ (trying, can)

Thus, all the relatively permanent factors that influence the effect but are not ascribed to the motivational factor—that is, the "trying" of the person—are lumped together and become the factor of "can." If a person can do something and he tries to do it, then he will do it (barring temporary circumstances). Common expressions are: "He could do it if he only tried," "He tries very hard but he just cannot do it," or "I will do it as soon as I can."

Ichheiser (1933) says that the experience of "I can" is a knowledge that one is able to reach a goal or to produce an effect if one only wills it. This hypothetical clause, "if one only wills it," i.e., if one only really tries, if one exerts all one's powers, is important. If one tries one's best to produce an effect, and one can produce it, then the effect will come about (excluding, of course, cases of "bad luck"). Both "$p$ tries to cause $x$" and "$p$ can cause $x$" are conceived of as conditions of "$p$ causes $x$." Both are necessary but neither is sufficient.

Relating the roles of "can" and "try" in the action outcome to the effective forces of the person and of the environment, we can state the following: When we say: "He can do it, but fails only because he does not try sufficiently" then we mean that the effective personal force is smaller than the restraining environmental force only because the exertion is not great enough; with greater exertion he would succeed. The concept "can" means that if a person tries to do $x$, no environmental force away from $x$ is likely to arise that would be greater in its resultant effects than the effective personal force of $p$ toward $x$.

The word can has also been used in other senses than the personal can, the concept being explored in this chapter. We may say, as noted by Ryle (1949), "Stones can float (for pumice stones float)" (p. 126). But this usage is not to be confused with personal can.

*Constituents of can.* As already noted, can refers to the relation between the power or ability of the person and the strength of the environmental forces. The relationship might be further specified as:

can = $f$ (power, ability − difficulty of environmental factors)

If the task is easy, then even a person with little ability can do it; if it is difficult, the person cannot do it unless he has greater ability. Or, we may say, if a person succeeds, then his ability must be greater than the environmental difficulty; if he fails (and has maximally exerted himself), his ability must be less than the environmental difficulty. We see, therefore, that though "can" is a function of ability or power, it is not identical with it.

To avoid possible confusion, we wish to make explicit that the term power is used not only to express a meaning different from can. In ordinary conversation, the sentence "$p$ has the power to do $x$" is often used as identical in meaning to the sentence "$p$ can do $x$." In our formulation, however, "can" refers to a relation between the person and the environment; the nonmotivational factors contributed by the person are encompassed by the generic term, power. Yet, in some places in the discussion that follows, it will be seen that we have used power and can more or less interchangeably. This occurs when, to all intents and purposes, the environmental factors can be disregarded. Furthermore, our use of power differs from the topological one in which power is restricted to social power, that is to the case "$p$ can cause $o$ to do something."

**The cognition of can through action.** The most direct recognition that $p$ can do something is given by his actual behavior. If he causes a change in the environment, we conclude that he can cause this change. Ichheiser (1933) has also pointed out that we get to know what we can do through realization, i.e., by transforming the potential can into real action. In reality testing or testing the limits, a person may attempt a task in order to learn just what he can and cannot do, or what he may do without suffering negative consequences. On the other hand, if a person only talks about effecting a change in the environment, that is if he only expresses his intention of doing something, then we may attribute the absence of the action effect to the absence of the can, one of the necessary conditions of action. A person who only threatens harm but does not execute his threat is judged feeble; the one who carries out the threat, strong. In the first case it is concluded that the person cannot harm me, in the second case that he can. "Actions speak louder than words" is an expression not only applying to intentions, but also applying to abilities.

However, action outcome as the criterion for the determination of can is sometimes misleading. A person's failure is often seen as proving that the task is too difficult or that he lacks the requisite ability, i.e., can factors, when actually motivational factors are mainly responsible. Or a particular success, when a matter of luck, may sometimes be erroneously ascribed to can. The boy who accidentally hits the bull's eye may feel that he is a good marksman.

As we shall see later, in addition to the perceptual data given by the outcome of an action, there are other bases for believing that a person can or cannot do something. Not all of these are equally reliable. For example, a strong need may lead to an unjustified belief that one is able to do something. Factors that indirectly influence beliefs about can will be considered in the following sections which deal with the personal and environmental properties significant in can.

As with most psychological phenomena, what a person can do is not always apprehended in consciousness. As Stern (1935) has suggested, much of the time "can" exists as a background, like a mental set (pp. 570 ff.). We walk, recount events and digest food without at the same time having a conscious experience that we can do these things. However, when what one can do becomes problematic, then we tend to think about it and become aware of it. The question of what can and cannot be accomplished with an arm prosthesis is in the foreground when a person is being fitted with it for the first time. The insecure swimmer will wonder whether he can swim the lake when he is put to the test. The confident student is sure that he can solve the equation when challenged by another. Questioning, wondering about, and knowing the can are all conscious experiences of can. But the can that does not penetrate into our consciousness also belongs to the explication of the concept of can.

In the events of everyday life, we are interested not only in what people can do. We want to know whether what a person can do is primarily due to his own characteristics, his abilities for example, or primarily due to favorable environmental conditions. Such knowledge enables the person to profit from experience as well as to influence the outcome of actions involving other people. Let us suppose that the speeches of a certain politician were poorly received. He might ascribe the failure to the shortcomings of the speeches, that is, to his own creations and therefore to himself: they were too rough, too highbrow, too emotional, too general, or too factual. He might ascribe the failure to his appearance or to the fact that he was not enough of a regular guy, or that he got stage fright. On the other hand, the source of the failure might be placed outside himself, on the audience, for example. He might feel that it was too primitive, that it fell only for slogans, or was too prejudiced. He might attribute the failure to the physical setting: the acoustics were poor, it was too cold, the seats were uncomfortable. In any case, he would then try to avoid that to which he attributes his failure and strengthen that to which he attributes success. The learning, of course, may be based on the experience of others. If the politician sees another man succeed or fail, he will try to imitate that to which he attributes the success and avoid that to which he attributes the failure.

Attribution, the linking of an event with its underlying conditions, involves a kind of unit formation. In the case of "can" a unit is formed between the possibility of success or failure and person or environment. If the success "belongs" to the person, then the person is felt to be responsible for it; if it belongs to the environment, then the environment is held accountable. Therefore, though "can" is a resultant of two contributing sources, it is sometimes ascribed more to the person and sometimes more to the environment. We shall now inquire into the conditions of attribution to one or the other source and also examine further the properties of the person and of the environment that are important in can.*

***Difficulty—an important dispositional property of the environment.*** Often, as we have just seen, the success or failure of an action provides the raw material for the perception of "can." If a person successfully completes an action, we say, "He can do it" but the implications are very different if we conclude "He can do it because it is so easy" or "He can do it because he has such great ability." In both instances the personal force is permanently greater than the environmental force but in one case the reason is that the environmental force is small and in the other case that the personal force is great. That is, the superiority of the personal force is attributed either to the person or to the environment.

An important basis for such attribution is the following. If we know that only one person succeeded or only one person failed out of a large number in a certain endeavor, then we shall ascribe success or failure to this person—to his great ability or to his lack of ability. On the other hand, if we know that practically everyone who tries succeeds, we shall attribute the success to the task. The task is then described as being easy. If hardly anyone succeeds it is felt to be difficult.

Sometimes the knowledge concerning group performance and the appraisal of task difficulty is inferred from the performance of a

---

* In the sectional headings below, sometimes "power," sometimes "environment," and sometimes "can" appears. Where the factors under consideration apply more or less clearly to one of the components of can, namely power or environment, the corresponding term designates the section. Where, however, ambiguity as to attribution exists, or where "can" as such is being emphasized, then "can" is used.

single individual. If a child, for example, successfully bakes a cake or reads a book, we conclude that the recipe or book was easy. In effect we have made use of the postulates linking can with power and environmental difficulty: (1) Since success has occurred, the task difficulty must be smaller than the ability. (2) Since a child has effected the success, we presume that the ability is low. (3) Therefore, we conclude that the task is easy and that most adults would be able to accomplish it.

Exertion, often, is the dominant clue for inferring task difficulty. When we see a person performing a skilled act, like dancing or diving or playing a musical instrument with elegance and ease, we may well feel that the task is probably not so hard after all. Only our rational knowledge about "what it takes" checks us from this tempting conclusion; we modify our interpretation and say, "It looks so easy." The high pressure salesman effortlessly demonstrates a new gadget in order to convince a gullible public of the simplicity of the operation, when in reality considerable skill may be required. As for self-exertion, if I find that I can do something with little effort, I am likely to judge that the task is easy unless I think I have special ability. If it takes considerable application, then I judge it to be difficult. But unless I place my ability in the framework of others' I will not be able legitimately to predict how another will fare with the same task.

The unit forming character of attribution is clearly seen in judgments concerning task difficulty. If $p$ is the only person who can do a certain act, or if there are only a few other people who can do it, then the task is difficult and the action belongs in a peculiar way to $p$. A strong unit between the possibility of success in this action and $p$ is formed. If, however, the task is felt to be so easy that anyone could do it, then the possibility of the action lies in the environment. Speaking topologically, some regions of the individual's space of free movement are common to the spaces of free movement of many people; others have a closer connection with the person.

We shall see later that the assumed difficulty of a task may also be established by such influences as suggestion, needs, task stereotype, etc. In any case, difficulty is one of the important properties assigned to the environmental side of the can complex; it is invariably connected with an object or situation. Even so, there is an implied relation to a person acting. When we say "this is an impossible task," we do not merely mean "it is impossible that this happens." The meaning most important for us is that "If any person tries to do this he is bound to fail," or "No matter how hard I try, I cannot succeed."

Finally, difficulty has a dispositional quality (cf. pp. 80–82).

Referring to a permanent characteristic of the task helps us predict the action outcome on future occasions.

*Opportunity and luck—the more variable environmental factors.* As stated before, man is interested in the invariances of the environment and of the person so he can establish himself in a stable world in which the future can be anticipated and controlled. It is therefore important that a person "diagnose" the temporary conditions that disturb the more permanent coordination between outcome and the dispositional properties of the task and person.

On the environmental side two terms are commonly used to designate the more temporary states. One of these is opportunity. Another is luck. If the strength and direction of the environmental factors fluctuate, the person may wait until they are optional for reaching his goal; i.e., he waits for a good opportunity to do $x$. Likewise, a person is felt to succeed because he is lucky when the resultant environmental force in the direction of the goal is at a maximum, or when the force away from it is at a minimum. Thus, when the success is attributed to luck or opportunity, two things are implied: First, that environmental conditions, rather than the person, are primarily responsible for the outcome, and second, that these environmental conditions are the product of chance; at least this is true for "luck."

As with difficulty, there is a diversity of conditions that lead to the cognition of luck. One of these is consistency, or conversely, variability, of performance. If a person succeeds only once in a great number of trials we will attribute the success to luck, especially if it is followed by a number of failures so it cannot be interpreted as "He has learned it at last." If he fails only once and succeeds at other times, the failure is attributed to bad luck (sometimes temporary personal factors are held accountable). In line with the dispositional character of can, the unusual is attributed to luck and not to the permanent "can" constituents. Whyte (1943) reports that the members of the Norton Street gang judged a bowler not by his strikes—knocking down all the pins with the first ball—but by his ability to get spares, that is, to knock down the pins remaining after the first ball; the strike, a highly inconsistent occurrence, was considered merely a matter of chance (p. 17).

Drawing upon the more lasting properties of the person and environment for judgments concerning "can" serves in effect to make such judgments more realistic. If a person has failed consistently in 50 trials and then suddenly shows a success, it would be very unrealistic to change one's opinion about his ability or about the environmental difficulty: it is more realistic to attribute the success to chance.

Whether or not the outcome of an action is attributed to luck also depends upon our ideas concerning the person's abilities (again a dispositional property). For instance, if we have a very low opinion of a person's ability then any success will be attributed to luck. Whyte says about the high-prestige members of the gang:

Good scores were expected of them, and bad scores were accounted for by bad luck or temporary lapses of form. When a follower threatened to better his position, the remarks took quite a different form. The boys shouted at him that he was lucky, that he was "bowling over his head." The effort was made to persuade him that he should not be bowling as well as he was, that a good performance was abnormal for him. This type of verbal attack was very important in keeping the members "in their places." (Whyte, 1943, p. 24.)

There are other conditions that favor the judgment of luck (cf. p. 284), but these examples suffice to draw an analogy between action attribution and attribution in the case of other phenomena in which dispositional and more transitory, situational factors play a role. The following parallels with the phenomena of color constancy may be drawn:

1. The raw material or datum in the case of action is success and failure, in the case of color phenomena the retinal color.

2. Attribution of this raw material may in both cases be referred to dispositional factors; the abilities of the person or environmental difficulty in the case of action and the object color in the case of color.

3. Or, attribution of the raw material may in both cases be referred to temporary situational factors: luck in the case of action and illumination in the case of color.

The important point is that correct attribution, whether to the stable or to the vacillating conditions underlying an event, always serves to build up and support the constancy of our picture of the world. Naive psychology has therefore found it necessary to isolate those wavering, more fortuitous conditions that interfere with this constancy. Sometimes these conditions are designated luck; events that deviate from constancy are then relegated to good or bad luck depending upon whether or not they favor the person's fortunes. If action outcome is correctly made accountable, then future performance becomes more predictable.

*Ability—a main power factor.* Thus far in the discussion, "power" as the personal contribution to "can," was represented by ability, and for good reason. First of all, ability is clearly a property of the person. Though environmental factors may augment or deplete ability, it describes the person and not the environment. Also, ability is a dispositional concept. It characterizes a person over time and therefore its use is in line with the general tendency to analyze experience in terms of underlying invariances. At the same time it is to be noted that certain facets of ability, for example, knowledge (knowledge is power), are less permanently an integral part of the person than others, as for example, intelligence or strength. We may become shockingly aware of how easily knowledge has been kept from us or with what facility we forget what we have learned. Last but certainly not least, ability, both mental and physical, plays a frequent and significant role in determining a person's power. A person with strength and skill can row the boat farther than one less favorably equipped. A clever man can do more things than a stupid one.

Degree of ability, as has already been pointed out, is sometimes determined by relative standing in the group as measured by success and failure on particular tasks. If $p$ is among the few people who can do a task, his ability is high; if he is among the few who fail, his ability is low.

In addition, ability is sometimes judged by a more irrational spreading of ability in one area to ability in other areas. This halo phenomenon is more fully described in a subsequent chapter as a process characterizing unit relations (cf. pp. 182–184). It involves (1) an assimilation of the whole person to the part and vice versa: If a person shows himself able in one field, he may be considered an able person in general. Or, if he is considered an able person he will be expected to show good ability on a particular task. (2) Sometimes the spread may occur from one area directly to another without the intervention of generalization to the whole person, as when a person who understands grammar is expected to be proficient in spelling as well. Spelling and grammar are assumed to belong together and so display the unit characteristic of spread.

The same spread phenomena occur on the negative end of the ability dimension. A dunce in one field tends to be similarly judged in other fields. We suspect, though scientific evidence is lacking, that an ability that is not especially outstanding one way or the other is less potent in its spread effects than one that is more uniquely characteristic of the person. The term, prestige suggestion, familiar in social psychology, has been used to refer to certain kinds of spread phenomena.

In certain cultures there exists the belief that "mana" or general power, may be transmitted from one object to another. For instance, power is acquired by eating the meat of powerful animals. This phenomenon can also be seen as involving a kind of unit formation between two objects.

There are many other factors that influence the perception of a person's abilities. Some of these, such as the influence of personality traits, attitudes, and suggestion, are brought out in the sections below. The relation between a dispositional ability and a concrete action is also discussed by Ryle (1949, p. 45).

**The contribution of personality traits and attitudes to power.** Personality traits and attitudes are also personal factors that have an important bearing on what a person can do. Power is not merely a matter of physical and mental ability skills. It is also highly affected by attitudes of self-confidence, attitudes that assert, "I can do something worth while here. Thinking new thoughts and carrying out new activities belong to my space of free movement."

The feeling of one's power or lack of power on a particular task may be connected with a pervasive mood of competence in which one feels that one can do anything, or with a despondent mood in which one despairs of one's powers and abilities. Sometimes the feeling of personal power may encompass a philosophical view of the course of world events as a whole in which, at one extreme, one feels that the world can always be changed in such a way that it fits one better; or, at the other extreme, one may feel that one can do nothing, that one must remain at the mercy of imposed forces. Literature abounds with plots whose dramatic effect pivots around the world outlook of the superman and of the fatalist.

Many psychologists have stated that one can do more when one is confident, less if one mistrusts one's own power. The impact of personality traits is pointed up when a person with high ability is made powerless in a group because of his diffidence. Moreover, there is ample clinical evidence that even so stable a characteristic as a person's abilities may be grossly and permanently affected by attitudes of self-confidence. When a person's self-confidence is destroyed, his abilities may also be. He becomes the person he thinks he is.

Certainly a person's apparent self-confidence often influences our judgment of his abilities. The candidate who is sure of himself casts the most favorable light on his abilities. This may decide for which presidential aspirant we vote, which job applicant we hire. Naive psychology is so clear about these connections that the person himself, aware that manifest self-confidence often speaks for underlying abilities, may consciously feign this attitude as the core of his strategy.

**Some variable personal factors affecting power.** Just as on the environmental side of the can matrix, vacillating, unpredictable chance events were set apart from the more consistent characteristics, so the less persistent power factors are recognized on the personal side. Fatigue and mood, for instance, represent for the most part temporary states, and unless they should persist, their effect on the power component of can is likely to be temporary also.

Since can tends to be used as a dispositional concept, when failure is attributed to fatigue, the conclusion is usually not drawn that the person cannot do the task. On the other hand, success, even when understood as due to a transitory positive state in the person, often leads to the conclusion that the person can do the task. As an illustration we may draw upon the performance of an alcoholic or psychotic who is able to hammer a nail, read a book, and so on only on a rare day of lucidity. We are led to feel that he can do these things even though there are few occasions when he can actually do them. It is as though we perceive the "real person" through his chronic alcoholic or psychotic state and coordinate the ability to this.

We now come to certain factors less univocally attached to the person or the environment than are those discussed above.

*Can as affected by social and legal status.* Often social and legal status define the may and may not (cf. pp. 84–85) rather than the real can. A member of a lower caste *may not* open a conversation with one of higher caste. If he does, he will be punished. On the other hand, the can may also be determined. A member of a certain caste *cannot* live in the area reserved for the privileged. No matter how hard he tries he will not succeed.

Social and legal status may sometimes be thought of as belonging to the environmental side of the can matrix. Not only its genesis, but also its control, lies outside the person. Society confers status and can take it away. Moreover, social and legal status often affects what a person can and cannot do by determining the strength of the environmental forces. A veteran, for example, can become a civil servant with a lower test score than can a nonveteran.

Nevertheless, social and legal status is often felt to be a personal characteristic. It "follows the person around" in a wide variety of situations and in this sense becomes attached to him. John is a citizen, a high officer, or a social outcast, for more than momentary periods. However, should one be "Queen for a day," the status is not considered a personal characteristic.

Attribution of status, therefore, is less univocal than is attribution of ability, personality, or attitudes. The latter generally "belong to" the person. But a person's status may sometimes be felt to be part of his essence and in other cases to be detached from him as a person.

Regardless of its attribution, however, social and legal status is important in naive psychology precisely because of its bearing upon can and may.

**The connection between possessions and can.** Often, possessions, such as tools and money, enable a person to do something which otherwise he could not. Without the telescope I cannot see the star. With an automobile I can travel to distant places.

The question of attribution of such action possibilities is not as clear-cut as it may seem. Though possessions are definitely "outside the person's skin" and typically are felt to be a part of the environment, not infrequently the actions they permit are ascribed to the person. Ichheiser, in discussing misunderstandings in human relations, has emphasized the point that

. . . we experience as our "own" those of our potentialities which we owe, let us say, to money we possess, in the same way as we experience those we owe to intrinsic psychological and physical characteristics. (Ichheiser, 1949, p. 48.)

Dembo, Leviton, and Wright in a discussion of personal characteristics versus possessions, point out that the boundary between them is often obscure:

Clothes may be thought of as a material possession, and "being well-dressed" as a personal characteristic. Where some judges would perceive a man who owns a house, others would perceive a "homeowner," a substantial and responsible member of the community. (Dembo, Leviton, and Wright, 1956, p. 22.)

Their conclusion is that "whether something is seen as a part or characteristic of a person or as a possession seems to depend upon the judge," especially upon the values he holds (p. 22). A contributing factor to this determination is that under certain conditions there is a tendency to attribute the outcome of an action to the person even though its source may reside in the environment. A pointed example, given by Ichheiser (1949), is that of the unemployed whose "misfortune is being ascribed to him as a manifestation of his alleged personal defects" rather than to situational factors beyond his control (p. 48; cf. also Heider, 1944).

**Physical position and can.** Physical position is an important determinant of both the possibility for, and outcome of action. The fact that I am in the Midwest means that I cannot swim in the ocean. The child who has driven his adversary against the wall or into a corner is at an advantage. We sit close to the stage in order to be able to hear the dialogue or see the actors.

Strictly speaking, physical position implies a relation between the person and the environment. To be in the Midwest, against the wall, in the corner, or close to the stage requires the existence of two entities, the person and his physical surrounding. Similarly, a relation to a person was found to be implicit in the concept of task difficulty and may well be extended to the environmental properties of opportunity and luck. Notice, however, that we speak of the difficulty of a task, but the position of a person. This semantic difference leads us to suspect that naive psychology generally assigns position to the personal element in can and difficulty to the environmental element. Yet, the position of the person, unlike task difficulty, is not necessarily a dispositional property; it may be highly stable or it may be fleeting. If the former, it may become a dispositional property and be used to characterize the person, for instance, having lived in Kansas for some time, a person may be thought of and think of himself as a Kansan. When, however, the relation between the person and his surrounding is transitory, position is not used to characterize the person, though it may be used to describe the person's temporary state. We say, "I am sitting close to the stage," but would be quite startled to be called a "close-to-the-stage sitter."

**Can influenced by opinion and suggestion.** What we can do is influenced by what we think we can do, and what we think we can do is influenced by what other people think we can do. Therefore, what we can do is influenced by what other people think we can do. Such is the syllogistic sequence behind the fact that the opinion of other people, their suggestions, prejudices and stereotypes often determine what a person can do.

This determination may occur by way of influencing the person's perception of task difficulty or of personal power (ability). A child may decide that arithmetic is a hard subject once he learns of its reputation. All of us have at some time doubted our ability to carry through a particular action the moment it was doubted by others. Homans, in discussing Whyte's observations on bowling and social rank, points out that the actual abilities, and not only the person's cognition of them may be affected to some extent:

Clearly the group, and particularly the leaders, had a definite idea what a man's standing in bowling ought to be, and this idea had a real effect on the way he bowled. . . . When you have only one or two pins left standing, and your opponents are shouting, "He can't pick it up," then you most need the confidence that will take the tension out of your muscles and give you smooth control. . . . Above all you will have confidence if your teammates have made plain by comments, past and present, their belief that you can make the shot. On the one hand, your bowling ability helps to form their good or bad opinion of you. . . . On the other hand, their opinion is crucial in determining how well you bowl. (Homans, 1950, p. 167.)

The opinions of others may have a lasting effect on a person's over-all feeling of what he can do. Then it is that the syllogistic sequence becomes mediated by a change within the personality as a whole. It is well known that inferiority feelings may become fixed because of inexpedient treatment by those around the person.

The cognition of can in another person is also influenced by stereotyped judgments. The syllogistic sequence is of the following order:

Men in general can do *x*.
John is a man.
John can do *x*.

All sorts of expectations about can are based on this sort of inference: Age and can connections—we expect three-year-old Bobbie to be able to ride a trike because other three-year-olds can master this feat. Sex and can connections—we expect Bill to be able to change a tire because men (particularly American men) are mechanically adept. Occupation and can connections—we expect Dr. Jones to be able to cure the patient (particularly in case of ordinary illness) because that is the function of a physician.

**The impact of needs on can.** Many wise sayings stress the importance of needs in the cognition of can. La Rochefoucauld (1665) declared: "We have more strength than will; and it is often merely for an excuse that we say things are impossible" (p.7). Laziness, fear of consequences, aversion, all may lead to the belief that an action is impossible. That the wish is father to the thought holds as much for can as for cannot. Children with a strong urge for independence are convinced that they can do many more things than actual test will confirm and certainly many more than their more timid peers. *The Little Engine That Could* has become a classic tale for children to illustrate the moral, "Where there is a will there is a way."

Even the attribution of can may be strongly influenced by the needs that are served. It is reported that Cocteau, when asked if he believed in luck, replied, "Certainly. How else can you explain the success of those you detest?" We need only to recall how often the poor workman blames his tools to realize that the attribution of can, as well as its cognition, is not always as objective as might be desirable.

**Summary.** The diversity of relations described in the foregoing sections form part of our naive theory of "can." Can is recognized as one of the two necessary conditions of action. For each combination of the underlying constituents of can (namely, environmental difficulty and personal power) there are corresponding manifestations in actual behavior. This schema is part and parcel of our interpretations of success, of our expectations of success, and of our own behavior directed toward influencing the actions of others. Such everyday applications have been illustrated throughout the text. Further examples are introduced as summary elucidations.

The action manifestations, together with other "raw material" become the data that allow us, in a kind of factor analysis, to assess the role of the factors contributing to can. We assess when we attribute action outcome mainly to the person, mainly to the environment, or to a combination of both. Only then do we understand. Only then are we able to predict future action, for even when relatively momentary factors make an action possible, by circumscribing these factors, one acknowledges the existence of the more invariant and reliable personal and environmental conditions.

But we not only diagnose the constituents of can from their manifestations; we are also led to expect certain manifestations when the constituents are given. Thus, if a task is easy, or if a person has good ability, then we expect the person to be able to engage successfully in the action. Or, if we know that $p$ lacks the necessary powers to do something, such as ability or endurance, then we shall not expect him to do it. Moreover, if the action occurs, we may conclude that he did not do it. We form a similar conclusion in the absence of the environmental conditions necessary for action. Thus, in order to make $p$ responsible for an action, the opportunity has to be ascertained (its lack is known as the "alibi" in legal parlance), and the personal powers assessed. This, of course, is not all that is necessary for conclusively associating $p$ with an action, but at least we do not blame someone for a crime we know he could not have committed.

Knowledge of can as a necessary condition of action also enables us to influence and control the actions of another. We focus on the power component when a person's abilities are enhanced through teaching, training, and practice. We focus on the environmental component when we create favorable opportunities, remove environmental barriers, decrease task difficulty, and so on. We change what a person can do by confiscating his property, exhausting his energy, demoting his rank. Frequently information is withheld or made public according to whether action is desired or not. Suggestions concerning task difficulty and personal ability are often guided by the action consequences. In short, attribution of action, expectations concerning action, and the control of action will require apprehension of can as a concept.

We have thus far attempted to make explicit the constituents of "can" as grasped by naive psychology and to point out some important factors that bear on them. The second essential component of action remains to be discussed, namely the motivational factor that becomes manifest in trying, the factor that propels and guides the action and gives it its purposive character. This is the feature par excellence that distinguishes instigation by a person from other "causes" of events. It is so central to the interpretation of actions that we shall introduce the analysis of trying by a rather full consideration of the difference between personal and impersonal causality.

## Personal and Impersonal Causality

**Intention, the central factor in personal causality.** What we have designated as personal causality refers to instances in which $p$ causes $x$ intentionally. That is to say, the action is purposive. This has to be distinguished from other cases in which $p$ is a part of the sequence of events. For example, $p$ may cause $x$ unintentionally merely because his physical or social being exerts some influence on the environment. He may cause a board on which he stands to break or he may act as a social stimulus for others. Sometimes the statement, "He did it" is really a short cut for "It was the weight of his body that caused the board to break." But unless intention ties together the cause-effect relations we do not have a case of true personal causality.

A more complicated case which is also excluded from personal causality occurs when $p$ causes $x$ because $x$ is an unintended consequence of a change $y$ which is intended; $p$ may or may not be aware that $y$ leads to $x$. For instance, $p$ may acquire an object that $o$ also desires. If the true goal of $p$ is only to obtain the object, then the fact that this has negative consequences for $o$ is not part of $p$'s intention. Of course, the fact that the aftereffects of the action were not intended by the person does not mean that we can neglect them in the analysis of action, or that they are irrelevant for psychological processes. The person himself and other persons will react to these effects in a specific way which will derive precisely from the fact that they are not intended. A case in point is an outcome that is very injurious to the person and is the aftereffect of an action from which the person hoped to gain great benefits. This often produces the impression of tragic fate; that the person causes his own destruction is an element in many tragedies (Reardon, 1953).

True personal causality is restricted to instances where $p$ tries to cause $x$, where $x$ is his goal. This, by the way, does not exclude unconscious action; often, it is precisely because such action displays the features of personal causality as delineated below that inferences are drawn concerning unconscious motivations and unconscious goals. But cases of personal causality must be distinguished from effects involving persons but not intentions. The latter are more appropriately represented as cases of impersonal causality. They not only are different phenomenally from cases of purposive action, that is, in the way in which we experience them, but the causal nexus that links the person to the effect is also different. Consequently, to influence the outcome of an action in these cases one would have to change a different set of conditions.

**The causal network in personal and impersonal causality.** When I am threatened by a danger from a nonpersonal source, all I usually need to do is change the conditions in order to escape the danger. If I am threatened by falling stones on a mountain, I can get out of the danger area and seek shelter. The stones will not change their paths in order to find me behind the shelter. If, however, a person wants to hit me with a stone and he can run faster than I can, I am exposed to the danger of being hit to a much greater degree and I have to use very different means in order not to be hit: I can hit him back and disable him before he has hit me, I can ask for mercy, or I can try to move in such a way that he will not know where I have gone.

In other words, if I meet a person who has certain intentions in regard to myself—for instance, who wants to get me into a certain state—that means that my environment contains conditions that are convergently directed towards this state, and if the person has enough power, this state will sooner or later be brought about whatever I do. In short, personal causality is characterized by equifinality, that is, the invariance of the end and variability of the means. Vicarious mediation with respect to an end point is an essential feature of the operational definition of purpose (Tolman, 1932; Brunswik, 1952).

Yet this is not the only characteristic of personal causality, for we must distinguish the equifinality in this case from that which sometimes occurs in physical systems, for instance, a system like a pendulum or a marble in a bowl which, in the end, will always come to rest at the lowest point regardless of where it started. In the inorganic world where a particular end state may be enforced, the forces leading to that unitary effect are not controlled by any part of the system. There is no power hierarchy, no leader-led distinction between the parts, and the process is understood in terms of the whole system. On the other hand, in the case of personal causality, the invariant end is due to the person. Because the person controls the causal lines emanating from himself, he not only is the initial source of the produced change, but he remains the persistent cause. Here, if anywhere, one can speak of a local cause, the second characteristic of the causal network in personal causality. Actually, within a wide range of environmental conditions, the person may be thought of as the one necessary and sufficient condition for the effect to occur, for within that wide range the person changes the means to achieve the end, the end itself remaining unaltered. However, equifinality is characteristic of personal causality only within certain limits, and these limits define what the person "can" do if he tries.

On the other hand, in the case of impersonal causality, a wide range of environmental conditions will lead to a wide range of effects. Since no one condition bears the responsibility for creating other conditions necessary for a particular effect, any specific effect of a complex process requires the presence of a great many specific conditions. The more conditions required, the more unlikely it is that the same effect will occur. Thus, if I see leaves on the ground arranged in the form of a neat square, I will conclude that a person created this effect and not that it was an accident of nature. The same is true when we find pictures of bisons in caves, or statues buried in the ground. In some places little piles of stone are used to mark a path. In all these cases we are confronted only with inorganic matter; but this inorganic matter is distributed in a way that would be most unlikely to occur except through the agency of a person with intention and with the possibility of guiding effects in accordance with this intention. Attribution to personal causality reduces the necessary conditions essentially to one, the person with intention, who, within a wide range of environmental vicissitudes, has control over the multitude of forces required to create the specific effect.

It is possible to use topological terms to represent the meaning for $p$ of personal causality that has its source in another person. The goal of being in a certain state or producing a certain effect can be represented by what Lewin has called the "hodological" space, the space of the paths toward the goal (Lewin, 1938). This hodological space represents the fact that wherever $p$ is located in the space, a force will act on $p$ in such a way that he will take the means that most quickly bring him to the goal. Again we see that within a wide range of environmental conditions, the person is the sufficient condition to effect the change. If there are obstacles in his way, the goal-directed person will circumvent them. Moreover, his own actions will take into account changes in the environment.

In an analogous way one can represent the fact that it is $o$'s goal for

$p$ to be in a certain state. Then, wherever $p$ is located in the space $o$ controls, $o$ will apply a force on $p$ in such a way that $p$ will be most quickly pushed toward that state. One can say that $p$ is then caught in a field of push forces all of which are directed toward the same point and have their source in the acting person, and especially in the intention of the acting person.

This, then, is the essence of personal causality. It is characterized by equifinality and local causality. Not only is the end state enforced by a convergence of independent forces to a unitary effect, but also, the convergence is effected by a unique part of the totality of conditions involved in the events that transpire, namely the person and especially his intentions.

**Personal causality compared with perception.** The distinguishing features of personal causality become even more outstanding when we compare purposive action with the impersonal causality involved in another function of the organism, namely perception. Instances of impersonal causality previously considered involved the effect of things on things. The aspect of perception that belongs to impersonal causality is confined to the effect of things (the environment) on persons. We do not consider here that the person's needs and personality may affect what he perceives.

Let us start by comparing the initial focus (the stimulus conditions that set off the train of events), the terminal focus (the end point), and the conditions mediating them.

INITIAL FOCUS. In perception it is the environment; in personal causality it is the intention.

TERMINAL FOCUS. In perception it is the person's awareness of the environment; in personal causality it is the change that is produced by the action.

MEDIATION. In both personal causality and perception we find what Brunswik (1952) has called a "wide-arched dependency" of the terminal focus on the initial focus (p. 19). In both the mediation is characterized by the following three features:

1. The mediation is "atomistic"—that is, the parts of the mediation in themselves are relatively independent of each other. They do not, in the ideal case, form what may be called internally conditioned units (Heider, 1926; Barker and Wright, 1955, pp. 182 ff.). With action, for instance, the way I move my fingers to shingle the roof is only in small measure directly determined by my previous finger movements. It is more closely conditioned by my intentions as related to the demands of the task. In fact, to the extent that the sequence of finger

movements is determined by its own properties, that is, internally conditioned, to that extent the hand fails as an ideal mediator of intentions. For this reason the hand is generally much more efficient as an action medium than is the foot whose movements are relatively less responsive to the intentions of the person. In a case of perception, the separate light rays emanating from the tree are relatively independent of each other. They are produced by the properties of the tree and the surrounding illumination. The character of one light ray is not affected by the neighboring rays.

2. In spite of the atomistic mediation the terminal effect can be described as a unitary entity. When someone builds a wall the many part actions which are independent in themselves are combined by the intention of the person to produce the unitary object. This is what may be called "concerted action," the causal lines of the part action converging toward the outcome of the action. In perception, the mediating causal lines which are independent of each other bring about the unitary percept of the object.

3. The mediation is vicarious—that is the same terminal focus may be reached by different paths. With action, for instance, the intention to have the roof fixed (initial focus) and the actual roof in repair (terminal focus) may be bridged by such diverse routes as doing the work oneself, paying to have it done, using wooden shingles or asphalt, and so on. Likewise with perception, the tree outside my window (initial focus) and the awareness of that tree (terminal focus) may be mediated by different intensities of illumination, a reflecting surface, and so on. This relation of foci to medium has been described by Brunswik as follows:

. . . both for reception and for action, it turns out that the special manner in which anything is mediated (or done), is not especially essential or significant. One and the same means-object may be represented at different times by very different stimulus configurations. And one and the same goal may be reached equally well by very different kinds of movements and means-object manipulations. (Brunswik, 1936, p. 125.)

Thus there are two kinds of convergence in personal causality: on the one hand there is the convergence of different means by which the same goal may be reached. This can be called equifinality, since the converging lines represent a number of different instances of reaching the goal. On the other hand there is the convergence of different part actions of a single means toward the goal. In this case the convergence, which might be designated unifinality, refers to the fact that the part actions all combine to produce a unitary effect.

One of the most important differences between perception and purposive action concerns the control over and responsibility for the events that transpire, that is, with local causality. This can most pointedly be seen if we divide the sequence of events in both perception and purposive action into two parts: a divergent part, that is, the initial phase in which the mediating events emanate or radiate outward from the initial focus; and a convergent part, that is, the second phase in which the mediating events are brought together towards their final outcome. Let us make these phases concrete by considering the processes involved when a man sees a wall and when a man builds a wall.

In the case of perception, the relation between the initial focus, the objective wall, and the medium manifold of atomistic light waves, the "offshoots" that diverge from it, is one of coordination rather than control. The offshoots are coordinated to the objects according to simple physical laws. But the objects do not guide the offshoots. The waves that are sent out are entirely independent of the object in their further fate. This means that the initial focus has nothing to do with the second phase of the causal network. As we know, the offshoots are not guided by the wall in such a way that they converge on a person in front of it and are converted into a percept of the wall.

If purposive action were like perception in this respect, that is, if only the divergent part of the causal network were coordinated to the initial focus, then we would only have to make a plan visible to the world and let effects of it radiate out into the environment; the things would perceive our intention and would obediently change in such a way that the intention would be realized. Instead, where purposive action occurs, the initial focus, i.e., the plan, the intention, controls both the divergent and the convergent phases in guiding the mediation to a unitary effect. In some way the initial focus is responsible for the whole arch. The entire mediation from start to finish is guided by it. If this were true of perception, if both the divergent and convergent parts of the process were controlled by the initial focus, it would mean that the objective thing would have to paint a little image of itself in the life space.

In short, the organism controls the convergent part of the process in perception, whereas in action it controls both the convergent and the divergent parts. To put it another way, the initial focus in perception controls nothing, though the divergent part of the process is coordinated to it. In purposive action, the initial focus controls everything, that is both the convergent and divergent parts of the action sequence. It is true that very often with action, part of the sequence of events that terminates in the goal change is also not directly guided by the organism. We have to distinguish between two types of action that may be exemplified by putting and by throwing. In both, the motion of an object is caused by a person. But when someone puts a stone in a certain place, he controls the motion of the stone along the whole path, imposing it by the movements of his hand which is in contact with the stone. On the other hand, when a person throws a stone in order to get it to a certain place, he controls the motion of the stone by direct contact only up to the moment when the stone leaves his hand. He imparts kinetic energy to the stone, after which the environment takes over; the events then run off without further interference by the person. The person sets the stage, plants the conditions, initiates the change, and then thinks he is assured, or at least hopes he is assured, of the intended terminal effect. Examples of only part of the sequence of events leading to an intended effect being directly controlled by the person are: telling $o$ about $x$ because we anticipate that when he knows he will do something about it; benefiting a person because he will in turn benefit $p$; instances of ulterior motive. The true goal in these cases is a necessary or probable consequence of the changes we directly influence: we sow in order to reap.

One might think the causal structure of this kind of "throwing" action is, after all, not so very different from that of perception, for is it not true that only the divergent but not the convergent part of the process controlled by $p$? However, though the person, when he throws a stone, does not guide it the whole length of its course, he does nevertheless in an important sense control the motion of the stone even after it has left his hand: he plants the conditions in such a way that the intended aim is reached; the further conditions that might influence the movement are taken into consideration (wind, gravity); the person, surveying the situation, gets a feedback from it by way of perception, and he imparts to the stone such speed and direction of movement as will get it where he wants it to be.

Of course, the more variable the conditions that influence the course of events following the person's direct action, the smaller will be the probability that the goal will be reached. We know that the person cannot control the outcome in throwing to the degree that he can in putting. Even a very skilled person is often unable to throw a stone in such a way that it lands exactly in a certain position. In building a wall, the person will not throw the bricks on it from a distance; he will place them so that the end position of the brick is exactly controlled by direct or proximal influences. A certain stability in the coordination between starting conditions and outcome is necessary to make actions reach distant goals with better than chance probability.

But in spite of this, as we have seen, there is a certain control by the person over the whole course of events in actions that have been exemplified by throwing, through the purposeful planting of the starting conditions. This is not true for perception; there the initial focus, the perceived object, does not plant the light rays in such a way that they are bound, or even likely, to produce a percept in a person. When the light process has left the object it is completely uninfluenced by the object; it is neither guided step by step, nor have its conditions been set in such a way that a certain result is probable. In "throwing" actions, however, though part of the process is not directly controlled by the person, it is still controlled to such a degree that we again have to ascribe the outcome to the person as the local cause.

**Diagrammatic summary of personal-impersonal causality.** We have stressed that personal causality represents a certain kind of structure of events in the system comprising the organism and the environment, namely, a structure in which equifinality and local causality both appear. These characteristics typically do not describe the causal network in impersonal causality. Where equifinality characterizes an instance of impersonal causality, it represents the function of the entire system rather than any local part of it.

The main differences between personal and impersonal causality are represented in Figs. 1 and 2. The diagrams show only a few conditions and a few effects. In reality, of course, there are always a great many possibilities. Figure 1 depicts the case of impersonal causality. Here $x$ stands for an impersonal event which, with circumstance $c_1$ leads to effect $e_1$, with circumstance $c_2$ leads to effect $e_2$, etc. Notice that the effects are all different; for example, a falling stone, depending on the conditions, will hit a man ($e_1$), fall on the ground ($e_2$), start an avalanche ($e_3$). Equifinality does not occur. We are excluding the

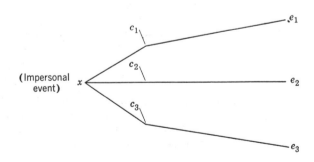

**Figure 1.** *Multifinality in the case of impersonal causality.*

special case of equifinality in physical systems, where multifinality is the typical situation.

In Fig. 2, $x$ represents a source of personal causality, that is, a person with the intention of producing $e$. If circumstance $c_1$ is given, $x$ will choose means $m_1$ to reach the goal $e$. If circumstance $c_2$ prevails, he will choose means $m_2$, etc. The means are variable, the end the same. Equifinality exists. Moreover, the equifinality rests upon local causality. The causal lines are seen to emanate from $x$ and to be controlled by $x$ to their final outcome $e$.

The consequences of the represented differences are significant. For example, in the case of impersonal causality, a source outside the given situation can influence the outcome by altering any one of the circumstances $c_1$ to $c_3$. Thus, if a person exposed to the effects of $x$ does not like $e_1$, he can change $c_1$ to $c_2$, as when he steps aside in order to avoid the falling stone. On the other hand, where personal causality operates, a source outside the situation cannot as simply change the outcome. The outcome will not be altered merely by changing $c_1$ to $c_2$ or to $c_3$. Another person will succeed in influencing $e$ only by altering $x$, that is the intention of the agent, or by creating a circumstance $c_4$ that makes it impossible for the agent to produce $e$.

It should be clear that the intention of the person, that is what he is trying to do, usually refers to the point where the causal lines that represent vicarious means-actions converge. Any aftereffect that results, even if it is an inevitable consequence under a variety of intervening circumstances, cannot strictly be considered a part of personal causality.

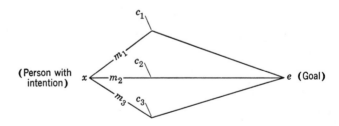

**Figure 2.** *Equifinality in the case of personal causality. In the particular case depicted, each single means with its circumstance represents a sufficient condition for the goal change. In the case of what may be called concerted action, that is, where several different actions in combination are required to produce the effect, the diagram would have to include a corresponding differentiation within the causal lines connecting x with e.*

Figure 3 represents the causal lines leading to the aftereffects. They diverge and produce different consequences under different circumstances. If the circumstance $c_a$ is given, the goal change will have aftereffect 1. If circumstance $c_b$ is present, aftereffect 2 will result. The causal lines beyond the goal change do not show the convergence of equifinality.

Now we are ready to examine the concept of trying. Personal causality characterizes trying and it is this fact that carries great weight in our interpretations of actions and what we do to influence the actions of others.

## The Concept of Trying

Early in this chapter we noted that the outcome of an action, $x$, is commonly acknowledged to be a function of factors that reside in the environment and in the person. The effective personal force was dissected yet further and the constituents of action realigned in such a way that "$p$ tries to cause $x$" and "$p$ can cause $x$" became the two conditions of $x$. These conditions are almost always taken into account in considering the actions of other people. Both are necessary but neither of them is sufficient.

In the condition "$p$ tries to do $x$" the factor of personal causality may be recognized. The local cause of the event $x$ is the person. His trying is the central factor that controls the forces exerted on the environment to produce the equifinality. The condition "$p$ can do $x$" points to the possibility of an action. The distinction between can and try is related to the distinction between learning and motivation in scientific psychology.

**Intention and exertion: the constituents of trying.** "Trying" has a directional aspect and a quantitative aspect. In describing it we have to define first what $p$ is trying to do, and second how hard he is trying to do it. The first aspect is usually called intention, the second

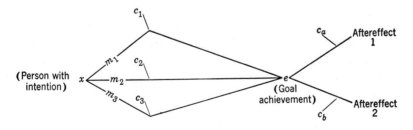

**Figure 3.** *Multifinality following goal achievement.*

exertion (Allport, 1947). In psychology they are often thought of as the direction and strength of motivation. As expressed in "trying" they make up the vectorial component of action.

In ordinary usage, the term intention is also used in other senses. For instance, intention does not merely refer to the direction of an action in progress. We may have the intention of trying to do something tomorrow. When the intention, however, takes over the action system, then we characterize this motivational aspect of action by saying "He is trying to do it." Intention is also often taken as the equivalent of wish or wanting. If I know that a person is trying to do something, I frequently assume that he wants to do it, that it is his own wish that is propelling the action. Conversely, if it is shown that a person had a motive and the opportunity for the deed, he becomes a likely suspect. In general, when we know that a person very much wants $x$ to happen and that he can effect the change, then we expect him to do it, or, if $x$ has occurred then we are inclined to assume that he brought it about. It is in this sense that "can" and "want" may be viewed as the conditions of successful action.

But to do so introduces a certain conceptual ambiguity and inconsistency in the effects of these conditions. For one thing, there are reasons other than personal wish for doing something. One may try because one feels that one ought, for example. (Cf. Chapter 5, p. 126.) Furthermore, a wish does not necessarily produce trying. I may wish that something would come about, and I may even have the conviction that I am able to bring it about, but I may not have the vaguest notion what particular behavior will realize it. It may be that I do not yet think at all about tactics and have only the feeling that I will eventually find some means to obtain the goal, or it may be that I have ready a great number of possible means. Again, I may withhold action, knowing that my wish will be realized without my efforts. Or, I may even wish for something to happen that I cannot influence in any way. Or, finally, a particular wish may be held in abeyance because of restraining forces, such as fear of punishment or because preference is given to a second desire that conflicts with the first. All the while there is certainly a motivational state but it cannot be identified with any particular action. In the interest of conceptual clarification, therefore, we shall use the term intention to refer to *what* a person is trying to do, that is to the goal or action outcome, and not to *why* he is trying to do it. The latter applies more particularly to the reasons behind the intention. To be sure, a frequent reason for trying to do something is one's own wish, and occasionally in the discussion of trying we have found it expedient to use "want" as a special case of intention. In any case, it is the intention, whatever its source, which gives to trying the characteristic features of personal causality.

As for exertion, it varies directly with the difficulty of the task and inversely with the power (often taken as ability) of the person. Or:

$$\text{exertion} = f\left(\frac{\text{difficulty}}{\text{power}}\right)$$

This means that where different people have the same power, the minimum exertion needed to succeed in a task will vary with the difficulty. It also follows that if the task is held constant, the person who has less power or ability will have to exert himself more to succeed. The greatest exertion will be needed when the person has little power and the task is difficult.

Transposing the terms in the equation so that power becomes the dependent variable, we have:

$$\text{power} = f\left(\frac{\text{difficulty}}{\text{exertion}}\right)$$

Thus, if two people exert themselves to the same degree, the one who solves the more difficult task has greater power. The one who has to exert himself more to solve a task of given difficulty has the lesser power. And the greatest power or ability will be shown by the person who solves a difficult task with little exertion. This, by the way, is the theoretical basis for including timed problems in tests of intelligence. The person who can solve a problem quickly does so with less exertion than the one who takes considerably longer and therefore should be given added credit toward his total intelligence score.

*Influence of p can on p's intentions.* In some cases, motivational forces toward a goal seem to be aroused by the appearance of the idea, "I can attain that goal." We shall not try to answer the question whether the recognition that "one can" really creates the intention, or whether it only channelizes motives that have always been present but were not connected with concrete goals. But there is no doubt that "I can" frequently influences "I want" (or "I ought," cf. p. 226) and thereby "I intend."

A case in point is the teen-age boy who, though he has begun to drive his father's car, has not yet thought of himself as a potential car owner. Then one of his friends gets a job and buys a secondhand car with his earnings. The fact that the boy now sees owning a car as a possibility may suddenly create the situation where this becomes a goal and all his efforts are directed toward attaining it. Similarly, one reads of the bank teller who has lived for years in daily contact with money far beyond his own income without any thought that it could be his. He hears of another man in his position who has found a way to divert a small part of the money he handles for his own use and so leads a life of greater ease than he had known before. In such a case the knowledge that this could be done may serve to make it seem possible, and perhaps even desirable, to the man who has heretofore not thought of it. This reminds us of Fritz Redl's (1949) description of the form of contagion in which $p$ imitates $o$ because $o$'s behavior has demonstrated that a certain act is possible or that it can be done with impunity, and therefore $p$ wants to perform the same act.

There are, of course, also indirect effects of can on motivation. The ability to do something leads to satisfying experiences, which then lead to new activity in the same direction.

Though "can" may influence $p$'s wants, action does not necessarily take place. Remember that can and trying, strictly speaking, are the two conditions of action, and not can and want. However, since trying is often instigated by a wish force, "can" frequently influences action by influencing motivation. It can even be said that if a person wishes for a certain effect and thinks that he can achieve it, he is apt to attempt it. In this sense can and want may be thought of as the two conditions of trying.

***The conditions of action and personal responsibility.*** It has already been stressed that intention is the central factor in personal causality, that it is the intention of a person that brings order into the wide variety of possible action sequences by coordinating them to a final outcome. Therefore, if we are convinced that $o$ did $x$ intentionally we generally link the $x$ more intimately with the person than if we think that $o$ did $x$ unintentionally. By the same token, if we account for an act by a person's stupidity or clumsiness, that is by ability factors, we tend to hold him less responsible than if we take the act as an indication of his motives. Thus it is that the question of premeditation is important in the decisions regarding guilt.

Ability is also attributed to the person, but not in the same way as motivation. If a person tries to help but cannot, then it may not be considered his fault if he does not help. People are held responsible for their intentions and exertions but not so strictly for their abilities. William Stern (1923), who distinguishes between dispositions of direction and those of equipment (abilities), says that "strivings form the center of personal causality, abilities belong more to the periphery" (p. 85).

Moreover, as we have seen in the naive analysis of action, the change $x$ is not always attributed to the person. Sometimes it is attributed to luck, for example, or at least partly to such environmental factors as task difficulty. Personal responsibility then varies with the relative contribution of environmental factors to the action outcome; in general, the more they are felt to influence the action, the less the person is held responsible. One may consider the different forms in which the concept of responsibility has been used as successive stages in which attribution to the person decreases and attribution to the environment increases.

At the most primitive level the concept is a global one according to which the person is held responsible for each effect that is in any way connected with him or that seems in any way to belong to him. For example, a person may be accused of the presumed wrong doings of his church or his country for centuries back. Similarly, a person may be congratulated upon the victory of his school's football team.

At the next level anything that is caused by $p$ is ascribed to him. Causation is understood in the sense that $p$ was a necessary condition for the happening, even though he could not have foreseen the outcome however cautiously he had proceeded. Impersonal causality rather than personal causality as we have defined it, characterizes the judgment of responsibility at this level. In an "achievement ethics" the person is judged not according to his intention but according to the actual results of what he does. A bad deed exerts a sort of polluting effect even when it is not intended, a good deed an enhancing effect. (Cf. Westermarck, 1932, pp. 162 ff.) This is what Piaget (1932) refers to as objective responsibility, and it represents an earlier developmental stage in contrast to subjective responsibility where motives become the central issue.

Then comes the stage at which $p$ is considered responsible, directly or indirectly, for any aftereffect that he might have foreseen even though it was not a part of his own goal and therefore still not a part of the framework of personal causality. For instance, $p$ may be perceived as having done it because he was stupid, negligent, or morally weak. He is held responsible for the fact that the restraining forces that a wider field would exert were lacking. Thus, $p$ may be accused of bringing harm to $o$, though this was not $p$'s intention. That he was not deterred from pursuing his goal by the thought of harm to $o$ is taken as a sign that he is ruthless, though not necessarily malicious. A nicer person would not have carried out the action. The moral restraining forces were lacking in $p$.

Next, only what $p$ intended is perceived as having its source in him. This corresponds to what Piaget has called subjective responsibility and pertains to actions whose structure may be described by personal causality.

Finally there is the stage at which even $p$'s own motives are not entirely ascribed to him but are seen as having their source in the environment. We may say about an action of $p$'s, "It is not his fault that he behaves like that. He has been provoked." We mean by this that anybody would have felt and acted as he did under the circumstances. The causal lines leading to the final outcome are still guided by $p$, and therefore the act fits into the structure of personal causality, but since the source of the motive is felt to be the coercion of the environment and not $p$ himself, responsibility for the act is at least shared by the environment. The criminal may blame the environment for his ill-fated career and thereby excuse himself. We view traitorous acts committed under duress differently from those that are premeditated. In extreme cases in which the act coerced by the environment does not fit the individual's personality organization, the behavior appears alien and the person is described by himself and others as "not being himself."

It will be recognized that the issue of responsibility includes the problem of attribution of action. That is, it is important which of the several conditions of action—the intentions of the person, personal power factors, or environmental forces—is to be given primary weight for the action outcome. Once such attribution has been decided upon, the evaluation of responsibility is possible.

Attribution of action or the cognition of the conditions of actions is also basic, as has already been emphasized, in our expectations and in the control of future actions. Attribution as applied to can was considered in the first half of this chapter. We shall now consider some of the factors that influence our perception of the intention and the exertion involved in the trying component of action.

*Cognition of trying.* The structure of personal causality is used, in effect, to discover what another person is trying to do. We may want to know whether an outcome produced by a person was intentional or not, or we may want to know, given a particular action, what was the intention behind it. Different clues are available to us. We can observe the action and note whether the person tries other means of reaching the same goal when he is thwarted in one attempt, whether he gives up trying when he has produced a certain change, or whether the different coordinated means actions all converge on an identical end. In these cases, the features of equifinality and local causality seem to define the intention. The intended goal is the point at which the converging causal lines of the different possible means actions meet.

Short of direct observation of the action structure itself, we may make use of knowledge from other sources about it. We may, for example, learn later of the person's behavior during the course of the action. There are also means actions which usually lead to only one goal. If we see a person performing one of these actions, we will assume that his intention is to reach that goal. For instance, when a person orders a dinner in a restaurant we have little doubt that his intention is to eat it. When we see a person buying a railroad ticket to a city we will assume that he intends to go there. This assumption will be strengthened if the city is far away and we observe that he is carrying a suitcase. In every concerted action, that is an action whose success demands a number of coordinated means actions, the clues provided by the means actions can point to the goal in a redundant way. If we know that a person packs his suitcase in a hotel room, pays his bill, orders a taxi to the station, we can be fairly certain that he intends to leave town. In many jokes the means action results in an entirely different outcome from the one redundantly indicated. The story is told of a man who waited weeks so that complicated arrangements could be made for a cake to be baked precisely in the shape of a capital S, who kept inquiring anxiously about the progress of this achievement, only to eat the prized production himself in the baker's shop.

There are other clues revealing intentions that pertain, perhaps, less directly to the action structure itself. One of the most common of these is the report of the person himself of what he is trying to do. We also make use of knowledge about the person. Thus, in figuring out whether a particular action outcome was intended by the person or not, we may note whether it is in line with his character and usual motives or whether it was provoked by the particular situation. Intentions are also inferred from our knowledge about people in general. If a person brings about a number of changes in the environment, and one of them is generally considered much more attractive than the others, we will assume that it was the person's goal. Thus, we will take for granted that it is the fish and not the seaweed upon his line that the fisherman is seeking, even before we have a chance to learn what he does with them. The property of the goal determined by common practice has provided the basis for our inference concerning personal intention.

Just as a mistake may be made when we infer intention from means action, so we may also err when conclusions concerning intention are drawn from the action outcome. Since "can" and "try" are conditions of action, we sometimes make these relations reversible in the following inferential logic: If we know that a person produced a certain environmental change, then we infer that he tried to produce it and that he could produce it. Neither of these inferences, however, is necessarily true. In the discussion of "can" we mentioned that success does not always imply a permanent can; the person may have had exceptional luck. And in the discussion of personal causality it was pointed out that not all aftereffects fit the structure of personal causality and therefore the imputation from them that they were purposely caused or intended by the agent may be erroneous. One cannot, therefore, always conclude from the fact that a person has produced a certain change that he tried to do it. He may have caused the aftereffect, but not necessarily intentionally.

Nevertheless, since $a$ (can) together with $b$ (try) implies $c$ (outcome), if $a$ and $c$ are given, in everyday life we often do infer $b$. Likewise, if $a$ and not $c$ is given, we often infer not $b$, though here again we may be in error. Consider the case where I know that (1) a certain person is aware that he could easily help, but (2) he does not help. Though I may rashly conclude that $p$ has not tried, I may be in error for a variety of reasons—his efforts, for instance, may have been rebuffed. Moreover, the error may be further compounded when the intention in try is made equivalent to wish. Thus, I am prone to conclude that the person does not wish to help, when in fact, any lack of trying or intention to help may stem from other considerations, such as whether he ought to help. In this case "$p$ can" and "$p$ does not cause" are given and we infer "$p$ does not try" or even "$p$ does not wish." If "$p$ tries" and "$p$ does not cause" are given, we infer "$p$ cannot." But, if both *not a* and *not c* are given, we cannot make any inference with respect to the absence or presence of $b$. Thus, if a person does not succeed (*not c*) and we know that he did not try (*not a*) we cannot conclude anything about his ability ($b$). In testing abilities, therefore, motivation must be controlled.

Finally, inferences concerning intentions may be false because the perception of the actions that took place, of "what happened," may be distorted. What the other person actually did is not only perceived on the basis of local cues given by the movements of the person, but also on the basis of what we think we know about the situation and about the person. In the following example, taken from Maupassant's story *The Piece of String*, the combination of situational clues external to the action itself plus the presumed character of the acting person serve to define the action for the observer: Mr. Hauchecorne picks up a worthless piece of string in the street. He notices that he is seen by Mr. Malandain with whom he is not on very good terms. He gets embarrassed, and hastily hides the piece of string in his blouse. Malandain, who hears later that somebody had lost a wallet containing money, is then convinced that he "saw" Hauchecorne pick up the wallet.

We shall see later that the cognition of intention is also conditioned by the needs of the perceiver. But here let us restate the important point that when we attribute an action to a certain intention, we diagnose the family of possible equifinal changes to which the action belongs. The one concrete action then represents a manifold of vicarious means changes which all lead to the goal change. Such terms as "personal causality" and "intention" refer to concepts that presuppose a manifold of possible events. They have no meaning if one restricts the problem to a single concrete process or means action.

The exertion aspect of trying is sometimes perceived directly, and sometimes through inference. We may see a person *struggling* to move a heavy weight or *easily* lifting it. Or sometimes we infer the amount of effort put forth by the relations between effort and other concepts, such as task difficulty and ability. If a person with little ability accomplishes a difficult task, we feel that he must have tried very hard. (Cf. pp. 85–86.) Exertion, and not only intention, is also gauged from the structure of personal causality. If we know that a person has tried many different possibilities in attempting to solve a problem, we conclude that he has worked hard at it. If he gives up quickly, we feel that he has not exerted himself very much.

The cognition of both intention and exertion has important bearing on our interpretation of action. We have seen, for instance, how the diagnosis of intention may affect the judgment of responsibility and the appraisal of ability. Above all, it is the goal of an action, its source in the intention of the person, that often determines what the person really is doing, or what really is happening. The situation is quite different, and carries different implications for the future, if something is done to me intentionally or accidentally. It is the difference between a stone accidentally hitting me and a stone aimed at me. The particular path the stone travels might be the same in both cases; still the events are very different because the movement of the stone is only a part of the whole event to which we react and which is of vital importance for us. The position of intention in the expectation and control of action has been elaborated in the main discussion of personal causality.

Less obvious, perhaps, is the fact that the cognition of exertion also may have important repercussions on the meaning of an act. For one thing, exertion circumscribes the degree of motivation or intention, that is, how much a person wants something. The cognition of exertion even helps differentiate genuine intention from the more superficial or less sincere variety. For instance, if a person gives up easily, we might conclude that he was not really interested. Or, if a benefit does not presuppose some self-sacrifice on the part of the benefactor, that is, if the necessary exertion was minimal, then the recipient may discount the benefit and feel little obligation to reciprocate. Exertion also, as has already been pointed out, may be taken as an indicator of both ability and intelligence (cf. p. 111). As a matter of fact, the most convincing raw material for the perception that "*o* cannot do it" is to see someone trying very hard and not succeeding. Dembo and her associates have stressed that effort may even be taken as a main criterion for the evaluation of the total person. Often the person who tries very hard is applauded. But,

. . . under certain circumstances, of two persons who reached the same performance level, the one who did so with greater ease is considered the better. He is seen as potentially a better producer than the one who had to work harder. Thus, effort is not always considered a positive value but, paradoxically, sometimes as a liability. (Dembo, Leviton, and Wright, 1956, p. 40.)

It is, of course, then taken as a sign of low ability.

   *Egocentric cognition and attribution in the case of can and try.* Sometimes the data make it very clear in the absence or failure of action, whether it is the "can" or the "try" that is the missing condition. But sometimes the data are sufficiently ambiguous so that the person's own needs or wishes determine the attribution.

   An example of such egocentric attribution is the sour grapes fable. The fox pretends, or perhaps is even convinced, that he does not want the grapes rather than that he cannot get them. He attributes the failure to the "not want" (and the "not intend" and "not try") instead of the "not can," since in this case the former is neutral as far as his self-esteem is concerned, and the latter is damaging. Another example is the thief who, having no opportunity to steal, considers himself an honest man. In reality he does not steal because the condition "can" is lacking: he has had no opportunity. However, he attributes the not stealing to the fact that he has no intention to steal and is thereby able to claim credit for being law abiding. Examples of egocentric attribution to "cannot" are not hard to find. The child affirms that he cannot do the chore when in fact he does not wish to. (Cf. also p. 227.)

   Finally, when a person wants to absolve himself of responsibility for the action outcome, he may find a good ally in fate. If neither of the personal contributions to action—namely, the ability factor in "can" and the intention in "try"—is manifestly suspect, he may blame the tricks or commands of fate for what he has done: he could not do otherwise. The following pronouncement, taken from *King Lear*, illustrates this point:

*Edmund:* This is the excellent foppery of the world, that, when we are sick in fortune, often the surfeit of our own behaviour, we make guilty of our disasters the sun, the moon, and the stars; as if we were villains on necessity; fools by heavenly compulsion; knaves, thieves, and treachers by spherical predominance; drunkards, liars, and adulterers by an enforc'd obedience of planetary influence; and all that we are evil in by a divine thrusting on. An admirable evasion of whoremaster man, to lay his goatish disposition to the charge of a star! (Act I, Scene 2.)

Not only are personal actions a fertile field for egocentric attribution; the actions of others are likely candidates too. We may think erroneously that another person can and intends to do something just because we wish it to happen.

An experiment reported by A. Pepitone (1950) is relevant in this connection. His subjects, high school sophomores, were told that they would be interviewed by a board of three coaches and that if the results of the interview were satisfactory, they would receive tickets to games. After the meeting, the subjects were asked to rate the coaches on social power (power to influence the evaluation of the subjects) and on approval (whether they seemed to be friendly towards the subjects or not).

The judges were carefully instructed as to the roles they should play. In one set of conditions, the appearance of equal power was established while the friendliness varied, one coach seeming very friendly, one neutral, the third unfriendly. In another set of conditions the three behaved in equally friendly fashion, but one was obviously the boss whose opinion would be decisive, while another one always asked permission of the other two board members for questioning the subject, etc.

The main result was that the judgments of power and of friendliness showed a kind of assimilation. In the equal-power situation, that is, the situation in which the raw material, the data, were carefully arranged so as to give the impression of equal power, the friendly coach was judged to have most power, the unfriendly one to have least power. In the same way the different degrees of power (as actually presented in the stimulus situation) affected the judgments of the objectively equal friendliness. One explanation might be that because of a halo effect, a person correctly judged to be positive in one trait is then also judged to be positive in the second trait. Pepitone, however, does not accept this explanation, because some of his results contradict it. He proposes a theory of "facilitative distortion":

> From the standpoint of a subject wanting to reach the goal these are facilitative perceptions. Obviously, to perceive Mr. Negative as less disagreeable than he actually is, and to perceive the same board member as having less power than he actually expressed, are estimations which characterize a better state of affairs for the subject. (Pepitone, 1950, p. 71.)

In other words, if I want an effect, I will want the essential conditions to be realized; in wishful thinking, I will tend to see the conditions as being realized. In the Pepitone experiment, the two conditions favoring the desired outcome concerning the board's recommendation are (1) the coach has the power to influence the board, he can do that; this condition is represented by the power rating. And (2) the coach wants and therefore intends to influence the board favorably; this condition is represented by the friendliness rating. Thus, if it is apparent that one condition is present, the subject will wish to have the other condition realized, and where the raw material is sufficiently ambiguous he will be influenced in his judgment by this wish.

A good example of egocentric cognition in which the needs of the perceiver help to determine the perception of *o*'s intentions is the tendency to see ourselves as the focus of the other people's actions. This tendency may be strong enough to counteract the objective action structure which points to a different terminal focus, and it is especially noticeable when the actions of another involve us in some way. Thus, we are inclined to assume a "for our sake" attitude even if the person benefited us unintentionally, and an "against us" attitude when the harm was unintentional. Bertrand Russell (1950) has remarked that "One of the odd effects of the importance which each of us attaches to himself is that we tend to imagine our own good or evil fortune to be the purpose of other people's actions . . ." (p. 151). In these cases, an egocentric point of view has been adopted, so that, of several changes resulting from the action of the person, the perceiver has selected the one important to himself rather than the one significant to the agent and which has in fact guided the actions of the agent. Let us say that change *A* implies changes *B*, *C*, and *D*. If *B* is most important to me by virtue of the fact that it has personal effects upon me, then I have a tendency to assume that *A* was produced in order to bring *B* about even though *C* may actually have been the intention.

One might say that, on the whole, attribution of action will be such that one's idea of the environment or of one's relation to the environment is kept inviolate or even supported. Since one's idea includes what "ought to be" and "what one would like to be" as well as "what is," attribution and cognition are influenced by the mere subjective forces of needs and wishes as well as by the more objective evidence presented in the raw material. Especially important is the point of view adopted—whether one perceives and interprets according to one's own outlook or whether one is able to assume the position of the person who is the source of the action in question.

**Coping with the can and want of hostile others.** Needless to say, the attribution of action to can and try, and the cognition of these components does not always respond to our preferences. Sometimes the reality as perceived is so unyielding that even when it runs counter to our own well-being we have little choice but to acknowledge it. Then it is that we may attempt to change the can and want, not by wishful thinking, but by doing something about the situation. Knowing that two conditions are necessary for another person to act, we may try to eliminate one of them in order to prevent an undesirable action. Specifically, if $o$ can do $x$, $p$ has to induce "$o$ does not want to do $x$" in order to prevent $x$, or at least he has to be careful that the wish does not become activated as a force toward $x$. Or, if $p$ knows that $o$ wants to do $x$, then $p$ has to be careful to prevent $o$'s being able to produce $x$.

These considerations can be applied in the analysis of basic premises underlying Karen Horney's (1945) description of types of neurotic behavior. However, the logic also applies to non-neurotic behavior, to everyday adaptations in interpersonal relations.

According to Horney (1945), the basic situation as seen by the neurotic is one of "being isolated and helpless in a potentially hostile world" (p. 41). The two conditions for the possibility that he will be harmed, namely "$o$ can harm me" and "$o$ wants to harm me" are fulfilled. If he can remove one of them, he will be safe. This he attempts to do by either moving towards people or against them. In moving towards people he tries to remove the condition "$o$ wants to harm me," by changing the relationship to "$o$ likes me." In moving against people he tries to change the condition, "$o$ can harm me," to "$o$ cannot harm me." Horney states,

When moving *toward* people he (the neurotic) accepts his own helplessness, and in spite of his estrangement and fears tries to win the affection of others and to lean on them. Only in this way can he feel safe with them. If there are dissenting parties in the family, he will attach himself to the most powerful person or group. By complying with them, he gains a feeling of belonging and support which makes him feel less weak and less isolated. (Horney, 1945, p. 42.)

The significant relations can be shown graphically:

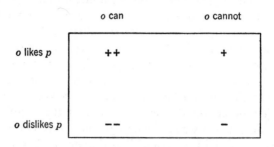

The square presents a field in which the vertical dimension means degrees of liking ranging from "*o* likes *p*" (the other person likes *p*) to "*o* dislikes *p*"; the horizontal dimension at the same time indicates the degrees of the power of *o* to cause benefit or harm ranging from "*o* can" to "*o* cannot." The positive and negative signs within the square refer to the degree to which the situation conforms to *p*'s wishes.

The whole square thus contains all the possible pictures *p* can have of *o* in regard to the dimensions of can and want (as indicated by like). For instance the situation represented in the upper left hand corner of the square is one in which *o* can help or harm *p* and in which *o* likes *p*. In such a case there is no question but that *o* will help *p*; the situation is the most favorable one possible and on our diagram is marked by a double plus. In the lower left hand corner, on the other hand, the situation is represented in which, though *o* again can do something positive or negative for *p*, he dislikes *p*. In this case it can be assumed that *o* will do harm to *p*; this situation is the most negative one possible and is marked by a double minus. It is the situation characteristic of Horney's neurotic.

Unless the situation is the most positive one, forces in the direction of something more positive, or at least less negative, will be aroused. In the case in which *o* likes *p* but at the same time has relatively little power (upper right hand corner) *p* will wish that *o* had greater power, and may try to augment it. If it is given that *o* has great power but that his attitude toward *p* is less positive than it might be (lower left hand corner), then the force will be in the direction away from *o* dislikes *p* toward *o* likes *p*, i.e., *p* will wish that *o* liked him better and may "move toward" *o* to accomplish this. If it is obvious that *o* dislikes *p*, then the force will be towards *o* *cannot* harm or toward a lessening of *o*'s power (lower right hand corner); *p* may attempt this by "moving against" *o*. Though this situation may still be far from positive, in the sense that it is not agreeable to be disliked even by a person who has no power over our fortunes, it is much better than having *o* dislike *p* coupled with *o* can harm *p*, the situation in which we are at the mercy of someone who dislikes us.

In brief, when *p* becomes convinced that *o* cannot harm him, then he doesn't have to be so concerned about whether *o* wants to harm him or not; *p* can even arouse *o*'s hostility with impunity. By the same logic, when *p* becomes convinced that *o* will never want to harm him, then he doesn't have to worry about whether or not *o* can harm him; *p* may even put himself in the power of *o*. The principle guiding *p*'s efforts clearly focuses around the can and want: If other people cannot harm me because they are in my power, or do not want to harm me because they like me, then they will not harm me.

## Summary

We have attempted to show the complexities, the wisdom, and the failings of the naive psychology of action by making explicit what is not always phenomenally explicit. In the analysis, "can" and "trying" were shown to be the two necessary and sufficient conditions of purposive action. Each is analyzable into constituent elements: can into personal power and environmental factors; trying into intention and exertion. The nature of dispositional properties as well as the meaning of personal causality were singled out as being of special significance in the understanding of these concepts. Factors that influence the conditions of action and their constituents were also discussed.

The naive factor analysis of action permits man to give meaning to action, to influence the actions of others as well as of himself, and to predict future actions. The framework of the many examples in the chapter rests on the fact implicit in naive psychology that can and try are the conditions of action. Thus, our reactions will be different according to whether we think a person failed primarily because he lacked adequate ability or primarily because he did not want to carry out the action. In the first case, we will expect him to succeed as soon as the condition "can" is fulfilled. Moreover, we may bring this condition about by making the task easier, by removing obstacles, by teaching the person requisite skills, and so on. In the second case, however, we will not expect the person to perform the action even when such changes are realized.

Only by affecting the want is there a possibility of establishing the necessary condition, try. Consequently, the direction of our efforts will be quite different. We may attempt to convince the person that this is something he wants to do, we may highlight the positive features of the goal, or appeal to ethical considerations. In this case, the conditions of motivation become the focus. In addition to differences of expectation and control in the two cases, our value judgments may be quite different also. The person may be held far more responsible for the action outcome in the one case than in the other.

The above example seems obvious. But after all, our intention was to show the connections given by naive psychology that permit action and the interpretation of behavior in everyday interpersonal relations. At the same time, in delineating the "logic" of the naive analysis of action, we do not imply that the conclusions based thereon always fit objective reality. Sometimes, as we have seen, erroneous inferences are made when the conditions of action are only partially given or when egocentric influences distort cognition.

It is quite remarkable that the naive psychology of action works as well as it does and applies to such a wide range of cases involving action. It permits statements about the attribution of action, the cognition of its components, and the prediction and control of behavior. Similar functions were seen to emerge from the naive analysis of perception and in this area as well as that of action, man's meaningful association with his environment and control over it is thereby widened.

# CHAPTER 5

# Desire and pleasure

INSOFAR AS THE DISCUSSION of trying was restricted to intention, i.e., what a person is trying to do, and to exertion, i.e., how hard he is trying to do it, we were dealing with motivation at a relatively superficial level; we did not consider the question of why he is doing it. Intention and exertion were conceptualized as the constituents or aspects of trying, not as the conditions of trying. But, as we have pointed out more than once, man has a strong urge to push toward deeper levels of understanding, those levels that reveal the conditions behind the events with which he is confronted. In this chapter we shall trace a few outlines of the way one of the conditions of trying—desire, and its counterpart, pleasure or enjoyment—is managed in interpersonal behavior.

Scientific psychology, in spite of considerable thinking and research in the area of motivation, has not yet succeeded in establishing a generally accepted vocabulary. It is not surprising, therefore, that the vocabulary of naive psychology, which bases its concepts on a much wider range of phenomena, is not altogether clear either. The experience of pleasure has hardly been touched by systematic psychology. As Henle has observed,

Contemporary motivation theories are theories of striving to reach goals; their interest stops once the goal has been achieved. Even hedonism seems to deal only with the pursuit of happiness and to have little place for happiness itself. (Henle, 1956, p. 299.)

But naive psychology hasn't neglected pleasure. As we shall see, by relating desire and pleasure within a system of concepts, man is enabled to think and do many things involving motive and affect.

## Own Wish and Induced Motivation

The following are a few examples of motivating behavior commonly apprised in everyday life. They are neither exhaustive nor mutually exclusive:

1. The most obvious reason for $o$ trying to do $x$ is his own wish. He likes to do it; the goal in itself is attractive to him.

2. He may do $x$ for the sake of some ulterior goal. Then $x$, a means to reach this goal, may be neutral or even disagreeable.

3. He may have been asked to do $x$ by a friend.

4. He may do it for somebody he likes without having been asked.

5. He may do it because somebody in authority told him to do it.

6. He may do it because he thinks he ought to do it, because he feels obliged to do it.

7. He may do it because he wishes to establish or maintain a certain reputation, being helpful or courageous for example.

In distinguishing the first reason, the own desire to do $x$, from the others, one has the feeling that it stems more strictly from the person himself and depends less on outside factors. Most, if not all, of the other reasons require an entity outside the person and his immediate goal $x$. Thus, if I do something because I am commanded to (reason 5), the existence of an authoritative person is necessary. The relation between $p$ and $x$ is not the primary consideration, but rather the relation between $p$ and other factors. Sometimes the difference between the own desire and other motives is sharpened when they stand in opposition. We say, "I wish I could do that but it would not be right." Or, "I don't want to, but I have been ordered to." In these cases, the own force is opposed in direction by the force of other considerations. These other considerations, to use the topological term, are induced forces. Of course, they need not be in conflict with the own wishes. One may like to do what one ought or is commanded to do.

At the same time, the distinction between own wishes and induced motivations is not always clear. What is the outside entity in doing something because of ethical considerations? It may be argued that ought requirements are attributed to an authority beyond oneself, but in another sense these requirements may be very much a part of the person. And yet, even in this latter sense, behavior dictated by duty is felt to be in a different class psychologically from that guided by own desire. The conceptual ambiguity in the distinction between own desire and induced motivation is again seen in the following case. Doing *x* may be a means to benefit a loved person, the real goal. But just because of its means character it may actually become very attractive. In fact, without its means-end significance, doing *x* may even be negative. A hated task may become a pleasure when done for someone one loves. Though the force toward *x* is induced by its means character, depending, therefore on a different goal, one might be reluctant to exclude this case from those expressing own wishes. In general, if one goes back to the conditions behind the conditions, many desires can be seen to have been induced by all sorts of environmental influences, such as the requests and suggestions of other persons in the distant past, means-end relations over a period of time, and so on. The theory of the functional autonomy of motives derives the existence of the variety of motives in the adult from what originally are but means actions (Allport, 1937).

In spite of the conceptual ambiguity, we shall attempt to explore some of the conditions and effects of the motivational state variously referred to as desiring, wishing, and wanting. At least in a global sense we can say that this state is directed toward a goal that in itself is attractive to the person. Intention, as we have used it in the preceding chapter, is a different concept from desire. Both are directed toward a goal, but intention is identifiable solely by the structure of personal causality which points out what a person is trying to do or has succeeded in doing without regard to the meaning it holds for the person. Desire refers to one of the motives that gives meaning to an intention. Other motives, such as those dependent upon request, command, and ethical considerations are considered elsewhere in this work (Chapters 8, 9, and 10).

## The Relation of Action to Desire

In scientific psychology, motivational concepts analogous to wish or desire have often been directly referred to the particular action by which one tries to satisfy it. Holt (1916), for instance, defines the wish as "*a course of action* which some mechanism of the body is *set* to carry out, whether it actually does so or does not" (p. 3). The opinion that a wish is a potential action, is, of course, an outcome of the behavioral viewpoint. But not all theoretical psychologists tie wishes to action. Murray, for instance, says,

Among the commonest subjective experiences is that of conflict between desires, and that of having one desire inhibit another. If psychology limits itself to concepts which refer only to external movements, there will be no way of formulating important psychological events of this sort. (Murray, 1938, p. 65.)

In naive psychology, also, wishes are not necessarily linked to actions. There are several important features of the concept of wish as it is commonly understood which support this view. First, one and the same wish may lead to very different means actions according to the requirements of the environment. The particular action by which the person tries to reach the goal is a consequence of the wish *and* the way the person sees this goal embedded in the causal structure of the environment (means-end beliefs). The person, or some mechanism in his body, could not be set to carry out all the different possibilities of reaching the goal under all possible circumstances. In accordance with this consideration Lewin makes the following proposal concerning the relation between force, which is coordinated to the way a person tries to reach the goal, and need or tension, which corresponds roughly to wish:

> Instead of linking the need directly to the motoric, the need is linked with certain properties of the environment. The environment then determines the motoric. . . . The theory obviously separates need and directed actions much more than did the previous theories. . . . Psychology has proved increasingly that a given need might lead to a great variety of different or even contradictory actions in accordance with the specific environment. (Lewin, 1938, p. 108.)

Another reason for the common-sense separation of wish and action is that a wish may exist long before a specific action is taken to satisfy it, or without its ever being actualized in action. This point has already been made in connection with the constituents of trying (cf. Chapter 4, p. 110); in brief, it refers to the fact that a wish may exist even though no action on the part of the person is evident, either because no action is necessary, or because the person withholds action for certain reasons.

Finally, naive psychology does not coordinate desire too closely with action because of the recognition that wishes can have other effects besides action. The most important of these is the emotional reaction to the fate of the wished-for event, even though no action of the person is involved, the events being entirely due to environmental factors. If the wish is fulfilled, a positive affective state ensues—happiness, satisfaction, pleasure, enjoyment; if it is thwarted, the affect is quite different—disappointment, frustration, displeasure. Murray, who again and again calls attention to the connection between need, outside events, and satisfaction, designates as "gratuities" the changes that fulfill a need but are not produced by the person (Murray, 1938, p. 62).

Some persons may be disturbed about such mysterious internal states as desire, pleasure, and dissatisfaction which may be accessible phenomenally, but which are not always directly manifested in behavior. It is our belief that even as purely phenomenal states, they are real and therefore worthy of study. However, though they cannot be linked with specific action patterns, they certainly can have behavioral effects that are widespread and often indirect. For instance, if something occurs that I have wished for, I will be pleased. This state of happiness might lead to all sorts of actions. I might give presents to my friends; I might be very friendly toward a person whom I do not like very much; I might decide to be very good and act more in accordance with what I think is my duty, etc. All these actions, though not intrinsically connected with the realization of the wish, are correctly explained by naive psychology in terms of desire and pleasure. Naive psychology shows little reluctance in using these concepts as intervening variables.

In fact, we very often infer *o*'s motives from his behavior. If *o* does something most people like to do, or if *o* is obviously pleased, it will be assumed that he wished to do it. On the other hand, if we know that the action and its outcome is in itself disagreeable we will look for other reasons to explain it. Depending on the real or imagined facts at our disposal, we will infer that he was ordered to do it, that he did it on his own initiative for someone he loved, that he considered it his duty, and so on. The chief point is that an action may be taken as a sign for the existence of a motive even though it cannot be said that the existence of a wish requires its coordination to an action.

In summary, we cannot say that a wish is characterized by any one of the actions that may bring *x* about, nor by the sum total of all such actions. But we can say that a wish largely determines the person's reaction to the vicissitudes of *x*. If *x* occurs or does not occur, if it is likely to occur or is impossible, if its occurrence is facilitated or hindered by other people, the reaction to all these possibilities will largely be determined by whether I want *x* to occur or not. We shall now examine more carefully the connection between desire and the affective reaction to wish-fulfillment.

## A Priori Connection Between Desire and Pleasure

In naive psychology, the concept desire is not linked in every case to action, but it is linked to pleasure upon the fulfillment of the desire, thus: desire for *x* plus obtaining *x* leads to pleasure. This is a postulate that connects a motive with an affect and as such may erroneously be thought to express a hedonic theory of motivation. But the postulate says nothing about the *source* of the motive. It merely states that when a desire exists, its fulfillment will be satisfying, not that desire arises because of anticipated pleasure. Hedonic theories, on the other hand, specifically attribute motives to pleasure-pain consequences. P. T. Young (1955), for instance, affirms that primary motivation lies in the affective processes and "As human beings we are aware of feelings of delight and distress, of anger, anxiety, embarrassment, et cetera, and we repeatedly interpret our actions and the actions of others in terms of conscious feeling" (p. 193).

The a priori connection between desire and pleasure is variously applied in everyday life. It provides us with a working definition for the detection of wish-fulfillment. It specifies at least one effect of the fulfillment of desire, the crucial one of positive affect. It also defines certain conditions of pleasure. The following, therefore, seem axiomatic: if one could have what one wishes one would be happy; if one sees a person happy who had been consumed by a wish then we assume that he got what he wanted; if we want a person to be happy we will want to find out what his wishes are, being quite certain that if they are fulfilled he will be pleased. Moreover, as we shall soon see, the connection between wish-fulfillment and pleasure belongs to the a priori content of naive psychology and cannot be contradicted by experience, just as the relation between can, try, and success cannot be negated.

*The inviolability of the connection.* Two questions can be asked about the connection between desire and pleasure. First, does the fulfillment of a desire always and necessarily lead to pleasure? Second, does the arousal of pleasure always depend upon wish-fulfillment? More formally, are desire and obtaining $x$ the necessary and sufficient conditions of pleasure?

With respect to the first question, our answer is in the affirmative, meaning that wish-fulfillment *always* leads to pleasure, or, in the language of logic, that desire and obtaining $x$ are sufficient conditions of pleasure. But, you may argue, what if the anticipated pleasure is not forthcoming? Is not this a common experience? Our reply is that even under these circumstances we never doubt for a moment that there is an a priori connection between desire and pleasure. Yet, if this connection is to be preserved, something must be doubted. As a matter of course, therefore, we either analyze the situation in an attempt to determine which of the underlying conditions is lacking, or we reappraise our reaction and conclude that our disappointment was unjustified.

Let us discuss this phenomenon through a concrete example. Suppose that I desire a juicy, tasty apple and purchase one at the store only to be displeased upon eating it. If we insist that desire for $x$ (the apple) existed and that $x$ was in fact obtained, then the resulting displeasure is strange indeed. But in naive psychology we have little trouble with such a problem. The following reconstructions are open to us: (1) The apple was not really desired in the first place. We only thought we wanted it. In this case the desire itself is challenged. (2) The apple obtained is like the desired one in appearance only. In actuality, for instance, it is mealy and tasteless. Or, if it had the anticipated qualities, an additional factor, perhaps the information that it had been contaminated by a poisonous spray, enters, and again the conclusion is formed that a genotypical $y$ instead of a phenotypical $x$ was purchased. Here, the second condition, that pertaining to the realization of $x$, is challenged. (3) The reaction was unjustified. We are really pleased. The initial disappointment was based on some detail, either false or insignificant. Or, particularly when the reactions of another person $o$ are in question, we may feel that the displeasure is feigned for ulterior purposes. The enjoyment is really there, but it is covered up by a masochistic need, for example, or by ethical requirements. In any case, the perceived affect undergoes the necessary change in conformity with the desire-pleasure postulate.

Which of the underlying conditions the lack of the affect will be attributed to depends in part on cognitive factors. If I wanted a juicy apple and received one that is dry and mealy, I am likely to attribute the disappointment to the nonrealization of $x$. If, however, the apple clearly met all the specifications, the desire itself will be questioned. Since a flaw in only one of the conditions is sufficient to account for the lack of pleasure we usually rest the case upon one such discovery. From the point of view of the desire-pleasure postulate, it would be redundant to doubt both conditions, i.e., the desire and the getting of the desired. If, however, both conditions survive such a scrutiny, then the manifest affect itself is suspect. In any case, the connection between desire and pleasure remains unchallenged.

The same reasoning backward and reappraisal without reconceptualizing occurs in case of the a priori relation between can, try, and success. If a person feels he can do $x$ and upon trying to do $x$ fails, he may conclude that he cannot do $x$. That is, the lack of the expected effect is attributed to the lack of one of the conditions, not to the incorrectness of the relation.  Or conversely, if the person, convinced that he cannot do $x$, is forced to try and succeeds, he may reappraise his abilities; or he may feel he has incorrectly assessed the outcome and has actually failed.  In brief, the relation "can plus try leads to success" holds unconditionally.  Similarly, if the desire for $x$ really exists, and if the person really obtained what he desired, then he must be pleased.

As for the second question, namely whether pleasure always pre-supposes wish-fulfillment, our answer is in the negative.  We often experience events full of pleasure or displeasure that was not expected. A happy surprise beyond our fondest wishes may come our way; sudden disasters we had never thought of as possible may strike us.  In a word, though desire and obtaining $x$ are sufficient conditions of pleasure, desire, at least, is not a necessary condition.  Whether obtaining $x$ is a necessary condition is somewhat unclear.  On the phenomenal level, it seems that the experience of pleasure may arise "out of the void," without being pointed toward any specific event.  Usually, however, it is connected with a source (cf. the section below).

The inviolability of the connection between desire and pleasure has not gone unchallenged.  Seeman and Buck (1952), in referring to the popular notion that the nature of a wish is such that its fulfillment must be attended by an introspectively experienced pleasant affect, make the point that "... even in popular experience there is acknowledgment that this *need* not be the case.  It is, after all, recognized that Alexander the Great, having satisfied his wish to conquer the world, did not smile, he wept!" (p. 18).  Oscar Wilde goes so far as to say: "When the gods wish to punish us they answer our prayers" and "In this world there are only two tragedies.  One is not getting what one wants, and the other is getting it."  In the light of the preceding discussion, it becomes clear that these examples are only seemingly contradictory. In the natural order of things, as viewed by common-sense psychology, one does not weep upon the fulfillment of a desire.  One may weep because of other factors separate from the desire—in wish-fulfillment, one may have to give up something dear; one may have to accept negatives together with the desired object.  The weeping is over the negatives, not because the desire is fulfilled.  In regard to the admonitions of Oscar Wilde, it is necessary to draw a distinction between the phenomenal experiences of desire and pleasure on the one hand, and other requirements pertaining to one's well-being.  What gives pleasure may adversely affect one's conscience or health, for instance.  This issue is considered more fully in a later section dealing with disharmony.

**The connection cognitively rooted.** One might also phrase the relation this way: when $p$ desires $x$, that does not imply that he will enjoy it, but it does imply that he thinks he will enjoy it. Anticipated pleasure, then is an essential component of desire.

Desire and pleasure generally have a belief content about possible events. They are usually not given simply as states; "$p$ desires $x$" implies that $p$ believes that the realization of $x$ will bring him satisfaction. (This is to be distinguished from wishful thinking in which "$p$ wishes for $x$" leads to "$p$ believes in the reality of $x$.") Only when desire represents a vague wish for something undefinable, only when pleasure represents a generalized joy over something without content, might we say that these states refer to sensations devoid of cognitive aspects. Even then, one may consciously seek for a cause, for something on which to focus the desire or affect, as when, in the words of Scheler (1927), "...one asks oneself: why am I in this or that mood today? What has caused this happiness or sadness in me?" (p. 263).

Since pleasure is anticipated upon fulfillment of desire, one may speak about correct and incorrect desires or even foolish wishes. If the desire becomes actualized in pleasure, one has desired "correctly." The person was not misled. If a negative or neutral reaction occurs, one has desired "incorrectly." If everyone could have told the person he would be disappointed, his desire may even be considered foolish.

It is important to realize that it is the cognitive-like aspect of desire and pleasure that makes it possible for the a priori connection between them to hold even when the actual events are not in the expected direction. It is then that the perception of the events changes, not the relation itself.

## Incompatibility with Other Requirements: Disharmony

We have seen that when the mutual requirement between desire and pleasure remains unfulfilled, disharmony results. The situation is then brought into proper perspective by re-evaluating the motive, the affect, or the object to which these states are directed. In addition to the disharmony contingent upon the a priori relation of desire and pleasure, there are other sources of disturbance involving these states.

A frequent source of disturbance is the incompatibility of desires and pleasures with more objective organismic requirements. Disharmony results when something that is felt to be objectively positive is disliked; cases in point are just punishment and bitter medicine. It also results when something that is felt to be objectively harmful is enjoyed; the various drug addictions come to mind. Even when I desire something I do not need and need something I do not desire, I may experience a certain uneasiness.

In the present context the term "$p$ needs $x$" means that $x$ is necessary to $p$'s good functioning. This may be an entirely objective fact, like "This machine needs oil," or "The trees need more water." The relation among the terms is: need for $x$ plus obtaining $x$ leads to organismic improvement. It will be recognized that this relation parallels that of the desire-pleasure postulate and like it, cannot be contradicted by experience. By definition it becomes self-evident that an organism will be in a better state when it has obtained what it needs. And, as with desire, the relation is used to infer conditions from effects as well as to predict effects from conditions. Thus, if obtaining $x$ and better state are given, if we know that right after getting $x$, $o$ improved, then we infer that there was a need for $x$; if need is given and we know that $o$ will get $x$, we can predict an improvement in $o$. If we know that $o$ had a need for $x$, and that he suddenly improved, we may conclude that he must have gotten $x$. If need for $x$ is given and $p$ wants to improve $o$, he will give him $x$; if he wants to prevent an improvement of $o$, he will try to prevent $o$ from getting $x$. All this is analogous to the inferences, predictions, and applications to action which are made on the basis of the relation between can, try, and success.

Frequently, if not usually, what we desire is not inconsistent with what we need, and vice versa. Then, upon obtaining $x$, pleasure as well as improvement of the organism results. But such harmony does not always hold. The chain smoker desires a cigarette, achieves satisfaction from the smoke, and yet knowingly suffers the harmful consequences. That the pleasurable is incompatible with the good has even become a principle of certain religious and philosophical viewpoints. Medicine must be bitter to be medicine. In any case, pleasure may be contaminated by concern over the fact that the organism is at the same time being harmed. The conflict may be so extreme as to take the joy out of pleasure entirely and leave in its wake negative and disturbed feelings. The person fails to enjoy his pleasure because of his preoccupation with these other matters. The a priori relation between desire and pleasure, however, remains intact insofar as the person knows that the pleasure would be experienced in full measure were it not for the troublesome and interfering issues.

The judgment that a wish is foolish is often based on the fact that there is marked incompatibility between it and the person's needs, between the implied pleasure and the well-being of the organism. One is foolish in one's desires if the pleasure of fulfilling them leads to major trouble. A person may even be thought stupid if he seeks something everyone but himself knows will lead to inevitable disaster, whether or not the anticipated pleasure occurs.

In addition to considerations concerning the more objective biological well-being of the organism, there are other requirements that may be in conflict with one's own desires and pleasures. To mention but a few, disharmony results when I desire and enjoy something that goes against my ethical convictions, something that is opposed by someone I like, that is dependent upon the good offices of an enemy, etc.

When the disturbance is sufficiently acute, some readjustment is necessary. As with other psychological disharmonies, this may be accomplished through re-evaluation (cf. Chapter 7). Thus, I may decide in favor of my desires and persuade myself that the presumed harm is but a tempest in a teapot. Or, better judgment may hold sway and lead to a waning of the desire itself, or at least I may try to convince myself that I have no taste for the $x$ in question. Or, I may decide that the pleasure is worth the price; the disharmony is not resolved. It is simply of manageable proportions.

In substance, there will be harmony when what is wished for is sought, is enjoyed, is objectively positive for the organism, is in line with ethical prescriptions, is supported by one's friends, and so on. Where conflict occurs, balance may be restored by a re-evaluation of the factors in question.

## The Cognition of Desire and Pleasure

Though desire and pleasure are states only the person himself experiences directly, it does not mean, of course, that they are undetectable by another person. As a matter of fact, it can happen that the person himself is less cognizant of his wishes and affective reactions than a second person is. The boy who speaks glowingly and at every opportunity about a certain girl may even deny his interest in her himself, though those around him know better. Murray notes that "... satisfaction is an affective state which is likely to manifest itself objectively as well as subjectively. It is no more difficult to diagnose than anxiety or anger..." (p. 456).

In everyday life we often form definite opinions about whether a person enjoys an object or a situation from his expressive behavior. Smiling, laughing, lively interested behavior, what he says and how he says it, are all indices of the person's reaction. If the person seems chagrined or angry when an object is taken away, we may assume that he enjoyed it.

Desires may also be disclosed by what a person does and how he does it. If a person tries this way and that to retrieve a coin outside his reach, we will certainly conclude that his intention is to obtain the coin. More than that, since a coin is a valued object, we are likely to assume that the intention represents a personal desire unless contrary evidence leads us to realize, for instance, that he is acting under the commands of another. The reader will recognize in this example the structure of equifinality (cf. pp. 100–109) representing the important behavioral manifestations of the motive.

Sometimes it is the a priori connection itself between desire and pleasure that is the primary basis for inferences concerning the existence of the two states. Since desire for $x$ and obtaining $x$ are the sufficient conditions for pleasure, when we know that these conditions are given, we also feel sure that the person is enjoying himself. By the same token, $o$'s happiness is sometimes taken as a sign that his wish is fulfilled or that his fear is now groundless. If we know what wish or fear occupied him, we may make very definite conclusions, though not necessarily correct ones, about what happened to produce the sudden change in mood. For instance, the relaxed look of a student who feared failure may tell us that he has passed. The gaiety of a daughter may inform the mother that the suitor had declared himself. These examples refer to the cognition of "obtaining $x$," i.e., of wish-fulfillment, and require prior knowledge of the wish in question. The desire itself, however, is sometimes cognized from the manifest joy. The mother may realize for the first time that her daughter wanted a formal when she observes the daughter's ecstasy upon receiving one. The host may be struck by how much his guest desires friendship when the invitation is acknowledged with excessive gratitude. As we said before, the cognition of desire, obtaining $x$, and pleasure, on the basis of the desire-pleasure postulate is similar to the cognition of can, trying, and success on the basis of their a priori connection (cf. pp. 114–118, the cognition of trying). In both cases conditions are inferred from effects and effects from conditions.

It hardly needs pointing out that the apprehension of desire and pleasure in another person may be incorrect. One source of error is that the behavioral clues themselves may be misinterpreted. The smiling of contempt may be mistaken for the smiling of pleasure, for example. Therefore, the cognition is more apt to be accurate when it is redundantly based upon a variety of behavioral clues, for instance, sayings and doings in addition to the smiling.

Another source of error is the fact that the behavioral clues may be intentionally feigned. As a matter of fact, training in the conventions includes training in formal pretense. We acknowledge a gift "with pleasure" when we consider it nothing but a white elephant. Nonetheless, people are often quite perceptive in distinguishing the real from the pretended. Thus, the verbal statements of another person are not always taken at face value. In the following, the critic of a eulogy given at the death of a college head perceives an underlying and certainly not intended enjoyment: "The uncomfortable nature of the speech was that he made it with such tremendous gusto; he was enjoying himself too much" (Snow, 1951, p. 233).

When a person says, "I don't enjoy that at all" we do not always believe him, especially when it is clear from his face and behavior that he just loves it. When in addition we have reason to believe that *o* wishes to hide his enjoyment, our grounds for suspicion become firmer. Perhaps liking *x* is not quite proper, or it may imply that *o* is obligated for the benefit, or it may signify a giving in, a confession that *o* was in error in anticipating dissatisfaction.

Cognitions based on the desire-pleasure postulate are also not without hazard. We infer desire from enjoyment even though the first is not a necessary condition of the second. We are therefore bound to be in error at least on occasion: The daughter may never have wanted a formal until it was hers to have and to keep. Also, we may be misinformed about one or another of the conditions, and so draw an erroneous conclusion about the affect. For instance, we may believe that the young man is pleased since (1) he wanted a watch and (2) he received one. In actuality, he may already have received a watch and so no longer desires one, or it may have been lost in the mail. In either case, the pleasure we expect or even perceive is not matched by reality.

There are other sources of cognitive error. The structure of equifinality which spots the person's intention may be mistakenly equated with the person's own wishes. Then there is the complex interplay of the perceiver's own needs and wishes which can produce a distorted picture of another person's motives and reactions: The father may be sure his son wants to go to college because the father so desperately wants him to. The girl may be certain the boy is enjoying her company because she fervently wishes this to be the case (cf. egocentric attribution, p. 158).

Desires and pleasures, as this brief review indicates, may be apprehended correctly or incorrectly by diverse processes, just like the cognition of can and trying previously discussed. The principles, in fact, are similar.

## *Value and Distance Relations Between* p *and* x

It has already been pointed out that neither desire nor pleasure are merely states with a peculiar quality; both have cognitive aspects that have far-reaching implications. One kind of cognitive meaning may be referred to as the value relation between $p$ and $x$. With desire, the value relation means that if I get $x$ it will give me satisfaction. Even if it is bad for me (or my conscience), it has at least this one positive consequence. In the case of enjoyment, the value relation between $p$ and $x$ is also a positive one, the pleasure centering on $x$. In short, desire and pleasure imply the apprehension of a quality of $x$, the quality of being satisfying to the person.

But a positive relation between $p$ and $x$ characterizes not only desire and pleasure. Consider the sentiment, liking. If $p$ likes $x$, there is also something positive or satisfying about $x$ for $p$. The same holds true if $p$ hopes for $x$ or fears that he will lose $x$. A second cognitive relation between $p$ and $x$, the distance relation, is helpful in distinguishing and at the same time interrelating a variety of emotional relations between $p$ and $x$. The distance dimension includes such relations as having or being in contact with $x$, not having $x$, possibly getting it, possibly losing it, and almost getting or losing it.

In addition to its conceptual usefulness, the distance dimension is important for interpersonal relations because one way of influencing another person's emotions or state of happiness is to change the nature of the contact between the person and his goal. We can benefit a person by giving him what he wants, or harm a person by preventing him from attaining his wish, for instance. Usually it is more difficult to change the fact that something has a positive or negative value for a person than to control whether he gets it or not.

Various thought models have been proposed to describe the distance dimension. We shall mention these briefly before proceeding to a discussion of the role of the distance dimension in a variety of emotional reactions involving $p$ and $x$ and in the control of pleasure in interpersonal relations.

*Models for conceptualizing the distance dimension.* Several thought models have been used to describe the nature of the contact between $p$ and $x$ that is characteristic of desire and pleasure. One such model in theoretical psychology is consumption. According to this analogy, enjoyment but not desire involves some kind of consummatory process. This model is obviously taken from the consumption of food in which the goal activity implies the destruction of the object involved. It is questionable, however, and especially alien to the thinking of naive psychology, that consumption is an adequate general term. What is consumed when a person takes pleasure in benefiting someone he likes or buying something attractive? There may be many wishes that involve another person or thing but where nothing is really consumed.

With food, as it happens, the most typical activity is consumption, but even there, other activities are possible. A person might enjoy cooking food. Does he consume the cooking?

Another model differentiating the states of desire and pleasure along the distance dimension is ownership, having or not having, getting or not getting. This model is often used in naive psychology. We give a person attention; we give him love; we give pleasure; we give a person what he wants. However, when a person enjoys something he does not always "have" it. One can enjoy a landscape or a person without having it, owning it or getting it.

Still another model is a spatial one, namely, being away from the goal or in contact with it. Lewin (1936), for example, speaks of being *in* the goal region, not of consuming the goal nor of having it. Though it is not entirely satisfactory, we have found this model conceptually useful. Problems arise especially if the spatial concept is identified with physical space. When a desired event occurs, as when the hoped for peace is concluded, one is not inclined to say that the person is *in* the goal region in a physical sense, nor that he is in contact with it. But if we do not restrict the model to physical space, then its usefulness is enhanced considerably. Time may then also be considered in spatial terms. Since being in the goal region requires the contemporaneous existence of $p$ and $x$, one can enjoy only what is present. Even if thoughts of some future event give pleasure, these thoughts must be present. Similarly, the probability of an event may also be considered in spatial terms. An event that is more probable may be thought of as closer psychologically than one that is less likely to occur. Of two events equally distant in the future, perhaps expected tomorrow, the one that is expected with certainty is as good as attained; it is "in the bag." And the person may experience, not the pleasure of anticipation, but the pleasure of an event that has virtually occurred. Psychologically at any rate, he is in the goal region. In spite of its shortcomings, the spatial model appears useful as a first approach, though it is not as precise as we might like. Essentially, this is the model that appears in our exposition of the distance dimension.

***Affective reactions determined by distance between p and x.*** DESIRE, PLEASURE, LIKING, AND OTHERS. Desire and pleasure express not only a value relation between $p$ and $x$ but also a distance relation. In desire, the person and the valued object are separated; in pleasure they are in some kind of contact. The value relation between $p$ and $x$ independent of the circumstances pertaining to distance is represented by liking. If someone likes $x$, we know that there is a positive relation between $p$ and $x$, but we do not know anything regarding the conditions of contact—whether he has $x$, will have $x$, can never have $x$, etc.

Liking, therefore, is more dispositional as a concept than is desire or pleasure. Even though liking may be affected by change within the distance dimension, as when "absence makes the heart grow fonder," conceptually, liking does not disappear and reappear with the vicissitudes of contact. In general, liking withstands changes within the distance dimension. Depending on conditions of contact, however, it is manifested as either desire or pleasure. By and large the following relations hold: if $p$ likes $x$ and is in contact with it, he will enjoy it; if he is separated from it he will be apt to wish for it.

Certain parallels in terms of distance may be drawn between the affective states of liking, desire, and pleasure and the cognitive functions of knowing, thinking about, and perceiving. Desire may be likened to thinking about insofar as separation between $p$ and the $x$ that is desired or thought about occurs. Pleasure is analogous to perception since in both instances contact with $x$ is required. And liking may be viewed as analogous to knowing or believing. Both are independent of the distance dimension and refer to a more invariant relation between $p$ and $x$.

The relations between liking on the one hand, and enjoyment and desire on the other, are important because they too form part of the matrix of beliefs on the basis of which we cognize or predict pleasures, desires, and sentiments of other people and on the basis of which we influence them. Just as knowing may be created by perception, so liking may be created by enjoyment. We may also infer from the present enjoyment of $o$ or the desire of $o$ for $x$ that $o$ likes $x$. Moreover, when we want to induce pleasure in $o$ we will give him something he likes or we will produce a change that he likes.

These are natural, harmonious relations between liking, desiring, and enjoying. As such they are used to detect the correctness or incorrectness of a person's likes. As believing may be confirmed or contradicted by perception, so liking may be "reality tested" by the enjoyment or displeasure aroused by the direct contact. A person may state to others and even to himself that he likes something though he does not really enjoy contact with it; he is subconsciously relieved when the contact ends. If somebody says that he dislikes another person $o$, but it is obvious that whenever he is with $o$ he experiences great enjoyment, then something is felt to be wrong. In order to make the pieces fit, once again re-evaluation takes place. We may decide, for instance, that $p$ really likes $o$ but doesn't realize it.

The emotional life of the person is yet further differentiated according to the future prospects of the distance variable. Fear arises when the person, in contact with and enjoying $x$, recognizes the possibility of losing $x$. Hope arises when the person, separated from $x$ and desiring $x$, believes that $x$ will come within his reach.

Shand conceives of desire as containing an emotional system in accordance with the relative proportions of pleasure and pain arising from circumstances to which the desire is subjected, and which, in our terms, can be seen to depend upon the distance relation between $p$ and $x$. He points out that

. . . we feel Hope when the chances of accomplishing our desire seem good, or when we cling to these in thought; Confidence when we feel certain of its accomplishment; torturing Anxiety, when the event is long in suspense; the pang of Disappointment when the event has been expected and is not fulfilled; Despondency when we fail to make progress; and Despair when hope is shut out because attainment is impossible . . . these peculiar emotions arise in desire and nowhere else. (Shand, 1920, p. 462.)

We should like to interject that such a system of emotions may perhaps more properly be conceived as belonging to liking rather than to desire, since liking, pertaining as it does to a dispositional value relation between $p$ and $x$ independent of the conditions of contact, can also include within its system desire, which corresponds to but one among several variations along the distance dimension.

It is as if the positive quality of the object is discerned through such different avenues as remembering with pleasure, enjoying, desiring, hoping for, etc. We see, so to speak, the same hedonic property of the object from different points of view. Furthermore, when we once have seen it from one point of view, we expect to find the same quality when the object is seen from a different point of view. In other words, all these relations between $p$ and $x$ imply the positive quality of $x$ for $p$ designated by "$p$ likes $x$." The difference between them concerns only the relative positions of $p$ and $x$. In enjoyment $p$ and $x$ are in contact; in remembering with pleasure the contact was in the past; in desire $p$ and $x$ are separated; in hope the contact is expected in the future; in fear loss of contact is a possibility.

THE "ALMOST-SITUATION" AND EMOTIONAL CONSEQUENCES. When a person almost obtains what he desires or almost loses what he is enjoying, additional emotional nuances occur. A near success leads to exasperation, heightened frustration, the feeling of being teased, of being unfortunate. A near miss produces a feeling of relief, of being blessed, of being warned.

The especially sharp negative reaction to almost succeeding is due to the fact that the degree of desire depends to some extent on the possi-

bility of wish-fulfillment. Possibility, to recapitulate, may be conceptualized along the distance dimension, the distance between $p$ and $x$
shrinking with increasing possibility. When a person wishes for something and finds out that the wish cannot possibly be fulfilled, that $p$ and
$x$ will remain forever separated, the wish is likely to die out. When a
person finds out that something that had never before entered his mind
is possible, a wish for it may be aroused. The more it becomes possible
the more the wish may increase.

In the frustration-aggression hypothesis of theoretical psychology the
relation between wish and frustration is expressed in the following way:
the amount of frustration varies directly with the strength of instigation to the frustrated response (Dollard *et al.*, 1939, p. 28). Therefore,
the more the person believes wish-fulfillment possible the greater the
frustration will be. The belief influences degree of desire, which in
turn influences degree of frustration. A relevant example is given in
Dembo's (1931) study of anger—the subjects showed more anger when
they *almost* succeeded in the task, which involved throwing ten rings
on a peg, than when the failure was clear-cut. Dembo explains this in
the following way: if during the course of the series of throws a success
was indicated, the expectation reached a high degree; if, at this stage of
being almost sure of the success, the subject is confronted with failure,
the failure is felt more intensely. This explanation involves a time difference between the experience of coming close to the goal and the
experience of failure. It assumes, as do other frustration theories, that
frustration has to act on a force already present to produce the negative affect. Though this assumption accounts well for the reaction
in Dembo's situation, it cannot be applied to other situations in which
an interval between expectation of success and the failure does
not exist.

Consider the following situation. If somebody holds number 5304
in a lottery and he learns that 5305 is the winning number, this near-
success is probably harder to bear than if there is no winning number
anywhere near his own. Phenomena of this sort are pointed up by
Fielding in *Tom Jones:*

Nothing more aggravates ill success than the near approach to good. The
gamester, who loses his party at piquet by a single point, laments his bad
luck ten times as much as he who never came within a prospect of the
game. So in a lottery, the proprietors of the next numbers to that which
wins the great prize are apt to account themselves much more unfortunate
than their fellow sufferers. In short, these kind of hairbreadth missings of
happiness look like the insults of fortune, who may be considered as thus
playing tricks with us, and wantonly diverting herself at our expense.
(Fielding, 1749, Vol. II, pp. 157–158.)

One could say that, because of the possibility that the stroke of luck might have happened, the intensity of the wish simultaneously increases with the evidence of failure. Consequently, the frustration becomes intensified. But how can a wish become stronger because of a possibility which can no longer exist? The deed is done. In terms of the distance dimension, how can a wish be strengthened when the distance between the person and the goal is unbridgeable because of the events of the past? One way out of the difficulty might be the following:

A near approach to what we desire seems to make its attainment more possible either in the here and now or in terms of what might have been or even "should" have been. In some magical way the present will become transformed into the wished-for reality, or what might so easily have been becomes the existing preoccupation. In either case, the strength of the desire as a *current state* becomes augmented by virtue of its psychological though not realistic proximity to goal satisfaction. The evident failure, consequently, leads to heightened frustration. In effect, there is a feedback from the experience of failure, particularly from the cognition of almost succeeding, which either intensifies a wish that actually did exist before or which arouses a wish that had no prior apparent existence at all. Psychologically, the distance between $p$ and $x$ has shrunk even though "a miss is as good as a mile." To express this point in yet another way, we can say that there are different kinds of distances between $p$ and $x$. There is the objective distance and the one the person experiences. It is the latter which is directly related to wish intensification and frustration effects. Or, we can say that objective distance affects frustration only as it is mediated by psychological distance.

Analysis in terms of psychological distance also makes somewhat clearer why a misfortune appears less negative when it is thought of as necessary than when it is seen as something that could easily have been prevented. In the former case, the distance between the person and the preferred state of affairs is inexorably bound by the force of necessity. Often the negative event fits in with a host of other facts or events, making its existence stark and unyielding. As long as the person experiences the misfortune as inevitable, both his contact with it and the separation from the more fortunate state are the unchanging facts relating to the distance dimension. In the case of an avoidable misfortune, however, the distance is determined by an irrelevant trifle, a mere mischance. The bulk of the evidence, in fact, points to a different distance relation. It is then easy to wish that it had been otherwise. "If only I had done this, if only $x$ had happened, I would have been spared this misfortune." The more the evidence points in a more favorable direction, the stronger the wish, and the more one wishes, the more one suffers the lot of the unfortunate.  Thus we can say with a certain nonchalance, "Either that bullet has my number on it or it doesn't." In saying this we are implying that chance and necessity have different effects on the meaning of events that happen to us.

In the same manner near misses, such as hairbreadth escapes from accidents, provoke deep emotions and personal interpretations.  In this case $p$ "should have been" separated from $x$, the region of safety.  All the evidence points to such a distance relation.  Yet the fact that the distance relation is different must mean that something intervened to prevent tragedy.  The unwarranted yet favorable turn of events is then often perceived as the act of a person-like entity, and can be interpreted either as a warning—"Here, I will show you what might have happened to you; now be more careful next time"—or as meaning, "My life is charmed; somebody watches over me; anybody else would have had an accident, but in my case a special factor prevented the accident." A personal force is felt to have prevented completion of the almost-event.  Since this corresponds to a reality that is exceptional, one feels peculiarly blessed.

***Control of pleasure through manipulating the distance between o and x.***  The most obvious way to affect the happiness of another is to help him achieve what he desires or to hinder him; that is, the distance between $o$ and $x$ is actually altered.  But the fact that the desire-pleasure postulate applies to psychological reality and not to objective reality, opens up an entirely different approach.

When we wish for a certain event, this wish will cease and enjoyment take its place as soon as we become convinced that the event has happened.  The object of the enjoyment is the real event; the enjoyment is directed toward it.  But the occurrence of the event is mediated to the person in different ways.  He may see it happen; he may infer its occurrence from other events; he may be told about it.  As long as he believes that the event has taken place, whether or not the belief is valid, he will experience the pleasure of wish-fulfillment.  (If he does not, re-evaluation of the desire or of its fulfillment, or of the apparent affect occurs, cf. p. 131.)  Similarly, if the event which has actually occurred remains unknown to the person, it will not be accompanied by pleasure.  Thus, though the wish was directed toward the event, it is not the actual occurrence of the event but rather the belief that the event has occurred that is the necessary and sufficient cause for the change of wish to enjoyment.

This fact introduces hazards of cognition into enjoyment.  We can enjoy something prematurely, or "incorrectly," in the sense that the belief that the wish is fulfilled is incorrect.  Our enjoyment may be based on a wrong judgment or perception of what has happened, which may be the result of wishful thinking or wishful perceiving. It may also result in "fearful thinking," as when a pessimist does not enjoy the fulfillment of his wish because he cannot believe that the wished-for event really happened. But the point of special interest to us here is that since belief is the necessary and sufficient cause of enjoyment, one person can make another happy or unhappy by telling him something—p can bring good or bad news to o. If p likes o he will delight in bringing him good news and he will avoid bringing him bad news. If p is hostile to o the opposite will be true.

Information can thus play the role of benefiting and harming. Sometimes the real intention of the reporter may be merely the dissemination of information. As a messenger, for instance, part of his job is to convey information. He may not even be aware that the report has any relevance for o personally. Or, his real intention may be the benefit or harm done to o. One might hesitate to apply the words benefit and harm in this case since the act consists in o's being informed of an event that has already occurred rather than the execution of the event itself. However, since there is often a confusion between ultimate cause and mediation, the messenger is frequently experienced by both parties as being at least partly responsible for the pleasure or displeasure. In stories of the past the messenger with bad news was sometimes killed by the king. Nobody wants to bring bad news to a person who might hold it against him.

The reporter or informer can also knowingly report something that is not true. In doing so, he acts on the basis of the conviction that if o believes x certain consequences will follow: o will do something; he will have a good opinion of p; he will dislike q; or he will feel pleasure or displeasure because he thinks that what he wished for or feared came true. Since belief is often the immediate cause of an affect and a trusted person can create beliefs in another person through verbal communication, he can also to a certain extent control the affect.

As enjoyment is influenced by beliefs concerning what happened, so it may be influenced by beliefs concerning what will happen. The possibility of an event first acts on the wishes, strengthening them as the distance between p and x shrinks with increased possibility (cf. p. 139). The role of possibility is similar, as we have seen, in the case of trying. When p wants to influence o's efforts, he may tell o how easy the job is or how impossible it is depending on the direction of influence. Likewise, in order to arouse a wish, p may tell o that something nice may occur; in order to intensify a wish p may lead o to believe that his chances of realizing his wish are greater than he imagined. The affect will be correspondingly heightened, either as a positive reaction in the case of wish-fulfillment, or as a negative reaction in the case of wish-denial. Sometimes a wish may even be activated for the sole purpose of frustrating it.

The almost-situation in connection with emotional reactions of the person himself has already been discussed (cf. pp. 141–144). Control of pleasure through such manipulation of the possibilities in a situation is familiar to the naive psychology of interpersonal relations as well. Tempting, luring, tantalizing, certain kinds of teasing and flirting, all involve a belief in a kind of goal gradient, a belief that the intensity of a person's desires or the strength of a valence is influenced by the distance between the person and the desired object, by the possibility of wish-fulfillment. These techniques also imply the additional postulate that the more intense the wish, the greater the frustration when the wish is not fulfilled. Thus, to make a person really suffer, the goal is made to seem within reach of the victim. In an old story, a prisoner is allowed to *almost* escape in order to make his punishment greater. At the last moment, he is picked up by the guards who had watched him all along. In the Greek myth, Tantalus stands in water up to his chin. But when he wants to drink, the water recedes. Fruit hangs on boughs close to him. But when he tries to pluck them, the boughs recede. It is interesting to note that when fortune is described as playing tricks, the sequence of events is patterned after the structure of one kind of teasing to present a tempting goal and then to withdraw it.

### Attribution of Desire and Pleasure

It is not surprising that the question of attribution should arise in connection with motives and affects as it has with perceptions and actions, and as it will with other psychological phenomena yet to be discussed. Man wants to know the sources of his experiences, whence they come, how they arise, not only because of intellectual curiosity, but also because such attribution allows him to understand his world, to predict and control events involving himself and others.

The type of attribution both common-sense psychology and scientific psychology find satisfying, has, among others, the following two features: (1) It points up the invariancies in nature—the enduring properties of objects, people, and events, those properties that are felt to be characteristic of them. It is these dispositional properties that make behavior understandable, predictable, and controllable (cf. pp. 80–82). (2) Attribution of psychological phenomena is directed toward the dispositional properties of the environment and the person.

In the phenomena under discussion, the contribution of the environment is represented by the object $x$. It should be clear that object $x$ can also mean event or situation $x$. The contribution of the person refers to special properties within the subject which have evoked the desire or led to the enjoyment. Person-environment attribution is sometimes referred to as attribution to the subject and object poles. The principles of attribution discussed below apply equally to desire and enjoyment, though for the most part enjoyment is taken as the illustrative material.

***Significance of attribution to subject and object poles.*** Our judgment of a situation and its possible future development may depend greatly on whether we attribute the psychological phenomenon to the subject or to the object. If a person enjoys an object it may be because the object is very enjoyable or it may be because of very personal reasons located in him.

If the former, any person who has commerce with the object will find it satisfying. This is a judgment about the value of an object and refers to a more invariant disposition of the object. Once this judgment is made, a host of expectations that guide our actions are possible. If I want to make a person happy, I will present him with the object, for instance. If I want to annoy him, I may prevent him from obtaining it. Believing that the object is desirable, I may attempt to make someone envious by flaunting it. I may welcome identification as its creator in order to be admired or liked. I myself will attempt to interact with the object again, the interaction taking various forms depending on further conditions. I may try to have physical contact with the object or I may talk about it or think about it. It will be recorded in my belief-value matrix as something I like. These are some of the implications of the attribution of enjoyment to the object, implications that encompass an ever-widening field as one investigates the network of conditions and effects. In all of them, the enjoyability of the object remains constant, and the varied possible effects of this object-disposition form the expectations of many kinds of behavior.

If $p$ believes that the source of enjoyment is located in $o$ and not in the object, however, very different expectations arise. They depend upon the presumed facts about $o$ implied by the enjoyment and with which the attribution is connected.

For example, when we see that a person obviously enjoys hearing good news about others we will think him a kind person. Conversely, if we believe that he delights in the misfortunes of others, we will judge him unkind. Attribution to the person could also mean that $o$ is easily satisfied, that he is a peculiar person, that he has sophisticated taste, that he is like me, etc. These "facts" implied by the enjoyment of *o* are personality traits, the dispositional properties upon which expectations are based. Thus, if I attribute *o*'s enjoyment to his sophistication, then I may expect him to enjoy a different but equally artistic object, to dislike something that is trite, to enjoy the company of a connoisseur, etc. In each of these expectations, it is the object or situation that varies, but the dispositional property of the person remains the same.

Attribution of pleasure to the person, of course, does not mean that object *x* plays an insignificant role in enjoyment. On the contrary, as has previously been stressed, enjoyment typically refers to the enjoyment of something. The cognition that I am pleased by *x* is usually an intrinsic part of enjoyment, but this is quite different from attributing the pleasure primarily or solely to the object or to the person. Notice that in the formulation "I am pleased by *x*," there is both an "I" and an "*x*," and it remains for a psychological factor analysis to establish their weights.

Likewise, desires are attributed sometimes to the person, sometimes to the environment. We may think a person wants to do something, just anything, no matter what, because of the state he is in, or that he wants something because it is so attractive.

In order to see more clearly how predictability is dependent upon attribution to dispositional properties, different types of enjoyment are discussed in order of their complexity. First, let us take as a simple fact that "*o* enjoys *x*." If we have no idea whether the relation between *o* and *x* is a permanent one, that is, whether it is dispositional, then we are unable to make any predictions at all. However, as soon as we ascribe it to a permanent relation between *o* and *x*, even without further attribution to the person or to the object, certain predictions are possible. At least we can expect that *o* will enjoy *x* again and that he may be annoyed if it is taken from him. Parenthetically, it is notable that such a nonpolarized dispositional relation, though theoretically possible, does not ordinarily seem to occur. The perception of a relation as enduring and its attribution to one or another of the variables seem to go together. In any case, if we know what caused the relation between *p* and *x*, that is, if we attribute the enjoyment either to the subject or to the object, many other predictions, as we have seen, can be made. Without such attribution, enjoyment remains an ambiguous local experience. The enjoyment of a satiated person eating something very appetizing and the enjoyment of a hungry person eating something less appetizing may represent the same degree of biological elation or tension, but the equivalence of the two experiences ends as soon as identification with one or the other of the two poles is made. Thus, an event that remains undefined as to its dispositional character tells us very little. One whose dispositional character is further defined by attribution to causal factors tells us much.

Of course, we may mistakenly identify enjoyment with the wrong dispositional property. For instance, one might enjoy the noise of one's own son (how full of spirits the boy is), but the same noise produced by the child of a disliked person would be perceived with displeasure. This is so because the quality of an experience, the attractiveness of $x$, is influenced by the cause to which it is attributed. We may still be correct in predicting continued pleasure upon contact with the particular $x$, the son's noise in this case. But we will err in predicting enjoyment from similar $x$'s or in predicting the pleasure of others.

The cause-effect relation implied by the attribution of enjoyment to the person or to the object should be distinguished from the cause of the event of contact itself. That is to say, the contact between the person and the object of enjoyment may have been brought about by the person or by the environment. If $p$ enjoys some food that he has bought then the resulting enjoyment is, in one sense, caused by $p$ through his own action. But in the more usual sense the source of the hedonic quality of the experience does not lie in his person, unless we feel that he is enjoying the food because he is hungry or that he is such a peculiar person that he enjoys this kind of food. Rather, $p$ may be felt to enjoy the food because of its objective quality of excellence; any discriminating person would enjoy it.

Like predictability, learning is helped by dispositional attribution. For example, if a person has adequately analyzed past enjoyment into the subjective and objective poles, the fact that he has profited from this learning is demonstrated in his use of the experience for producing future enjoyment. Let us assume that once, in a very hungry state, he enjoyed a particular food very much, but erroneously attributed the enjoyment to the food. Later, wanting to pamper himself again, he eats the same food, but is disappointed in the gustatory results, not realizing that the experience had originally depended largely on his own appetite. In order to profit from experience, one has to analyze the event correctly into the underlying invariables, otherwise no adaptation to the environment is possible—unless, as Brunswik puts it, the mediation is channelized. Then a number of conditions are constant and the true source is correlated on a one-to-one basis with the experience (Brunswik, 1956, p. 9).

In Dewey's differentiation between the ideas of "satisfying" and "satisfactory," the significance of attribution of pleasure to the object is seen. He points out that to say something ". . . is satisfying is the content of a proposition of fact...." Let us add that it is equivalent to the datum of enjoyment that has not yet been aligned with the subject or the object as the entity primarily responsible for the affect. In Dewey's words,

> To say that something satisfies is to report something as an isolated finality . . . [However,] to assert that it is satisfactory is a judgment, an estimate, an appraisal. . . . It defines it in its connections and interactions. . . . (Dewey, 1929, pp. 260–261.)

We might add that it is equivalent to object-attribution in which the dispositional property of the object makes definition of connections and interactions possible. To say that something is satisfactory is to say something about the object pole of a number of occurrences.

Not all personality theorists hold the view that attribution is significant to phenomenal experience or behavior. For example, Angyal's basic motivational concept is what he calls biospheric tension. This is a transactional process that goes on between two poles, the person and the environment, and as such is consistent with the position of those who view behavior as a function of both. However, Angyal believes that it is only a matter of convenience whether one conceptualizes this process in terms of one pole or the other:

> Tensions are inherent in the undivided biospheric occurrence in which the subject and object factors can be separated only by abstraction. Tensions can be described, however, from various points of view. One may choose as a point of reference either the subject or the object. . . . Biological tensions viewed from the subject as a point of reference are considered as *drives*. Viewing the same tensions from the object side as the point of reference, one obtains something similar to what Kurt Lewin calls the "field forces" or "demand qualities" of environmental situations. (Angyal, 1941, p. 128.)

He concludes that

> ... we cannot speak of drives and environmental attraction as two different phenomena: they both refer to a single phenomenon, to the biospheric occurrence viewed at times from the side of the subject and at other times from the side of the object. Neither of the two ways of considering the phenomenon has a greater justification than the other, and we cannot say that one is a realistic and the other a metaphorical description. To use one or the other type of description is a matter of convenience. (p. 151.)

Angyal further argues that his point of view

> . . . is comparable to the relativity in physics. A physical motion is a unitary process consisting in the change of the spatial relationship between two physical bodies. The point of reference for the description of the motion can, however, be either of the two bodies. (p. 128.)

It is our opinion, however, that though such relativity describes the purely mathematical aspect of motion, from the point of view of the psychological meaning of action (motion) it may make all the difference whether *A* moves and *B* is still or vice versa, whether Mohammed goes to the mountain or the mountain moves to him. The meaning of an interpersonal approach may entirely depend on whether Tom approaches Jane or Jane approaches Tom. In the case of enjoyment, as we have seen, my entire relationship with *o* may hinge on attribution. Those pleasures attributed to him as a person reveal the kind of person I believe him to be and I am accordingly drawn to him or repelled.

Using the language of the psychology of perception, we could say that the biospheric occurrence, that is, the fact of enjoyment, belongs to the level of raw data; in the enjoyment itself the contributions of the subject and the object are combined, as the factors are combined in a mathematical product. As such it gives us only very incomplete information about the facts that interest us most, namely, under what circumstances we or other people will meet such enjoyment again, or how we can produce it for ourselves or others. It is comparable to retinal color that does not tell us very much about the possibilities of the environment.

Ideas like enjoyable, satisfactory, desirable, belong to the object world; ideas like easily satisfiable, personality, and character belong to the subject world. These terms refer to the stable world, to the dispositions of objects or persons. If we correctly analyze the raw data in such terms we know much more about the event itself and about future occurrences. A highly general statement that can be made is: If we know that our present enjoyment is due to the contribution of the object because it is an intrinsically desirable one, then we can expect anyone who has contact with it to enjoy it; on the other hand, if the enjoyment is attributed to our own personality, then at most we can expect only persons who have a similar personality to enjoy it.

Dispositional attribution is so crucial in interpersonal relations, to say nothing of personal behavior, that once again we will review some of the factors important in the determination of attribution as specifically applied to desires and pleasures.

***Attribution based upon condition-effect changes.*** Enjoyment as such can be viewed as an ambiguous local stimulus; i.e., remaining unattached to any source, its stimuli operate diffusely within the skin. For the ambiguity of enjoyment to be replaced by a more structured experience in which the contributions of the object and subject poles are determined, a stimulus pattern of raw data is necessary. We are reminded, for instance, of Gibson's (1950) concept of "ordinal stimulus," the data syndrome necessary for adequate depth perception (p. 56).

We shall start with the data pattern fundamental in the determination of attribution, namely: that condition will be held responsible for an effect which is present when the effect is present and which is absent when the effect is absent. This principle underlies Mill's methods of experimental inquiry and was seen to operate in the case of the attribution of perception and of action to the subject and object poles (cf. pp. 60–69 and pp. 82–84).

Now let us see how this principle operates in the case of the attribution of enjoyment to the object. If I always experience enjoyment when I interact with an object, and something other than enjoyment when the object is removed (longing, annoyance, or a more neutral reaction, for instance) then I will consider the object the cause of the enjoyment. The effect, enjoyment, is seen to vary in a highly coordinated way with the presence and absence of the object.

In this example, the object $x$ represents a particular thing that does not change in the course of repeated contacts with it. Attribution to the object can also occur, however, if the object of the enjoyment undergoes certain variations. Let us first consider an example in which the same object may be characterized by different states, as when a place is transformed by seasonal conditions. As long as the enjoyment is closely connected with the presence and absence of the particular state the object is in, then the latter will be seen as the cause of the effect. Thus, if one always enjoys Kansas more in winter than in summer then one will attribute the reaction to the seasonal variation. In addition to varying the object by altering its state, variation can take place by substituting one object for another. The substitution may take place within a class of objects, as when one replaces a particular toy by another toy. The substitution may also take place across classes, as when one substitutes food for the toy. As long, however, as the enjoyment is coordinated to the presence of the class or classes of objects in such a way that the absence of enjoyment is also experienced when an object representing the class or classes is absent, then object attribution will take place. Thus, the judgment "It is enjoyable," instead of being confined to a particular object, or to a particular state of the object, is now extended to a class or several classes of objects. The varieties of attribution to the object may be seen concretely in the following judgments: (1) The object itself: the automobile affords a great deal of pleasure. (2) The state of the object: when the automobile is in good repair, it affords a great deal of pleasure. (3) Class of objects: vehicles in general, such as cars, airplanes, and boats, afford a great deal of pleasure. (4) Classes of objects: most broadly of all, the world in general affords a great deal of pleasure. This last case is nicely expressed by Robert Louis Stevenson's classic couplet: "The world is so full of a number of things, I'm sure we should all be as happy as kings." In each of these cases, the source of the enjoyment is primarily accounted for by the object world.

Now let us see how the principle operates in the attribution of enjoyment to the person. If I sometimes enjoy the object and sometimes do not, then the effect varies, not with the object, but with something within me. I may or may not be able to define that something, but I know that the effect has to do with some fluctuating personal state. It may be my mood, my state of hunger, etc., which, though temporary in character, are often detectable as the conditions highly related to the effect. Notice that in this type of attribution, a temporary state and therefore a more or less nondispositional property of the person is singled out as the source of the pleasure. As a matter of fact, if a dispositional property of the person were causally connected with the effect, if for instance, the person were always hungry and consequently always enjoyed the food, then the pleasure would not be attributed to the person at all, but, on the basis of the data at hand, it would be attributed to the object. This is so because, according to our principle, the pleasure comes and goes not with the person but with the object.

When enjoyment is attributed to a dispositonal property of the person, additional data pertaining to the reactions of other people are necessary. Concretely, if I observe that not all people enjoy the object, then I may attribute the effect to individual differences. (We use the more restricted term, may, rather than the inclusive term, will, for reasons that will become clear later. Cf. p. 158, egocentric attribution.) That is to say, the effect, enjoyment in this case, depends upon who the person is. With $o$ enjoyment is present, with $q$ it is absent. We sometimes, then, speak about differences in taste. The important point is that the presence and absence of the enjoyment is not correlated with the presence and absence of the object, but rather with the presence and absence of different people. Therefore $o$ is felt to enjoy $x$ and $q$ to be dissatisfied with $x$ because of the kind of person each is.

The same type of analysis holds when the data pertaining to individual differences refer to differences among groups of people and even among such broad classifications as separate species and genera. We then have such judgments as "preschool children enjoy large motor activity" or "man alone enjoys aesthetic experience." Thus, attribution of enjoyment to the person may refer to an individual, a state of the individual, a group of people, or to wider classes. Parallel variations were seen to hold for attribution of pleasure to the object.

In the examples presented thus far, attribution of enjoyment to the object or to the person, but not to both, occurred. It is possible, however, that two conditions, one pertaining to the person and one to the object, may be present when the effect is present and absent when the effect is absent. Then both poles are seen to play a role in the enjoyment. Such bipolar attribution frequently occurs when a temporary state of the person is responsible for the effect, for though the enjoyment then varies with the state, it also comes and goes with the object while the person is in that state.

We might expect bipolar attribution to represent a more sophisticated approach to understanding than attribution to one or the other pole, for after all, the former requires taking into account of more than one pattern of condition-effect interaction. This is one reason why in everyday life we burden the environment or subject with the whole responsibility for the effect in question, only to recognize the contributions of both upon more careful examination. Kurt Lewin has proposed the general formulation that behavior is a function of the person and the environment. This may appear to be a truism, yet it must be held to the fore as a constant reminder lest the tendency to unipolar attribution lead to the neglect of one or the other factors. How often do we feel that we have only to describe the person or the object to explain the enjoyment or other behavior in question.

The cases of attribution discussed in this section all require a data pattern in which the presence and absence of the effect is correlated with the presence and absence of the condition (or conditions) held responsible for the effect. This principle reminds us of Wertheimer's factor of common fate in perceptual unit formation. The common fate of the cause and its effect is reflected in their coordinated changes; what happens to one happens to the other. It is this common fate that brings the two variables together as a cause-effect relation, a kind of unit formation.

The valid identification of such a common fate—the mutual appearance and disappearance of a condition and an effect—is made more certain by repeated instances of the reaction of $p$ (or persons) to $x$ (or objects). We say "valid identification" rather than simply "identification," for although a series of exposures between $p$ and $x$ is helpful, it is not necessary in order for attribution of enjoyment to occur.

Let us consider an example in which during a single experience attribution is established spontaneously and definitely. In the example of Scheler (1927), one "feels the beauty of snow-covered mountains at sunset" as a feeling immediately and directly related to an object (p. 263). Examination will show that a data pattern still exists involving the coordination of change of effect with the presence and absence of the object. This is so even if we omit any past affective experience with such phenomena as part of the data upon which the attribution is based. The bare facts are that the enjoyment was absent before the scene came into view and emerged only with its presence. The data pattern therefore consists of one instance of joint absence of the object and effect and one instance of joint presence. This shall be referred to as the minimum data pattern.

Attribution based on a minimum data pattern is more common than one might suppose. Generally, we don't postpone attribution until we tally a series of joint condition-effect changes. We judge the *book* to be good, the *food* to be excellent, the *child* to be nice, the *scene* to be beautiful, because we experienced pleasure upon the specific and single contact with it. Instances of attribution of the effect to the person can also be found in cases of a single experience. Thus, I attribute my sudden displeasure with the food to my attack of indigestion if, during the course of what started out to be an appetizing meal, I find myself preoccupied with physiological distress. Since the food is the same, the change in affect cannot be ascribed to it. Or, I attribute my pleasure over the examination to my realization that I can pass it, if a moment before I had been filled with dread.

We do not wish to imply that any condition at all that appears and disappears with the effect in a minimum data pattern will become attached to the effect. If a child leaves the room at the moment when I become aware of my sudden disinterest in the food, it will be most unlikely that I will ascribe my displeasure to this factor. A certain cogency in the connection between a condition and an effect is undoubtedly taken into account. But because such fortuitous joint changes of condition and effect become less likely with the number of interactions between $p$ and $x$, it is clear that on these grounds alone, attribution based on many $p$-$x$ contacts is more apt to hold up than attribution based on the fragmentary evidence of a minimum data pattern.

The tendency to assume that we shall enjoy again what we enjoyed once now becomes clearer. The single contact often leads to attribution of enjoyment to the object. Since attribution in general tends to become connected with dispositional properties, the enjoyability of the object is felt to be more or less enduring. Thus, we will expect continued pleasure upon repeated encounters with it. We shall see later that the invariant enjoyability of the object also leads to the expectation that other people will enjoy the same things we do, an expectation which is the core of a common type of egocentric attribution.

**Tendency to attribute enjoyment to the object versus the person.**
It has often been pointed out that there is a tendency for attribution in general to be leveled at the environment. Let us attempt to arrive at some basis for better understanding this tendency. It is not sufficient to use the fact that enjoyment is usually directed toward an object as explanation for this tendency, for after all, when one says, "I enjoy the book," the "I" is as much in evidence as "the book" and the pleasure is quite differently understood when it is attributed to the "I," personal taste for example, or to the book, its intrinsic value.

We know that when we are in a good mood we think every object and every person is wonderful. We usually don't attribute our joy to our mood. In the words of Maine de Biran:

What one calls strokes of fortune contributes generally much less to our unhappiness or uneasiness than do the unconscious disorders our frail body is subject to. . . . When the lack of equilibrium of fluids and solids makes people fretful and melancholy, they attribute their experiences to external causes and, since their imagination, which is tuned to a dismal strain, shows them only distressing objects, they think that the cause of their trouble is in the objects themselves. But when a favorable change in their physical state occurs, the scowls suddenly disappear, the sad faces brighten up. From where does this metamorphosis arise? Nothing has changed in their environment; the cause of their misery, therefore, was not outside of themselves. (Maine de Biran, 1927, p. 57.)

Two different judgments as to the source of the pleasures and displeasures are presented in this quotation, one given by the author and one by the person he is talking about. The author, an outsider viewing the situation of another, rests his case on attribution to the person, whereas the person himself holds to attribution to the object. In the case of the observer, the data noted are: "*o* is elated with practically anything. I know that many of the *x*'s are not that attractive. Some, in fact, are downright repulsive." The data pattern, then consists, not only of *o*'s reaction to the *x*'s, but also the reaction of the observer himself, and other people as he surmises it. We have a situation where the effect, elation in this case, varies not with the object, but with the person. Even if the outsider had never observed *o* in a depressed state so that change in the effect with change of the state of *o* is excluded from the data pattern, the case for attribution to the person is still adequate. Change in *o*'s mood with concomitant affective change simply extends the data pattern and lends additional support to the attributive judgment already made. However, if the observer also considered the many *x*'s to be intrinsically attractive, then he, too, would attribute *o*'s elation to the object. Attribution to the person would then occur only if *o*'s mood changed so that he no longer enjoyed the *x*'s. In this case, the observer would bring in the special state of *o* to account, not for *o*'s pleasure, for that was due to the object, but for *o*'s displeasure.

Another highly interesting and relevant phenomenon pertains to the changes that occur in *p*'s perceptual field when his mood changes. On objective grounds, he ought to see, as pointed out in the Maine de Biran quotation, that since nothing has changed in his environment, his altered reaction must be due to something in himself. This objective view, sometimes identified as the rational one, is not taken, since "nothing has changed in his environment" is not the way the person sees the situation. To a greater or lesser extent, what a person sees is conditioned by what he is tuned to see. In the words of Maine de Biran, " . . . imagination, which is tuned to a dismal strain, shows . . . only distressing objects." When our previously elated person becomes enveloped in the depths of despair, he "picks on" the morbid conditions around him and remains oblivious to the brighter side of life. Even the same objective circumstances can be seen in a positive or negative light depending on the person's mood. The "glass that is half full" suddenly becomes the "glass that is half empty" when one is depressed. That the person himself has changed is more readily observed by an outsider.

Thus, it is not accidental that the outsider, in the above example, favored the judgment of attribution to the person whereas the person directly affected leaned toward attribution to the object. The outsider generally has at his disposal not only the reaction of the one observed, but also at least what he surmises his own reaction would be in the situation. Thus, the issue of variation of the person pole readily presents itself to him. Should the outsider and *o* have the same reaction, attribution of *o*'s enjoyment to the object is natural. Where the reactions differ, attribution to the person of *o* follows; however, here the outsider arrives at two attributive judgments, one pertaining to the source of *o*'s reaction and one to the source of his own. The former is to the person, the latter to the object, and not the other way around. We can now state, in more differentiated terms, the polar tendencies in attribution. The person tends to attribute his own reactions to the object world, and those of another, when they differ from his own, to personal characteristics in *o*.

The saying "hunger is the best cook" contains an insight about attribution, or about the factors of enjoyment. It says that the enjoyment gotten from eating indifferent food when one is hungry is as great as that gotten from eating very good food when one is not hungry. At the same time the proverb seems to refer to a tendency for environmental attribution, as if the meaning were: if you eat any food when you are hungry you will think it is exceptionally good. The enjoyment which actually should be attributed to the person will be attributed to the object.

**Egocentric attribution.** The implications of attribution of enjoyment to the object provides an important source of one type of egocentric attribution. Attribution to the object, whether based on a minimum data pattern or a pattern more varied in form, means more than the dependence of $p$'s pleasure on the object. It also means that there is something enjoyable about the object. The attractiveness is a quality of the object, just as is the sweetness of a fruit or the roughness of a terrain. Consequently, $p$'s expectations, and therefore beliefs, refer not only to his own reactions to $x$ on future occasions, but also to the reactions of other people. The basic scheme is as follows: "Since my pleasure was aroused by $x$, $x$ is positive, and therefore everyone will like it." An expectation of *similarity* between the reactions of others and the self is thus egocentrically determined.

The perception of how much another person is enjoying something, also very often stems from just this kind of egocentric attribution. If $p$ has a definite preference for one object over the other, and consequently thinks that the former is objectively better than the latter, and $o$ finds them equally appealing, $p$ will perceive $o$ as liking the one too little and the other too much. More than that, $p$ will perceive $o$ as reacting differentially. A parent who prefers one child and rejects the second will see the other parent as persecuting the first and spoiling the second even though the spouse treats the children equally.

Attribution of enjoyment to the object, so natural and "logical" as we have seen when one is viewing the data of personal experience, leads to an expectation of *similarity* between the reactions of others and the self. Where such similarity actually obtains, no one is put out—$o$ does not accuse $p$ of being egocentric (though indeed he is as long as his expectations, independent of their "correctness," are based solely on a personal point of view), nor does $p$ feel that $o$'s reactions are bizarre. When, however, disagreement results, then $p$ (to say nothing of $o$) is faced with a discrepancy which needs to be accounted for. Either $p$ can maintain his original position by concluding that $o$ is a peculiar person, that his reaction is unjustified, or $p$ can shift and attribute the enjoyment to individual differences. In the former case, enjoyment still rests upon the object quality, and the displeasure (or absence of pleasure) of *o* is attributed to *o*'s idiosyncrasies. Because the attributive judgment is based on *p*'s evaluation of *x* as the standard and *p*'s evaluation alone, it remains egocentric. In the latter case, *p* has clearly modified his attributive judgment to accommodate the point of view of another person.

Thus far we have been considering egocentric attribution as a consequence of the attribution of enjoyment to the object. Enjoyment may also be egocentrically attributed in such a way that the enjoyment fits our wishes and the picture we have of ourselves or the way we think things ought to be. For instance, to enjoy the misfortune of another person, or to enjoy a biting remark about an envied person may not be considered proper by *p*. Consequently, he may attribute the very real enjoyment he feels to some other cause so that the interpretation becomes innocuous. This can also be true of the attribution of *o*'s enjoyment. If *o* is liked, *p* is apt to assume praiseworthy sources, but if *o* is disliked, reprehensible ones. To take another example, *p* may think he enjoys *x* greatly because it is intrinsically valuable, although he really enjoys it because he made it himself. In these cases, the positive or negative affect is given, and *p* seeks to direct it toward an object (source) that will not violate personal needs and wishes. One might speak of "displaced" enjoyment in these cases.

It may also happen that the object or situation is given and the emotion must be fitted in accordance with what is proper. One may have to pretend, even to oneself, that the emotion is the correct one. If the self pretense is not effective, one may suffer guilt and remorse: "... for instance we are sad that we could not enjoy an event as much as its felt value deserved; or, that we could not grieve as much as for instance, the death of a loved person requires" (Scheler, 1927, p. 266).

We mentioned above that the discrepancy in the reactions of *p* and *o* to *x* may be reconciled in different ways. The original attribution of enjoyment to the object may be shifted to the person, the reactions being seen as a matter of personal taste; or attribution of enjoyment to the object may be maintained by dismissing *o*'s reaction as unjustified. Which of these will be selected depends partly upon additional facts perceived by *p* with which the judgment is connected that *x* is positive.

For illustrative purposes, let us suppose *p* feels that a particular movie was delightful, the enjoyment being attributed to the movie, the *x* in question. If this reaction stands alone, unsupported by any other considerations, it is relatively easy to reattribute the pleasure, in the light of differing evaluations of others, to "*x* is positive for me, but not intrinsically so; it is a matter of personal taste." But if additional perceptions support the original attribution, such a shift is less likely.

Examples of supporting "facts" are: the acting was excellent, the plot was masterfully designed, the costuming was perfect, etc. In addition to such cognitive "facts," special needs of the person may also serve to maintain the original position. The person may not wish to lose face by shifting his judgment, for instance. If, then, other people find the film dull, the person may ascribe their negative reaction to their ignorance. The ones who do not enjoy $x$ simply do not realize its good points. The connection of "$x$ is positive" to other cognitions or needs may be so strong, that even if $p$ knows that everyone else is displeased with $x$ and he alone enjoys it, he can have the feeling that he is right and others are wrong. In short, he continues to attribute the enjoyment of $x$ to its intrinsic excellence and not to his own personality.

Phenomenally, enjoyment is directed toward an object. But the object may not be responsible for the enjoyment. We may not have insight into the true reasons for our pleasure or that of others. As in cases of perceptual attribution, a hedonic experience of either $p$ or $o$ may be attributed to a condition in such a way that it fits our own view of the world, the state of affairs as we wish them or as we think they should be.

## Effects of Enjoyment

Enjoyment is not only an effect of certain conditions, but it also has effects of its own. A survey of these effects points up the diverse and basic significance of enjoyment in man's relation to the world of objects and people. The first two of these effects have already been discussed:

1. Enjoyment has behavioral manifestations from which enjoyment in another is cognized (cf. pp. 135–137).

2. Enjoyment is attributed to different sources, notably the person and the object; the consequences of such attributive judgments are legion (cf. pp. 146–160).

A third point may be mentioned:

3. The effects of enjoyment are the goals we attempt to reach when we use enjoyment as a means.

With respect to the last point, we again have a wealth of illustrative material from everyday life upon which to draw:

Knowing that enjoyment leads to liking, $p$ may try to have $o$ enjoy $x$ so that $o$ may be positive toward it or desire it in the future.

Realizing that the sentiment toward the source (cause) of $x$ is often largely determined by the attractiveness of $x$ (cf. Chapter 7 on sentiment), *p* may try to get *o* to enjoy *x* if he wishes *o* to be positive toward the people who made *x* possible.

Realizing that the pleasure or displeasure of one person also affects others perceiving these reactions, *p* may attempt to have *o* enjoy something just because he wishes to please a friend of *o*, or annoy *o*'s enemy.

Being aware that enjoyment is attached to an object and very often is attributed solely to the object, *p* may show *o* how much *q* is enjoying *x* in the hope that *o*'s attraction for *x* will be enhanced accordingly.

Believing that enjoyment leads to a feeling of well-being in general, *p* may give *o* something desirable in the hope that it will take his mind off disturbing thoughts and help him overcome depressed feelings.

Believing that enjoyment leads to a feeling of expansiveness and generosity, *p* may wish to make *o* happy so that *o* will be more ready to do him or someone else a favor.

These examples by no means exhaust the ways enjoyment is used to bring about desired ends. Yet as a sample, they serve to show how the naive psychology of enjoyment consists of a system of concepts that not only refers to the conditions of enjoyment, but also to the effects of enjoyment.

## Summary

The path connecting desire and pleasures in the naive psychology of motivation led us to explore some of the more compelling signposts along the way. The major ones read:

Desires or personal wishes are to be distinguished from induced motives, though the distinction is not always clear.

Desires are not invariably coordinated to actions.

The fulfillment of a desire is thought to be invariably coordinated to pleasure, though not vice versa.

When necessary, re-evaluation of conditions and effects occurs in accordance with the desire-pleasure postulate.

Desires and pleasure may conflict with other requirements perceived by the organism. Harmony may be restored through re-evaluation.

Conceptually, there are two relations between the person and the object to which the desire and pleasure are directed, namely, value and distance.

The value relation is designated by the sentiment, *p* likes *x*. It is uncoordinated to conditions of distance between *p* and *x*.

The distance relation between *p* and *x* pertains to the distance as perceived by *p*. It is a psychological distance conceptualized as a spatial relation between *p* and *x*.

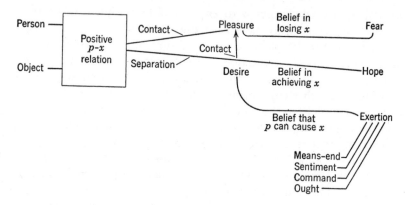

**Figure 1.** *Desire and pleasure in the naive psychology of motivation.*

The conditions of distance between $p$ and $x$ differentiate the affective reactions of $p$. Desire, pleasure, hope, fear, the frustration of a near success, the relief of a near miss are examples.

Control of pleasure in another person may be accomplished by manipulating the distance between $o$ and $x$—$o$ may be correctly or incorrectly informed of wish-fulfillment or wish denial; he may be teased by manipulations leading to near successes.

The attribution of desire and pleasure to the underlying subject and object poles has far-reaching consequences. It is essential for understanding. Through attribution an experience leads to further beliefs important for prediction and control.

Adequate attribution requires an adequate data pattern of condition-effect changes.

Attribution to the object or to the person can depend on whether experiences of the self or those of another are being considered.

Attribution of enjoyment to the object provides the basis for one kind of egocentric attribution.

Personal wishes and propriety may also lead to egocentrically determined incorrect attribution.

Enjoyment has certain aftereffects. These may be the ends sought by $p$ in bringing about pleasure.

Figure 1 represents some of the above features, a basic skeleton as it were, which provides the outline for the rich detail and vast scope encompassed by the naive psychology of desire and pleasure. Beginning at the left, we find the person and the object as possible reasons for the positive relation between $p$ and $x$. This positive relation, a dynamic $p$-$x$ relation designated as liking, together with the distance relation, determines the experience. When $p$ is in contact with $x$, pleasure will result, when $p$ is separated from $x$, desire. A somewhat different view of the same underlying dynamics is given by the connection, desire plus contact produces pleasure. Beliefs in the future possibilities of the distance variable will further influence the outcome: if with contact the belief in the possibility of losing $x$ is given, fear will arise. With separation, the belief that $x$ will be secured leads to desire with hope. The belief that $p$ can cause $x$ will lead to exertion and action. But exertion can also be caused by other sources: $p$ can exert himself to produce $x$ not only because it is intrinsically attractive to him, but because of extrinsic motivation derived from a means-end relation, from sentiment, command, or ought forces.

# CHAPTER 6

# Environmental effects

EVENTS CAN HAVE THEIR SOURCE in the environment, and the many ways such events affect the individual have already been discussed. We examined at some length how the other person as perceiver is able to evaluate and control his environment, which can have major consequences for $p$. Environmental conditions bearing upon the attribution of success, such as task difficulty, luck, and opportunity were discussed. That environmental circumstance may alter the distance between $p$ and his goal, and thereby affect his desires and pleasures, was shown to be of theoretical and practical interest. In later chapters, especially Chapter 10, "Benefit and Harm," the significance of environmental effects will be examined further. In the present chapter we wish to present a few considerations relevant in a general way to all such environmental effects on the person. The problem can be seen as one in which personal action is contrasted with what happens to us: pushing versus being pushed, being the hammer versus being the anvil, in general, activity versus passivity.

In discussing environmental effects we shall not be concerned with the more general influences of the social or physical milieu which may shape personality but rather with concrete events which are caused by the environment and with which the person has to cope, such as what another person does to him, the strokes of fortune or misfortune, etc. It should be clear that events originating outside the person include those instigated by another person as well as those stemming from the inanimate environment.

Angyal refers to such events as heteronomous events in contrast to autonomous happenings which have their source in the person himself.

The autonomy of the organism is not an absolute one. Self-determination is restricted by outside influences which, with respect to the organism, are heteronomous. The organism lives in a world in which processes go on independently of it. . . .

Autonomy and heteronomy refer here only to the source out of which a process is governed. In this study, by autonomy is meant "self-government" and by heteronomy "government from outside." Thus, for example, when two animals A and B are engaged in a fight, what animal A does to animal B is heteronomous for B, in spite of the fact that it originates from an organism. (Angyal, 1941, pp. 37–39.)

## Heteronomy as Treated by Lewin and Murray

It should be mentioned that in the topological psychology of Kurt Lewin (1936) heteronomous events are of less central importance than events that have their source in the person. The typical process handled topologically is that of a person proceeding through means-actions toward a goal. He is the agent of his actions, and only in a limited sense the recipient of environmental effects.

Topological psychology represents heteronomous events in the life space, albeit restrictedly, by the use of barriers, by the concept of alien facts, and by the concept of behavior induced by the power field of *o*. It is significant that since action is the main thought model in topology, heteronomy appears mainly in the shape of external obstructions to action. Barriers express the fact that external factors can stop an event that has its source in the person. The concept of alien facts refers to heteronomous events that are not represented in the life space, not even in unconsciousness. If we experience an unforeseen event, a sudden change in our life space occurs that could not have been derived from the previous state of the life space. Insofar it is an intruding, alien fact. But, of course, heteronomous events cannot be equated with alien facts, for the simple reason that the former are often clearly present in the life space. One can anticipate a good or a bad fate, one can hope for it or be afraid of it; one can feel the pressure that is being exerted on oneself and can resist or yield to it; and the fact that we have been pushed into fortune or misfortune is represented in our life space. Whether a past change, a past locomotion has been caused by us or by an external, heteronomous force is of the greatest importance for the reaction. We can internalize heteronomous forces and make them part of our life space. The concept of induced force, representing that the behavior of *p* may be induced by the power field of *o*, is also relevant to, but not the same as, the concept of heteronomy. It is not the same because induction, referring to social induction, excludes inanimate environmental events as a source of change, and refers to the environmental source of *p*'s actions, not to the source of, for instance, *p*'s affects or emotions. Thus, that the child complies on command is an example of induced behavior; that his emotions may be drastically influenced by the dictates of fortune is not.

Murray's system, on the other hand, provides a central position for heteronomous events, particularly in his concept of "press." His view of environmental effects, actually, is very similar to our own in which benefits and harms in their broad sense are major psychological concepts. Murray suggests that

. . . it is convenient to classify the SS [stimulus situation] according to the kind of effect—facilitating or obstructing—it is exerting or could exert upon the organism. Such a tendency or "potency" in the environment may be called a *press*. For example, a press may be nourishing, . . . or restraining, or amusing or belittling to the organism. It can be said that a press is a temporal gestalt of stimuli which usually appears in the guise of a *threat of harm* or *promise of benefit* to the organism. (Murray, 1938, p. 40.)

Thus, an object or a situation is represented according

. . . to its effect (or potential effect) upon the subject. . . . By "effect" here we *do not mean the response that is aroused in the subject* . . . we mean what is done to the subject before he responds (ex: belittlement by an insult) or what might be done to him if he did not respond (ex: a physical injury from a falling stone), or what might be done to him if he did not respond by coming into contact with the object (ex: nourishment from food). . . . [It is therefore advisable to] classify an environment in terms of the kind of benefits (facilitations, satisfactions) and the kind of harms (obstructions, injuries, dissatisfactions) which it provides. (pp. 117–118.)

Murray (1938) coins the term "pressive perception" for "the process in the subject which recognizes what is being done to him at the moment (that says 'this is good' or 'this is bad') . . ." (p. 119).

In the following quotation, Murray specifies some of the important presses with which individuals are confronted:

What we want to know is how people in general, or how people of a given type or category, respond to situations such as these: frustration, postponement of gratification, social rejection, injustice, despotic coercion, moral condemnation, erotic advances, flattery, appeals for help, and so forth. (Murray, 1951, p. 459.)

The kinds of press important in interpersonal relations are uncovered by probing certain areas:

In formulating an interpersonal proceeding, for example, the task would be that of defining the need-aim of the object [the other person] (just as one would define the need-aim of the subject). The question is, what is the object doing to the subject, or intending to do, or capable of doing under certain circumstances? Is the subject being rejected or accepted, attacked or assisted? Are his tastes being criticized or praised? (p. 459.)

These are the presses to which the person is subjected, and they can be classified as benefits, harms, lacks, and barriers. Also important for interpersonal relations is the concept of "potential press."

Many situations are not definable as press (which have already been exerted), but rather as signs of *potential press*—promises of benefits or threats of harm. In such cases, the subject will predict to himself or expect that the alter will respond with an agreeable or beneficial press if he is properly treated, or that he will exert a disagreeable or harmful press if the subject comes within reach of him or acts in a provocative manner. (p. 459.)

## Heteronomy and Causal Attribution

The concepts of heteronomy and autonomy, in referring to the origin and governing source of an event, designate its causal attribution. The diversity of conditions leading to a judgment concerning the cause of an event has already been indicated in the analysis of different types of interpersonal relations. We can refer, for instance, to the discussions of personal and impersonal causality (p. 100), problems concerning the attribution of can (p. 87) and of trying (p. 114), the source of a perceptual experience (Chapter 3), etc.

Of particular importance, is that the origin or cause of heteronomous events may be referred to different sources depending upon whether one is concerned with the facts immediately presented in a concerte instance or with the dispositions underlying a whole group of events. For example, a particular action may be ascribed to *o*, or upon deeper analysis to *o*'s sentiments toward *p*, the mainsprings of *o*'s action. Thus, a phenotypically single event may bespeak a hierarchy of heteronomous events depending on its causal attribution. The distinction between the more proximal and the more distal was discussed earlier in connection with perceptual phenomena (cf. pp. 23–35). What is more immediately given as raw material is referred to more distal contents so that the situation may be grasped more fully. This point also has bearing on the scope of the situation that is taken into account, the so-called local and total relevance in causal attribution; its relation to proximal and distal phenomena are elaborated in Chapter 10, "Benefit and Harm."

The question of the reality of an event—whether in fact it has been caused or not—which arose in connection with the control of pleasure in interpersonal relations, also has general application to all heteronomous events. There it was pointed out that the event that brings about pleasure must have psychological reality and not necessarily objective reality: "...though the wish was directed toward the event, it is not the actual occurrence of the event but rather the belief that the event has occurred that is the necessary and sufficient cause for the change of wish to enjoyment" (p. 144). Thus, though $p$ may mistakenly believe that a harmful or beneficial event has occurred to him, nonetheless, the effects are real and can have major consequences for his actions and feelings. For the onlooker, who is informed of both the actual events and the mistaken beliefs of the affected person, this discrepancy often causes strong impressions of irony or tragedy, and is used as such in literature.

On the other hand, the person may not be aware of an environmental event that has actually taken place. He may only after some time be informed of something that is of great importance to him, such as the death of a close friend or loss of property. A change in his life space is then suddenly produced by knowledge about something that was there all the time. Objectively, of course, nothing has changed and though the person realizes this, the change in his life space has the character of a heteronomous event.

It is necessary to add, however, that an environmental change of which the person is not aware may affect him indirectly and in this sense has psychological significance. For instance, another person may have knowledge of the event. He may even classify it as a fortune or misfortune for $p$, and in looking forward to or fearing the moment when the person concerned will realize the event, may act in a special and unusual manner toward $p$. In this way, by altering interpersonal relations involving $p$, the environmental change is made to play an important part in $p$'s life.

There also appear to be individual differences in the tendency to attribute the cause of events to the self or to outside sources. Rosenzweig's concepts of intropunitive and extrapunitive reactions are cases in point (Murray, 1938, pp. 585 ff.). The intropunitive person is inclined to blame himself for unfortunate events, i.e., he sees himself as the cause, whereas the extrapunitive person is apt to react by blaming someone else or environmental circumstances. Typically, the causal attribution is to such condemnatory features in $p$ or $o$ as a hostile intent in $o$ or a fault (a weakness, stupidity, or moral defect) in $p$. It may be mentioned that Epictetus had a notion that these reactions showed change with education:

It is the action of an uneducated person to reproach others for his own misfortunes; of one starting his education to reproach himself; and of one completely educated, to reproach neither others nor himself. (Epictetus, trans. 1865, pp. 377–378.)

Intropunitive and extrapunitive tendencies specifically apply to negative events. Putting the case of causal attribution more generally so as to include positive and neutral events as well, one could say that people differ in their propensity for heteronomous versus autonomous attribution, a difference that may be subsumed under individual differences in perceptual attitude (cf. p. 56).

## Attribution of the Significance of an Event

The significance or meaning of an event as well as its cause can, as we have seen, be attributed either to the environment or to the person. An important basis for such differentiation is provided by data bearing upon condition-effect changes (cf. Chapter 5), the data being comparable to the methods of experimental inquiry. A corollary of this principle is that the effect an environmental change has on the average person is attributed to the environmental occurrence as a property, the nonaverage or idiosyncratic effect being attributed to the person. Thus, though an event may be heteronomous (causal attribution), the way the person reacts to it may or may not be environmentally determined, i.e., attributed to the objective world. This is another way of saying that environmental effects on the organism are "biospheric," to use Angyal's (1941) term; they involve an interaction between the organism and the environment.

When naive psychology classifies events as intrinsically fortunate or unfortunate, it is making a statement about the "objective" qualities of the environmental circumstances experienced by $p$. Consequently it is expected that anyone undergoing the situation would or should feel fortunate or unfortunate, as the case may be. This represents an instance in which the significance of the event is attributed to the environment and not to the person. If, however, a person struck with misfortune should not act like an unfortunate person, but instead should appear quite composed, his happiness or contentment is attributed to him as a personal characteristic, or else he is felt to be shamming.

It is notable that in everyday life our judgment of personality traits generally depends on gauging the "objective" qualities of what the person experienced; it is made on the basis of the attribution of certain properties to the object. When we say, "This man is easily pleased," it implies that we first assess the objective situation as not especially pleasing, even though it is so satisfying to him. Likewise, such cognitions as "he takes it too hard," "he keeps up his chin," "he doesn't know when he is well off," all require a judgment about the objective state of affairs.

Just as there are individual propensities for heteronomous or autonomous causal attribution, there are those who primarily perceive the affective significance of an event as intrinsically and objectively determined, whereas others attribute it to a much greater degree to the person. To be sure, the former, which sees in fortune and misfortune objective events that happen to the person, is by far the more typical approach, but supporters of the second point of view are not lacking. Epictetus (trans. 1865), for example, says: "Men are disturbed not by things, but by the views which they take of things. Thus death is nothing terrible...the terror consists in our notion of death, that it is terrible" (p. 377). This seems to be more or less the view of the existentialists. Epictetus also admonishes: "Demand not that events should happen as you wish; but wish them to happen as they do happen, and you will get on well" (p. 378).

We are reminded of the findings in level of aspiration experiments which show that the feelings of success or failure do not depend on the actual achievement as such, but on the relation of the achievement to the level of aspiration. Thus, whether a certain outcome is a "fortune" or a "misfortune" is determined by the subject, by the choice of his goal. The level of aspiration refers to the expectation of the result of one's own actions. There is also a level of expectation in regard to heteronomous events; not what one expects to achieve but what one expects to receive. This is influenced by what one has received in the past, and by what others with whom one compares oneself have received. This is also true of our judgments of the good or bad luck of others. Very often these judgments are relative to the heteronomous events with which the majority of people are confronted. While we can usually influence what happens to $o$ more easily by managing his environment, i.e., the objective factor (cf. Chapter 5, pp. 144–146), we can often influence the meaning of what happens to ourselves by changing the personal factor, the choice of goals.

### Interaction between Causal Attribution and Affective Significance

In distinguishing between the attribution of an event to a causal source, and the attribution of the positive or negative quality of the experience, we do not mean that causal attribution and the affective significance of an event do not influence each other. Actually, they are highly interdependent. For instance, the affective significance depends greatly on the causal attribution. One has only to recall the example of the parent who finds the noise of his own son entirely endurable and that of his adversary's child irritating. The reverse of this situation in which the causal attribution is determined by the affective significance often represents the dynamics underlying rationalization. For example, if one person $A$ antagonizes several persons one after the other and there arise difficulties between him and them, then an onlooker observing only the difficulties, will attribute them to $A$ as the constant factor in the situation. However, $A$ himself may be reluctant to put the reason for his negative reception into his own person; that would undermine his self-esteem. So, in order to explain the common attitude, he may come to the conviction that there is a conspiracy among the others, or that one person has contaminated all of them by spreading untrue stories about him. If they all independently came to dislike him, that would leave only himself as the source. In this way the affective significance of the event is seen to markedly influence its causal determination.

In the following examples used by Bertrand Russell the factors significant in the interaction between causal attribution and affective meaning are highlighted:

I am, we will say, a playwright; to every unbiased person it must be obvious that I am the most brilliant playwright of the age. Nevertheless, for some reason, my plays are seldom performed, and when they are, they are not successful. What is the explanation of this strange state of affairs? Obviously, that managers, actors, and critics have combined against me for one reason or another. The reason, of course, is highly creditable to myself: I have refused to kowtow to the great ones of the theatrical world, I have not flattered the critics, my plays contain home truths which are unbearable to those whom they hit. And so my transcendent merit languishes unrecognized. (Russell, 1930, p. 68.)

Analysis: The datum, the raw material the playwright $p$ faces is that other people by their words and actions imply that $p$'s plays are not valuable. Consequently, $p$ as a person feels devaluated, and since he thinks highly of himself, a reason for the contradiction must be found. It is possible that $p$ will revamp his own self-image in conformity with the presumed verdict of others, but this is a less pleasant alternative, and not the one chosen. Besides, there may be, as some writers believe, a resistance against altering the self-concept (Rogers, 1951). It is also possible that $p$ will conclude that the critics lack the depth to appreciate true art, but this introduces an additional fact the playwright does not accept. Perhaps it is too flagrantly denied by reality. The alternative chosen is that his critics really think well of him as a playwright, but they want to harm him. This conclusion demands justification. Taken by itself, it is an incomplete explanation. Possible reasons for the presumed intention to harm $p$, which at the same time are highly creditable to him, are: (1) the others are jealous because of his great ability, and (2) they are taking revenge because, being themselves conceited and untruthful, they feel harmed by $p$'s intrinsic sincerity and honesty. The second reason is the one selected by the playwright. The underlying cause of his unfavorable reception is placed in the positive value of $p$ and the negative value of his critics.

A similar analysis showing the interdependence between causal attribution and affective significance is given in this further example from Russell. Here jealousy and fear are made to account for the slight:

> You make a speech, let us say, at some public dinner. Photographs of some of the other speakers appear in the picture papers, but there is no picture of you. How is this to be accounted for? Obviously not because the other speakers were considered more important; it must be because the editors of the papers have given orders that you were to be ignored. And why should they have given such orders? Obviously because they feared you on account of your great importance. In this way the omission of your picture is transformed from a slight into a subtle compliment. (Russell, 1930, p. 73.)

In both examples we see how a given datum is connected by chains of reasons with a number of possible underlying causes belonging to the level of relatively invariant traits or attitudes. From these possible underlying causes the one will be selected that best fits the ideas and wishes the person has about himself and other people. The examples also show the major influence of self-attitudes on the interpretations of the actions of other people. Misinterpretations occur especially often when the effect of the actions has great import for us but when we know very little about the person who acts. We are confronted with a poorly structured situation, but at the same time a need exists to structure it. We cannot believe we are so unimportant to the agent that he failed to act courteously if not deferentially to us. A plausible reason that fits in with our self-attitudes must be found.

Thus, there are two factors that determine the selection of the acceptable attribution: (1) the reason has to fit the wishes of the person, and (2) the datum has to be plausibly derived from the reason. The first refers to the affective significance of an event. That reason is sought that is personally acceptable. It is usually a reason that flatters us, puts us in a good light, and it is imbued with an added potency by the attribution. The second factor is that of the "rationality" in every "rationalization." What is selected as acceptable cause is not just anything that fits with the personal needs and wishes of the life space. It also has to fit the cognitive expectations about connections between motives, attitudes, and behavior, etc. It has to fit the system of naive psychology; the less far-fetched the rationalization is, the better it will follow this system.

It is probably correct to assume that the factor of plausibility shows greater universality than the factor of personal acceptability which, connected as it is with the needs, wishes, and values of the attributer, represents the more projective part of the attribution. In order to investigate the factor of plausibility, therefore, one can reduce the projective factor by placing the subject in a situation he can view with a certain detachment. Thus, one can confront subjects with social problem-solving situations in which an action is specified, the task being to find a plausible motive for this action. The situation can be made as complex as one wants by adding other conditions. Especially, the problem can be made more and more difficult by excluding the more obvious solutions.

For instance the subject may be presented with the datum that $o$ intentionally benefits $p$. The question is posed, why does he do it? Since one of the most common answers is, "Because $o$ likes $p$" let us add the condition that $o$ dislikes $p$. Possible reasons then are: $o$ benefits $p$ for $q$'s sake and in the end the benefit is harmful to $p$; $o$ wants to obligate $p$; $o$ feels he ought to benefit $p$; etc. This problem can be made more difficult by adding that $o$ benefits $p$ secretly so that no one else knows about it. Then such solutions as he wants to get approval of other people, or he seeks reciprocation from $p$, are excluded. Most of these solutions are means-end solutions; $o$ benefiting $p$ cannot be intrinsically satisfying to $o$ because $o$ dislikes $p$; therefore it must be a means to some further end. The solutions also show the influence on the interpretation of $o$'s actions of the perceived attitude of $o$, i.e., of the dislike of $o$ for $p$.

## Summary

These few considerations were meant to point up the fact that the world outside the person is the source of many events that are evaluated by the person in terms of their causal and affective significance. Heteronomous events are perceived in such a way that they tend to fulfill the requirements of what may be called the person's objective or rational system of understanding as well as to fit in with the dynamics of his personal life. Within this interplay between causal attribution and affective significance, the person concentrates on the more invariant, dispositional properties of his world and extends his field of interpretation to include the factors he considers relevant. It is what he believes to be true that directly influences his reactions, the actuality having psychological significance only indirectly if at all.

# CHAPTER 7

# Sentiment

SENTIMENTS ARE SUCH an integral part of interpersonal relations that one hardly need explain why they are to be discussed in such a book as this. Many of the actions that occur between people can be understood only if one has an appreciation of the feelings that guide them.

A sentiment refers to the way a person $p$ feels about or evaluates something. The "something" may be another person, $o$, or an impersonal entity $x$. Sentiments may be roughly classified as positive and negative. We shall speak of positive sentiments in a relation of liking between $p$ and another entity, and of negative sentiments in a relation of disliking. Finer distinctions among sentiments such as those between like and love or between dislike and hate will be disregarded for our present purposes.

## Naive Psychology and Scientific Psychology in the Study of Sentiments

Naive psychology is fairly certain about the meaning of the sentence "$p$ likes $o$." There can be doubt whether a particular person likes a certain other person, but there is hardly any doubt as to the meaning of the words "to like." This is the more remarkable as it is rather difficult to state explicitly what the conceptual properties of this naive construct are.

For one thing, sentiment is not coordinated to a single kind of emotion nor to a single action. The variety of behavior and emotions connected with a sentiment is pointedly illustrated by Shand in regard to love:

. . . the situation of presence contrasts with that of absence, and prosperity with adversity, and love responds to the one with joy, and with sorrow and longing to the other. The anticipation of the future changes; and, in correspondence with it, love is sometimes full of hope and sometimes sunk in despondency. The remembrance of the past changes; and, responding to it, love is sometimes filled with thankfulness, and sometimes with remorse. The situation of danger contrasts with the situation of security; and, responding to the first, love feels anxiety, and to the second, confidence. The plots of .enemies contrast with the help of friends; and love responds in the one case with suspicion and anger, and in the other with trust and gratitude. The situation in which love is placed may be any one of those referred to; and, in the course of its history, it may pass successively through all of them. Love, therefore, cannot be reduced to a single compound feeling; it must organize a number of different emotional dispositions capable of evoking in different situations the appropriate behavior. (Shand, 1920, pp. 55–56.)

The point is clear. Different situations give rise to different actions and feelings that in some way are appropriate to the sentiment. Shand puts it this way:

Every sentiment tends to include in its system all the emotions, thoughts, volitional processes and qualities of character which are of advantage to it for the attainment of its ends, and to reject all such constituents as are either superfluous or antagonistic. (p. 106)

That is, the sentiment is the connecting link between the variety of situations on the one hand and the events that transpire on the other.

How, then, does one go about bringing order into the infinite diversity of possible situations and the manifold of events? Aside from the urge of the scientist to reduce the complex to the simple, naive psychology itself tells us that there is order and coherence in the way sentiments function. We have no trouble understanding a parent's pleasure over the success of his son and sorrow over his defeat. The totally different reactions of pleasure and sorrow do not leave us with a feeling of chaos or of unfathomable complexity regarding the vagaries of human nature. The factor that brings order into heterogeneity is the perceived sentiment, namely the fondness of a parent for his son. The sentiment is the more or less underlying invariance, the disposition which gives a stability within fluctuating circumstances and behavior.

Naive psychology does more than tell us that there is order in the way sentiments function. In providing a superabundance of psychological events, it points to the way in which we must look for that order. But naive psychology cannot do the whole job of explanation, because it does not provide the principles (or laws in their more rigorous form) underlying the phenomena. Scientific psychology attempts to provide this not only by drawing upon the generous offerings of naive psychology, but also by seeking insights from all possible sources, whether from other scientific fields or from other laws and facts in psychology itself.

### Unit Formation and Balanced State

The two main concepts we have utilized to account for the variety of events linked by naive psychology to positive and negative sentiments are unit formation and balanced state. Briefly, separate entities comprise a unit when they are perceived as belonging together. For example, members of a family are seen as a unit; a person and his deed belong together. The concept of balanced state designates a situation in which the perceived units and the experienced sentiments co-exist without stress; there is thus no pressure toward change, either in the cognitive organization or in the sentiment. We shall have a good deal more to say about these concepts later, but this brief description will suffice to point up their relevance to the events of naive psychology demonstrated in the following experiment (Esch, 1950):

Subjects were given short descriptions of social situations and were asked to write down the most probable outcome, that is, "what would happen nine times out of ten when something like this occurs." One situation was the following:

Bob thinks Jim very stupid and a first class bore. One day Bob reads some poetry he likes so well that he takes the trouble to track down the author in order to shake his hand. He finds that Jim wrote the poems.

The 101 subjects consisted of high-school and college students and other adults.

In the situation presented to the subjects the poetry was liked whereas its author was not. Such a combination of positive and negative entities produces an unbalanced situation. The subjects resolved the disturbance in the following ways: (1) Forty-six per cent changed the negative author to a positive person, e.g., "He grudgingly changes his mind about Jim." In this way both entities became positive and balance was achieved. (2) Twenty-nine per cent changed the value of the poetry, e.g., "He decides the poems are lousy." In this way balance was achieved by transforming the unit into one that was consistently negative. (3) Five per cent challenged the unit formation itself, e.g., "Bob would probably question Jim's authorship of the poems." (4) Two subjects altered the unit by differentiating the author in such a way that the unit comprised only the positive part of the author and the admired poetry, e.g., "He then thinks Jim is smart in some lines but dumb in others." (5) The rest of the subjects did not resolve the disharmony, but some were definitely aware that the situation presented a conflict—"Bob is confused and does not know what to do. He finally briefly mentions his liking of the poems to Jim without much warmth."

That sentiment, unit formation, and balanced state have something to do with each other can be stated as a general hypothesis, namely: the relationship between sentiments and unit formation tends toward a balanced state (Heider 1944, 1946. A theoretical approach similar to the one presented here has been suggested by Osgood and Tannenbaum 1955; in regard to the relation between cognitive structure and sentiments, cf. also Adams 1953). Our ultimate task is to make some headway in accounting for a variety of phenomena involving sentiments in terms of this hypothesis, but we must first pause to detail some of the facts and assumptions related to its main terms.

## Units and Cognitive Organization

**Unit-forming factors.** In the foregoing discussion we have indicated that when two entities are seen as belonging together, that is, when they make up a cognitive unit (like Bob and his poetry), consequences important for the interpersonal relationship follow. A first task, therefore, is to consider the conditions that lead to unit formation. Many of these conditions have been systematically investigated by the gestalt psychologists who demonstrated that the formation of units is an important feature of cognitive organization. The gestalt experiments often involved the perception of simple figures in the demonstration of such unit-forming factors as similarity, proximity, common fate, good continuation, set, and past experience (Wertheimer, 1923).

Thus, in the following line we see the stars in groups of two because of the factor of proximity:

$$** \quad ** \quad ** \quad ** \quad ** \quad **$$

The factor of similarity makes us see, for instance, similar figures forming groups in a line of figures with equal spaces between them:

$$* * - - * * - - * * - - * * - - * *$$

Koffka summarizes the unit-forming properties of similarity and proximity by noting that "two parts in the field will attract each other according to their degree of proximity and equality" (Koffka, 1935,

p. 166). It has also been shown that some of these factors can be considered as forming social units (Koffka, 1935, pp. 654 ff.).

Unit-forming factors particularly relevant to groupings involving persons can be seen in the following: Things that are made by a person, or that are his property, belong to him. Changes that are attributed to a person as effects of his action also belong to him in a certain sense. A person may be seen in a cognitive unit with other persons because of kinship, nationality, or religion. One may feel close to another person because one is familiar with him, or because one has interacted with him frequently.

***The influence of the surrounding on unit formation.*** Whether two entities are seen as making up a unit depends not only on their relation to each other—whether they are similar or close to each other—but also on the properties of the surrounding. This can easily be demonstrated in figural perception. If two crosses are surrounded by circles, they will form a strong unit as a pair; if they are surrounded by other crosses, the pair unit as such will not be perceived. Köhler says that

. . . for the most part similarities of various degrees will occur in one perceptual situation; and then specific perceptual units will be formed not simply because their members resemble each other, but because their mutual resemblance is greater than is that of such members and any other parts of the situation. (Köhler, 1940, p. 135.)

This influence of the surrounding entities can also be shown in regard to the factor of proximity. If we compare the two letter sequences:

abcd efgh     and     a b c  d e  f g h

we see that *d* and *e* form a pair in the second sequence and not in the first. This occurs in spite of the fact that the distance between *d* and *e* is exactly the same in both examples. The difference is brought about only by the change in distances between *d* and the preceding letters and between *e* and the letters that follow.

The dependence of unit formation on the surrounding holds also for units consisting of people. If two Americans meet among people of other nationalities, they readily stand out as a pair, whereas if they are surrounded by other Americans, this grouping does not occur. Homans (1950) offers the general hypothesis that ". . . the nature of the relationships between the individuals *A, B, C*, . . . is always determined in part by the relationships between each one of them and other individuals, *M, N, O*, . . ." (p. 113). Thus, as so often happens, the formation of friendship groupings may be influenced as much by dislike of others as by liking within the group.

The influence of a new person on a pair formation is considered by Wiese and Becker (1932): "An existing pair relation is either weakened or strengthened by interaction with another person, rarely if ever does the degree of association or dissociation remain unchanged" (p. 524). In the pair $mn$ the unit will be weakened if another entity is added that is very similar either to $m$ or to $n$. Thus, if we have the unit $mnn$ the two $n$'s make a pair and $m$ is the outsider. But if the added entity is dissimilar to both members of the original pair, as in $mn5$, then the unity of the letter pair is apt to be strengthened by its difference from the figure.

Theoretically, the degree of unit formation between the members of the original pair should change least if the affinities of 1 to 2, 2 to 3, and 1 to 3 are the same (taking 1 and 2 as the original pair and 3 as the new entity). If, however, 1 is closer to 3 than 1 is to 2 or 2 to 3, for example, then 1 and 3 will "gang up" against 2. The greater probability of inequality in the affinity of the different pairs might be one reason for the precarious balance of a triad, and why organizations of two against one develop so often. Simmel (1950) had discussed the effects of a third person on a dyad in similar terms (pp. 135 ff.). See also Mills (1953) for experimental tests of Simmel's theory.

More complicated are the cases in which two units can be classified in different ways. For instance, $a$ and $A$ can be seen as two examples of the first letter of the alphabet and thus as belonging to one group. Or, they can be seen as one lower-case and one upper-case letter belonging to two different groups. Again, the surrounding can determine the unit formation by pointing up one or another aspect. In the sequence $aaaaAAAA$, the two letters belong to different groups; in the sequence $XXXXaAXXXX$, they may easily be seen as belonging to one group. If a New Yorker and a Bostonian meet in a party composed half of New Yorkers and half of Bostonians they will very likely feel they belong to two different units. But if they meet in a party in which no one else is American they will feel they belong together.

Ichheiser (1949) points out that the situation enters the "choice we make among different possibilities in classifying an individual in one particular way and not in another" (p. 34). He offers the example of two people who are thought of as doctor and patient when seen in the physician's office, as radical and conservative when seen at a political rally, and as two Englishmen should they meet in Italy.

The effect of the surrounding on unit formation is involved in the following question: A Kansan boasts about the Empire State Building. Where is this most likely to happen, in Topeka, New York, Paris, or Chicago? The obvious answer is: in Paris. Boasting implies that the person who does the boasting and the object about which he boasts form a unit. This is equally true, for instance, of being proud or ashamed of something. For the Kansan this unit with the Empire State Building would exist only outside of the United States, or at least it is much more likely to occur there.

## Phenomenal Properties of Balance and Imbalance

By a balanced state (or situation) is meant a harmonious state, one in which the entities comprising the situation and the feelings about them fit together without stress. That naive psychology has little difficulty detecting situations of imbalance can be seen in the following examples:

$p$ hates $o$ because he is so similar to $o$.
He always imitates people he dislikes.
He always hates people with whom he has to work.
He hates $q$ because $q$ is similar to his friend $o$.
He avoids people he likes.
Jones is very conceited and vain. His best friend is Smith who is very fond of him. They always get on very well because Smith likes to insult Jones. Jones is especially proud of his children. Smith thinks they are very obnoxious and says so openly to Jones.

In some way we sense that the factors in the situation "do not add up"; they seem to pull in different directions. They leave us with a feeling of disturbance that becomes relieved only when change within the situation takes place in such a way that a state of balance is achieved.

That harmonious situations tend to be preferred to those that are unbalanced has been experimentally shown by Jordan (1953) in a study that dealt directly with the theory of balanced states to be developed in this chapter. On p. 204 a description of the experiment is given.

On the other hand, there may also be a tendency to leave the comfortable equilibrium, to seek the new and adventurous. The tension produced by unbalanced situations often has a pleasing effect on our thinking and aesthetic feelings. Balanced situations can have a boring obviousness and a finality of superficial self-evidence. Unbalanced situations stimulate us to further thinking; they have the character of interesting puzzles, problems which make us suspect a depth of interesting background. Sometimes they evoke, like other patterns with unsolved ambiguities, powerful aesthetic forces of a tragic or comic nature.

If a novelist tells us that a person likes the things he makes, is uneasy if he has to live with people he dislikes, likes the child of his best friend, etc., all this seems obvious and we feel that we do not know much about the person as an individual. But if we hear of someone who dislikes everything he produces, who hates to own what he likes, and who always tries to live with people he dislikes, then immediately we have the feeling that here is a person who is different and at the same time interesting because of his psychological quirks. Stories in which the stress is laid on unbalanced situations are felt to have a deep psychological meaning. Dostoevski, for instance, describes again and again feelings full of conflict resulting from just such situations.

An assertion of a tendency contrary to the obvious one toward balanced situations is felt to be a paradox, and often a paradox that imports a sense of great psychological profundity. The statement, "people like to help their friends," sounds tautological and does not seem to have any great psychological significance. But when Oscar Wilde says, "Yet each man kills the thing he loves . . ." (*The Ballad of Reading Gaol*) we feel at once that there is a "deep truth" in this paradoxical statement.

Sometimes paradoxical statements have a quality of wit. Someone said: "I was able to do him a favor, which, I am sure, he never held against me." This statement implies that in general people dislike people who benefit them, and the fact that this supposition contradicts the obvious gives it the character of a witticism. Paradoxical statements function on two levels. On the one hand, measured by the standard of the obvious, they are nonsense. On the other hand, if one goes deeper some justification for this nonsense may be found.

Some people want a "happy ending" in the fiction they read, the happy ending being one in which a balanced situation is established—people who like each other are united; the good are rewarded, the bad punished. However, we often feel that such endings are superficial, and good taste revolts against them. Nevertheless, one might say that dramatic situations are unbalanced and require a solution. The existence of tragedy poses a problem—it ends in what looks at first glance like an imbalance: the admired person is destroyed. Probably that is why so many theories about tragedy exist, many of which attempt to show that the imbalance of the ending is only an apparent one.

Experiments would probably show a difference in the recall of balanced and imbalanced situations. The balanced situations should be more stable and therefore better remembered. Distortion of memory should also differ in the two cases. If the situation presents but a slight imbalance, distortion due to what has been called "leveling" should occur, thereby transforming the situation into a balanced one. If a striking imbalance exists, exaggeration of that imbalance should occur by the process known as "sharpening." The concepts of leveling and

sharpening were first introduced in an experiment on figural perception
in a paper by Wulf (see Ellis, 1939, pp. 137 ff.).

We shall now review a wide variety of balanced states and then attempt a more exact formulation of the theory of balanced states.  In
the review, evidence from literature, naive psychology, and experimental data will be introduced as appropriate to the particular case of
balance under consideration.  Seemingly contradictory evidence will
also be presented.  Whether the conditions that may account for the
exceptions invalidate the balance hypothesis will be considered later.

## Cases of Balanced States

**Homogeneity of the person.**  The study of figural perception
teaches us that a strongly unified part of the field tends to look as uniform as possible (Koffka, 1935, p. 135).  Krech and Crutchfield (1948)
offer the example of a series of black dots in a single row: they may
appear equally black in spite of the existence of minor differences in
shading among them (p. 95).  It is also true that under some conditions
exaggeration of the difference in the parts of a unit may occur so that
they appear as unlike as possible.  The first process is called assimilation
and the second is called contrast.  Krech and Crutchfield (1948) state
the hypothesis concerning the conditions under which each will occur:
"Assimilation appears when the differences between the substructure
and the major structures are small; contrast appears when the differences are large" (p. 95; cf. Werner, 1922, p. 115).

. The concepts of leveling and sharpening are also relevant.  Contrast
will be discussed later.  Here we shall consider the significance of assimilation for problems of sentiments.

It has often been stressed that assimilation occurs in the perception
of other people.  Ichheiser (1949) talks about the tendency to overestimate the unity of personality (p. 27).  Asch (1952) emphasizes
that our impressions of persons are often highly unified (pp. 207 ff.).
Stagner (1951) links these phenomena with homeostasis.  In regard to
sentiments this implies that we tend to have an over-all like or dislike
of a person.  Where several sentiments can be distinguished, they tend
to be alike in sign.  For instance, liking and admiring go together; the
situation is unbalanced if a person likes someone he disrespects.  In
other words, the unit of the person tends to be uniformly positive or
negative.  This is known as the halo phenomenon.  To conceive of a
person as having positive and negative traits requires a more sophisticated point of view; it requires a differentiation of the representation
of the person into subparts that are of unlike value.

As an example of the tendency to overestimate the homogeneity of other persons, let us consider the relation of external appearance to more central personality traits. The situation is balanced if external and internal characteristics correspond, if what looks good is also truly good.

Spiegel, on the basis of experiments, points out that for the child

The beautiful person . . . is the good person; the ugly person is bad. . . . The child forms a total concept which expresses the tendency that certain qualities or things "go together," or "belong together," such as beauty and goodness. The result of such an intellectual tendency is that a concept becomes a collection of qualities that "belong together" but which are not integrated into a unified whole in which the subordinate parts are inherently and necessarily articulated. This looseness obviously fits the child's concept of beauty; the beautiful person is good, rich, strong, healthy, has a car, can sing, dance, etc. (Spiegel, 1950, p. 21.)

Shakespeare is often concerned with the relation between virtue and beauty. In *Twelfth Night* he argues that appearance should be assimilated to the inner personality, and that the reverse assimilation is invalid:

Thou hast, Sebastian, done good feature shame.
In nature there's no blemish but the mind;
None can be call'd deform'd but the unkind:
Virtue is beauty; but the beauteous evil
Are empty trunks o'erflourish'd by the devil.
(Act III, Scene 4)

To summarize these remarks, we might say that if several parts, or traits, or aspects, of a person are considered, the tendency exists to see them all as positive, or all as negative.

In the foregoing, balance between sentiment and unit formation was considered in terms of the unit character of one entity, $o$. When all the sentiments toward that single entity are of like sign, balance obtains. In the following cases of balance, the relation of $p$ *liking* (L) $o$ (or $x$, an impersonal entity) and other unit-forming connections (U) between $p$ and $o$ (or $x$), such as similarity, will be considered. The situation is balanced if (1) $p$ likes $o$ with whom he is connected in some way, or (2) if he is not connected (notU) with a person he dislikes (DL).

If one relation is given, it can bring about the other concordant one. Thus, ($p$ U $o$) may be a condition or an effect. It can induce an harmonious ($p$ L $o$) or it can be induced by the sentiment relation. The word induce refers to a tendency or force towards the realization of the second relation rather than to its actual production inasmuch as forces against the tendency may exist in the situation. It is to be understood that the units refer to $p$'s experience of them rather than to the objective state of affairs, though often there is a substantial correlation between the two. For instance, $p$ may see himself as quite similar to $o$, though this may or may not be the consensus of those around him.

The cases of balance to be discussed are grouped according to the factors responsible for the unit formation. Not all cases are discussed under each type of unit relation, the basis of selection being the availability of experimental and other evidence, or the relevance of special points.

***Similarity between* p *and* o.** Similarity has appeared as a significant concept in many psychological theories. We have already pointed out that in figural perception similarity is recognized as a unit-forming factor. The early theories of association also drew upon similarity as a factor in association. An exceptionally cold day, for example, leads us to think of another like it years ago.

$p$ SIMILAR TO $o$ INDUCES $p$ LIKES $o$, OR $p$ TENDS TO LIKE A SIMILAR $o$. The relation between similarity and sentiments is observed in everyday life. That similar people tend to associate and to like each other is the point of many proverbs. Even in language a relation between similarity and sentiment seems to be recognized: the word "like," as a verb, refers to a positive sentiment; as an adjective, it means "similar." In regard to the formation of a new group, Koffka (1935) concludes that "Though surely not the only factor, the similarity between ourselves and the others seems definitely to contribute to this new organization" (p. 654).

The role of similarity in regard to marital selection has been noted by LaPiere and Farnsworth:

> The findings of almost all studies of assortative mating confirm the hypothesis of homogamy, namely, that there exists a tendency for "like to mate with like." More specifically those studies indicate that the "affinity of like for like" exerts a greater influence in marital selection than the "attraction of opposites for each other." (LaPiere and Farnsworth, 1949, p. 475.)

Sorokin (1947) who has studied extensively "the roles of similarity and dissimilarity in social solidarity and antagonism" (Section 7), points out that one is not justified in assuming that "solidarity and love in marriage or in any other social group is based always and entirely upon similarity" (p. 137). One can only assume that similarity creates a tendency towards liking. One can distinguish more definitely between the cognitive unit that is produced by similarity, and the social unit. One could assume that the cognitive unit is responsible for a positive sentiment, and this positive sentiment then often leads to a real "association," a social group. Such a course of events for example presumably occurred in the pattern of family visiting on the part of newcomers in a resettlement community. Loomis and Davidson (1939) studied a

Spanish-American community in which a group of ranchers and a group of farmers had been relocated from a dust-bowl area. Antagonism among the three groups at the time of resettlement was evident. After two years, the investigators found that ranchers predominantly visited ranchers, and farmers visited farmers, and the indigenous Spanish-Americans also tended to visit largely within their own group. That is, the social groupings tended to occur according to the background similarities in the community.

The tendency of similarity to lead to social unit formation may, of course, be counterbalanced by a force toward dissociation which results from possible disagreeable consequences of association. This happens, for instance, when twins choose to live in different cities in order to develop their individual personalities.

Experimental support for the existence of an association between similarity and liking is given in a study by Fiedler, Warrington, and Blaisdell (1952). Each of 26 fraternity men was asked to name the person in the group he liked best and the one he liked least (sociometric choice), to describe himself and his ideal self by means of a statement-sorting test, and to predict the self-descriptions of his best-liked and least-liked member. The results showed that the subjects *perceived* those they liked best as more similar to themselves as well as more similar to their ideal selves than those they liked least. However, whether the perceived similarity was the basis for the sociometric choice or vice versa cannot be determined from this study which was cross-sectional in character.

Notice also, the use of the term perceived similarity, for in fact, these men were not more similar to the actual self-descriptions of the best-liked than to the least-liked fellow member. They were only more similar to what they thought the self-descriptions would be. This result illustrates a point made previously—the unit-forming factors refer to $p$'s experience of them rather than to the objective state of affairs. In line with the additional statement that often there is a substantial correlation between the two, is the investigators' belief that the

. . . statements [in the sorting test] probably do not adequately sample all relevant areas of personality which might affect one person's preference for another. It is, therefore, not unreasonable to expect that other statements, or other methods, might demonstrate a relationship between [actual] similarity on certain traits and likings. (Fiedler, Warrington, and Blaisdell, 1952, p. 793.)

Zimmer (1956) conducted an experiment with largely negative results: he found no relation between the "behavior tendencies" (as measured by ratings on eight personality dimensions such as tense-relaxed, withdrawn-sociable) of members of harmonious and of discordant dyads. There existed merely a trend in the direction of greater similarity between the members of harmonious dyads than between the members of discordant dyads. There was also an absence of correlation between the subject's self-ratings and his perception of the partners he chose. However, it is possible that the results are specific to the eight personality dimensions used. Furthermore, the way the dyads were selected may have been an important factor. Airmen were asked to indicate those members of their group with whom they would like or not like to work; thus, a task-oriented selection was produced, and one can assume that it often happens that people like to work with persons whom they would not choose as friends. Fiedler (1953) concludes from studies he made "...that effective informal teams which want to get a job done must have members who prefer to work with men who are psychologically distant and task-centered" (p. 148).

Just as we noted that the factor of similarity can, under certain circumstances lead to dissociation, so it can evoke disliking when the similarity carries with it disagreeable implications. For example, a person with a disability who wishes to deny it, may dislike and even feel hostile toward another person similarly afflicted. The disagreeable similarity may serve as a reminder of the disability, and in other ways emphasize it. That the factor of similarity may also induce a conflicting liking is still possible, though the person may not be aware of this tendency when the hostility and anxiety dominate.

$p$ DISSIMILAR TO $o$ INDUCES $p$ DISLIKES $o$; $p$ TENDS TO DISLIKE A PERSON DIFFERENT FROM HIMSELF. Xenophobia is a relevant example. It is sometimes difficult to isolate the effects of dissimilarity from the effects of unfamiliarity since both may be evident in the situation. For example, does the child hesitate to make friends with the foreigner because the foreigner is different in his ways or because the child is unfamiliar with them? Likewise, people who are similar to us are also familiar to us in some way. In any case, similarity and familiarity (cf. pp. 214–215) as well as their opposites seem to have parallel roles in cases of balance involving sentiments and unit relations.

The apparent exception to the above relation between similarity and sentiment, namely, that dissimilarity can lead to liking and association if two people fit together because they complement each other, may turn out to be a verification of the relation, at least in some instances. A good deal depends on the criteria for the designation of similar, dissimilar, and complementary entities. Two apparently dissimilar entities may in one sense be considered similar when they lead toward a common purpose. This is one kind of complementary relation and may be exemplified when "opposites attract," as male and female. In terms of this level of analysis, then, the fact that dissimilarity can lead to liking is not necessarily an exception to the balanced case under consideration, since the apparent dissimilarity may in effect become supplanted by a similarity, that of purpose for example. The previous discussion of the influence of the surrounding on unit formation is also relevant—with shift in context dissimilar entities may appear similar. The dissimilarity according to one determination becomes a similarity according to another.

$p$ LIKES $o$ INDUCES $p$ SIMILAR TO $o$. There is a tendency in $p$ to increase the similarity between a liked $o$ and himself. The similarity can be increased by a change in $p$, or in $o$, or in both.

The increase can occur merely in the cognitive region: $p$ tends to see the similarity as greater than it actually is. In a study by Preston *et al.*, ratings by husbands and wives of their own and of the spouse's personality were examined. It was found that husbands and wives consistently rate themselves and their partners similarly on specific personality traits. Furthermore,

. . . while all spouses show such a tendency, happily married partners exhibit materially higher correlation on their ratings of themselves and their partners than do unhappily married partners. (Preston, *et al.*, 1952, p. 336.)

However, the self-ratings of husbands and wives reveal negligible correlation. The authors suggest that

. . . the foregoing results are a direct consequence of the fact that people on opposite sides of a conflict situation have more opportunities to take note of their opponent as different rather than similar to themselves, whereas persons with strong affective feelings (such as love) promoting a wish for identification, tend to see their partners as similar rather than dissimilar to themselves. (p. 336.)

In the study itself, however, the actual causal direction between the variables liking and similarity cannot be definitely stated, just as in the study by Fiedler *et al.* which showed a similar finding.

The increase in similarity can also be produced by actual changes in $p$ or $o$. To make the other person similar to oneself, or at least to try to change him in such a way that he is a fitting partner, is, one might say, the extrovert way of producing the harmony. To change oneself towards greater similarity would be the more introvert way. One is reminded of a remark of Angyal's which expresses these two ways of meeting a situation:

In the rearrangement of a constellation, the response may take place either by positional shifts close to the object pole of the biospheric occurrence or by positional shifts close to the subject pole. In this latter case, which is a sort of "change of attack," one speaks of *adaptation*. Behavior, as a rule, involves in various degrees both the manipulation of environmental factors and an adaptive rearrangement of the subjective factors, for the purpose of meeting the situation adequately. (Angyal, 1941, p. 285.)

There is a folk story in which a man with graying hair had two wives, an old one and a young one. The old one pulled out all his dark hair, and the young one all his gray hair, so that the poor man soon was completely bald. This example shows how complicated the motives can be for increasing the similarity of a partner. It is likely that the behavior of the two wives was not simply a manifestation of a positive sentiment evoking a wish for a more similar partner; the tendency to be seen with a suitable partner would also play a role. The young wife does not want to be seen with an old man, and the old wife may want to prevent the approach of other younger women.

The other possibility, namely that $p$ tries to change himself, is treated in a paper by Schmidt (1930). Schmidt notes that some people attempt to resemble the loved person as completely as possible, and others try to resemble the type most attractive to the loved partner. Instances of hero worship, where the admirer emulates the stance, speech, and dress of his idol are common.

Examples of the inverse case of balance, namely, $p$ tends to think that the disliked $o$ is different from himself, are also not hard to find within one's experience. Finally, imbalance occurs when disliking and similarity are both present, with the result that there is tension and a tendency toward change in the relations.

**Interaction and proximity.** These two relations often occur together because nearness increases the possibilities of interaction. It is true that two people can interact intensely, for instance by letters, over great spatial distances; or, conversely, two people working in the same office may not be on speaking terms with each other. But because there is often a close causal connection between the two relations, we shall treat them together.

$p$ IN CONTACT WITH $o$ INDUCES $p$ LIKES $o$. The tendency is for $p$ to like a person with whom he has contact through interaction or proximity.

A popular song echoes this relation in its refrain: "If I'm not near the girl I love, I love the girl I'm near." Homans notes:

The relation between association and friendliness is one of those commonly observed facts that we use all the time as a guide for action in practical affairs but seldom make an explicit hypothesis of sociology. We assume that if only we can "get people together," they will like one another and work together better. (Homans, 1950, p. 111.)

There are many investigations that give substantial support to this assumption. Homans (1950), in reviewing studies of small natural groups such as the Norton Street Gang (Whyte, 1943), states that the observations show that persons who interact frequently with one another tend to like one another. There is also an abundance of experimental evidence which is reviewed by Riecken and Homans (1954). Festinger, Schachter and Back (1950, pp. 153 ff.) showed that persons who had frequent opportunity to interact with one another, because of the strategic position of their apartments in a housing project, were likely to choose one another as friends. In a study of a boy's camp, Sherif (1951) showed that when the boys were divided into two groups, the number of likings for members of these smaller groups as indicated in sociometric choices tended to increase over what it had been before the groups were formed. Bovard (1951) found that in group-centered situations where there was greater verbal interaction than in leader-centered situations, the subjects showed greater positive interpersonal feelings on an affect scale than did the leader-centered subjects.

The dynamics of the connection between spatial or interaction closeness and sentiment may be linked to various conditions. Bovard, for example, explains his results by assuming that verbal interaction leads to a more correct picture of the other and the self-other relation. It is this cognitive clarification that produces positive interpersonal affects. That other factors may be involved is suggested by an experiment by Bieri (1953) who found that as a result of constructive interaction, members of a group came to perceive their partners as more similar to themselves. Bieri states that if one wishes to speculate about the nature of the interpersonal processes, the findings can be interpreted as indicating "identification" or "projection." According to the former, the partners, interacting in a friendly manner, begin to identify with each other. According to the latter, the contact favors attributing one's own characteristics to the partner. In either of these interpretations, cognitive clarification or the "correction of perceptual distortion," does not enter.

Whatever the explanation, it is clear that spatial proximity and interaction do not always lead to an increase in positive attitudes. Witness the saying, "The grass on the other side of the fence is greener." That changes can also occur in a negative direction, is experimentally demonstrated in a study by Wright (1937) which involved preference for objects. Waitresses, when selecting a piece of pie for a customer, tended to take the nearest one, whereas when the pie was for their own consumption they were more likely to select one from a back row fully 12 inches behind the front row.

The lack of a univocal relation between proximity or interaction and liking is also seen in the not uncommon negative attitudes that emerge between people living in close contact, such as neighbors, married couples, people living in one household or working in one office. Park and Burgess said long ago:

> Love and hate, longing and disgust, sympathy and hostility increase in intensity with intimacy of association. . . . The fact is, that with increasing contact either attraction or repulsion may be the outcome, depending upon the situation. . . . (Park and Burgess, 1921, pp. 283 f.)

It seems as if in some cases all the negative feelings of a person were focused on the person who is closest. One might venture the hypothesis that interaction and proximity increase the effect of similarity on sentiments, especially the effect of similarity or dissimilarity of beliefs and attitudes. With similar attitudes proximity will increase the degree of positive sentiment; with slight dissimilarity of attitudes a mutual assimilation might be produced, and with it an increase in friendliness; with strong dissimilarities the hostility will be increased. This would be valid, of course, only insofar as one disregards factors like displaced need for aggression, etc. For whatever reason, however, when dislike develops in an interaction a state of imbalance results. The disharmony is resolved either by dissociation or by a change in the sentiment relation.

$p$ LIKES $o$ INDUCES $p$ IN CONTACT WITH $o$, OR $p$ TENDS TO APPROACH A LIKED $o$. This reminds one of Murray and Morgan's (1945) "adient vector," a positive conative trend which is exhibited "by verbal or physical activity that brings the subject closer to the entity in order to enjoy it" (p. 13). It is often described as a desire for contact and it is a fundamental characteristic of mankind according to Crawley:

> . . . ideas of contact are at the root of all conceptions of human relations at any stage of culture; contact is the one universal test, as it is the most elementary form, of mutual relations. . . . In this connection, we find that desire or willingness for physical contact is an animal emotion, more or less subconscious, which is characteristic of similarity, harmony, friendship, or love. Throughout the world, the greeting of a friend is expressed by contact, whether it be nose-rubbing or the kiss, the embrace or the clasp of hands; so the ordinary expression of friendship by a boy, that eternal savage, is contact of arm and shoulder. More interesting still, for our purpose, is the universal expression by contact of the emotion of love. (Crawley, 1927, pp. 107–108.)

Homans (1950), who has given special attention to the relation between interaction and sentiment, concludes that ". . . if it is true that we often come to like the persons with whom we interact, it is also true that we are prepared to interact with persons we already like"

(p. 111). In support of this hypothesis Riecken and Homans (1954) have collated the findings of many experiments.

The relation between sentiment and spatial or interaction closeness underlies the concept known as "social distance." By social distance is meant the degree of interpersonal closeness one accepts. For example, one might not mind living in the same city with a particular person, race, or class, but would object to being neighbors. Or, one might accept neighborhood association, but resist membership in the same club. Acceptance of the marriage relation represents a minimal degree of social distance, community ostracism the other extreme. In short, on the basis of the attractiveness of a close interaction, sentiments are ranked on a positive-negative scale.

$p$ DISLIKES $o$ INDUCES $p$ AVOIDS $o$, OR $p$ WITHDRAWS FROM A DISLIKED $o$. Murray and Morgan (1945) speak in this case of an "abient vector," a negative conative trend which is exhibited by "activity that separates the subject from the entity" (p. 13). Crawley again notes the universal nature of this relation:

On the other hand, the avoidance of contact, whether consciously or subconsciously presented, is no less the universal characteristic of human relations where similarity, harmony, friendship, and love are absent. This appears in the attitude of men to the sick, to strangers, distant acquaintances, enemies, and in cases of difference of age, position, sympathies or aims, and even of sex. (Crawley, 1927, p. 108.)

$p$ LIKES $o$ AND $p$ NOT IN CONTACT WITH $o$ LEADS TO TENSION, OR $p$ IS UNHAPPY WHEN THE LOVED $o$ IS ABSENT. Absence or separation cannot be defined in simple spatial terms or in terms of perceptual presence. At least with a mature person, one must consider the possibilities of future interaction. It makes a great deal of difference whether $o$ leaves $p$ for one day, for one month, or forever, in spite of the fact that the momentary physical change, i.e., the disappearance of $o$ from $p$'s perceptual field, can be the same in the three cases. The actual not seeing or not being able to talk to another person is not so important as the possibility or impossibility of future contact. Of course, physical distance is one factor determining this possibility.

There exists the familiar contradiction between proverbs as to whether absence increases or decreases a positive sentiment. However, if one takes the adage: "Short absence quickens love, long absence kills it" together with La Rochefoucauld's aphorism: "Absence extinguishes small passions and increases great ones, as the wind will blow out a candle and blow in a fire," one would obtain the following hypothesis: the effect of absence on the sentiment depends on (1) the length of absence, (2) the intensity of the original sentiment.

*Familiarity between* **p** *and* **o.**   The effect of familiarity is closely related to that of proximity and interaction, since the latter lead to an increase in familiarity. We shall mention here only a few cases that have been treated in terms of familiarity rather than in terms of interaction.

*p* TENDS TO LIKE A FAMILIAR *o.*   In nonsocial perception, it has often been found that familiarity with an object leads to liking it. Maslow's (1937) experiment is particularly relevant. He familiarized his subjects with a variety of tasks and objects over a period of several days. The subjects then had to indicate whether they preferred the now familiar task or object or a similar but relatively unfamiliar alternative. For example, 30 Russian names were arranged in pairs, the members of each pair being as alike as possible. One list was read out loud on several evenings. The subjects were instructed to write the names down as they were read and to spell them as well as they could. For the crucial test, the 15 now familiar names and the 15 unfamiliar matched names were read in random order. The subjects rated each name according to two scales: like-dislike and euphony of the names. On both scales the subjects expressed a preference for the familiar names. The results of some of the other experimental tests were consistent with this finding, although some were less conclusive, possibly because of confounding factors.

In referring to experiments on recognition (recognition being a manifestation of familiarity), Titchener points out that recognition

. . . is variously reported as a glow of warmth, a sense of ownership, a feeling of intimacy, a sense of being at home, a feeling of ease, a comfortable feeling . . . we may go further, and find a genetic sanction for its peculiar warmth and diffusion; we may suppose that it is a weakened survival of the emotion of relief, of fear unfulfilled. To an animal so defenseless as was primitive man, the strange must always have been cause for anxiety; "fear" is, by its etymology, the emotion of the "farer," of the traveller away from home. (Titchener, 1909, p. 408.)

Allport (1940) has declared, "Sheer familiarity seems to engender positive valuing (demand) on the part of an organism" (p. 544). Murphy (1947) discusses the relation in connection with the concept of canalization (pp. 163 ff.).

However, we must emphasize again that the influence of familiarity on sentiment is not a simple one, and that it may have diverse effects particularly in combination with other factors. Sometimes it has only a negligible effect, as is suggested by Jennings' (1943) statement about leadership and isolation: "The subject who is relatively more or relatively less expansive towards others will react to them more or less independently of the length of time he is in association with them as far as this population goes" (p. 52). Maslow (1937) also reported the general impression that ". . . in certain of the choice tests, familiarity made no difference at all . . . simply because the choices were of no importance at all for the subject" (p. 178).

Further, Murphy (1947) states ". . . the pull *away from* the familiar, the demand for novelty and adventure, whether rooted in curiosity or challenge or the need to expand and grow, must never be minimized" (p. 191). There even appears to be a general personality type, the xenophile, who tends to reject the familiar and maintain an over-all positive orientation towards the foreign.

Xenophilia is based on an unconscious but rigid in-group-out-group distinction; it involves stereotyped, negative imagery and hostile attitudes regarding in-groups, stereotyped positive imagery regarding out-groups (often where he has had no direct experience with that out-group). The underlying dynamics of the Authoritarian and Xenophile are probably very similar. (Perlmutter, 1954, p. 295. Cf. also Perlmutter, 1956.)

Thus, familiarity can also become a condition favorable to the development of dislike. Sometimes security relations enter. Because we are comfortable and secure with the familiar person for example, we may feel freer to let go in front of him than in front of a casual acquaintance. The familiar person may have less potency in our life space than an unfamiliar person, and because we think we know him, we are not inhibited by the presence of the unknown and potentially dangerous. In letting go, we may say things and think things that are clearly antagonistic. This is one sense in which familiarity breeds contempt. Another revolves around the effects of similarity of beliefs and attitudes in much the same way that was previously postulated in regard to interaction and proximity. With the appropriate word substitutions, the statement reads: With similar attitudes, familiarity may increase the degree of positive sentiment; with slight dissimilarity of attitude a mutual assimilation may be produced, and with it an increase in friendliness; with strong dissimilarities hostility tends to increase.

*p* TENDS TO DISLIKE AN UNFAMILIAR *o*. Xenophobia, which has been mentioned in connection with similarity, is also relevant here. The negative effects of unfamiliarity may be assumed to occur as a result of at least two factors. First, an unfamiliar situation is full of possibilities that may be sufficiently threatening to an insecure person to turn him against it. An unfamiliar situation is cognitively unstructured; that is, the sequence of steps necessary to reach an objective is not clearly known. On the basis of the consequences of cognitive unclarity, the unstable behavior and the conflicts of such groups as the following have been explained: adolescents (Lewin, 1939), minority groups (Lewin, 1935a), autocratic groups (Lippitt, 1940), young children in unfamiliar surroundings (Arsenian, 1943), and persons with disabilities (Barker, *et al.*, 1953).

In addition, there is a second factor which has little to do with insecurity or danger. It is a more purely intellectual and aesthetic component of the resistance to the unfamiliar. The strange is experienced as not fitting the structure of the matrix of the life space, as not fitting one's expectations. The adaptation or change in expectations which is required by meeting the unfamiliar demands energy. It is more comfortable to wear old clothes and to talk with old friends.

*p* LIKES *o* INDUCES *o* FAMILIAR TO *p*, OR *p*'S LIKING FOR *o* BRINGS ABOUT GREATER FAMILIARITY WITH *o*. When we meet a person for the first time whom we like very much, we wish to become more familiar with him and to find out all about him; we wish to get cognitively close to him just as we wish to get spatially and interactionally close. Also, we may often have the feeling, "I have known this person for a long time," which is an illusion of familiarity.

*Ownership.* Here we shall mainly refer to the attitudes of *p* toward an impersonal entity *x*, instead of toward another person *o*, because ownership commonly involves a person-object relation. As the following quotation shows, ownership can also be felt in entities which are not physical things:

> Harold and Paul felt a keen sense of property in the nursery rhymes and songs they had heard at home, or in gramophone records of a kind they had there. No one else had the right to sing or hear these things without their permission. All the children felt that anything was "theirs" if they had used it first, or had made it, even with material that itself belonged to all. Duncan and others felt a thing was "theirs" if they had "thought" of it, or "mentioned it first," and so on. (One is reminded of controversies among scientific men as to the parentage of ideas, discoveries or inventions.) (Isaacs, 1933, p. 222.)

Two of the cases of balance which have been reviewed in connection with each of the preceding unit-forming factors will now be briefly considered in order to demonstrate the relation between sentiments and ownership.

*p* OWNS *x* INDUCES *p* LIKES *x*, OR *p* TENDS TO LIKE SOMETHING HE OWNS. Irwin and Gebhard (1946) concluded from their experiments with children that a clear majority of them "expressed a preference for an object which was to be given to them as compared with an object which was to be given to another child" (p. 650), and, "the results may illustrate some general principle whereby ownership enhances the value of an object to the owner" (p. 651). Ownership might be considered "one form of nearness" (p. 651).

Again it is worthwhile to ponder exceptions. The suitor may find his sweetheart utterly alluring until the moment she agrees to marry him. We may like a painting on the wall of a showroom but become very much disappointed as soon as we purchase it. Persons who cannot bear success and thus either destroy what they achieve or prevent its occurrence have been described in psychoanalytic literature.

$p$ LIKES $x$ INDUCES $p$ OWNS $x$, OR $p$ TENDS TO POSSESS SOMETHING HE LIKES. That we often buy, take, request or work hard for something we fancy hardly needs documenting. The tendency to possess something that is wanted may be so powerful as to overcome restraining social rules; the person then unlawfully acquires what he likes.

In our consideration of cases of balanced states thus far, we first dealt with a single entity where the balance referred to the state of homogeneously perceived parts, or, as applied to sentiments, to the tendency for an over-all liking or disliking of another person. The next steps included a variety of cognitive unit relations between the person and another entity and it was shown that these relations and the sentiment relation tend toward a balanced state. We shall now consider cases in which there are not one, but two external entities with whom the person has commerce, namely $o$, another person, and $x$, an impersonal entity. In this triad consisting of $p$, $o$ and $x$, we shall again see the tendency for cognitive and sentiment relations to achieve a state of balance. Only a few of the possible cases are considered.

**Similarity of beliefs and goals.** Just as a person and his deeds or possessions "belong" together, so do a person and his beliefs. With two persons, there are thus two unit relations involving $x$ ($p$ believes $x$, and $o$ believes $x$) and the question is how the third relation, the sentiment of $p$ towards $o$, is articulated within the $p$-$o$-$x$ triad. We find again a mutual dependence between the sentiment and the unit relations: we tend to like people who have the same beliefs and attitudes we have, and when we like people, we want them to have the same attitudes we have.

Beliefs and attitudes imply a reference to the objective environment. This reference plays an important role in the fact that commonality of beliefs leads to a harmonious situation. If we believe a proposition to be true, it cannot at the same time be untrue. The fact of representation (that is, the way a situation is pictured by the person) brings with it a new meaning of similarity: if two representations of the identical situation are different, they clash—provided one does not have the excuse that they refer to partial aspects of the situation or to different points of view. The disharmony occurs not only if two representations belong to different persons, but also if the two representations belong to the same person: if they are different then one or both must be wrong; or they are understood as referring to partial aspects of the situation in question. The power of similarity of beliefs or attitudes derives from the identity of the environment to which they refer, and from the fact that it is satisfying to find support for one's own view. (Cf. Asch, 1952, pp. 129 ff.)

Newcomb (1953) has stressed the advantages of what he has called co-orientation between two people, or the symmetry of their points of view toward $x$: it leads to a ready calculability of the other person's behavior and it performs the important function of validation which increases one's confidence in one's own cognitive and evaluative orientations (p. 395). These advantages form the basis for Newcomb's assumption that a persistent "strain toward symmetry" exists which underlies communicative acts.

In addition to these advantages Precker points out that similarity of attitudes operates according to definite mechanisms:

> Similarity of values allows for increased interaction, . . . allows for similarity of action . . . allows for a mutual language. . . . Similarity of values also operates in line with the defenses of the self—if values are rejected, then the self is rejected. In manifesting similar values, the leader is not only saying that "What is the Good (the True and the Beautiful) for you is also the Good for me," but also, "You are 'good' for professing (or moving towards) that which obviously is the Good, the True, the Beautiful." (Precker, 1952, p. 412.)

$p$ TENDS TO LIKE A PERSON WITH WHOM HE HAS BELIEFS AND ATTITUDES IN COMMON. Many experiments demonstrating this type of balanced state are reported by Riecken and Homans ( 1954. Cf. also Newcomb, 1953a, and Smith, 1957).

At this point it may be well to remind the reader that in our frame of reference, the conditions refer to the phenomenal world of $p$'s life space. As applied to the above experiments, this means that the objectively obtained similarity in beliefs of friends and wished-for associates was actually felt by $p$. Moreover, in regard to causal direction, we have assumed that the factor of shared beliefs favored the formation of friendships among particular subjects. At the same time, it is probable that the friendship itself contributed to the concurrence of opinion.

Closely related to the factor of similarity of beliefs affecting sentiments is the factor of similarity of goals. There are, of course, many instances in which the similarity of the goals of two people induces a mutual liking, but first we shall consider examples in which this does not occur. In situations of competition, jealousy, or envy, the fact that two people have apparently identical goals often leads to antagonism.

Paul may hate Peter, because he conceives that Peter possesses something which he (Paul) also loves; from this it seems at first sight, to follow, that these two men through both loving the same thing, and, consequently, through agreement of their respective natures, stand in one another's way. . . . (Spinoza, 1677, trans. 1936, p. 212.)

In essence, Spinoza resolves this difficulty by pointing out that the goals of Peter and Paul are, in fact, not identical; Peter wants Peter to have $x$, and Paul wants Paul to have it. In other words, the object is not considered positive in itself; only the possession of the object is positive. If Peter and Paul loved the same object in the sense of admiring its aesthetic qualities—then liking the same object would imply an agreement in attitude and might well lead to friendliness between them. Spinoza concludes his argument by saying:

We can easily show in like manner, that all other causes of hatred depend solely on differences, and not on the agreement between men's natures. (pp. 212–213.)

The effect of the relation between their goals on mutual sentiments of people toward each other has also been treated by Deutsch (1949). He distinguishes two kinds of goal relationships. If the goals are "promotively interdependent," then one person of a group can attain his goal only if all others attain their goals; if they are "contriently interdependent," then one person can attain his goal only if none of the others attain theirs. Cooperative situations are characterized by promotively, competitive situations by contriently interdependent goals. Deutsch states the hypothesis that there will be more friendliness among individuals in a cooperative situation than in a competitive situation. First he makes the assumption that the actions of the fellow members in a cooperative situation will be positively cathected because ". . . an entity will acquire positive valence or cathexis (become attractive) if that entity is seen to be promotively related to need satisfaction" (p. 138). Then, ". . . we would also expect the perceived source of these actions to acquire, to some extent, a cathexis similar to that held with respect to the sections" (p. 146). With contriently interrelated goals, there should be less friendliness among the individuals. Aristotle said:

And we like those who resemble us and have the same tastes, provided their interests do not clash with ours and that they do not gain their living in the same way; for then it becomes a case of "potter (being jealous) of potter." (Aristotle, trans. 1939, p. 197.)

*p* TENDS TO THINK THAT A LIKED *O* HAS THE SAME BELIEFS HE HIMSELF HOLDS. We have already seen that when *p* likes *o*, he tends to feel that he resembles *o*. Here we shall refer to experiments which more specifically concern similarity of beliefs or judgments. One by Horowitz, Lyons, and Perlmutter (1951), was designed to test a number of derivations from the theory concerning the relation between sentiments and cognitive units. They utilized a natural discussion situation to study the relation between liking among the participants and the degree of agreement that they felt between their views. Each subject first ranked the members of the group in terms of liking from best to least. This was followed by an hour and a half of free discussion. The subjects then listed the names of group members who they thought would or would not support each of three rather controversial statements made during the course of the session and indicated their own reaction to the statements. The main result in terms of the present context is that the subject was more apt to infer a similarity of opinion between another person and himself when he liked that person than when he disliked him.

Similar findings were obtained by Newcomb, who conducted an experiment in which subjects rated several issues in terms of importance (e.g., "civilian vs. military determination of international policy"), giving both own judgment and judgments attributed to various reference groups.

In highly significant proportions, the "issues" rated most important by subjects themselves were also those judged most important to attractive groups, such as closest friends, or "liberals" for subjects who described themselves as liberals. In lesser but still significant proportions the issues judged least important by subjects themselves were judged more important to unattractive groups, like "uninformed people" or "liberals" for subjects . . . in favor of the alternative "conservative." (Newcomb, 1953b, p. 154.)

Newcomb (1953b), employing the letters, *A*, *B* and *X*, for our *p*, *o* and *x*, presents the hypothesis that "the more *A* cares about *B* and about *X* the more strongly he is motivated to perceive similarity of his own and *B*'s orientations toward *X*" (p. 153). As support for this hypothesis he points to the findings of several experiments.

Many of the experiments on prestige suggestion are also directly relevant. Prestige is associated with such positive sentiments as admiration and respect. The research bears out the common experience that *p*'s opinions readily fall into line with *o*'s when *o* is a person of prestige. To be sure, as Asch (1948) has so ably demonstrated, this effect need not be a mechanical and irrational one; *p*'s opinions may change because he sees things in a new light. The sentiment relation, however, guides the cognitive processes toward bringing about a concurrence of opinion.

**Benefit and sentiments.** Formalistically, "*p* benefits *o*" can also be considered as belonging to a *p-o-x* triad. One might say that *p* benefits *o* is an example of *p* causes something *o* likes; since causing may be regarded as a factor producing a cognitive unit (Heider, 1944), we can say that a unit relation exists between *p* and *x*, and a sentiment relation exists between *o* and *x*. The third relation, namely the sentiment of *p* toward *o*, enters into the triad in such a way that the total situation achieves a state of harmony. This will be demonstrated in the following brief references to a few balanced cases.

*p* BENEFITS *o* INDUCES *p* LIKES *o*, OR *p* TENDS TO LIKE A PERSON HE HAS BENEFITED. This effect is sometimes mentioned in the literature, though the converse, which also represents a balanced case, is probably noted more often, namely, that people tend to dislike persons they have harmed.

*p* LIKES *o* INDUCES *p* BENEFITS *o*, OR *p* TENDS TO BENEFIT A LIKED *o*. Murray and Morgan (1945) designate a promotive vector, i.e., a tendency to promote the welfare of the other person, as one manifestation of a positive sentiment (p. 13).

This case of balance is so obvious that it is taken for granted. When it does not occur, other factors are seen as accounting for the exception to the rule. B. Wright (1942) experimented with children in a situation in which they could keep a preferred toy or give it to another child, either a stranger or a best friend. The results showed that eight-year-old children more often decided to give the toy to the stranger than to the friend. In other words, the special liking for the friend did not induce the subject to benefit him. This seemingly paradoxical result was explained by the assumption that the children acted according to their ideas of what one *ought* to do in such a case. One ought to be especially nice to strangers since one is in the position of host.

*o* BENEFITS *p* INDUCES *p* LIKES *o*, OR *p* TENDS TO LIKE A PERSON WHO BENEFITS HIM. A benefit caused by another person has often been considered the most important condition of a positive sentiment. Spinoza (trans. 1936) defines love as "pleasure accompanied by the idea of an external cause" (p. 140).

The fact that, if *o* benefits *p*, *p* will like *o*, could be conceived as a simple spreading of the positive character of the benefit to the cause of the benefit; *o* becomes positive because he is connected by a causal unit with the positive benefit. We then have an instance of the tendency towards homogenity in the perception of the parts of a whole. Or, the fact that *o* benefits *p* could mean to *p* that *o* likes him. Then the resulting positive sentiment toward *o* is based on the tendency toward symmetry of the L relation: *p* likes people who like him (cf. p. 205). If that is the case, then the positive sentiment should not result if *p* sees the act as not based on a positive attitude but on ulterior motives. In Chapter 10, we shall return to the discussion of the reactions to being benefited.

*p* LIKES *o* INDUCES *o* BENEFITS *p*, OR *p* WILL TEND TO BELIEVE THAT THE LIKED *o* BENEFITS HIM. As always, of course, there are a number of conditions that determine the way in which we perceive the act of another person. But it is assumed that, other things being equal, *p* will prefer being benefited by a liked person to being benefited by a disliked person. Furthermore, the difference between being benefited and being harmed might be greater for *p* if the source is a liked or admired person, than if the benefit or harm comes from a neutral person. That is, beyond the direct positive or negative significance of *x*, the harmony or disharmony of the whole situation will play a role in *p*'s reaction. This, of course, is the implication of Caesar's "Et tu Brute." It was after he saw the man whom he loved among his adversaries that he gave up.

There are a great many other concrete cases involving *p*, *o* and *x* which could be added to show that the relations among the entities tend toward a state of balance. We could, for example, detail the different cases of balance that involve another person's actions, *p*'s evaluation of them, and his sentiments toward *o*. It is sufficient here to mention that if an action *x* by *o* fits in with *p*'s values, then *p* will tend to like *o*. There is then a balanced situation consisting of one unit relation and two sentiment relations: a unit relation between *o* and *x*, and the sentiments of *p* and o toward *x*. Riecken and Homans (1954) have summarized the results of a number of studies (pp. 788–794) by just such an hypothesis, namely, a person chooses or likes another person to the degree that the other's activities realize the chooser's norms and values.

Actually, the variety of cases that could be adduced is considerable, and we shall be more parsimonious in our efforts if we pause to consider the over-all formal affective logic of relations involving *p*, *o* and *x*. (Cf. Heider, 1946.)

## Affective Logic of the Relations Among p, o *and* x

**Types of relations.** Relations between *p*, *o* and *x* are of two kinds. First, there is the *sentiment relation*. This refers to a person's evaluation of something, as when *p* likes or admires *o*, or *p* approves of *x*, or *p* rejects *o* or condemns *x*. L (like) and DL (dislike) are the generic symbols we shall use to refer to positive and negative sentiments. In addition, there is a *unit relation*. Persons and objects are the units that first come to mind; the parts of such units are perceived as belonging together in a specially close way. But also two (or more) separate entities can form a unit. The two entities may be related through similarity, causality, ownership or other unit-forming characteristics (cf. pp. 177–180). U denotes the cognitive unit between two entities, and notU the fact that the two entities are segregated.

For example, in the triad *p-o-x*, three specific relations are involved: (1) *p* to *o*, (2) *o* to *x* and (3) *p* to *x*. Each one of these relations has four possibilities: U, notU, L, DL. Depending on the situation, *p*, for example, may be in the same family with *o* (*p* U *o*), may feel different from *o* (*p* notU *o*), may like *o* (*p* L *o*), or may dislike him (*p* DL *o*). There are thus 64 combinations (4 × 4 × 4) of triadic relations. Only some of these represent balanced states.

**Assumption of balanced states.** By a balanced state is meant a situation in which the relations among the entities fit together harmoniously; there is no stress towards change. A basic assumption is that sentiment relations and unit relations tend toward a balanced state. This means that sentiments are not entirely independent of the perception of unit connections between entities and that the latter, in turn, are not entirely independent of sentiments. Sentiments and unit relations are mutually interdependent. It also means that if a balanced state does not exist, then forces toward this state will arise. If a change is not possible, the state of imbalance will produce tension.

**Sign character of the relations.** It will simplify the task of listing the harmonious combinations of relations in a *p-o-x* triad, or in a dyad between *p* and one other entity, if we make the assumption that the relations U and L can be treated as positive relations, and notU and DL as negative relations.

Cartwright and Harary (1956) have called attention to some difficulties connected with the notU relation. These authors have developed a generalization of the theory of balanced states utilizing concepts from the theory of linear graphs. This permits treating problems of balance in statistical terms and extending the theory to configurations other than those of sentiment and unit relations as they pertain to an individual. In regard to the sign character of a relation they point out that one has to distinguish between the complement of a relation and its opposite. The opposite of liking is disliking, while its complement is absence of liking, which can be disliking or a neutral attitude. "Not liking" is somewhat ambiguous: it can mean the opposite or the complement of liking. They say that

In general, it appears that ~*L* has been taken to mean "dislike" (the opposite relation) while ~*U* has been used to indicate "not associated with" (the complementary relation). (Cartwright and Harary, 1956, p. 280.)

They refer to Jordan who states:

Specifically, "$+L$" symbolizes a positive attitude, "$-L$" symbolizes a negative attitude, "$+U$" symbolizes the existence of unit formation, and "$-U$" symbolizes the lack of unit formation. (Jordan, 1953, p. 274.)

The question arises whether one can talk of a negative U relation, that is, a relation which is the opposite and not merely the absence of a unit relation. One might suggest that this can be done in cases of clear segregation or disjoining of the entities in question. Contrast, for example, the following situations: (1) $p$ is unfamiliar with $o$ who is seated next to him in the bus, and (2) $p$ is unfamiliar with $o$ whose ways and dress seem strangely different. In the first case, there is an absence of unit formation, the sign character of the relation being neutral rather than negative or positive—somewhat akin to that of indifference in the sentiment dimension. In the second case the relation may be thought of as a disunion; $p$ and $o$ are to some extent separated into two camps.

There may even be resistance to forming a unit and the outcome of such efforts may be rather unstable, as when $p$, though feeling different from $o$, tries to relate to him in some way, and then gives up. To attach the negative sign to such a relation seems phenomenologically appropriate. Unfortunately, we do not have very good criteria, other than the vague notion of resistance to unit formation or the qualitative feel of a situation, for determining whether mere absence or real disjunction characterizes the relation. For this reason notU as a first approximation is in general treated as a negative relation, though the balance situations dealt with here more strictly apply to disjunctive notU relations rather than to those representing mere absence of unit formation.

A more exact analysis of balance would have to take into account the difference between the complement and the opposite of the U relation, and also the related difference between a balance in which all relations fit together and one which consists only in the absence of not fitting relations. Cartwright and Harary (1956) call the latter "vacuously balanced" (p. 291).

**Conditions of balance.** DYADS. A dyad is balanced if the relations between the two entities are all positive (L and U) or all negative (DL and notU). Disharmony results when relations of different sign character exist.

TRIADS. A triad is balanced when all three of the relations are positive or when two of the relations are negative and one is positive. Imbalance occurs when two of the relations are positive and one is negative. The case of three negative relations is somewhat ambiguous and will be discussed later.

The conditions of balance are presented as hypotheses that can be tested either in the laboratory or in everyday life. They may also be regarded as propositions that can be derived from the general postulate that a unit is balanced if its parts are of like sign, that is, all positive or all negative. Notice that this postulate does not refer to relations among entities but rather to parts of a unit.

We shall now offer examples to illustrate the conditions of balance. This will be followed by discussion of preference for balance, induction of relations, and the direction of change in the event of imbalance.

### Examples.

1. $p$ feels neighborly to $o$    $(p \, L \, o)$   is a positive relation
   $o$ reminds $p$ of an acquaintance    $(o \, U \, x)$   is a positive relation*
   $p$ is fond of the acquaintance    $(p \, L \, x)$   is a positive relation
   Conclusion: The triad has three positive relations and is therefore balanced.

2. $p$ can't stand $o$    $(p \, DL \, o)$ is a negative relation
   $o$ made a record cabinet    $(o \, U \, x)$   is a positive relation
   $p$ thinks the record cabinet is
   made poorly    $(p \, DL \, x)$ is a negative relation
   Conclusion: The triad has two negative relations and one positive relation and is therefore balanced.

3. $p$ worships $o$    $(p \, L \, o)$   is a positive relation
   $o$ told a lie    $(o \, U \, x)$   is a positive relation
   $p$ disapproves of lying    $(p \, DL \, x)$ is a negative relation
   Conclusion: The triad has two positive relations and one negative relation and is therefore unbalanced.

4. $p$ is very fond of $o$    $(p \, L \, o)$   is a positive relation
   He admires him also    $(p \, L \, o)$   is a positive relation
   Conclusion: The dyad has two positive relations and is therefore balanced.

5. $p$ is dissatisfied with the lecture    $(p \, DL \, x)$ is a negative relation
   $p$ delivered it    $(p \, U \, x)$   is a positive relation
   Conclusion: The dyad has one positive and one negative relation and is therefore unbalanced.

6. John dislikes Mary who resembles his beloved sister.
7. John enjoys listening to his friend play the piano.
8. John doesn't like the way his teammate handles the bat.

---

* In this case $x$ stands for the acquaintance, a personal entity. If one wishes, the letter $q$ may be substituted for a personal $x$.

9. John hurts his favorite teacher.
10. John agrees with his assistant as to how to handle the sanitation problem.
11. John approves of the motion of his political opponent.
12. Mary loves to fondle her baby.
13. John buys the painting he thinks isn't any good.

(Examples 6, 8, 9, 11, and 13 are unbalanced situations; examples 7, 10, and 12 are balanced.)

**Preference for balanced states.** An analysis of the phenomenal properties of balance and imbalance as well as the experimental evidence relating to them supports the generalization that states of balance tend to be preferred over disharmony. This is also confirmed by the findings of an experiment by Jordan (1953), who set out to test certain of the implications of the balance theory. The subjects were asked to indicate the degree of preference for different triadic situations. The situations were presented in a rather abstract form, for example "I like O; I like X; O has no bond or relationship with X"; or "I dislike O; I have a sort of bond or relationship with X; O likes X." Thus, in each case the sentiment and the unit relations were indicated. The experimental design made it possible to give to one subject not more than 8 of the total number of 64 situations to judge. Each situation was rated 36 times. The number of subjects was 208. The results showed a statistically significant tendency for harmonious situations to be rated higher than unbalanced ones. Jordan also found that positive relations between a person and another person or impersonal entity were considered more pleasant than negative relations. Cartwright and Harary (1956) show that Jordan's results become even more consistent when one counts the "notU" relation ("$p$ has no sort of bond or relationship with $o$") as absence of any relation rather than as a negative relation. The average unpleasantness score of balanced situations is then 39, of not balanced situations 66, and the score of situations containing at least one notU relation, which they call "vacuously balanced," is 51. Kogan and Tagiuri (1957) reported on another test of the balance hypothesis in which they used as subjects members of groups of naval enlisted personnel. The S's were asked to indicate three members with whom they would most like to go on liberty, and to identify which three men each of the other members would choose to go on liberty with. In one group they also asked for the three persons the S's would least like to go on liberty with. Thus, only affective relations (like-dislike) were taken into account. Eight basic situations for the triads consisting of perceiver, other person, and third person result. Four of them are balanced, containing three positive relations, or one positive and two negative. Four are unbalanced, with three negative or one negative and two positive relations. Their basic hypothesis was that balanced situations should occur in the perceptions of the S's more frequently than chance would allow for, and also more frequently than the actual situation would warrant. That is, they assumed, for instance, if $p$ likes two other people he will think they like each other, though actually they dislike each other. The results confirm this assumption:

> Balanced cognitive units occur significantly in excess of chance and actuality baselines. Imbalanced cognitive units, on the other hand, appear significantly less often than would be expected by chance, though it should be noted that actual social units of this kind are also very rare. (Kogan and Tagiuri, 1957.)

***Induction of relations and equifinality.*** Induction will first be illustrated by an example. Suppose that $p$ likes two people, $o$ and $q$. He may then wish to bring them together. In this case, two existing relations $(p\ L\ o)$ and $(p\ L\ q)$, induce the tendency toward a third new relation $(o\ U\ q)$, which is in balance with the two given ones.

Types of induction may be distinguished according to the nature of the relations involved. The simplest type involves a relation that tends to become symmetrical, that is, when $(a\ R\ b)$ induces $(b\ R\ a)$. U is a symmetrical relation since $(p\ U\ x)$ implies $(x\ U\ p)$. Both $p$ and $x$ belong to the same unit, though the specific factor responsible for the unit formation may not be symmetrical. Causality is a case in point. $(p$ causes $x)$ as such is not symmetrical since it does not imply that $(x$ causes $p)$. The same is true of ownership; $(p$ owns $x)$ does not imply that $(x$ owns $p)$. But, $(p$ causes $x)$ and $(p$ owns $x)$ are symmetrical as far as the unit relation is concerned. In other words, $p$ belongs as much to $x$ as $x$ to $p$.

L is not a symmetrical relation since $(p\ L\ o)$ does not necessarily imply $(o\ L\ p)$. However, it tends to become symmetrical; that is, a balanced state exists if both $(p\ L\ o)$ and $(o\ L\ p)$ are true. We want people we like to like us, and we tend to like people who like us—and the parallel is true for negative sentiments. Janet (1929) says that social phenomena have a double aspect; if we dislike people we almost always have the feeling that they also dislike us—he calls this the "*sentiment reciproque*" (p. 208). The tendency toward symmetry of the L relation may be derived if we assume that $p$ likes himself, for then, if $(p\ L\ o)$ and $(p\ L\ p)$, there are two positive relations given, and, as will be explained below, these conditions induce a third positive relation. In effect we have substituted $p$ for the $x$ in the *p-o-x* triad.

It is also possible for one relation to evoke another of a different type.

That is, a sentiment relation may induce a unit relation and vice versa. Thus, I want to like what I own, to dispose of what I dislike, etc. (cf. pp. 184–195). Induction of this sort may be said to be characterized by a tendency towards the evocation of corresponding relations. As in the preceding type of induction, it presupposes a positive self-attitude, for only then is the tendency to evoke corresponding relations consistent with the general postulate that harmony exists when entities of equal sign value are united. In other words, for ($p$ L $x$) to induce ($p$ U $x$) both $p$ and $x$ must be positive; for ($p$ DL $x$) to induce ($p$ notU $x$), $p$ must be positive since $x$ is negative.

In triadic situations, the new relation may be brought about by a tendency toward transitivity of the relations. A relation is said to be transitive if ($a$ R $b$) and ($b$ R $c$) imply ($a$ R $c$). An example frequently used is the relation "greater than." If $a$ is greater than $b$, and $b$ is greater than $c$, then $a$ is greater than $c$. In the $p$-$o$-$x$ triad, the case of three positive relations may be considered psychologically (though not necessarily logically) transitive. For example, though ($p$ L $o$) and ($o$ L $x$) do not logically imply ($p$ L $x$), there is a psychological tendency for this to occur. Generalizing, we can state that if two positive relations are given (either one being U or L) then there is a tendency for the third to be positive also (either U or L).

However, three negative relations cannot be considered transitive. If two negative relations are given, balance can be obtained *either* when the third relation is positive or when it is negative, though there appears to be a preference for the positive alternative. This is illustrated by Jordan's (1953) finding that positive relations between $p$ and $o$ or $p$ and $x$ are considered more pleasant than negative relations. Moreover, common negative attitudes toward $x$ may readily bring about a feeling of similarity between $p$ and $o$. The resulting unit ($p$ similar to $o$) is in itself a positive relation, and as we have seen tends to induce a second positive relation, ($p$ L $o$).

With respect to the case in which one positive and one negative relation is given, e.g., ($p$ DL $o$) and ($o$ U $x$), there is a tendency for the third to be negative, for only in this way can balance be obtained. Thus, $p$ tends to dislike something his adversary made or owns. Or, should $p$ like $o$, he would tend to share $o$'s negative feelings about $x$.

The specific character of the new relation, regardless of the type of induction, depends not only on the tendency toward balance of the existing relations, but also on the possibilities in the total situation. For example, when $p$ likes $o$, the tendency towards $p$ U $o$ may take different forms depending on the circumstances: $p$ may try to meet $o$, but if $o$ lives far away, $p$ may be content to correspond with $o$ or to think about him occasionally.

This consideration of types of induction points up one important fact, namely, the system tends toward a balanced state no matter what condition it starts from. In other words, there exists a kind of equifinality, an end state with certain properties; in this case the end state is a balanced system whose relations are mutually dependent. Formulation in terms of equifinality is more parsimonious than formulation in terms of single conditions and effects. Certainly, one could also say that, in some cases, the sentiment of $p$ toward $o$ influences the attitude of $p$ toward $x$, in other cases the attitude of $p$ toward $x$ influences $p$'s sentiment toward $o$, etc. However, we would only obtain a great number of relations and their connection to each other would remain unclear.

The preceding discussion deals with the incomplete dyads and triads —one relation is given and the necessary second is induced or two relations are given and the necessary third is induced. The new induced relation was seen to be in harmony with the existing ones. We shall now turn to a consideration of the problem in which the existing dyadic and triadic relations are themselves out of balance.

**States of imbalance and the stress to change.** The assumption that sentiment and unit relations tend toward a balanced state also implies that where balance does not exist, the situation will tend to change in the direction of balance. An example was given on pp. 176–177 where the concept of balanced states was first introduced. Now we shall generalize the example to show more systematically the types of change compatible with balance.

Let us suppose $p$ likes $o$, and $p$ perceives or hears that $o$ has done something, which we call $x$; $x$ may be something $p$ likes and admires, that is which is positive for $p$, or $x$ may be something which is negative for $p$. If $p$ likes $o$ and $o$ does something positive, this situation is pleasant for $p$; it is fitting and harmonious. As a triad the situation presents a balanced case characterized by three positive relations: $(p \text{ L } o)$, $(p \text{ L } x)$, $(o \text{ U } x)$. However, if the liked $o$ does something that is negative, imbalance results: the triad contains two positive relations $(o \text{ U } x)$, $(p \text{ L } o)$ and one negative relation $(p \text{ DL } x)$. This is an unpleasant situation for $p$. Tension will arise and forces will appear to annul the tension (Fig. 1a).

The situation can be made harmonious either by a change in the sentiment relations or in the unit relations.

1. Change in sentiment relations.
   a. $p$ can begin to feel that $x$ is really not so bad, thereby producing a triad of three positive relations (Fig. 1b).
   b. $p$ can admit that $o$ is not quite as good as he thought he was. A

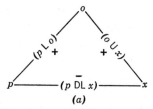

(a)

The given situation is unbalanced:
two positive relations and one
negative relation.

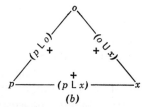

(b)

Change in sentiment relation
resulting in a balance of
three positive relations.

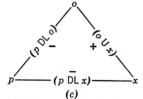

(c)

Change in sentiment relation
resulting in a balance of two
negative relations and one
positive relation.

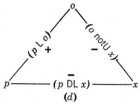

(d)

Change in unit relation resulting in
a balance of two negative relations
and one positive relation.

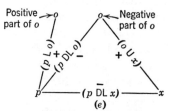

(e)

Change in unit relation through
differentiation resulting in a
balance of two negative relations
and one positive relation.

**Figure 1.** *Change toward balance within existing unbalanced sentiment
and unit relations.*

balanced triad of two negative relations and one positive relation
is thus established (Fig. 1c).

2. Change in unit relations.

   *a.* $p$ can begin to feel that $o$ is not really responsible for $x$. In this
way $x$ cannot be attributed to $o$ and the unit between $o$ and $x$ is
destroyed. We again have two negative relations and one positive
relation (Fig. 1d).

*b.* $p$ can resolve the situation by gaining a more differentiated picture of $o$. He says in effect, that $o$, like everyone, has good points and bad points; I still like him because of his good points, though I dislike part of his personality; $o$ has been differentiated in such a way that the unit with the negative $x$ now consists of just the negative part of $o$. A unit of two negative entities is thereby established and the triad in question revolves around two negative relations ($p$ DL $o$) ($p$ DL $x$) and one positive relation ($o$ U $x$). Of course, the $o$ in this triad refers to that part of him which is negative. Since the total $o$ must then consist of a positive part and a negative part, to this extent imbalance still exists (Fig. 1$e$).

As an example, we may quote from Hovland, Janis, and Kelley, who discuss the case in which $p$ is confronted with the fact that an admired $o$ expresses an attitude with which $p$ disagrees. In such a case, people

. . . are likely to deny that the source actually was responsible for the communication or to reinterpret the "real" meaning they believe the message to have. For example, if the message given by a highly respected source is repugnant to the audience's values, the source may be thought to be someone else capable of originating such ideas, or the message will be interpreted so as to be congruent with the actual respected source. (Hovland, Janis, and Kelley, 1953, p. 43.)

The authors also mention the possibility that

. . . where the assertion is repulsive to the audience and the source is only mildly respected, there is a tendency to change one's attitude toward the communicator in the direction of attributing less credibility to him or otherwise becoming more negative toward him. (p. 45.)

An example of an imbalanced situation producing tension is given by an experiment by Festinger and Hutte, who found that

. . . if persons in a group feel that those members of the group whom they like best dislike each other, this tends to make them uncertain and unstable about their interpersonal relations in the group. (Festinger and Hutte, 1954, p. 522.)

The experiment was performed in Holland and the United States, and the results for the two countries were very similar, which supports the view that these relations between sentiments and cognitive structure are independent of cultural differences.

The statement that unbalanced situations may be transformed into balanced ones by appropriate changes in the sentiment or unit relations also, of course, applies to dyads. Thus, if I dislike what I own, I may either begin to like it (change in sentiment) or sell it (change in unit relation).

*Exceptions and the Validity of the Hypothesis*

We have taken as a working hypothesis the assumption that there is a tendency toward balanced states in human relationships. This hypothesis provides us with a way of ordering, comparing, and examining data. It presents a language in terms of which we can capture a wide variety of phenomena which gain new meaning when they are described in these terms. At the same time we have seen that there are many cases which, at least if taken at their face value, do not fit the hypothesis. This in itself, however, is no ground for discarding the hypothesis. There can be many reasons for these discrepancies.

First of all, it is possible that the exceptions are the result of additional factors which have nothing to do with the hypothesis. The fact that birds fly does not prove that they are not attracted by the earth. The hypothesis regarding the relation between unit formation and sentiments states only that there is a tendency, or a force, toward the balanced situation; it does not state that in every case the defined balanced situation will actually be realized.

A second possibility in accounting for the discrepancies is that the hypothesis itself may allow for some factors which have not been considered in the formulations given so far; for example, attitude toward the self, contrast formation, determination of the unit-forming factor, its sign character, and unit implications.

Most of the examples discussed in this chapter presuppose a positive attitude toward the self. As we have seen, only then can one derive the harmonious case $(p \text{ L } x)$, $(p \text{ U } x)$—$p$ is united with positive entities —from the general proposition that harmony exists when entities with equal value are united. And only then can symmetry of the L relation be derived. However, the possibility of a negative attitude toward the self $(p \text{ DL } p)$ must also be considered. One would expect it to play a role contrary to that of $(p \text{ L } p)$. If $p$ dislikes himself he might reject a positive $x$ as too good for him; a negative $p$ and a positive $x$ do not make a good unit. Or, the minus character of $p$ may spread to the $x$ he has made; e.g., if his friend admires his work, he will think that the friend does so because of politeness. The tendency toward symmetry of the L relation would also be disrupted; if $p$ dislikes himself, he might easily think that $o$ dislikes him too, especially if he likes $o$. The conditions given are: $(p \text{ DL } p)$ $(p \text{ L } o)$, or one negative and one positive relation. According to the conditions of balance, such a combination tends to induce a third relation which is negative, in this case $(o \text{ DL } p)$.

The second point concerns contrast formation. So far we have considered only assimilation, that is, a harmony characterized as a whole with equal parts. But there may also exist a tendency toward "sharpening" or contrast, i.e., a tendency toward making differences between the parts of a unit as great as possible. It has been assumed, and with good support from experimental findings, that "Assimilation appears when the differences between the substructures [of a unit] are small; contrast appears when the differences are large" (Krech and Crutchfield, 1948, p. 95). Such a principle would again introduce many variations in the balance tendencies of concrete situations.

In other cases, ambiguity may arise in connection with the determination of the unit-forming factor. We have already spoken of the possibility that apparent or surface dissimilarity may in some instances be compatible with a more underlying similarity, as when the dissimilarity supports a common purpose. Thus, the precise but less inspired scientist may work harmoniously with the creative scientist in a common search for truth. The sentiment which is then induced is coordinated to the similarity of purpose rather than to the dissimilarity of temperament. Likewise, apparent similarities may be only the phenotypic expression of more basic dissimilarities.

As has been pointed out above, the sign character of the unit relation is ambiguous in some cases. Results that deviate from the balance hypothesis may be due to the fact that the situation is characterized by an absence of unit formation rather than a clear disjunction of the entities.

The state of balance may also be influenced by what we have called implications between unit relations. Sometimes the existence of a particular unit relation in a situation precludes the occurrence of a second unit relation which may be induced by the tendency toward balance, the end result being one of conflict rather than harmony. An example of ownership will help clarify this point. Let us assume $o$ owns something that $p$ likes. According to the rules of balance, these positive relations, namely, $(o \cup x)$, $(p \, L \, x)$ should foster a liking on the part of $p$ for $o$ $(p \, L \, o)$. However, often the reverse occurs. Instead of a positive relation toward $o$, $p$ may envy $o$ and in other ways feel at odds with him. This exception can be derived from the fact that ownership is ordinarily a one-many relation: "$o$ owns $x$" excludes "$p$ owns $x$," or $(o \cup x)$ implies $(p \, \text{notU} \, x)$. But, since $p \, L \, x$ may tend toward $(p \cup x)$, conflict is introduced.

In the same way, conflict appears if $p$ and $o$ want to avoid $x$ but only one of them can do so. A simple example is one in which a disagreeable task must be finished by either $p$ or $o$. Then $(o \, \text{notU} \, x)$ excludes $(p \, \text{notU} \, x)$ and vice versa.

Last, conflict results when $x$ is positive to $p$ and negative to $o$, or vice versa, but either both must have it or both not have it; that is, both $p$ and $o$ must move together. This is often the situation with a husband and wife. The unit relation $(p \text{ U } x)$ excludes that of $(o \text{ notU } x)$ and since the latter also tends to occur because of $o$'s sentiments toward $x$, conflict ensues.

In each of the above three cases, there was conflict because a certain unit relation prescribed by the conditions of balance for one person was excluded by the existence of a unit relation on the part of another person. The reader may recognize these examples of interpersonal conflict as analogous to Lewin's (1935b) three types of conflict situation, which involve one person and two valences (p. 123).

After all is said and done, however, there is always the likelihood that quite a different reason accounts for the instances that do not fit the balanced case; namely, the theory is not 100 per cent perfect. But that should not bother us too much, if, in spite of its shortcomings, the theory aids scientific work.

## Remarks on an Organismic Theory of Sentiments

In some ways the balance hypothesis as described above leaves one dissatisfied. For one thing, the effects of the different unit-forming factors are not sufficiently understood. We noted, for example, that the conditions that lead to the mere absence of unit formation in contrast to the definite segregation of entities have not yet been specified. Continued theorizing and experimental work may be expected to lead to the gradual elimination of such unclarities. More important, perhaps, is the fact that the positive or negative character of sentiments has been treated as a simple quality, like color. There is thus the danger that sentiments will be seen as automatic reactions to the unit organization of a situation without otherwise being related to significant processes within the person. To avoid this danger we shall attempt to show how the balance hypothesis may be integrated within a more inclusive organismic point of view.

Spinoza's theory about sentiments is admirably suited to this purpose, for it considers sentiments systematically and in detail, and takes into account a great number of interpersonal relations. The theory is to be found in the third book of the Ethics which deals with the origin and nature of emotions. We shall present Spinoza's approach in terms which are more familiar to the modern psychologist. In some cases, our formulation may not be exact, but our purpose here is not to be historically accurate; we want to obtain help in the solution of problems.

Spinoza (1677, trans. 1936) attempts to define love and hate in such a way that their manifestations and their functions within human behavior can be derived from their definition (pp. 140 ff.). According to him, the person has a tendency toward a state of greater perfection. When an increase in perfection occurs, the person feels pleasure; when there is a decrease, pain is experienced. One might object here that the path toward greater perfection and maturity, in requiring the eradication or least sublimation of egocentricities, is often unpleasant; conversely, simply satisfying all the present needs of the person does not lead to greater perfection. This objection can be taken care of within Spinoza's theory by the argument that, in order for the person to attain a more encompassing harmony, some part structures may have to be eliminated or suppressed. Since the mind "endeavors to persist in its being" (p. 136), this elimination is painful. Spinoza's theory in general implies that the organism functions in a more integrated and harmonious way when it is in a state of greater perfection.

In addition to this affective reaction to change in the state of perfection, a sentiment towards the cause of that change is aroused. If the person attributes the change to an external cause, such as an object or a person, he will also love that cause. Conversely, hate or dislike is aroused for something seen as a cause of impairment in the state of perfection.

It is interesting to note that Spinoza always refers to the person's perception of the loved object, that is, to how the person conceives the loved object, and only indirectly to the real object in the external world.

The mind, as far as possible, endeavors to conceive those things which increase or help the body's power of activity . . . in other words, . . . those things which he loves. But conception [representation] is helped by those things which postulate the existence of a thing, and contrarywise is hindered by those which exclude the existence of a thing . . . therefore the images of things, which postulate the existence of an object of love, help the mind's endeavor to conceive the object of love, in other words . . . affect the mind pleasurably. . . . (Spinoza, trans. 1936, p. 144.)

The balance hypothesis, it may be noted, also refers to representations within a person's life space and only indirectly to the objective reality which affects the representations.

The cases of balance derivable from the theory of balanced states may be seen to fit Spinoza's understanding of the role of sentiments in the struggle towards greater perfection. This is readily demonstrated in the case involving benefiting, namely "*p* likes *o*" induces "*p* benefits *o*." According to Spinoza, the person wants that factor which furthers his own perfection and happiness to be strong, integrated, and at the highest possible state of perfection. The more perfect it is the more will it be able to exert a positive influence on the person.

He who conceives that the object of his love is destroyed will feel pain; if he conceives that it is preserved he will feel pleasure. He who conceives that the object of his love is affected pleasurably or painfully, will himself be affected pleasurably or painfully. (Spinoza, trans. 1936, pp. 144–145.)

It should be mentioned again that the factor that furthers the person's own perfection refers in the immediate sense to the *representation* of the loved object. But since the powerful functioning of this representation depends on the functioning of the real object, the person wishes to promote the welfare of the real object. Spinoza's propositions XIX, XX, and XXI deal with the promotive vector. To be sure, Spinoza talks in terms of feelings and not in terms of actions. But promotive action can easily be derived from his formulation since the person acts to bring about his own pleasure.

In this connection, it is important to emphasize that the action which brings about one's own pleasure need not presuppose conscious and calculating means-end reasoning nor that the person is selfishly oriented. Rather, the relation between sentiments and greater perfection requires that the person benefit the object of his love, the source of his advancement. In short, it is man's nature, as an expression of his search for greater perfection, to find pleasure in the pleasure of a loved object.

Likewise, the balanced cases involving interaction and spatial proximity with a loved object may be made accountable in Spinoza's system by his proposition that since a person wants to attain a state of greater perfection he will want to interact with the agent who has this effect. "...he who loves necessarily endeavors to have, and to keep present to him, the object of his love. . . ." (p. 140). Conversely, a person will wish to stay away from someone he hates, since such a person undermines his state of perfection.

We can also understand that interaction with a similar thing might lead to greater "perfection," and to a positive sentiment. Koffka, in discussing the role similarity plays in the communication between a process and a trace, says:

. . . the particular trace was selected because communication with it would lead to an improved process. At the same time, as we have seen, the selected trace derived from a process similar to the one now occurring, so that similarity and stability have become connected in our theory. Similarity is one way by which greater stability can be reached. (Koffka, 1935, p. 600.)

Of course, Koffka refers here to similarity between brain structures and their integration. But he himself applies these considerations to social groups as well when he discusses similarity and social unit formation. In somewhat general and vague terms one might say that in many cases similar entities fit together better than dissimilar ones, they more easily form an integrated and stable whole, and they support each other. This is especially true when representation, the reference to the environment, enters the picture.

We have already referred to the fact that two representations can either belong to the same life space, that is, they can be images or ideas of the same person, or they can belong to two different persons. If two representations that belong to the same person are similar, they will interact harmoniously, they will be easily remembered together, they will form a perceptual unit, and so on. If the two representations refer to the same thing, then identity is almost required, and if there are differences we try to resolve them by attributing them to differences in the point of view, as we attribute the differences in the images we have of an object to differences in perspective. Also, when two representations of the same object are located in different persons, similarity is necessary for harmonious interaction. Of course, when person $A$ sees the same object as person $B$, the two representations do not form a unit in the same way as when $A$ sees the object at two different times. But when $A$ and $B$ discuss the object that both see, there will be interaction between the two representations, and the more similar they are the more harmonious will the interaction be. The same is true for beliefs and attitudes which refer to the objective environment.

The influence of the factor of familiarity can also be brought into this framework. Familiarity usually rests upon interaction. During the course of an interaction, as $p$ gets to know $o$, mutual adaptation may take place. This adaptation to environmental entities brings about harmonious interaction, they have "grown upon one another."

The place of the balance hypothesis within such an organismic theory as Spinoza's may be defined in yet another way, namely, by the familiar comparison between the organism and a flame, which as Köhler (1938) has said, "is more than a poetical metaphor" (p. 320). Spinoza's ideas may then be paraphrased in the following way: Each organism has the tendency to burn as brightly as possible. Part of the flame which represents $p$ are $p$'s conceptions or representations of things in the environment. If the representation of $o$ as part of this flame intensifies it, then $p$ likes $o$ and vice versa. Moreover, as part of the flame $p$, the representation of $o$ may itself be compared to a flame; the more intense it is the more intense will the flame $p$ be. But, the organism cannot remain a closed system content with its representations of things which are congenial to the flame, for then its outcome would be an "entropic death." Instead it needs environmental support for these representations. "The organism is not a closed system; it is part of a larger functional context..." (Köhler, 1938, p. 323; cf. also Bertalanffy, 1950).

Thus, the intensity of the part-flame depends on the state of the external object to which the representation refers. The more the real person flourishes, the more will that part of the flame corresponding to the representation of $o$ flourish, and thus the flame $p$. Through representation in $p$'s life space, the functioning of $p$ depends on the functioning of $o$. This is where unit relations enter. The flame within the flame $p$ can be nourished not only by promoting $o$, but also by combining it with other fitting structures, or also by a more intense interaction between $p$ and $o$. On the other hand, interaction might lead to the building up of such a part-process within $p$. In awareness, the fitting of the part-process into the larger flame $p$ is experienced as a positive sentiment. Sentiments and unit relations are thus interdependent and in their tendency toward balance serve the organism in its striving for greater perfection.

The general starting point of Spinoza's theory, namely, that the life processes in man have a direction which reaches out toward ever higher states of perfection, has much in common with certain modern viewpoints. We are reminded of Goldstein's (1947) ideas on self-actualization, the main supposition being that "...the organism has definite potentialities, and because it has them it has the need to actualize or realize them" (p. 146). In this way the urge to perfection is derived for "...an organism is governed by the tendency to actualize its individual capacities as fully as possible" (p. 141). To the extent that the balance hypothesis was shown to be consistent with Spinoza's views, it is also consistent with Goldstein's. Balance between sentiments and unit relations may be said to be in accord with the process of self-actualization, for

... various actions occur in accordance with the various capacities which belong to the nature of the organism, and in accordance with those instrumental processes which are the necessary prerequisites of the self-actualization of the organism. (Goldstein, 1947, p. 142.)

Angyal is another personality theorist who believes that the life processes of an organism have a general dynamic trend. For Angyal the trend is towards greater self-expansion and self-determination.

Life processes do not merely tend to preserve life but transcend the momentary status quo of the organism, expanding itself continuously and imposing its autonomous determination upon an ever increasing realm of events. (Angyal, 1941, p. 48.)

This is the "system principle" against which situations, objects, other persons, are evaluated by the subject. If they fit the system principle, then they will be experienced as positive.

To this list of personality theories which offer unifying principles of personality functioning could be added Lecky's (1945) views on self-consistency of personality organization, Stagner's (1951) use of the concept of homeostasis, and others. Our intention, however, is not to review such personality theories, but rather to show the place of the balance theory of sentiments within broader, holistic theories of personality. Whatever the merits of such an integration, it must be remembered that the balance theory, because of its specifications, can still be tested in the laboratory as well as in everyday life.

## Summary

In this chapter a hypothesis concerning the relations between unit formation and sentiments was proposed. Stated briefly, it assumes that a state of harmony or balance exists if entities which belong together are all positive, or if they are all negative. If two closely related entities are of different sign, a state of disharmony or tension results, which can be resolved in different ways. A number of unit-forming factors relevant for interpersonal relations, and the way the surrounding influences unit formation were discussed.

A main section of the chapter was devoted to the different specific instances of this interrelation between unit formation and sentiments, that is, the way in which different relations between entities interact with liking or disliking them. Thus, the relations of similarity, interaction, proximity, familiarity, and ownership were explored from this point of view.

A theoretical analysis of the hypothesis was attempted and the different possibilities of resolution of states of disharmony were considered. At the end we tried to place the hypothesis in a broader frame of organismic psychology.

# CHAPTER 8

# Ought and value

WE OFTEN HAVE THE FEELING that someone ought to get a reward or a punishment, that we or other people should do something, that someone does not deserve his bad or good luck, or that he has a right to act in a certain way. These oughts or obligations play a major role not only in the evaluation and determination of behavior and its consequences, but also in the fashioning of the content and the emotional quality of experience. Instances of this have been given before in regard to the psychological phenomena we have already reviewed. We saw, for example, how the attribution of pleasure and of can may be influenced by ought requirements. In a subsequent chapter we shall also see how an act of harm or of benefit may be instigated by considerations of justice and how the recipient may accept the harm if he feels that it is warranted, or accept the benefit without any feelings of gratitude if he believes it was "coming to him," and even reject a benefit purporting to express a relationship of liking if he interprets the benefit as being offered from a sense of duty.

We shall now try to discuss some of the basic properties of the concepts of ought and value.

## Properties of Ought

Wertheimer (1935) and Köhler (1938) use the concept of required-ness to describe a situation in which we feel that something "ought to happen." To exemplify this, Asch presents a number of situations in which the experience of should is produced. He points out that all of them

> . . . contain a gap or disjunction; the person was in need of help, or action was called for in a given case. The situation was in some sense incomplete; our apprehension of the facts and their relations, or of the need of the situation, laid a claim upon us to improve or to remedy it, to act in a manner fitting to it. Action that fits the requirements we judge to be appropriate or right; to fail to act appropriately we experience as violating a demand, or being unjust. (Asch, 1952, p. 357.)

Requiredness, according to this view, is rooted in the gap or incompleteness of the situation. Acting in accordance with this implicit injunction, acting in a manner that brings about the necessary closure, then becomes identified with the right.

Yet, it is not strictly correct to equate gap-induced requiredness with ought requiredness, for clearly there may be many occasions in which the person may experience the tension of an incompleteness in the situation, without at the same time experiencing the tension of an ought. For instance, the person may realize that he wants $x$, the situation being incomplete in the sense that his desire is unfulfilled, and yet that he ought not have it. Or, in interpersonal relations, the person may recognize that someone else wants $x$, but unlike the case in which $o$ needs help, filling in the gap by satisfying his wants does not necessarily coincide with what ought to be done.

As a first approach, the content of "I (or $o$) ought to do $x$" may be said to be fashioned after the idea "somebody wants or commands that I (or $o$) do $x$." In the case of ought, however, it is not a particular somebody that is felt to want or command people to do $x$, but some suprapersonal objective order. It may also be experienced as a supernatural being who personifies this objective order. In any case, when $p$ has the conviction that he ought to do $x$ he recognizes a vector in the environment, a vector which is like a wish or a demand or a requirement on the part of some suprapersonal order and which has the validity of objective existence. True enough, when $p$ has the conviction that $o$ wants him to do $x$, he also recognizes a vector in the environment; the desire of $o$ is also felt by $p$ as being objectively existent. But the desire has its source, or is located, in only a part of the environment, that is, that part which consists of person $o$.

First of all, oughts are impersonal. They refer to standards of what ought to be done or experienced, standards independent of the individual's wishes. This is not to say that personal wishes do not influence the perception of ought forces; it is rather that they "should not," that in principle the ought is established by objective requirements. What *p* or *o* wants is his personal affair—though of course someone else might feel with him—but what he ought to do has a significance beyond personal concerns. It is true that *p*'s wishes may be objective in the sense of being recognizable by others, but in contrast to the wishes of the objective order, one cannot say that they are impersonal. Asch says

> . . . we distinguish between personal preferences or aversions and right or wrong. It is one thing to desire an object and quite another to have the experience of should. (Asch, 1952, p. 355.)

Westermarck uses the term "disinterestedness" to refer to the impersonal nature of ought. He says that a moral judgment always has the character of disinterestedness and concludes that the judgment of an act should be the same whether *p* himself or whether an *o*, with whom *p* has no relation whatsoever, is affected by the act:

> If I pronounce an act . . . good or bad that implies that I assume the act to be so independently of the fact that the person concerned is my friend or my enemy. (Westermarck, 1932, p. 93.)

We shall soon see that a moral judgment may in fact be altered just because of the social relations involved, but as long as this is not due to personal wishes but rather to objective requirements which may be modified in light of these social relations, it may still legitimately retain its ought character.

Moreover, oughts are dispositional in character. They refer to invariant standards, to "laws of conduct" which hold in spite of many variations in incidental or momentary factors. When Wordsworth says:

> I feel the weight of chance desires;
> My hopes no more must change their name,
> I long for a repose that is ever the same.
> *(Ode to Duty)*

he contrasts the shifting personal desires with the invariancy of an objective ought. Spinoza makes the same point in his Ethics when he says,

> Men can differ in nature, in so far as they are assailed by these emotions, which are passions . . . and to this extent one and the same man is variable and inconstant. (Spinoza, 1677, trans. 1936, p. 211.)

And we want to be secure in an unchanging eternal "good" and "beautiful" no less than in an eternal "true."

The dispositional character of oughts, however, is far more complicated than a simple constancy which holds no matter what. There are limits to the invariance of oughts. The same ought holds among a variety of situations as long as the variation is felt to be incidental, or extrinsic as far as the ought requirements are concerned. But as we know, a particular aspect may be so crucial as to change the meaning of a situation in such a way that the ought judgment is altered. "Thou shalt not steal" for some people means "under any circumstances"; for others it holds only as a general guide; particular circumstances such as dire need may modify it. Even if killing is usually considered a crime, it is felt to be less reprehensible when it is done in self-defense. In the extreme case, it is even possible that an ought force applies to one person alone because of the special nature of his situation. A person may feel, for example, that he and no one else in the community ought to undertake the particular assignment. The ought in this case still represents a dispositional wish of the objective order insofar as it would theoretically apply to anyone else who happened to fulfill the appropriate conditions.

Sometimes a judgment of what ought to be changes with the situation because the interpretation of the act in question changes. This has been concretely demonstrated in an experiment by Albert (1956) in which subjects had to make moral judgments about actions in which the social relation between the agent and recipient of the action varied. It was shown that certain provocative acts, such as playing a practical joke, criticising, kidding, or disagreeing vocally, were considered to be less acceptable morally when directed against a stranger than a friend. In the former case the acts tended to be interpreted as harms with overtones of hostility or aggression, whereas in the latter case the act was not interpreted as real harm. The same general difference in interpretation and moral judgment depended on whether the social relationship involved disliking the recipient or liking him.

In substance, it can be said that oughts are invariant to the situation as long as differences among the situations do not alter what are perceived to be impersonal objective requirements. Ought constancy may be expected, therefore, to be less limited in children than in adults, the less mature individual being less differentiated with respect to cognitive issues which would affect the perception of objective requirements. Piaget (1932) has shown this to be the case. Young children, for instance, tend to feel that the person who inadvertently breaks something is just as guilty as the one who does so intentionally. Special circumstances are disregarded.

That the concept of ought refers to an invariance or constancy lying behind incidental aspects of the situation can also be seen with examples that are not necessarily linked with ethical or aesthetic values. One can say: "I ought to go to the dentist, but I don't want to." One has to choose between two disagreeable experiences: going to the dentist right away, or having greater trouble but relatively far in the future. If a person has no ought constancy, he will feel the present vector in its full size, while the one far away will be felt as being small. But if he weighs them against each other as they would appear with their objective weights regardless of distance, then there is no question that he "ought to" go to the dentist.

The constancy of ought has certain features in common with the constancies of size, shape and color, constancies well known in the psychology of perception (cf. pp. 28–31). In all cognitive pursuits, from simple perception to scientific activity, we tend to look for the enduring properties of objects and events, so we try to attain the invariant dynamic requirements of oughts. What a person ought to do holds in spite of wide variations of expediency and preference.

The objectivization of ought as an impersonal, dispositional concept also implies that ought has interpersonal validity. Not only should ought disregard personal desires, not only does ought in principle appear unchanged in spite of incidental situational factors, but it is also universal and should look alike to everybody. Just as when enjoyment is attributed to the object, one assumes that people in general will find the object enjoyable, attributing ought to an objective order requires that people in general should concur in its directives. One might say that ought arises out of a tendency to equalize the life spaces of different persons as well as the different moments of the same life space. If $p$ sees $x$ and $o$ sees $x$, the $x$ of $p$ and the $x$ of $o$ belong together even though they are seen in different ways. The two $x$'s form a unit and therefore cannot have contradictory properties. The establishment of cognitive and dynamic reality rests on a synthesis of these different aspects, a synthesis furthered by the intersubjective validity of ought.

All people, then, should perceive the same ought requirements in a particular situation. Whether or not they will obey them is another matter. If $p$ accepts the vector which is given by the objective order and acts accordingly, he feels that he is a "good" person. He may even expect praise. But if he violates the directives of this vector, he may expect punishment.

Thus we see that even in this first approximation, the meaning of ought, as with other meanings of life-space content, is not a mystical quality somehow attached to the word. It can be defined by investigating the functional role it plays in our thinking and our reactions. We have suggested that it can be represented as a cognized wish or requirement of a suprapersonal objective order which has an invariant reality, and whose validity therefore transcends the point of view of any one person.

## Other Concepts Related to Ought

A number of concepts have reference to the impersonal order of ought and will be briefly mentioned.

Since the objective order is very powerful, its wishes are often reacted to as commands; "duty commands." The duty of a person is what he "ought to do"; if he does not do his duty then he does not act according to the wish or command of the impersonal order. But duty does not encompass all the actions conforming to the impersonal order; it is merely a minimum. Somebody can act in a praiseworthy way "beyond the call of duty." Not doing this act does not mean disobeying an objective wish; desisting would not be an action against the objective order. But doing it is acting for the objective order, even beyond what it commands the person to do.

Very often our ideas about what we or other people deserve are of decisive importance for our actions. The statement "*o* deserves *x*" can be restated "*o* ought to have or experience *x*." It refers to the relation of imposed experiences, or heteronomous events, to the objective forces. When the *x* in question is positive, one also feels that "*p* has a right to *x*." Punishment may also be deserved, though then one doesn't speak of *p*'s rights. People often have definite feelings about whether what happens to them is just and fair or not. The recipient, especially, likes to think that any negative experience is unjust. Sometimes, of course, it may be. The tendency, however, to perceive misfortune as punishment, a tendency that is in conformity with the balance between reality and ought (cf. p. 235 below) may be so strong as to deny the recipient such comfort.

The concepts *may* and *may not* also have reference to the wishes of an impersonal order. If it is true that the objective order, through moral laws or other ought requirements, does not wish me to avoid doing *x*, then I may do it. The impersonal order permits me to do *x* but because it does not require me to do so, not even to a slight degree, the situation is not an "ought." Therefore the act receives neither commendation nor condemnation. It is neutral. With *may not*, however, the act in question is no longer neutral. The *may not* means that the objective order wishes me not to do *x* and thus becomes equivalent to ought not. If I commit the act anyway, the requirements of the objective order are defied, and I become subject to punishment.

## Ought and Value—Force Fields

We shall use the term value as meaning the property of an entity (*x* has values), or as meaning a class of entities (*x* is a value) with the connotation of being objectively positive in some way. The attribution of value to the object, then, has the same consequences as the attribution of other phenomena (enjoyment for instance) to the environmental side of the biospheric interaction: We would expect that the value of the object will be recognized on subsequent encounters with it and that other persons will agree with us about its value. If they do, they show good judgment and are wise. If they don't they are misled, because of their own stupidity, or bad character, or lack of information about the true nature of the $x$ in question. Any strictly impartial observer, particularly one who is well informed and wise, would recognize it as being positive.

It is possible, of course, that our personal sentiments are different from the objectively required attitude. We then may feel that $x$ is valuable but that we personally do not like it. If we consequently reject $x$, we do not necessarily deny its value. We may merely be ready to forego it in favor of our personal preferences.

There are two cases which may appear to contradict the invariances implied by the objectivization of value. First, is it not possible that $x$ may have value solely for $p$ (or a few persons)? If $p$ and $p$ alone requires special medication, is not that medication a value to $p$, though it is not so to anyone else? Conversely, may not something have value for everyone but $p$? Even if we answer both of these questions in the affirmative we are not violating our belief in the objectivization of value, for in both the presumption is that all sufficiently informed persons would concur that, in the one case, $x$ is valuable for $p$, and in the other that $x$ is generally valuable although $p$ does not need it.

In distinguishing value from ought, we can begin with the idea that value is linked with actions in a much less specific way than is ought. That is, "$p$ values $x$" can give rise to many different actions, or to none at all, whereas "$p$ ought to do $x$" means there is an actual objective force present. The relation between "$p$ values $x$" and "$p$ ought to do $x$" is analogous to the relation between "$p$ likes $x$" and "$p$ wants to do $x$." Both value and like belong to the dimension of potentiality; that is, they can exist even though no force is present; at the same time, under proper conditions, they may evoke oughts or wishes. This functional role also holds for the cognitive concepts of belief, attitude, and knowledge, which therefore also belong to the dimension of potentiality. On the other hand, both ought and want belong to the dimension of force or force field. They refer to an actual process, like enjoyment or perception.

Angyal (1941) has also stressed the importance of distinguishing psychological phenomena that have the character of a force field from those that do not. He makes a distinction between valence (the attractive or repulsive character of something which implies the existence of a surrounding field of force) and relevance (also a property of an object as it is relevant to the person, but lacking the chacter of a force field). Relevance, like attitude and value, does not belong to the dimension of valence or force field, at least not as this concept has been used by Lewin (1938). Angyal notes:

> For the sake of terminological clarity it seems desirable to speak of the valence of an object when it exerts an actual prompting influence upon the organism and of its relevance when the object has the potentiality to exert such influence under proper conditions. (Angyal, 1941, p. 156.)

Only in combination with other conditions do psychological phenomena of the order of relevances, attitudes, sentiments, and values give rise to tendencies toward a number of different actions. There is a difference between "I like *x*" and "I want *x*," a difference that revolves around the existence of a field of force. The same difference differentiates "I value *x*" from "I ought to do *x*." If we continue the fiction of treating the objective order like another person, then we can say that a value is that which the objective order likes, or that which is of relevance to the impersonal reality, whereas an ought is that which the objective order wants.

It is illuminating to examine Lewin's ideas about values. He says:

> Values influence behavior but have not the character of a goal (that is, of a force field): For example, the individual does not try to "reach" the values of fairness but fairness is "guiding" his behavior. It is probably correct to say that values determine which types of activity have a positive and which have a negative valence for an individual in a given situation. In other words, values are not force fields but they "induce" force fields. That means values are constructs which have the same psychological dimension as *power fields*. [Power fields refer to the power of another person to control the behavior of *p*.] It is interesting to consider from this point of view the psychoanalytical theory that values are "internalized" parents. Independent of whether this statement in regard to the genesis of values is or is not correct we can at least say that values and persons are equivalent insofar as both can be represented by power fields. (Lewin, 1944, p. 14.)

This quotation, first of all, makes clear the difference between the actual force field and the potentiality implied in the value concept, a difference which Angyal, as we have mentioned, tries to define when he distinguishes between valence and relevance.

In regard to the analogy between the power field of a person and value, however, some objections might be raised. Without doubt, a cognized value can influence the actions of the person; but it does not necessarily do so. If value consists in having power over the person, then what is the status of a recognized value that does not influence behavior? One could answer that though the person does not act in accordance with the value there will nevertheless be a force induced by the value. However, is it not possible that $p$ only believes that he ought to do $x$, but there is no real force in the direction of doing it. Perhaps it is a terminological question as to whether one should then conclude that $p$ really does not hold the value.

In any case, the power of a value to induce behavior should not categorically suggest that the person is forced to do something by an outside power. It is in $p$'s power to go against duty, he "can" violate the objective order. When he obeys duty, he does so because he wants to be in agreement with the objective order or because he is afraid of punishment. In the latter case, the person may sometimes feel the ought as an imposed force, he may feel that psychologically at least he has no choice, because he *cannot* do otherwise, because the fear of punishment is so overpowering. Usually, however, the person does feel free to choose either to obey the objective order or to go against it. Then behavior in the direction of duty has its source in $p$; it is not as though $p$ is carried by a stronger person without being able to do anything about it. (Cf. G. Allport's (1955) analysis of the difference between must and ought, p. 72.)

In brief, the ought can be considered a cognized force with objective validity; value can be considered a cognized positive property of something, a relevance with objective validity. These cognized forces and relevances have, of course, a great influence on $p$'s own forces because in most cases there will be a strong tendency to be in harmony with them.

### Ought and Can

These last remarks bring us to a consideration of the relation between the concepts of ought and can. Rationally the concept of ought is applicable only when the person is a possible source of an event. It does not make sense to say that a person ought to do something if he cannot do it. Then, the not doing cannot be attributed to him. It is not his fault if he does not do it.

One could say that in this case there is no ought force with the point of application on $p$. If $x$ ought to be done, then $x$ is, according to the previous discussion, a valence or force field for the objective order. If we conceive of this valence as lying in the center of a causal space, then there will be a force acting on all the means that might bring $x$ about. And if $p$ can cause $x$, and the objective order wants $x$ to happen, then the objective order will want $p$ to cause $x$. This is analogous to the following: If $p$ wants $x$ to happen, and he knows that $o$ can produce $x$, then $p$ will want $o$ to do it. But if $p$ knows that $o$

cannot produce $x$, then the force toward $x$ should not imply a force toward "$o$ causes $x$." The goal force should be transmitted only to those regions that represent means to reach the goal. If I want only $x$ I have no interest in doing $z$ which does not lead to the goal. $p$ causing $x$ can be conceived of as a means the objective order uses to attain the effect $x$; but if p cannot do $x$, then $p$ as a means is useless, and no ought force rationally applies to him.

In the same way, there should be no great merit in doing one's duty if one is coerced by threats or lured by rewards. Then the force responsible for the action is not derived from the tendency to agree with the ought force, but from the valences of threats or rewards.

At the same time, we are not always rational. We do not have to look far to uncover instances in which $p$ feels that he ought to do something which he knows he cannot: A father feels guilty because his disability prevents him from playing ball with his son; a mother feels the child ought to get better grades though "deep down" she is aware that already he is doing as well as he can. In such instances the wish "to be able" is so strong that it seems to spread and engulf an "ought to be able" as well. The father then feels, "I cannot play ball but I ought to be able to play' ball."

When the wish is out of line with the ought, however, such an irrational juxtaposition of ought and cannot is less apt to occur. For example, if under ordinary circumstances I ought to study for an examination, but cannot because of illness, then the fact that I don't really want to study anyway makes for alacrity in shifting the point of application of the ought force away from the self. This has, for instance, the effect that one may wish for an insurmountable obstacle if one ought to do something one dislikes very much or is afraid of. An example of this is given in the following instance:

Martha doesn't intimidate me . . . only her parents or my father prevent me from kissing her. . . . Deeply in me another boy congratulated himself for these spoil sports. He thought: What luck that I am not alone with her! Because I would not dare to kiss her even then, and I would have no excuse. (Radiguez, 1923, pp. 34–35.)

If one does not wish to do $x$, but one is commanded to do it by another person in authority or by duty, one will wish for the excuse of a barrier. Barriers produce frustration only when they obstruct own forces; if they obstruct induced forces alone and support the own forces, then one is not frustrated, one is often relieved. Witness Benchley's feeling of deliverance upon discovering that he couldn't, after all, go to the dentist:

. . . that afternoon you look up the dentist's number in the telephone book. A wave of relief sweeps over you when you discover it isn't there. How can you be expected to make an appointment with a man who hasn't a phone? The thing is impossible! . . .

Bright and early Monday morning you make another try at the telephone book and find, to your horror, that some time between now and last Tuesday the dentist's name and number have been inserted. Fortunately the line is busy, which allows you to put it over until Tuesday. . . . (Benchley, 1942, pp. 73–74.)

Viewing the possible as impossible is the one way of avoiding the applicability of an ought force. Only if the induced ought force is accepted, that is, if it produces a desire in the same direction, will one feel frustrated should fulfilling the ought requirements be obstructed.

## The New Order of Reality Created by the Ought

The supra-individual reality of value and ought is a phenomenon of a new order of complication. It is an emergent social phenomenon which has to do with the exclusion of individual wants and likes, and which brings with it new constant functions, new perceptions and new possibilities of action. In this way it is similar to the emergence of the objective reality of objects for the individual. The ought is not merely a feeling, some esoteric quality that can be glimpsed by the phenomenologist in a happy moment. It influences real events.

Mead (1934) has made this clear with his concept of the "generalized other." The attitude of the generalized other represents the attitude of the whole community. The individual is confronted with the attitudes of the generalized other, attitudes that have greater objectivity than his own personal wants and attitudes. The individual can put himself in the place of the generalized other, and that assures the existence of a universe of discourse. Thus, the individual's conduct is guided by principles, " and a person who has such an organized group of responses is a man whom we say has character, in the moral sense" (Mead, 1934, p. 162). Mead illustrates this taking over of the attitude of the generalized other by reference to the notion of property. Property exists only on the basis of such common attitudes. Property is that "which the individual can control himself and nobody else can control" (p. 162). If the attitudes referring to property are shared by the community, then all the different rights and duties in regard to property are established, and new ways of functioning are prescribed for the individual. If $p$ owes something to $o$, then the objective order wishes $p$ to give it to $o$.

Hollingworth (1949) has distinguished ten varieties of oughts, each of which implies new functional relations of a nature that transcends individual wants and likes. A few examples follow: The ought in "This ought to be enough material for a coat" is a logical one, more or less factual. The ought in "We won the game and we ought to celebrate" implies a larger pattern or gestalt which calls for the act mentioned for the sake of completion. The ought in "Every man ought to keep his promises" often refers to a moral injunction. The ought in "The wedding ring ought to be worn on the third finger of the left hand" represents the propriety of a convention. These oughts, however diverse, all refer to the wish or requirements of an objective order, a reality independent of whimsical notions, a reality that makes a difference in one's expectations, evaluations, and behavior.

One might say that man can operate in the physical environment only when physical laws hold; in the same way, laws of conduct greatly increase man's possibilities of action in the social world. Obedience to the supraindividual norms insures invariances of behavior and stabilizes it against the shifting impulses and wants of the moment.

## Establishing the Cognitive Objectivity of Value

Psychologists generally agree that in the early part of the life of the individual there is a lack of separation between the ego and the environment, that is, between the personal and impersonal entities of a biospheric occurrence. If this is the case, then the differentiation between the want and the ought, or between "$p$ likes $x$" and "$x$ is a value," both requiring a differentiation of the personal from the objective, must also involve a developmental process.

Social intercourse, talking to other people and becoming involved in their point of view, is considered of great importance for the establishment of cognitive objectivity. Rapaport says

> The significance of communication in particular, and interpersonal relationships in general, for the development of human thinking, has been little appreciated and less explored. To my knowledge, besides Piaget only Sullivan . . . and Bernfeld . . . has a clear perception of its significance. . . . Sullivan coined the concept of "consensual validation" . . . to say that concepts and thinking become reality-adequate only by being tested in interpersonal communication. (Rapaport, 1951, p. 161.)

It is reasonable to assume that evaluation also becomes more objective through social intercourse.

In the chapter on sentiments, we discussed the fact that the reference to an objective reality, which is implied in beliefs and values, implies a special meaning of similarity. While it is pleasant to share personal likings with others, the identity of values is required; if $p$ values $x$ highly and $o$ disvalues it, then $p$ feels that either he or $o$ must be wrong.

Asch expresses this clearly in regard to perceptions in the following passage, which is applicable also to values:

> Under certain conditions . . . the trend to reach agreement with the group is a *dynamic requirement* of the situation. It is based first on a clear and reasonable view of the conditions; each assumes that he sees what others see. On these grounds he expects to reach substantial agreement. These cognitive conditions generate the striving to come nearer to the group. This striving, far from having its origin in blindly imitative tendencies, is the product of objective requirements. (Asch, 1952, p. 484.)

Because values, just as perceived objects, are considered to belong to an objective reality that is the same for everybody, we want other people to have the same values that we ourselves have. If *o* flouts my values he is a thorn in my flesh, he does not recognize what is reality for me. As long as somebody else, especially a person who is in some way connected with *p*, does not see reality as *p* sees it, there will be conflict, and a tendency either to make the other see as *p* sees, or, if the other has great prestige, to change *p*'s own ideas. The conflict in viewpoints may lead to the recognition that the views are only partially true and thereby to a greater objectivity.

If no agreement can be reached, *p* will think that *o* is wrong—*o*'s ideas will not be attributed to his openness to reality, but to some defect in his person, to his stupidity (cussedness), perversion, or plain badness. Ichheiser says that people

> . . . seek to restore their peace of mind in facing political disagreements by achieving a pseudounderstanding of the real motivations of the opponent. We are saying that they restore in this way their peace of mind, for now they can feel that they themselves are "right" and that "something is wrong with the other,"—to believe which is one of the most essential conditions of happiness in life. . . . Each of them is equally convinced of seeing the one world "as it really is" and of being faced by other people who, having a "confused mind" or being misled by "bad men" and "wrong ideas," are unable to see things "as they really are." (Ichheiser, 1949, p. 39.)

In visual perception, there are certain actions that have the purpose of establishing greater constancy, like, for instance, changing the point of view in which the object is seen by moving the head. Similarly, in comparing two values, we look at them from different sides and try to get an objective evaluation. Consequently, people's conflicting valuations may lead to a separation of personal considerations which influence the judgment from more objective ones, in other words, of what should be attributed to the subject from what should be attributed to the object. In his autobiography Goethe relates how, when each of a group of young people considered his own poem the best, he was greatly troubled by the thought that obviously only one of them could be right. He then grappled with the problem of an intersubjectively valid criterion.

Since there is only one truth but many different ways of being in error, there is more likely to be agreement between two people with object-adequate cognition than between two people with egocentric and subjective cognition. The same might be said of attitudes. Two people who always assess the environment in a fair and objective way have more chance of having concordant attitudes than people whose views are mainly determined by their personal situation. Spinoza (1677, trans. 1936) expresses this in the following propositions: "In so far as men are assailed by emotions which are passions, they can be contrary to one another" (p. 211). But "In so far only as men live in obedience to reason, do they always necessarily agree in nature" (p. 213).

In connection with the objectivization of value, it is interesting to consider the theory of Adam Smith concerning the propriety of emotions and of emotional expression. He points out that we have a tendency to be egocentric in the sense that we are very strongly affected by what happens to us, and only mildly affected by what happens to others. But, at the same time, we want to feel about things as other people do, we want to be in agreement with others.

Nothing pleases us more than to observe in other men a fellow-feeling with all the emotions of our own breast; nor are we ever so much shocked as by the appearance of the contrary. (Adam Smith, 1759, p. 10.)

In order to attain this fellow-feeling in the emotions, the principal sufferer must try to weaken his emotion, or at least its expression, while the spectator has to heighten his sympathetically induced emotion. In this way a certain common level of feeling is attained. The person principally concerned can only hope to obtain sympathy

. . . by lowering his passion to that pitch, in which the spectators are capable of going along with him. He must flatten, if I may be allowed to say so, the sharpness of its natural tone, in order to reduce it to harmony and concord with the emotions of those who are about him. (p. 23.)

For the sufferer, "virtue" consists in not giving vent to his emotions in an uncontrolled way, while for the spectator it consists in having a great degree of emotional compassion. Thus, there are on the one hand the personal, egocentric forces which make for great inequality of emotions, and on the other hand the need for communality of emotional feeling which leads to the formation of some suprapersonal standard by which equality of emotions is made more certain. In this way more "objective" emotions are established. Analogously, we can say that values that are not invariant to the person, that lack inter-subjective validity, tend to be re-examined and modified until greater objectivity is realized.

### Determining the Ought as a Motivating Factor in Action

What moves a person to act in a certain way is frequently a crucial matter in interpersonal relations. It is one thing if one person helps another because he considers helpfulness a good thing, and quite another if he helps because of promise of reward or fear of punishment, or because he is commanded to do so, or because the action itself is something enjoyable independent of its effect on another. We want to know if a person is really virtuous, or if it is merely expedient for him to act virtuously. Only in the former case, where the ought force is so internalized that its strength and direction may be said to be generated from within, can we count on the person's continued good will. Only then does the behavior have the distinction of a meritorious act.

When other possible motivating factors may be discounted in a particular situation, then we can feel more certain that the ought force has been accepted by the person as his own, that the act in question truly stems from the requirements of an impersonal objective order. Thus it is that when a person does something which is clearly unpleasant in itself, which runs counter to the individual's own wish, selfish motives may be ruled out. One feels appreciative not only because of the realization that the person has sacrificed himself, but also because of the conviction that he acted solely in the interests of ought requirements. The disagreeableness of the task, therefore, is sometimes a clue for the assigning of ought credits.

Another clue is the power of the person, insofar as fear of punishment can be eliminated as a major motivating factor. It can be stated that there are two kinds of force counteracting a tendency toward morally bad action; one the one hand conscience, or the generalized ought force, and on the other hand the force derived from fear of punishment from the outside world. With the powerless person both forces may be active so that if he refrains from doing evil we do not know to which force to ascribe it. With a powerful person the second force is minimized; he does not have to fear punishment. Therefore his doing or not doing something bad is a much better measurement of the generalized ought forces or of his own "character." Plutarch has said,

It is an observation no less just than common, that there is no stronger test of a man's real character than power and authority, exciting, as they do, every passion, and discovering every latent vice. (Douglas, 1940, p. 1348.)

## Balanced Situations

In the chapter on sentiments, the meaning of balanced situations and harmony was discussed in some detail. Instances of balance and imbalance in the psychological world of the person have been presented throughout the text in regard to the specific matter under discussion. So it is not surprising that balance phenomena also influence the fate of oughts and values themselves as well as how much requirements of the objective order affect other sentiments and perceptions. The following general statement can be made: There exists a tendency to be in harmony with the requirements of the objective order. Thus the situation is balanced if one likes to do what one ought to do, if one likes and enjoys the entities one believes are valuable, if happiness and goodness go together, if $p$ admires the person he likes and likes the person with whom he shares values, if what ought to be conforms to what really is, etc.

James, with reference to aesthetic and moral judgments, points to certain harmonious relations, though he dismisses them as being relatively unimportant:

. . . these judgments express inner harmonies and discords between objects of thought; . . . whilst outer cohesions frequently repeated will often seem harmonious, all harmonies are not thus engendered, but our feeling of many of them is a secondary and incidental function of the mind. Where harmonies are asserted of the real world, they are obviously mere postulates of rationality, so far as they transcend experience. Such postulates are exemplified by the ethical propositions that the individual and universal good are one, and that happiness and goodness are bound to coalesce in the same subject. (James, 1890, p. 675.)

One might disagree with James when he calls the feeling of harmonies a "secondary and incidental function of the mind," and rather be inclined to assign to them a central position with considerable power to influence what man sees, feels, believes and does.

A few of the interesting manifestations of balance phenomena as applied to oughts and values will now be reviewed, some briefly, others more fully.

**Personal wishes and objective requirements.** Balance between likes or desires on the one hand, and values or ought prescriptions on the other, has already been discussed at some length in preceding chapters (cf. Chapter 7, p. 182; Chapter 5, p. 135). Balance exists if the personal preference points in the same direction as the objective requirement.

Here we should like to add to the discussion by considering a psychological complication that arises because of the problem of establishing the ought as a motivating factor in behavior, a problem which has already been touched upon. Certainly it is true that one often receives far more credit for doing something one ought to do when it is counter to one's personal wish than when it is in accord with it. If merit is coordinated to the ought forces, it becomes necessary to rule out other motivating factors, such as the person's own wishes. If credit were merely a function of the agreement between behavior and ought forces, then these wishes could be disregarded. But such is not the case. Thus, though a person who likes to do (or who wants to do, desires or enjoys doing) the activity in question independent of its ought character is in a situation of harmony, it is not one which necessarily merits praise. If he does what he ought to because he likes doing it anyway, he may not get praised for it.

On the other hand, if the preference derives from the ought force, if for example, one gets pleasure from helping another because the act is helpful, then there is little question that the situation is both a harmonious and praiseworthy one. This is merely another way of saying that the ought force is then also the person's own force and not one that operates through rewards and punishments. It is then that happiness and goodness, which are often thought of as belonging together, can be understood as necessarily coexisting. If one likes the ought, one will achieve pleasure from following it. The adage, virtue is its own reward, is applicable.

To like the "ought to," or, to put it another way, to enjoy the valuable, may be psychologically different, however, from valuing the enjoyable. Both represent harmonious situations but the difference resides in the direction of influence between the two halves of the relation. In the first case, the oughts and values are given and the harmonious personal affective reaction is induced, whereas in the latter case, the influence is the other way around.

The harmonious coexistence of personal preferences and objective requirements may be fostered by a need to justify and make sense of one's desires and pleasures. Then the tendency to make the more personal enjoyment coincide with impersonal values may be aided by the need to gain the support of objective reality. Dewey emphasizes this balance tendency when he says:

> By way of self-justification and "rationalization," an enjoyment creates a tendency to assert that the thing enjoyed is a value. This assertion of validity adds authority to the fact. It is a decision that the object has a right to exist and hence a claim upon action to further its existence. (Dewey, 1929, p. 263.)

**Justice, happiness and goodness.** Happiness and goodness are often thought of as belonging together for intrinsic reasons, not only as a consequence of the derivation of the one from the other. They are also in harmony as two positive states which reflect the requirements of justice. When they coexist, we feel that the situation is as it should be, that justice reigns. On the other hand, the coexistence of happiness and wickedness is discordant no matter how much the person likes his wickedness. Happiness, reward, fortune are far more befitting to virtue than to evil. Scheler (1927) expresses a popular way of thinking when he says, "... only the good person is necessarily also the blissful person, and the bad person the necessarily despairing person" (p. 361). Common-sense psychology tends to hold that any imbalance represents a temporary state of affairs, that the wicked may have their field day now, but that they will eventually be punished and the good rewarded.

The relationship between goodness and happiness, between wickedness and punishment is so strong, that given one of these conditions, the other is frequently assumed. Misfortune, sickness, and accident are often taken as signs of badness and guilt. If *o* is unfortunate, then he has committed a sin. (Cf. Znaniecky, 1925, pp. 146-147; Kelsen, 1946, pp. 97 ff.)

**Ought and reality.** Aligning goodness and happiness, wickedness and unhappiness can also be seen as a tendency towards balance between the realms of the ought and existing reality. When we think that the wicked will be punished, our idea of "what is" is influenced by our idea of "what ought to be." The reverse is true when we interpret harm as punishment. Being unfortunate or suffering means that reality moved in a direction opposed to the wishes of the person. If the ought forces are thought to be in conformity with the real event, then it is seen as a justified punishment.

Coordinating the "ought" and the "is" applies to other areas as well, and is probably one reason tradition is so potent in preventing change. Tradition represents the existing reality made solid by a long history in which it becomes identified with the just, the ethical, the "should be." It is also one reason we often fail to perceive abuses in the world around us or why we become apathetic to them. The "is" takes on the character of the "ought" or the deviation from the ought becomes less obvious.

This mutual interaction between ought and reality is paralleled by the interaction between want and reality. In wishful thinking, reality, as we see it, is assimilated to our wants; in "facing the facts," adaptation, or getting to like our fate, our tendencies are adjusted to what "is."

*Liking and admiring: a value-oriented sentiment in interpersonal relations.* The statement "*p* admires *o*" means that *p* believes that *o*'s being, *o*'s acts and wishes, are valuable and in agreement with the objective order. An admired person is thought of as being objectively positive; he ought to be appreciated. Admiring is the more indirect, rational, and impersonal evaluation, and liking is the more personal reaction. In naive psychology, admiring belongs to the head, liking to the heart. Scheler (1913) says that one can give reasons for admiration but not for love (p. 149). Moreover, liking, but not admiration, is related to the warm-cold dimension. One has a cool admiration for a person when one admires him but does not like him very much. If one talks about "warm admiration," a certain degree of liking is implied.

The basic balanced situation exists if *p* likes the people he admires and admires the ones he likes. The tendency to bring the two attitudes into harmony can be readily understood. When we like somebody we want to be able to admire him because then our personal direct evaluation gains the support of being in agreement with the objective order. If we like somebody whom we cannot admire, then "our instincts have led us astray." It implies that we are "wrong" in some way and has a meaning that goes beyond a mere conflict between a like and a dislike.

The research presented in Chapter 7 dealing with the balanced situation of liking between *p* and *o* and their beliefs is relevant here. There it was said that *p* tends to like an *o* with whom he has beliefs or attitudes in common.

Philosophers, too, have considered the relation between liking and admiration. In this connection it is interesting to consider Scheler's theory of love. It is his view that the propensity of love to perceive and bring out the highest values in the loved object does not lead to imaginary virtues:

Such illusions do of course occur, but they are certainly not occasioned by love for the object, being brought about by the very opposite of this, namely the inability to free oneself from partiality to one's *own* ideas, feelings and interests. (Scheler, 1913, trans. 1954, p. 160.)

As a matter of fact, Scheler argues, the perception of values in the loved one is in many cases illusory only in the eyes of the detached observer

because he fails to recognize the particular *individual* values present in the object, but discernible only to the sharper eye of love. . . . Indeed, the essence of individuality in another person, which cannot be described or expressed in conceptual terms (Individuum ineffabile), is *only* revealed in its full purity by love or by virtues of the insight it provides. (p. 160.)

Furthermore, the lover himself reaches his highest value only in love.

> . . . love is the movement wherein every concrete individual object that possesses value achieves the highest value compatible with the nature and ideal vocation; or wherein it attains the ideal state of value intrinsic to its nature. (p. 161.)

We are again reminded of Spinoza (*Ethics*) who says that the loved object causes the mind to pass to a state of greater perfection.

It is interesting to note that Aristotle (*Nicomachean Ethics*) considered a friendship based on virtue as the most permanent and stable relationship and a friendship based on utility or pleasure imperfect and unstable. Virtue provides an invariant anchoring point:

> virtue is a permanent quality . . . the good are both good absolutely and profitable to each other . . . everyone is pleased by his own actions, and therefore by actions that resemble his own, and the actions of all good men are the same or similar. (Aristotle, trans. 1939, pp. 461–462.)

Harmony between liking and admiring (or between friendship and value attitudes), need not always imply a balancing process in which these two ways of experiencing entities are, at first, established separately and only gradually become more similar. Rather, the source of liking (or desiring, or enjoying) may be ascribed to the object. The reader is referred to the discussion of the conditions and process of attribution as applied to desire and pleasure, for it bears upon just this point (cf. pp. 146–160). Thus, at first liking and admiring are closely connected. The less differentiated and the more egocentric a person is, the less liking will be distinguished from admiring, but with greater sophistication the distinction between the two reactions becomes more clearly defined. Then, should conflict between the two emerge, a tendency toward adjustment in line with the balance hypothesis will occur.

However we think about this connection, it is true that liking and admiring are closely linked, and that the harmony situations that hold for liking, are also valid for valuing. There exists a tendency to value that with which one is connected, whether because it is similar to oneself, or because one is familiar with it and used to it, or because one has produced it (cf. Chapter 7). We have the wish to be in agreement with the objective order in everything that belongs to us in any sense.

## Power: An Important Value in General Adjustment

Now that we have examined some of the properties and functional roles of oughts and values in general, we should like to explore a specific value from the point of view of the adjustment of the person as a whole to the world about him. Power (or to use other terms such as ability and strength) was selected because it has to do with a naive concept that has already been analyzed, that of *can* (cf. Chapter 4). Power refers to what a person *can cause*, either because of his individual physical or intellectual capacities, or because of his position in relation to other people—in general because of the nonmotivational factors ascribed to him as a person.

The possibility of inducing changes in the environment, when it is ascribed to the person and not to the environment, is related to evaluation, though not in a simple way. On the one hand, it is a commonplace to say that people in general admire strength or power and despise weakness and impotence. We try to show off our powers or brag about what we can do; we have a tendency to hide our weaknesses and defects. Adam Smith talks about the corruption of our moral sentiments in this regard:

> That wealth and greatness are often regarded with the respect and admiration which are due only to wisdom and virtue; and that the contempt, of which vice and folly are the only proper objects, is often most unjustly bestowed upon poverty and weakness, has been the complaint of moralists in all ages. (Adam Smith, 1759, p. 84.)

This complaint will be felt especially justified when the power of a person is not intrinsically connected with him as a person. Lippitt, *et al.* (1952) observed in their study of children in camps that "high power boys are liked better and identified with more than other group members" (p. 57). To be sure, the authors state that one cannot decide on the basis of their results whether power led to popularity, or popularity to power.

On the other hand, there is also an opposite tendency. Power may engender suspicion, rebellion, and hostility, and weakness may lead to positive sentiments. Spencer (1873) even said that we have an inborn love of the helpless, stimulated by the perception of "smallness joined, usually, with relative inactivity being the chief indication of incapacity" (p. 624).

Related to this ambivalence toward power are the conflicting values of aggression. Fite examined parents' attitudes toward aggression in children. She found

> . . . that the parents themselves were not always too sure of their own standards. Even when most sure that they preferred for their children peaceable means of settling difficulties, they tended to become anxious and uncertain of their standards when the children did not stand up to aggressions of others. They became frightened at this apparent timidity on the

part of the child and felt confused as to what point of view they should take. (Fite, 1940, pp. 309–310.)

The relation of the person's attitudes toward power, strength, or aggressiveness to his personality has often been noted. For instance, Horney (1945) distinguishes between the compliant type, who avoids any kind of aggressive behavior, and the aggressive type, who worships power and strength. Frenkel-Brunswik studied those who scored high in ethnic prejudice on a questionnaire and those who scored low. She found that

. . . as in other interpersonal relationships, the highs tend in their relations to the opposite sex toward a *"power-orientation;* exploitive-manipulative (concrete benefits)" type of attitude. This contrasts with the *"love-seeking* (warmth and affection)" attitude in the lows. . . . (Frenkel-Brunswik, 1948, p. 271.)

The relation of these attitudes not only to personality, but also to cultural differences, has been stressed.

Certainly, personality factors often determine whether the individual follows more a power-logic or a love-logic. But it may also be illuminating to consider these two attitude-structures as two possible ways of living which are based on the functional meaning of power and aggression in life adjustment. One cannot simply say that for one reason individual power is positive, for another power is negative. The positive attitude toward strength or power is different from the positive attitude toward weakness, and concerns a different dimension. We may respect strength but we do not respect weakness. There is little doubt that strength, as an abstraction devoid of special circumstances, evokes a positive evaluation and weakness a negative one. Metaphorically we speak of the strengths of a person as meaning his positive qualities, not his shortcomings. The positive attitude toward weakness has more to do with love, pity, sympathy, and with the actions of helping and giving support.

Angyal's (1941) distinction between two very general tendencies of the organism may be seen to account for different reactions to power and aggression independent of personality factors. The one he calls the trend toward autonomy. It is the tendency toward self-determination, towards mastering oneself and the environment. The person's own self should be the source of changes, and should not be at the mercy of the environment. The other is the trend toward homonomy, a trend to fuse and be in harmony with superindividual units, to be in accord with forces from the outside which impinge upon the person. These tendencies seem to exist not only at the level of personal wish forces of the individual but also on the level of objectively required forces. People not only want to attain greater autonomy and homonomy, but they also think that men in general ought to strive in these directions. Around each of these tendencies a whole system of value attitudes can be built up.

Thus, aggression can be felt as something positive. It can be a sign of spirit and strength. We expect and demand a certain amount of autonomy of people; it is not "right" if they are too unresisting, yielding and weak—at least that is the normal reaction in our culture. Life should not be at the mercy of heteronomous imposed forces. The individual should be able to take care of himself and defend himself. Lapie (1902) says "Any being that, in spite of pain, fights against nature, proves not only its power, but also its autonomy, that is to say, its value" (p. 101). He also holds that "an act or agent is the more valuable the more it is really a cause" (p. 77), that is, the more it has autonomy. On the other hand, because aggression conflicts with the trend toward homonomy, it can also be negative. The requirement that people should unite as harmonious and equal parts of superindividual wholes may be interfered with by aggressive acts. Inflicting injury separates people and is a manifestation of opposition.

Similarly, considerations involving means-end relations and utility may be seen to play a role in the positive significance of strength and power. Power implies the possibility of causing events that are beneficial to $p$, and preventing events that are harmful to $p$. Also, strong people with whom we are united will do us no harm; they will benefit us. Power, therefore, is a good attribute; it is positive in itself. One arranges one's sentiments and evaluations in such a way that they coincide with the structure of causation.

Thus far we have treated aggression and power as being equal. When their relations to the principles of autonomy and homonomy are considered, however, an important difference emerges. Both aggression and power may be activated in the service of the trend toward autonomy. A certain amount of both is necessary for the defense of one's own person and the establishment of control over the environment. However, the aggression of $p$, but not necessarily his power, restricts the autonomy of $o$. One man's gain is another man's loss. To put this another way, aggression, signifying opposition and separation between people, conflicts with the trend toward homonomy. Power, on the other hand, in itself is neutral as far as the principle of homonomy is concerned. It can be used to further both social and antisocial ends.

We said above that the tendencies toward autonomy and homonomy can be considered to have the character of required forces. People seem to feel that everybody ought to strive in these directions, though the extent of the striving varies greatly with culture and personality. One might add that the value of a trend toward homonomy in another person could be derived directly from the tendency toward homonomy in $p$: $p$ can be part of superindividual social wholes only if other people participate. However, it is not so easy to derive the value of the trend toward autonomy in others from the value of one's own autonomy. Autonomy is essentially egotistic and individualistic. Autonomy for $o$ frequently conflicts with autonomy for $p$. Although two persons liking each other are in harmony, two persons trying to dominate each other will get into difficulties. One possibility of solving this problem has been suggested above. Admiring the strong person, and living in harmony with him, may in some cases have real means value for the autonomy of $p$.

But this may not be the only reason for the positive significance of strength in others. Hume refutes the notion that personal or selfish interests are always behind valuing a trait in another person when he talks about qualities which are useful only to the person possessing them, but which are also esteemed by the spectator.

> . . . as these advantages are enjoyed by the person possessed of the charac-
> ter, it can never be *self-love* which renders the prospect of them agreeable
> to us, the spectators, and prompts our esteem and approbation. . . . All
> suspicion, therefore, of selfish regards, is here totally excluded. It is a
> quite different principle which actuates our bosom, and interests us in the
> felicity of the person whom we contemplate. Where his natural talents
> and acquired abilities give us the prospect of elevation, advancement, a
> figure in life, prosperous success, a steady command over fortune, and the
> execution of great or advantageous undertakings, we are struck with such
> agreeable images, and feel a complacency and regard immediately arise to-
> wards him. The ideas of happiness, joy, triumph, prosperity, are con-
> nected with every circumstance of his character, and diffuse over our
> minds a pleasing sentiment of sympathy and humanity. (Hume, 1741, pp.
> 218–219.)

Thus, as we see, Hume uses the principle of association to solve the question of the positive evaluation of power in $o$.

One might also suggest that the strong and able person is in some way in harmony with reality. The superindividual objective world in a sense acknowledges him as being right. It is interesting to consider from this point of view the three properties happiness, power, and value. They belong together in the sense that when they appear together in one person, the situation seems harmonious. There exists a tendency not only to admire the powerful person, but also to think that he is happy. Philosophers have again and again felt the need to counter the spontaneous association of these attributes by emphasizing that great power or riches do not assure happiness.

The coexistence of the three properties happiness, power, and value, brings into harmony heteronomous forces, autonomous tendencies, and ought forces. (1) Heteronomous forces. With the happy and fortunate person, the environmental forces or changes are in the direction of his wishes. (2) Autonomous tendencies. With the powerful person, the structure of the environment is such that the person is the source of events within a causal network. (3) Ought forces. The good person acts in conformity with the superindividual objective requirements. Power, as a value, is then seen to be in harmony with other values, to fit in with autonomous and homonomous strivings of the individual, to make possible the achievement of the good and worthwhile.

### Summary

As a framework for discussion, oughts and values were conceptualized as impersonal objective requirements which are also dispositional in character and intersubjective in validity. They were distinguished by the concept of force field, the ought representing an actual process, a field of forces, and value belonging to the dimension of potentiality so that it evokes behavior only under proper conditions. The concept of force field also helps clarify the fact that rationally an ought has application only where the person is able to fulfill the requirements of the objective order. The effect of personal wishes on the perceived application of oughts and on the creation of barriers to action (i.e. establishing the cannot) was also pointed out. That oughts and values increase the possibilities of action in the social world was shown to stem from its conceptual properties.

The importance of communication among people in the establishment of the cognitive objectivity of values and oughts was examined in terms of the fact that objectivity requires intersubjective consensus. The absence of consensus may in fact direct the person to take a new look at his beliefs concerning oughts and values, the re-evaluation leading to the possibility that distorting personal considerations may be discarded. Where consensus is not achieved, the person tends to discredit the disagreeing member, thereby preserving the significance of the requirement of intersubjective validity.

Because behavior stemming from the wish to satisfy the objective order may not "look" any different from behavior arising from other motives, determining the ought as a motivating factor is not always simple. The significance of the disagreeableness of the task and of the power of the person were discussed in this connection, the one eliminating personal wishes as a possible motive, and the other eliminating fear of punishment from the outside world.

Harmony between the impersonal requirements of the objective order and other areas in the person's life space, was discussed at some length. The cases of balance were considered under the following headings: personal wishes and objective requirements; justice, happiness, and goodness; ought and reality; liking and admiring. Some of these cases could be seen as a logical consequence of the person's attempt to establish himself in a meaningful and stable world. Others may not primarily represent a process of rational determination, but all have major consequences for the content of oughts and values and how they affect other sentiments, perceptions, and actions.

Finally, a specific value, power or strength, was discussed in an attempt to explore how values are connected with man's over-all efforts to adjust to the many events about him when these events do not all conform to his personal wishes and welfare.

# CHAPTER 9

# Request and command

ONE PERSON CAN INDUCE ANOTHER to do something by producing conditions of action in the other person. The schema used in the interpretation of action and its motivation (Chapters 4 and 5) is used not only in assessing the sources of behavior in $o$, but also for the purpose of bringing about actions of $o$.

## Cases of induction of action

That the action schema can be used as a means-end relation was discussed at the end of Chapter 4. In the example analyzed there, $p$ wanted to prevent an action of $o$, namely, the harming of $p$. But, of course, the use of the action schema as a means-end relation is not restricted to the prevention of action; the conditions of action can serve as means by which an action of $o$ is brought about as the desired end.

Thus, $p$ knows that trying and can are the two conditions of action. If $p$ knows further that $o$ wants to do $x$ but cannot, he will try to affect $o$'s "can," by putting him in a position of being able to do it, or by influencing any of the conditions of can which were mentioned in Chapter 4. If, on the other hand, $p$ knows that $o$ can do $x$ but has no wish to exert himself in the direction toward $x$, he will try to bring about $o$'s action by influencing one of the conditions of trying, which were discussed in Chapter 5.

We are not considering here cases in which $p$ is the unintentional source of the behavior of *o*, for instance, in prestige suggestion, when *o* sees *p*, his admired superior, choose something which then becomes positive for *o*; or, when *p* wants something for himself and thereby arouses the competitive envy of *o*. We are concerned only with what Lippitt *et al.* (1952) call a direct influence attempt, which they define as "A social interaction in which one child consciously and deliberately tries to get another child to do something, in such a way that the research observer is aware of the intent" (p. 41). They distinguish it from behavioral contagion (a term first used by F. Redl, 1949) which is defined as "An event in which a person's behavior is changed to resemble that of another person. This change occurs in a social interaction situation in which the person acting as the 'initiator' has not communicated intent to evoke such a change in the other" (p. 41).

We will enumerate some of the main cases of *p* inducing *o*'s action which result from the general scheme of the conditions of trying:

1. It is possible that *p* changes a proper valence for *o*. Something that was unattractive to *o* suddenly seems attractive because of *p*'s action; *o* wants to do it, and he is induced to think that *x* is good for him. It is possible for *p* to produce this change in the proper valence for *o* if he can manipulate the different conditions for the establishment of a positive valence by praising *x*, by persuading *o* that *x* is good, or by demonstratively enjoying *x*. In the mind of *o*, *p* only shows what is good; he is not the source of the valence but only the cause of *o*'s realizing the valence. The real source of the valence is in the properties of *x*; it is intrinsically good, and *p* helped *o* to become aware of it.

2. *p* shows *o* the consequences of *x*. That is done very often in persuasion. No new valences are created; *x* merely attains a new derived valence for *o*. By showing that *x* has a positive *y* as its effect, *p* creates a derived positive valence of *x* for *o*.

3. *p* can also use derived valences in another way in order to control *o*'s actions. Not only can he call the attention of *o* to consequences that are given, he can also create consequences for *o* by promising reward or punishment. The power of *p* to produce actions of *o* is then derived from his power to cause events that are positive or negative for *o*. He does not create proper valences for *o*, he does not change the agreeableness or disagreeableness of activities for *o*. He only creates derived valences by setting up if-so connections when he promises rewards or threatens punishments. He does not have to be stronger than *o* in general; he can coerce *o* if he has only the power of causing a particular positive or negative event for *o*, for instance, using blackmail, or a child controlling his parent by bed-wetting. Also,

*p*'s attitude or state can figure as the reward or punishment if *p* says, "I will love you more if you do that," or "I will be happy if you do that."

4. *p* can request *o* to do *x*. In the cases discussed so far the own valences of *o* play a role, either directly or through derivations based on ground-consequence connections. The valence derivation that underlies the effectiveness of a request refers to a positive sentiment, and is based on the fact that *o* tends to benefit a *p* whom he likes. In asking, *p* does not arrogate to himself the ability to push *o*, no clash of wills is involved. Rather, *p* tries to move *o* by the tactics of deference and submission, he makes himself small. When he asks *o* to do something, he implies that he is dependent on *o*'s good will; *o* should do it because of a positive attitude toward *p*.

5. *p* may command *o* to do *x*. In this case the force in *o* toward doing *x* is created through the power relation between *p* and *o*. It may be that it is always finally based on the power of *p* to reward or punish *o*. However, in many cases, *o* accepts completely *p*'s right to tell him what to do or not to do. This case is treated in topology by means of the concepts of induced force and power field. The instance that has been most often taken to exemplify these concepts is that of the adult prohibiting an activity to the child. Lewin says:

A force induced by a person *P* on a child *C* can be viewed as the result of the power field of that person over the child. The person having power over the child is able to induce positive and negative valences by giving orders. (Lewin, 1954, p. 941. An interesting discussion of power given by French, 1956.)

There are no sharp boundaries between asking and commanding. If a superior person "asks" *o* to do something, it can have the meaning of commanding, though it may not be phrased as a command. Nevertheless, there exist the typical cases of asking and commanding, based on sentiments and power relations respectively.

### Attribution of Induced Actions

When *p* causes *o* to do *x* in one of these ways, then *x* is directly caused by *o*, and indirectly by *p*. Naive psychology attributes the act sometimes to the influence of *p*, sometimes to conditions located in *o*. When *o* does what his superior tells him to do, or when he is coerced at the point of a gun, the event is usually seen as being caused by *p*—*o* could not help doing it, and the act has, in a way, the status of a heteronomous event that happened to *o*, and not the status of an event whose source is located in *o*. Others, and *o* himself, may react to it as to an action for which *o* cannot be blamed. On the other hand, if *p* merely points out to *o* the advantages to be gained by doing *x*, and *o* then does it, it is more likely that *o* will be seen as the originator of the act, even if it is clear that *p* wanted *o* to do *x*.

The case is, in a certain respect, similar to that of simple object perception. There, too, we attribute the "responsibility" for the stimulus pattern to a certain place in the causal sequence, and usually we do not attribute it to the proximal medium. We do not "blame" the light rays for what they do to our eyes. They are only the mediators, they are forced to arrange themselves in certain patterns by the objects in which we locate the source of the stimuli. In perception, the attribution is determined mainly by the facts of constant coordination, which are in some way taken account of by the perceptual apparatus. The stimulus pattern is attributed to the objects and not to the medium because the properties of the stimulus pattern are coordinated to those of the objects and not to those of the medium.

Similarly, we find with the attribution of an induced action, that the caused event will be attributed to whatever is most closely coordinated to the event (cf. Chapter 4, p. 91). For instance, a person has performed a reprehensible action under threat. If we feel that almost every normal person would act in the same way, we will attribute the act to the person who threatened *o*. On the other hand, if we think that almost everybody would be able to resist the threat we attribute the act to *o*'s fear. That the attribution takes into account the reaction of a normal person in *p*'s place can be seen from the definition of "duress." According to Webster, duress is

Compulsion or constraint by which a person is illegally forced to do or forbear some act. This may be by actual imprisonment or physical violence to the person, or by such violence threatened. . . . The violence or threats must be such as to inspire a person of ordinary firmness with fear of serious injury to the person (loss of liberty, or of life or limb), reputation, or fortune. (Webster's Dictionary, 2d. ed., 1935.)

As is usual with attribution, in the attribution of an induced action, the whole causal structure is taken into account and not merely the proximal conditions. We have discussed attribution in previous chapters. Here we want only to add a few remarks in regard to the causal structure of an induced action. If *o* causes *x* through the mediation of another person, that is, for instance, by commanding him to do it, then this mediation is different from the mediation usual in perception or simple action which occurs by means of a manifold of processes which are independent of each other. The mediation in an induced action uses as means a system with representation, the person who carries out the command has to understand it, in other words, he has to integrate the sequence of stimuli sent out by $o$.

It seems that the event is more likely to be attributed to $p$ when he threatens $o$ with harm than when he bribes $o$ with a benefit. This may be partly because it is, on the whole, easier for $p$ to produce negative than to produce positive experiences, especially experiences of a high degree of relevance (cf. Chapter 10, p. 262). For instance, $p$ frequently has the physical power to kill or injure $o$, but only rarely is it in his power to save $o$'s life. The power to make other people unhappy may be more general than the power to make other people happy.

It may also be that it is more difficult to resist threats of extreme harm than to resist promises of extreme benefit, or at least that is the general opinion. When $o$ does something because $p$ threatened a vital injury if he does not do it, that will be counted as "duress" or coercion; $o$ is pushed "against his will." The force away from the harm is more often regarded as a "being forced" than the force toward the benefit.

### Conditions of and Reactions to Requests

When $p$ asks $o$ to do $x$, he tries to cause $o$ to cause $x$. Whether $p$ asks $o$ to do $x$ or not, will depend first of all on the valence of $x$ for $p$. Other things being equal, the more $p$ wants $x$ to happen, the more likely he will be to ask $o$. It will also often depend on the valence of the means to do $x$. The more disagreeable the bringing about of $x$ is for $p$, the more likely he will be to ask $o$ to do it; also the means valence for $o$, as $p$ sees it, plays a role. When $p$ knows that doing $x$ is negative for $o$, he may not want to impose on $o$. Further, the relation of what $p$ can do to what $o$ can do is important—$p$ will not ask $o$ to do $x$ if he knows that $o$ cannot do it, and usually he will not make the request if it is something that he can easily do himself. One can usually assume that when $p$ asks $o$ to do $x$ it is something that $p$ believes $o$ able to do and something that would be difficult for $p$ to perform for himself. At least one can make these assumptions in considering events between a mature $p$ and $o$. With a young child the matter of asking may have different meaning. On the whole, a request is more likely to be directed to a person superior in power, a command to one inferior in power. Lippitt *et al.* (1952) made the hypothesis in their study of children in camp that attempts to influence a person considered to have high social power are more likely to be nondirective in manner. They found that to be true for one camp, though not for two other camps (p. 49).

Thus, when $p$ asks $o$ to do $x$, e.g., to give him something, the asking often implies something about the power or strength relation between $p$ and $o$. It may imply a submission to the other person, or a recognition of superiority. When one asks for help, one admits that one is too weak to help oneself, and one may be embarrassed about it.

Ought forces can also play a role in the situation of asking. For example, $p$ may feel that $o$ owes him a benefit, and that $o$ ought to help him. It is then possible that the request implies not so much an admission of weakness as a reminder to $o$ of his duty. It can also be that $p$ feels that $o$ ought to do what he asks him to do, not because $o$ owes him a benefit, but because $p$ is superior to $o$. The request then becomes similar to a command; and the assumed power relation underlying the request is then opposite to that of a person in distress asking someone for help. That is, $p$ is not dependent on $o$'s help but he has the right to avail himself of it if he wants to.

Whether $o$ does what $p$ asks him to do will depend on, among other factors, whether $o$ likes or dislikes $p$. It is possible that $o$ complies with the request without question, $p$ is his friend and he likes to do something for $p$. He may have been asked to perform a disagreeable task which he would never think of doing as such, but because it is for $p$ he is glad to do it. The task becomes positive because it is a means of helping $p$. $o$ may even count it as a great favor to be asked by $p$ to help him.

Complying with $p$'s request and benefiting $p$ have in common the characteristic that $o$ acts in the direction of $p$'s wishes, that is, $o$ acts "for" $p$. Not doing what one is asked to is impolite or unfriendly because it implies that one does not want to act in the direction "for $p$," and it implies that there is a lack of positive sentiment toward $p$. The assumed condition for $o$'s compliance is "$o$ likes $p$." Therefore, refusal of the request is easily taken as a sign of "$o$ does not like $p$," or even as an act of aggression, and $o$ may comply in order not to give that impression, though he actually does not care much for $p$.

Often, compliance or resistance is not so much influenced by sentiments, as by the power aspect that is involved. We saw that a request can imply that the one who asks is in a superior or an inferior role. Similarly, complying with a request may have the character of granting a favor which confirms the superior position of $o$ who complies, or it may be a sign of weakness and give the impression of yielding to a pressure exerted by $p$. In the latter case the emphasis is on the fact that in complying, $o$ is influenced in his action by a heteronomous factor. One dislikes to give the impression of being weak, and if one has to yield to a request one likes to imply that one does it, not because one is weak but because one wanted to do $x$ anyway. Frank (1944) conducted experiments to study what happens when one person tries to influence another to do something he does not want to do. In this experiment E tried to make the S's eat crackers. He found that in one variation of the experiment the main cause of the resistance was that the subject defined the situation as a personal clash of wills; eating the crackers meant a defeat for the subject.

> The defeat character of eating . . . is further emphasized by the tendency for S's who do not resist to find a reason for eating of their own free will, to avoid the implication that they are eating under compulsion. One S said he liked the crackers and was hungry. . . . One S implied that by eating he showed himself to be E's superior in courtesy. . . . (Frank, 1944, p. 39.)

In these cases, the situation is structured in such a way that the autonomy of the person is preserved. That is, *o* performs the requested act because he wants to do it and not because he cannot resist the pressure that *p* puts on him. The source of doing *x* is put into the person and not into the environment. This is analogous to the sour grapes fable. The fox says, "I don't do *x* because I don't want to, not because I am unable to do it." In this case again the reason for not doing is put into the person; to put it into the environment would be a sign of weakness.

To comply, in these cases, is taken normally as implying a negative value of the self (weakness). In order to preserve the self value, either the request is refused, or, if *o* complies, he does it in such a way that the implication of negative self value is reduced. He may do what he is asked to do because of the consequences his compliance implies. For instance, he may think that if he complies, *p* will like him; people will say he is a good person; people, and especially *p*, will benefit him in return. He may also fear the consequences of not complying.

A more involved example from *Tom Jones* shows the relation between complying and creating an obligation:

> With reflections of this nature she usually, as has been hinted, accompanied every act of compliance with her brother's inclinations; and surely nothing could more contribute to heighten the merit of this compliance than a declaration that she knew, at the same time, the folly and unreasonableness of those inclinations to which she submitted. Tacit obedience implies no force upon the will, and consequently may be easily, and without any pains, preserved; but when a wife, a child, a relation, or a friend, performs what we desire, with grumbling and reluctance, with expressions of dislike and dissatisfaction, the manifest difficulty they undergo must greatly enhance the obligation. (Fielding, 1749, Vol. I, p. 11.)

An obligation of *p* toward *o* is an ought force in the direction for *o*, caused by a previous act *x* of *o* for *p*. The strength of an obligation is a function of the negative value of *x* for *o*, and the positive value of *x* for *p*. The greater the negative value of *x* for *o*, the more will *p* be obligated to *o*. In the example from Fielding, the negative value of *x* for *o* is demonstrated by *o* to *p* by "grumbling and reluctance." The grumbling is a means of making *p* feel obligated, and to gain a certain measure of ascendance over *p*.

To put it briefly, *o*'s force toward or away from complying with *p*'s request will depend on: (1) the value of *x* for *p* and for *o*; (2) what *p* and *o* can cause; (3) *o*'s sentiment for *p*; (4) the power relation between *p* and *o*, and (5) the consequences of the act.

## Command

A few words may be added in regard to actions that are induced by command. In these cases the power relation is more important than the sentiments. When *o* does what *p* commands him to do, he does not "grant" the command, as he can grant a request; he obeys the command. If *o* obeys, he is considered the source of the act much less than when he grants a request. Of course, he may also try to give the impression of acting autonomously. In a power hierarchy (e.g., manager, foreman, worker) it can happen that *q* commands *p* to command *o* to do a disagreeable task. If *p* does not want to appear as if he is being pushed by *q* and is weak, he may rather take upon himself the bad repute of being a domineering person himself than admit that *q* made him do it. On the other hand, if the sentiments are more important to him than the power relations, he may blame his superiors for having to give the command to *o*.

## Summary

In this chapter, how one person *p* gets another person *o* to do something was discussed. Underlying *p*'s attempts to influence *o*'s actions is the general action scheme (Chapter 4), that is, in order to make *o* act, *p* produces what he sees as the conditions of *o*'s actions. Different cases were distinguished on the basis of which condition *p* uses as means.

Induced actions are sometimes attributed to the immediate agent, sometimes to the person who made the agent execute it. In this attribution a number of factors play a role, and the way in which the event is placed in the surrounding causal structure is taken account of.

In exploring the character of requests, their relation to power, ought forces, sentiments, and self-esteem was treated. A few remarks on the role of commands were added.

# CHAPTER 10

# Benefit and harm

BENEFITING AND HARMING apply in a general way to a wide and colorful range of human interaction. Praising, helping, teaching, protecting and encouraging, for example, are considered actions generally benefiting a person unless special circumstances are taken into account. Usually for instance, helping is considered as a worthwhile and benefiting action, though if the one who is helped needs to learn through his own efforts, the help may be rejected as harmful. More typical instances of harming are seen in insulting, hindering, hurting, condemning, and breaking a promise.

## A Basic Definition

We may begin by noting the almost platitudinous statement that when $o$ benefits $p$, he causes something, $x$, that is positive for $p$, and that when $o$ harms $p$, he causes a negative $x$. Very quickly, however, it becomes apparent that this statement requires further specification in order to clarify its ambiguities. Yet it is a fruitful starting definition, for in the process of clarification some psychologically meaningful principles emerge.

The definition includes a causal factor, namely that $o$ causes $x$, and an evaluative factor, whether $x$ is positive or negative for $p$. Let us consider some of the variations that may be represented by "$o$ causes $x$." For example, $o$ causes $x$ but does not mean to do so; $o$ causes $x$ but $p$ does not realize it; $o$ causes $x$ accidentally, and $p$ thinks he did so intentionally; and even *o* did not cause *x* but *p* thinks he did. With regard to the evaluation of *x*, decisive differences may again be specified: *o* may have intended a positive *x* but the resulting action resulted in something negative; *p* and *o* may or may not misjudge the way the other evaluates *x*; *p* and *o* may agree or disagree as to the evaluation of *x*; though *p* and *o* may agree, the evaluation of *x* may differ from that determined by another person, *q*, or the standards of law and ethics; *x* may be negative in its immediate effects and positive from a long-term point of view, or vice versa.

Common-sense psychology leaves no doubt that there are important differences in these cases of causal attribution and evaluative judgment. The differences are recognized by such ordinary comments as: he tried to help me but he didn't know how; he did it because he had to; I refused his gift; he didn't mean to hurt me; his kind words are insincere; it is a blessing in disguise; his present is really a bribe.

## p's *Life Space as Perspective*

If all the possible variations of benefit and harm subsumed by *o* caused *x* and by the evaluation of *x*, were listed, the result would be unwieldly. From the theoretical point of view, we shall not do violence to this variety if we restrict the cases by adopting the point of view of *p* with respect to the harm or benefit of *o*. That is to say, we shall share *p*'s life space and interpret the event *x* in terms of his perception of its causal and evaluative connotations. If, for example, *p* feels that *o* wanted to harm him, it will not matter for our purposes whether *o* would concur in this belief or not. Of course, as the social relations between *p* and *o* progress, *p*'s understanding of the event *x* may well become affected by *o*'s real intentions, but our analysis would then proceed from *p*'s now altered life space. In the interest of ease of presentation, however, the event *p* perceives as caused and intended by *o* will be assumed to be so, unless otherwise indicated, and the evaluation of *x* will be assumed to be objective as well as the same for *p* and *o*.

## *Local and Total Relevance*

As we have seen, the cases of benefit and harm revolve around variations in the implications that may be conveyed by *o* caused *x* and by *x* itself. These wider implications constitute what may be designated as the total relevance of an event, and *p*'s interpretation and reaction to the situation usually rest on this. In contrast, the local relevance of an event is restricted to the immediate nature of *x* and the simple fact that *o* has caused it.

For example, though it is true that benefit can be defined only by referring to positive events, and harm by referring to negative events, this does not mean that the whole experience of being benefited is always positive, or that of being harmed always negative. To undergo a painful treatment is certainly to suffer a negative event; but $p$ can desire it because of the positive consequences. By the same token, an event that may be positive in its local relevance may, because of its total relevance, be rejected. A pointed illustration of this is provided in Ladieu, Hanfmann and Dembo's (1947) analysis of the meaning of help to the visibly injured. Half of the subjects had more bad things than good things to say about being helped, and this relationship was reversed in only about one-fourth of the subjects. A frequent reason given for rejecting help was that though assistance may expedite the reaching of an immediate goal, the long range goal of learning to do for oneself is blocked. The cases in which local and total relevance disagree, that is, in which a benefit is refused or a harm is accepted, are especially useful to demonstrate the difference between them.

We can consider local relevance as involving the more proximal stimuli of a situation and total relevance as usually referring to the more distal stimuli. (Cf. pp. 23–35 for discussion of proximal and distal stimuli.) To exemplify this as well as to justify it, let us return to the case cited above of an event whose immediate effects are negative. There the painful treatment or negative $x$ (proximal stimulus, local relevance) is something that directly impinges on the organism. However, it is referred to further contents, the consequences of $x$ (distal stimulus, total relevance) which in this case happens to be positive. Proximal and distal differences also exist with respect to the factor "$o$ causes $x$." The perception that $o$ caused $x$ provides necessary, though not sufficient, data for such further interpretations as he had to do it, he wanted to do it, he did it accidentally. It is in this sense that the simple causal perception, the perception that "$o$ did it," is proximal with respect to interpretations concerning the intentions or sentiments of $o$. The latter are relatively distal and point to the total relevance of $o$ caused $x$.

We have seen that in visual perception the distal stimulus and not the proximal stimulus provides the more invariant features of the environment. Thus, though the patterning of light waves impinging on the retina (proximal stimulus) varies as the person moves with respect to the object (distal stimulus), the object is perceived as the same object. Likewise in the case of benefiting and harming, the total relevance of the event and not its local relevance gives that kind of stability and order which make adaptation and expectation possible. The fact that $o$ harmed $p$ would in itself provide but a precarious basis for action if $p$ did not relate this to such relatively distal and invariant factors as, for example, the intentions and sentiments of $o$ toward $p$.

However, it is necessary to note that sometimes the local relevance as such may determine the reaction.

There exists a "stimulus directed" perception and the phenomenal representations of local proximal stimuli, in some cases, retain their identity in spite of their being organized into different object units. This is also true in regard to the experience of ego-relevant facts. Pain is disagreeable in itself, and though its coloration can be widely changed by different attribution, its core of negative value persists. The meaning of frustration is changed by causal integration to a greater degree than that of pain. However, even the effect of frustration is to some degree independent of how it is embedded in the social environment. (Heider, 1944, p. 368.)

Maslow, in talking about the reaction to frustration, says:

A goal object may have two meanings for the individual. First it has its intrinsic meaning, and secondly, it may have also a secondary, symbolic value. (Maslow, 1941, p. 364.)

We also know that the relative potency of the local and total relevance of an event varies with maturation, the latter becoming more prominent as the child grows older. Piaget (1932), for example, has shown that young children tend to ignore intentions and to base their moral judgment on the actual injury sustained. Thus, when asked which of two children was the worse, the one who broke twelve dishes while trying to help, or the one who broke one dish just for fun, younger subjects blamed the former more.

*Levels of attribution.* The total relevance of the event $x$ encompasses a manifold of attributions of varying depth; that is, $x$ can be attributed to factors which are further and further removed from the original stimuli. In this sense attributions, or the presumed facts by which $x$ is made accountable and meaningful, may be considered interpretations. Levels of attribution have been discussed before (p. 81), where the interpretation of an agreeable experience was discussed. It seems worthwhile to amplify the previous remarks at this point by considering the case in which something disagreeable happens to $p$. The steps of attribution may occur as follows:

1. What is the source of $x$? Did it occur by chance? Did $p$ himself cause it? Let us assume that the source is perceived to be another person, $o$.

2. Then the question may arise as to whether the harm was intended or not. Perhaps the unpleasant occurrence was not at all intended for $p$. Perhaps $o$ did it to please someone else and so did not have any

personal wish to hurt $p$. Perhaps $o$'s true goal was to benefit $p$, but his means were in error. Or perhaps the harm was only a necessary means to helping $p$. When a parent punishes a child or when a physician hurts a patient, the harm usually is not the goal. But let us assume that $o$ wanted to harm $p$.

3. A yet deeper level of attribution may be probed by asking why $o$ wanted to harm $p$. Was it because he didn't like $p$? Because he is a hostile person? Because he sought revenge for a real or imagined wrong? Because $p$ deserved to be punished? If $p$ feels that $o$ dislikes him, he may in turn search for the cause of the negative relation: Perhaps the dislike stems from what $q$ has told $o$ about $p$. Or there may be an intropunitive interpretation, namely, $p$ feels he is disliked because of his own faults; $o$ is really right in not liking $p$.

It should be clear that the steps in attribution may not always occur in the same order. A deeper level of attribution may precede and influence a more superficial one. For example, the conclusion that the harm was intended (step 2) may depend on the realization that $o$ is a vindictive person (step 3). Perhaps it should also be made explicit that the concept of attribution levels does not presume a corresponding conscious process in the individual. Attributions may not be experienced as interpretations at all, but rather as intrinsic to the original stimuli. Of course, attribution can also be determined by the raw material itself, as when $p$ sees that $o$ threw the stone, for example, but in many cases a host of memory traces in addition to the stimulus pattern determines the attribution.

Source attribution is so fundamental to the meaning of a harm or benefit, that we should like to explore it further. Even the evaluation of $x$ itself is not infrequently affected by the attribution to a causal source, as when $p$ is pleased with the assistance offered by a friend and dismayed when it proceeds from an enemy. Moreover, whether the source is ascribed to a person or to an impersonal circumstance may be crucial in the reaction. Aristotle recognizes this when he says that

. . . the angry man must always be angry with a particular individual . . . and because this individual has done, or was on the point of doing, something against him or one of his friends. . . . (Aristotle, trans. 1939, p. 136.)

Dembo conducted experiments in which she compared anger directed against a personal cause with "impersonal" anger and found that the former was much stronger and that its aftereffects lasted longer. (Koffka, 1935, p. 673.) The authors of the frustration-aggression hypothesis state that

. . . the strongest instigation, aroused by frustration, is to acts of aggression directed against the agent perceived to be the source of the frustration. . . . (Dollard *et al.*, 1939, p. 39.)

The point we wish emphasized, however, is that in pushing toward deeper levels of attribution, the person is trying to grasp the relevant features of the situation confronting him and this is true even when the levels become further removed from the raw experience determined by the immediate stimulus pattern. We cannot understand these features without attribution, notwithstanding the possibility that bias may operate to distort them. Moreover, as has already been noted, the properties attributed to behavior and events provide a continuity or constancy in the reality which is necessary for meaningful action. If the negative event was brought about by *o*, and if *o* really meant to harm *p*, then *p* might avoid *o* or prevent him from behaving in the same manner again. Without attribution to causal source and intention, *p* could neither avoid nor prevent, but would be at the mercy of seemingly fickle events in the environment.

But the intentions of *o* are usually not given directly. Even if *o* insists that he did not mean to harm *p* or that he really intended to benefit him, *p* may have grounds for disbelieving *o*. These grounds may be given by other clues in the stimulus pattern—the acrimony of "sweet words" may be conveyed by expression and tone, for example. Or they may be given by properties that are not an intrinsic part of the situation. The intention of *o* may then be attributed to underlying dispositional factors. Of these, the following will be discussed more fully: The relation of liking and disliking between *o* and *p*, power and status relations, and ought forces. These, and other factors, will be considered later as co-determinants of retribution.

### Compatibility of Benefit and Harm with the Liking Relation: Conditions of Harmony

The relation between a benefit or harm and sentiments has already been discussed in terms of the balance hypothesis (cf. Chapter 7). In that connection it was pointed out that we usually tend to like persons who benefit us and are prone to benefit persons we like. A parallel statement holds for harm and dislike. Therefore, benefit belongs to love, approach, and a tendency toward union, and harm belongs to hate, segregation, and opposition.

With true benefit, *p* feels that the primary intention of *o*'s act was to please *p*, and to support him, that it is "for" *p* as a person; if the specific act is blocked, another will arise which is again directed towards *p*'s wishes and tendencies. One could say that the totality of *x*'s that are positive for $p$ constitute the means field (hodological space) for $o$'s goal of benefiting $p$. The benefit could even be administered secretly, for if the only wish is to benefit, a reward will not be expected. In short, the terminal focus of $o$'s action is to benefit $p$.

Likewise, an act of harm is felt to be "against" the person, for it implies that it was produced only because it was negative for $p$, and that any other act with a direction opposed to $p$'s forces might serve. The harmful act does not merely conflict with a particular wish of $p$'s; it represents an attack directed against $p$ as a whole.

In line with the tendency toward harmony, it can be stated that if we like a person we are more apt to interpret his act as a benefit; conversely, if we dislike a person we are more likely to interpret his act as a harm. This hypothesis is supported by Maslow:

> In the same way we may take a criticism from a friend in two different ways. Ordinarily the average person will respond by feeling attacked and threatened (which is fair enough because so frequently criticism is an attack). He therefore bristles and becomes angry in response. But if he is assured that this criticism is not an attack or a rejection of himself, he will then not only listen to the criticism, but possibly even be grateful for it. Thus, if he has already had thousands of proofs that his friend loves him and respects him, the criticism represents only criticism; it does not also represent an attack or threat. (Maslow, 1941, p. 365.)

The following points, brought out in a study by Albert (1956), also support the tendency toward balance between the liking relation and benefit and harm: If $p$ who dislikes $o$ also benefits $o$, the action will be suspect and ulterior motives will be looked for. The benefit is also less likely to be perceived as a deliberate act than as an accident. However, if $p$ who likes $o$ benefits $o$, there will be less exploration of motives. The benefiting act is more apt to be taken as natural and understandable.

The conditions of balance between the liking relation and unit formation as delimited in Chapter 7 (pp. 182–200) are used in many different ways in acts of benefiting and harming. Thus, $o$ can benefit $p$ by telling him that he has done a good deed, and that an act of $p$'s friend $q$ is good, that $p$'s friend $q$ likes $p$'s deed, that something good has been done by $p$'s child, that $p$'s enemy is not very admirable, that two friends of $p$ like each other, and so on. Likewise, since disturbing a balanced situation is negative for $p$, $o$ can harm $p$ in this way. He can tell $p$ he has done wrong, that an act of $p$'s friend $q$ is bad, etc.

## Power Relations and Status Implications in Benefit and Harm

A simple thought may well introduce the power factor. Since $o$ does something to $p$ in an act of benefiting or harming, the act is within $o$'s power; that is, it is one of the things $o$ can do. Yet, as so often happens in pursuing the obvious, we are led to more intricate relations which add to its significance. We shall see that the power of *o* is an important determinant of *p*'s general evaluation and reaction to an act of harm or benefit. Not only will *p*'s perception of who is responsible for the act be influenced, but also his understanding of the reasons motivating the act.

One of the most direct ways in which the perception of *o*'s power affects causal attribution is seen in the following ordinary example. If *p* is told that *o* effected the benefit or harm, and if he knows that *o* could not have done so—that *o* lacks the necessary acumen or physical prowess, for example—then *p* will either doubt the veracity of the report or at least will feel that additional circumstances, such as the assistance of someone else, played a role.

A nice experimental demonstration of the fact that the perception of *o*'s power influences causal attribution in an act of benefiting is given in a study by Thibaut and Riecken (1955). The results showed that where *o* is perceived as powerful, his acts are more apt to be seen as self-caused, that is as determined by his own wishes and intentions, rather than as coerced.

The subjects were college students. Each subject made the acquaintance of two men, unknown to the subject as experimental confederates. One was obviously of high standing, poised and confident, with a record of high educational leadership achievements behind him. The other was presented as self-effacing, of lower socio-economic and educational levels, and with but modest leadership experience. The perceived power was thus based upon the presumed personal competence and status of the individuals. The trio was then given the task of constructing crossword puzzles for a certain purpose. They were to work in separate rooms, but could pass around the two available dictionaries which "happened" to be given to the confederates. After some time, when the confederates did not spontaneously share the dictionary with the subject, the experimenter gave the subject a series of written messages which requested the dictionary and varied in forcefulness. These the subject could send to his associates. After the same three messages were delivered to each of the confederates, both dictionaries were surrendered. The subject was then questioned as to why he thought his partners gave up the dictionaries (i.e., benefited him in this way).

The first fact of importance is that the power difference between the partners made a difference in the perceived locus of causality for 80 per cent of the subjects (16 out of 21). Moreover, of the 16 subjects who perceived a difference in locus of causality, internal forces (he wanted to help me) were associated with the high power partner and external forces (I put pressure on him) with the low power partner (12 subjects) more frequently than the converse (4 subjects). The results were even more striking in a second experiment (18 vs. 1) in which the subject was forced to make a choice between the two causal alternatives by being asked "... Which one [i.e., of the partners] would you say you forced and which one just wanted to anyway?" (In this second experiment, the act, donating a pint of blood, benefited a generalized other and not the subject himself.) In other words, a person of power is more apt to be seen as commanding his own will than is a weak person. Conversely, the ineffectual person is more apt to be seen as being pushed into things than is the person with a strong will.

Thus far we have stressed the factor of power as influencing $p$'s perception of the source of the act—who did it and whether it was done on his own initiative. Power relations also play a part in still deeper levels of attribution, levels that answer the question why $o$ wanted to harm or benefit $p$. In this way power relations are an important determinant of $p$'s acceptance or rejection of the act.

First, the case of harm. If $o$ is stronger than $p$, $p$ may accept the harm as being in the natural order of things according to which the big ones always peck the little ones; it is, in a way, their "right" to do so. Or, especially if $p$ admires strength, he may see it as an act derived from a sentiment: "$o$ dislikes me justly, I deserve to be harmed." In other cases $p$ may reject the event; he thinks $o$ ought not to harm him even though $o$ is stronger, that $o$ is an insufferable bully; $p$ may yearn for revenge, but may have to content himself day-dreaming about it if he feels too weak to defy $o$'s power. Where $p$ is stronger than $o$, the situation becomes radically changed. He may still feel that $o$ is justified in attacking him for one reason or another, but he also may easily think, "What an impudence of $o$, he is a rebellious, quarrelsome fellow; he probably thinks he is stronger than I; I have to show him his place."

Similarly, the interpretation of benefit may be influenced by the power relation. If $o$ is stronger than $p$, the act may be interpreted by $p$ as being one without ulterior motives: $p$ thinks that $o$ likes $p$ and that he wants to be helpful to $p$. It also may be interpreted as an attempt on $o$'s part to show $p$ that he considers him weak and in need of help; $o$ wants to show off his strength; $p$ says, "I don't need his help. His offer to help me is an insult." If a weaker $o$ benefits $p$, then $p$ might regard it as the proper behavior of $o$, as his tribute in recognition of $p$'s superiority: "The weaker ones ought to pay tribute to the stronger ones." Or, $p$ may think that $o$ wants something from him, that *o* benefits him in order to obligate him, or that *o* wants to be liked and appreciated by *p*.

Thus, the interpretation of *o*'s true goal in benefiting *p* will partly depend on the power relation between *p* and *o*. Obviously, however, since different interpretations may arise within the same power relation, other factors also enter into its determination. It has already been pointed out that where *p* feels that *o* likes him, he will be predisposed toward interpreting the benefit as being truly in his own interests. A high self-regard on *p*'s part will also favor such an interpretation. Likewise, where *p* likes *o*, balance tendencies will predispose *p* to assume that *o* has benefited him because *o* likes him. In addition, the objective possibilities within a given power relation play a role. For example, if *o* depends on *p* and is inferior in power to *p*, that means that *p* is a possible source of positive or negative events for *o*. It will then be important for *o* to produce a positive attitude in *p*. Thus, it will be much more likely that *o* is motivated to get returns when he benefits a person on whom he depends than when he benefits a person who is dependent upon him; *o* will not try to polish the apple for a person who cannot influence his fortunes.

Because these status implications so often become the dominant feature of the situation, particular attention will now be given to this aspect of power relations. Not infrequently, the control a person has over his environment, that is, his power, also carries a status value. His power is not only judged according to whether it is adequate to the task, or as being greater or less than someone else's, but he is evaluated as a person according to a worthiness dimension whereby he is to be admired or disparaged.

The differential power relations between agent and recipient which may be implied in benefiting and harming may, therefore, provoke status questions which become the pivotal factor in *p*'s reaction. Ladieu, Hanfmann, and Dembo see this as a major factor in the evaluation of help by a person with a disability. In their study of the interpersonal relations between the visibly injured and those around them, they state that

> Help is an asymmetric social relationship, and, as such, it lends itself easily to becoming an expression of the superiority-inferiority dimension. . . . The person who is always the one to be helped is likely to be considered as inferior. (Ladieu, Hanfmann, and Dembo, 1947, p. 179.)

Most of the reasons given by the injured for rejecting help "have as a common denominator the feeling that being offered help or accepting it involves being in a position of lowered status" (p. 180). Among the reasons given are, that help means lack of recognition of ability, that it implies pity, that it points out the disability, or that it means being considered a person apart from and not equal in value to others. Though one might assume that with a person who has a handicap the ability aspect is likely to be especially prominent, the status implications of relative power that may be implied by a benefit is by no means restricted to the handicapped.

It seems that potentially unfavorable status connotations tend to be more potent in harm than in benefit. There are several reasons for this, but we may single out the point that in many cases, consummation of a benefit requires some measure of sanction by the recipient—$p$ may be asked whether he wishes to be helped, or he may refuse the gift, thereby keeping the actualization of the benefit within his own power. This means that a benefit may be regarded not only as evidence of $o$'s power; it may also give recognition to the power of $p$ whenever it is felt that $p$ can nullify the benefit. Being harmed, on the other hand, is usually a much less "cooperative" affair. Though $p$ may be able to prevent being harmed by defensive action, $p$'s permission is not asked as to whether he will accept the harm. The harmful act usually is taken to mean that $o$ feels that $p$ will not be able to defend himself, that $o$ does not fear $p$, that $p$ is weak and can be pushed around with impunity. One *bestows, confers,* or *gives* a benefit such as a gift, praise, or help, but one *inflicts, causes,* or *commits* a harm, such as an insult or injury.

If we distinguish between value stemming from power and value based on other properties—which we may call in this connection "general" value—then we might say that $o$ harming $p$ can imply that, for $o$, $p$ is low in both power value and general value; the harm is an expression of negative sentiment and of the belief that $p$ is weak. On the other hand, when $o$ benefits $p$, it is most likely that $p$ is high for $o$ in general value; at the same time it can very easily mean that $p$ is low for $o$ in power value, and that $o$ thinks $p$ is weak and cannot take care of himself.

Yet it is noteworthy that harm more often serves the purpose of demonstrating one's power than does benefit. One reason has already been given, namely, that to some extent $p$ controls the actualization of a benefit; it is usually within his power to reject a benefit, but this is not necessarily so with harm. Sometimes, as we know, $o$ thrusts unwanted hospitality, food, or presents upon $p$ and insists that he accept it, but usually one can avoid a benefit by declining it. Benefits are sometimes rejected just because $p$ does not wish to become obligated to $o$ or come under his power in any way. Second, harm provides a more direct and obvious arena for a power contest since $p$ can be counted on to retaliate if he sees a chance of victory (unless he is restrained by ought forces). Abstention on $p$'s part generally gives recognition to $o$'s superior power, and defeated revenge reaffirms it. Other factors, of course, also play a role in the fact that power lust is more likely to be associated with harm than with benefit.

Bacon (1597) says that one of the main causes of anger is the apprehension of the injury suffered as being an expression of contempt, "for contempt is that which putteth an edge upon anger, as much or more than the hurt itself" (p. 142). He says that in order to control one's anger one should reorganize one's perception of the harm suffered, insofar as its attribution is concerned; one ought

. . . to sever, as much as may be, the construction of the injury from the point of contempt; imputing it to misunderstanding, fear, passion, or what you will. (p. 142.)

For Aristotle, slighting is crucial to the anger reaction. He defines slighting as

. . . an actualization of opinion in regard to something which appears valueless; for things which are really bad or good, or tend to become so, we consider worthy of attention, but those which are of no importance or trifling we ignore. (Aristotle, trans. 1939, p. 175.)

Anger is defined by Aristotle as a

. . . longing, accompanied by pain, for a real or apparent revenge for a real or apparent slight, affecting a man himself or one of his friends, when such a slight is undeserved. (p. 173.)

Power and status implications are so central in benefit and harm that anything that may be symbolic of these aspects of an act receives special weight. Notice how cautious we are before giving money as a gift. It can too easily be taken to imply that $p$ *needs* money, that he is weak and poor. Because of this the recipient of charity often feels that he is an object of pity. At the same time, a handsome sum is "nothing to be trifled with," because it is in excess of what the person really needs, and $p$ may accept this as a sign of respect.

These examples also point toward a connection between power, status factors, and ought forces. Not infrequently, harm from a power figure is accepted as his prerogative. And just as naturally, the one harmed ought to accept it. Thus, power, as a factor in causal attribution, and as a factor connected with status implications and ought forces, has a tremendous impact on the meaning and acceptance of harm and benefit.

### Ought Forces and Benefit and Harm

Whether the benefit or harm connotes that $p$ is liked or disliked, weak or strong, admired or disrespected, $p$'s reaction will always be influenced according to whether he perceives the act as fitting in with the ought forces or as running counter to them. Thus, $p$ will not feel grateful for a benefit, and will not feel obligated when he accepts it, if he thinks that it was owed to him by $o$, that $o$ ought to benefit him, that it was $o$'s duty to benefit him. If $o$ thinks that he should be thanked very much, that implies that he thought his act was over and beyond the "call of duty." Also, $p$ may reject a benefit if he thinks he does not deserve it.

Similarly, the ought forces will play a role in the acceptance or rejection of harm done by $o$. As psychoanalytic theories emphasize, if $p$ feels that he deserves the harm done to him he may even welcome it. However, since harm is an event that usually goes against the wish forces of $p$, and since there exists the tendency to confound wish forces with ought forces, $p$ is very likely to feel that any harm that occurred to him ought not have happened and is against objective requiredness.

For this reason, harm often provokes not only a reaction of anger, the feeling that arises when one's ego has been slighted, but also indignation, the feeling that arises when the objective order has been slighted. Though a more thoughtful person may experience his own anger as unjustified, the more usual reaction is to perceive one's own anger as well warranted and that of the other fellow as personal and biased.

There is also a marked tendency to identify positive and negative heteronomous (imposed) happenings with reward in the one case and punishment in the other. Outside events may be looked upon as signs that the recipient has done something for or against the ought forces, the objective order. Thus, fortune or misfortune are, legitimately or not, in the position of mediators in the cognition of ought forces. The person becomes informed through them about objective justice. Addison writes amusingly about the tendency to attribute "our neighbor's misfortunes to judgments":

We cannot be guilty of a greater act of uncharitableness than to interpret the afflictions which befall our neighbors as *punishments* and *judgments*. . . . An old maiden gentlewoman . . . is the greatest discoverer of judgments that I have met with. She can tell you what sin it was that set such a man's house on fire, or blew down his barns. . . . She can give you the reason why such an one died childless; why such an one was unhappy in her marriage; why one broke his leg on such a particular spot of ground; and why another was killed with a back-sword, rather than with any other kind of weapon. (Spectator, No. 483: Addison *et al.*, 1712, pp. 36–37; cf. also Kelsen 1946.)

## Retribution

Throughout the discussion of benefit and harm, allusions to retribution have necessarily been made, for revenge is often a prominent reaction to harm, as gratitude is to benefit. Now our attention will be focussed on retribution as such. We shall see that the liking relation between $p$ and $o$, power relations, and status implications, as well as ought forces, which were shown to weigh so heavily in the interpretation of benefit and harm, also play a role in retribution. Additional factors that are prominent in certain theories of retribution will also be presented.

The remarks concerning life-space perspective, local and total relevance, proximal and distal stimuli, and levels of attribution which introduced certain problems posed by benefit and harm, have equal application to a discussion of retribution. These concepts will again appear from time to time in our review of a variety of theories that attempt to define the conditions giving rise to retribution. However, because attribution to source and intention is so important in this connection, as it was seen to be in the case of benefit and harm, we shall pause here to consider this aspect in its new context.

An everyday fact is that the feelings of both revenge and gratitude become markedly attenuated, if not completely dissipated, upon the discovery that the harm or the benefit was not the true goal of the agent. We do not feel grateful to a person who helps us fortuitously, or because he was forced to do so, or because he was obliged to do so. Gratitude is determined by the will, the intention, of the benefactor. Attribution to source and intention has similar significance in the case of revenge.

Moreover, it has often been stated that for the full attainment of the goal of revenge or gratitude it is necessary that the recipient, in this case $o$, realize that the harm or benefit has been caused by $p$ in requital. Aristotle (trans. 1939) quotes Homer to make this point; in the Odyssey, Odysseus makes sure that Polyphemus knows who blinded him, "as if Odysseus would not have considered himself avenged, had Polyphemus remained ignorant who had blinded him and for what" (p. 191). In Andromaque, Racine makes Hermione say that her revenge is in vain if her victim, when he dies, does not know that she killed him.

In this regard Adam Smith says that love and hatred are different from gratitude and resentment. When we like a person, we are pleased with his good fortune and we may help to bring it about.

Our love, however, is fully satisfied, though his good fortune should be brought about without our assistance. All that this passion desires, is to see him happy, without regarding who was the author of his prosperity. But gratitude is not to be satisfied in this manner. If the person to whom we owe many obligations is made happy without our assistance, though it pleases our love, it does not content our gratitude. Till we have recompensed him, till we ourselves have been instrumental in promoting his happiness, we feel ourselves still loaded with that debt which his past services have laid upon us. (Smith, 1759, p. 95.)

The same is true for resentment:

Resentment would prompt us to desire, not only that he should be punished, but that he should be punished by our means, and upon account of that particular injury which he had done to us. (p. 96.)

One might add that this is true only to a certain degree; the tendency toward retribution will usually diminish if the person having the resentment hears that the object of his resentment has suffered great misfortune.

Now we shall turn to specific points of view that attempt to account for the nature of retributive acts. Since gratitude has been treated less fully in the literature than has revenge, the discussion will center around the latter.

***Retribution as a derivative of the liking relation.*** One might consider deriving the tendency toward retribution from the harmony relations which coordinate benefiting and liking on the one hand, and harming and disliking on the other. If $o$ benefits $p$, $p$ will like $o$; that in turn will lead to $p$ benefiting $o$. Similarly, $p$ harming $o$ in retaliation can be derived.

However, it is questionable whether the typical tendency toward retribution can be derived in its entirety from a sentiment. For instance, revenge usually does not merely reflect $p$'s dislike for $o$ which had been aroused by the original harm. Rather, it often refers quite specifically to the event that ought to be redressed. One may have known all along that $o$ is hostile, and that he thinks he can harm $p$ at any moment. This in itself will not produce the tension toward revenge. A tendency toward revenge usually demands a definite change that obliterates a previous event. This is different from dislike which belongs to the dimension of potentiality and not to that of actual tendencies. Dislike can be in a sort of equilibrium, though $p$ may enjoy changes that confirm it or are in accordance with it.

Of course, a sentiment can be a factor in determining the strength of the tendency toward retribution. One might assume that with a positive sentiment, positive retribution will arise more easily than with a negative sentiment, and vice versa. But this cannot be used as an argument for a sentiment theory of retribution which implies that the sole tendency toward retribution stems from a sentiment that has been produced by the original act. This theory does not take account of the special feature of retribution which refers directly to the instigating event.

*Revenge as an attempt to influence the underlying cognitive structure of o.* Revenge may be conceptualized not only as a simple effect of the tendency toward harmony, but more specifically as a pointed attempt on the part of $p$ to counteract in some way the beliefs held by $o$ which gave rise to the act in the first place. As in the tendency toward harmony, a disturbed equilibrium is reinstated, but the means has particular reference to the belief-value matrix of the other person.

From this point of view, the situation to be righted does not concern only the concrete evil experienced. If $o$ throws $p$ into the water and $p$ gets dry again, or if $o$ hurts $p$ and the hurt has subsided, then the injury itself is redressed. Though $p$ does not feel any present effects of the injury, the harm remains. Nor is the harm necessarily redressed by retaliation in kind. What is necessary is that the deeper sources of $o$'s actions, the sources that impart the full meaning to the harm and that most typically have reference to the way $o$ looks upon $p$, should be changed. This is the level of attribution that guides the revenge. It points towards the crucial facts that concern $p$, facts that are far more distal and invariant than the immediately occurring injury, and that comprise the major portion of what is considered "totally relevant" (cf. p. 253).

The important point in this theory is that the harmful act represents a belief the return action attempts to refute. The act of revenge can then be understood as a means action whose terminal focus is change in the belief-value matrix of $o$. In naive psychology this purpose is often recognized by such expressions as: I will teach him; he has to learn that he can't do that; who does he think he is; I can't take this lying down —my honor is at stake, etc.

In accord with this view, Westermarck (1932) has stressed the means character of actions prompted by resentment: "Rightly understood, resentment is preventive in its nature, and when sufficiently deliberate, regards the infliction of suffering as a means rather than as an end" (p. 83). In other words, resentment is a wish to produce a change in the underlying belief-attitude structure of the attacker, and revenge is the means of realizing this wish. The changes that are intended by revenge concern, according to this description, $o$'s ideas about the relative power, importance, and value of the two persons, as well as his ethical evaluation of these relations.

The beliefs about the relative power of $p$ and $o$ are seen to be the major target of a frequent type of revenge as delimited by Nietzsche (1881, No. 33). According to him, the word "revenge" has many meanings. One of them refers to the involuntary, defensive hitting back whose meaning is only to stop the harming influence in the service of self-preservation. With another kind of revenge, the goal is to hurt the other person in order to restore one's honor. By harming us, the enemy proved that he was not afraid of us; in turn, the revenge strives to prove that we are not afraid of him. We have to show ourselves fearless. Therefore, the dangerousness of the revenge, as exemplified by the duel in serious cases, is an important condition for adequate vindication. In the first form of revenge, fear is the motive; in the second, to show absence of fear.

As has already been pointed out, the aspect of the power relation that often is of greatest moment to the total relevance of harm and revenge, is that bearing upon status implications. Moreover, the force toward revenge is given added impetus when $p$ believes that $o$'s ideas of power and status infringe upon ethical precepts. Adam Smith combines these views in his statement concerning the goal of revenge.

What chiefly enrages us against the man who injures or insults us, is the little account which he seems to make of us, the unreasonable preference which he gives to himself above us, and that absurd self-love, by which he seems to imagine, that other people may be sacrificed at any time, to his conveniency or his humor. . . . To bring him back to a more just sense of what is due to other people, to make him sensible of what he owes us, and of the wrong that he has done to us, is frequently the principal end proposed in our revenge, which is always imperfect when it cannot accomplish this. (Adam Smith, 1759, p. 139.)

Revenge, seen as purposeful action directed against the belief-value matrix of $o$, may also be considered an attempt to maintain $p$'s image of himself and of his relations to $o$. Thus, Stagner (1951), for instance, says: "The self-image (including the relations of self to environment) ...represents a 'constant state' which the organism seeks to preserve" (p. 12). The need to maintain the constancy of the self-image has also been designated as a factor that brings about resistance in psychotherapy. This need is said to be so strong that modification of the self-image is resisted even though the change may assume a favorable direction. According to this thesis, revenge is sought if the act implies attributing to $p$ certain characteristics $p$ does not perceive as his own. For instance, $p$ will avenge himself if he feels that he does not deserve the ill treatment, but will not retaliate if he agrees that he is unworthy.

Repentance provides good evidence that the revenge has been effective, for if *o* is sorry for what he did, he virtually attests to the error of his beliefs and intentions. Adam Smith has pointed out that

> The object . . . which resentment is chiefly intent upon, is not so much to make our enemy feel pain in his turn, as to make him conscious that he feels it upon account of his past conduct, to make him repent of that conduct, and to make him sensible, that the person whom he injured did not deserve to be treated in that manner. (Adam Smith, 1759, p. 138.)

If *o* apologizes, he repudiates the act. He tries to produce in *p* the impression either that he is not really the source of the act, and that he did not intend it or that he would not now intend it.

If *p* does not seek revenge he may be felt to concur with *o*'s view of him which is implied by the harm. His inaction may be regarded as a silent affirmation that he is, in fact, weaker than *o*, or that he has been justly punished. So it is that the absence of any form of counter action can bring reality to the aphorism, "Might makes right."

Forgiveness, however, does not always imply passive acceptance of the attitude implications of harm. It may be a peculiarly effective way of accomplishing the desired cognitive changes in *o*. By forgiving, *p* can assert in effect that he is so superior that he can afford to be forgiving. Or the forgiveness can imply that since *o*'s actions are based on untrue beliefs, why should *p* be bothered by taking them seriously and avenging himself? Rather it is the attacker who is to be pitied, and being forgiven through *p*'s magnanimity emphasizes *o*'s inferiority still more. Forgiveness can devaluate the attack, devaluate the attacker, and affirm the power and status of the forgiver. Thus Oscar Wilde's injunction: "Always forgive your enemies: nothing annoys them so much." Of course, forgiveness can also be a more humble expression of an ethical doctrine.

**Undirected aggression in revenge.** The theory of revenge as undirected aggression refers to a type of counterattack in which cognitive factors are minimized to such an extent that even *o* does not feature in the reaction. Rather, the invariant end in such counterattack is far less specific than the interpersonal relation between *p* and *o*. The only feature common to the wide assortment of behavior embodied by undirected aggression is that something is destroyed or injured. The tension toward this kind of retribution has sometimes been represented as a kind of damming up of energy in a particular need system which is brought about by the fact that a "need"—for instance, the need not to be hurt—has been frustrated.

The theory does not necessarily exclude other kinds or aspects of revenge. It simply proposes that there is a feature of counteraggression which can only be described as undirected. Thus, according to the "frustration and aggression" hypothesis as presented by Sears, the invariance in reaction to frustration is to be found partly in directed, partly in undirected aggression:

The strongest instigation is to acts directed against the agent which is perceived as having been responsible for the frustration, [but also] to some degree every frustration produces instigation to every aggressive act in the person's repertory. (Sears, 1946, p. 216.)

In analyzing the theory of undirected counteraggression, it becomes clear that one has to be more specific about the meaning of "direction." One speaks of "directed" aggression in an act whose terminal focus is injury to a specific person. An act whose terminal focus is injury to something, is called "undirected" aggression. However, as an act it still has direction. An invariant environmental change which is produced by it under different circumstances, can be pointed out, even though the specific object to be injured is left undetermined. The invariance does not consist in "injury to $o$," but in "injury to $x$." The idea that aggression is essentially directed can still be retained, for instance, if aggression that is not focused on the attacker is regarded as "displacement," as merely deflected from its original direction by additional conditions. Actually, one can properly speak of an "undirected" tendency only when there exists a general tension toward change, and when the nature of the change and the person who suffers it are both undetermined.

Though Steinmetz, according to Westermarck, states that revenge as a primeval reaction is "undirected," he gives it a definite purpose, that of enhancing the self:

. . . revenge is essentially rooted in the feeling of power and superiority. It arises consequent on the experience of injury, and its aim is to enhance the self-feeling, which has been lowered or degraded by the injury suffered. It answers this purpose best if it is directed against the aggressor himself, but it is not essential to it that it should take any determinate direction: *per se* and originally it is "undirected." (Westermarck, 1932, p. 65.)

It may be added parenthetically that Westermarck notes that he found no evidence for the existence of an undirected revenge, and that one cannot give the name revenge to all the different ways in which a person may try to enhance his self-feeling after having suffered an injury. In any case, the aim to enhance self-feeling gives clear "direction" to revenge.

*Revenge in terms of the expression theory of emotions.* We shall now leave the issue of direction in counteraggression and give some attention to observations concerning the expression and projection of the concomitant of emotions. The essential contribution of expression theory is to point out that there is a correspondence between what may be called the expressive or qualitative character of a retributive act and the emotional feeling behind it.

For instance, an act of harm, as noted previously, is felt to be *"against"* the person. Therefore, the act of revenge must also have this quality of being against something whether its target is *o* or just *x*. But, to be against something requires a conception of the natural tendencies in the entity that is to be harmed so that one can act counter to them. If the target is *o*, *p* will attempt to counteract what he perceives to be the wishes or best interests of *o*. If the target is an object, one can also assume a physiognomic perception in which things are endowed with a tendency toward self-preservation and self-activation. One can act for a thing by taking care of it, cleaning it, keeping it in good shape, and repairing it; or one can act against a thing by destroying it, breaking it, or making it dirty. According to the expression theory of revenge, the anger tension may therefore be discharged by a counteraggression directed against things. Each thing tends to be as good and as perfect as possible, and the meaning of breaking a thing is acting against this tendency.

It is noteworthy that a hard, resistant object is more suitable for the expression of counteraggression than is a soft, yielding object. This is so because the resistance of the object represents its opposition to *p*'s attack against its intrinsic tendencies. "Undirected" counteraggression is expressed by throwing dishes and not pillows. Expression theory also clarifies why a hard, resistant object is so appropriate for the expression of anger aroused by frustration. Pounding one's fist on the table is a representation or image, as it were, of what the person has just experienced, namely an action obstructed by an obstacle.

The aggressive response to harm and frustration may be seen to be partly similar and partly opposite to the instigating act. As for the similarity: in frustration, the aggressive response and the original event involve obstructed actions; in revenge they involve actions leveled against something. At the same time, the stimulating conditions and the reaction bear an opposite relation to each other: in both frustration and harm, *p* is the recipient of the original event but he is the agent in the subsequent reaction. The original obstruction or harm are heteronomous events not intended by *p*, whereas he seeks out an obstruction or injurious act in his counterattack.

Extending expression theory still further, one can say that harm (and frustration or other disturbances) are experienced disharmonies, which demand disharmony in the environment. A person, whose inner life is full of destruction and disharmony, will tend to perceive destruction and disharmony in the environment. He will enjoy and produce them. A harmonious environment would not fit into his life space. Thus, he creates out of disharmonies a super-harmony. Similarly, a person who is made happy by some event may show "undirected" benevolence.

**Retribution, objective requirements, and moral issues.** From time to time in the preceding discussions, it has been intimated that the decision to avenge oneself or to repay a benefit is not always felt to be a matter of choice. Sometimes the person is propelled, as it were, toward retributive action by requirements that are felt to be given by the objective order of things.

Simple reciprocation is a case in point. As Baldwin (1955) abstracts it, "... if another person imposes some event upon us, we are motivated to impose that same event upon him" (p. 155). An event that consists of $o$ doing something to $p$ seems to require a second event consisting of $p$ doing something to $o$. Though not all people feel this sequence as a requirement—and we can leave the question as to its "truth-value" unanswered—the fact is, that it is often felt as such. Furthermore, this sequence has represented a basic model for the thinking about requirement in general. According to Kelsen (1946), the more abstract ideas about causality were developed in Greece from the experience of retribution.

The close relation between retribution and objective requirement is also born out by the attempts of Adam Smith and Westermarck to connect moral emotions with retributive emotions. According to Westermarck (1932), who is greatly influenced by Adam Smith, moral approval and disapproval, the "moral emotions," have their root in retributive emotions. But the moral emotions are distinguished from the retributive emotions by the feature of disinterestedness.

A moral judgment always has the character of disinterestedness. When pronouncing an act good or bad, I mean that it is so quite independently of any reference it might have to me personally. (Westermarck, 1932, p. 90.)

... if I pronounce an act done by a friend or by an enemy good or bad, that implies that I assume it to be so independently of my friendly or hostile feelings toward the agent. All this means that resentment and retributive kindly emotion are moral emotions if they are assumed by those who feel them to be uninfluenced by the particular relationship in which they stand both to those who are immediately affected by the acts in question and to those who perform the acts. (p. 93.)

According to Westermarck there are three sources of disinterested retributive emotions: (1) We may feel them "on account of an injury inflicted, or a benefit conferred, upon another individual with whose pain, or pleasure, we sympathize...." (p. 95); (2) we sympathize with the reaction of another person to harm or benefit; for instance, we see him getting angry and get angry ourselves; (3) disinterested resentment may arise because of differences of taste, habit, or opinion. What is considered new, foreign, or unusual, is considered wrong, even if it does not harm anybody.

Whether or not moral emotions can validly be said to develop from retributive emotions, it is important to relate these two spheres. Westermarck mentions that at earlier stages of cultural development to take revenge for a harm is regarded as a duty; at later stages, this requirement is limited by the doctrine of forgiveness. And as we have already noted, *p* typically feels righteous in his revenge because of the confounding of wish forces with ought forces. The need "to get even," to repay in kind, to hurt the enemy, may be so compelling that it assumes the character of a must, an ought force which is right and proper. Furthermore, as discussed previously, ethical considerations enter when it becomes *p*'s mission to make *o* realize the injustice of his ways; *o* has violated ethical standards and the damage can be at least partly alleviated through remorse on his part, a remorse that establishes as a fact that the proper modifications within his belief-value matrix have occurred.

Conceptually, punishment can be considered as having the same dimension as revenge. Punishment consists in *p* harming *o* because *o* harmed, or acted against, the objective order as *p* understands it; revenge consists in *p* harming *o* because *o* unjustly harmed *p*. When retribution partakes of a moral injunction, it tends to become depersonalized, a dictate of authoritative forces outside the self, a requirement of objective standards.

When *p* feels grateful, however, he generally does not wish his recompense to be attributed to social amenities or ethical decree. Possible reasons for the fact that revenge often draws upon ethical support and that gratitude usually neither needs nor wants it are: With revenge, ethical support may counteract the opposing doctrine of forgiveness. Furthermore, *p* may augment his power by ethical sanction, whereas with gratitude, power is usually not an issue.

***The power relation as a restraining or facilitating force in retribution.*** Power has already been discussed as a factor in the causal attribution of harm and benefit and as a factor relevant in revenge. Here we should like to give some consideration to the power relation as a restraining or facilitating force in retribution.

With revenge, the point, simply stated, is that if a powerful $o$ harms $p$, $p$ will be less likely to respond with counteraggression than when a weak $o$ harms him. According to the theory of frustration and aggression, "...the strength of inhibition of any act of aggression varies positively with the amount of punishment anticipated to be a consequence of that act" (Dollard, *et al.*, 1939, p. 33). Not only will there be fewer aggressive responses directed against an instigator with greater punishment-threatening value, but the aggression is also likely to be less intense, as has been shown in a study by Graham, *et al.* (1951). The authors asked adolescents to complete statements that indicated the nature of an aggressive act against a person and the individual who had committed it, according to what they thought would be the most likely way for a person to act in such a situation. For instance, one of these statements was: "When John's mother hit him, he———." Two independent variables were used: (1) the degree of aggressiveness of the act, and (2) the type of instigator: parent, sibling, friend, authority (policeman or teacher), or inferior. Though these instigators vary in more than one dimension, the dimension mainly used in the evaluation of the results was the punishment-threatening value. The results showed that

Both the frequency and the degree of aggressiveness of the aggressive responses were a direction function of the degree of aggressiveness with which the attack had been made. (Graham, *et al.*, 1951, p. 519.)

The result that concerns us at this point relates to the punishment-threatening value of the person who made the attack: The greater this value, the less was the aggressiveness of the response.

With gratitude as a reaction to benefit, however, a powerful $o$ usually does not act as an inhibiting factor. A main reason is that $p$ does not have to be concerned with the possibility of defensive counteraggression on $o$'s part, as he would be in contemplating revenge. Sometimes a powerful $o$ might even facilitate the expression of gratitude, as when it is designed to elicit yet further benefits or when $p$ looks up to a person of power.

An interesting general theory of emotions, based on the interaction of positive or negative heteronomous events and power relations, has been proposed by Marston (1928). Marston calls the influence from the environment the "motor stimulus." This motor stimulus can vary in two dimensions: it can be antagonistic or allied, and it can be superior in strength to the own person, or inferior. When the motor stimulus is antagonistic and superior in strength, the person will react by compliance. He will move himself at the dictates of a superior force. When the motor stimulus is antagonistic but inferior in strength, the person will react by dominance, a superiority of the self over some sort of adversary. A motor stimulus that is "allied" to the self and inferior, will produce "inducement" in the person; that is, he will try to influence the other person in a friendly way. A motor stimulus that is "allied" and superior will make for submission, that is, for voluntary obedience to the commands of the person in authority. It is impossible to give, at this place, an idea of the wealth of material treated by Marston in these terms.

To sum up, the power relation enters retributive behavior from all sides. First, it is an important determinant of the meaning of the harm or benefit itself (cf. pp. 258–263). Then, revenge may be directed toward change in *o*'s cognition of this factor (cf. pp. 267–269). The power relation may also be decisive in the retributive outcome, particularly whether the tension toward revenge will be realized in action or not. Finally, power influences the selection of the means whereby revenge or gratitude is expressed.

***Theories of retribution and the homeostatic principle.*** The discussion of retribution has revolved around different aspects of revenge (and in some instances gratitude) which are emphasized in one or the other of several theories. In spite of the differences, however, the principle of homeostasis receives silent, if not explicit, confirmation in each of them. Briefly, this principle states that the self-regulating processes within the organism tend toward a state of equilibrium. Balance will be restored when it is disturbed. (Cf., for instance, Stagner, 1951.)

The homeostatic reaction to harm or benefit can take place on different levels. If, for instance, the event produced is a bodily wound, the homeostatic process will bring about its healing. If a property of the person has been damaged, he may attempt to restore it.

Where the reaction takes the form of revenge, the homeostatic principle is also evident. Thus, the theory that derives retribution directly from the liking relation makes use of the balance hypothesis. The theories that give emphasis to cognitive factors also assume an equilibratory process: The beliefs and values underlying the harm must be corrected; that is, they have violated (were out of balance with) what are considered true notions as determined by the self-image, ethical standards, or other criteria. Should the revenge be yet further stimulated by objective, ought requirements, the homeostatic principle is again manifested in the need to right a wrong, or need to "get even" which then "balances the score" and restores the status quo. Where revenge takes the form of "undirected" aggression the homeostatic process may be described as follows: the harm leads to an accumulation of tension which acts as a disturbance of the existing state of affairs; the person mobilizes himself to meet the disturbance through a discharge of the tension in diffuse aggression. In the expression theory of revenge, the homeostatic process may be linked with the fact that the emotional character of the revengeful act is in harmony with certain essential features of the instigating event.

The several points of view describing or deriving retribution are not necessarily contradictory. They merely emphasize different features that are considered invariant, or at least important. It is likely that each of the features plays a role inasmuch as retribution exists on different levels and takes part in different functions.

### Summary

In this chapter we considered the actions of benefiting and harming another person with emphasis on the person's reactions. If $p$ is benefited or harmed, his response will depend mainly on the way he interprets these events; therefore, we had to deal once more with attribution. The ideas of local and total relevance were discussed in this connection. For instance, an experience can be painful as such, that is, its local relevance is negative; but since it implies agreeable consequences its total relevance is positive. The relations of benefit and harm to sentiments, power, and ought forces were treated, as well as the way these relations influence our interpretation and expectation of actions by other people.

In the second part of the chapter the phenomenon of retribution was explored as an especially important kind of reaction to experienced benefit or harm. Different theories of retribution and factors influencing the tendency to retribution were considered: the derivation of retribution from the tendency toward harmony with sentiments; revenge as an attempt to influence the cognitive structure of $o$; revenge as undirected aggression; revenge seen as an expression of retributive emotion; the relation of ought forces and power to retribution; and retribution as homeostatic tendency.

CHAPTER 11

# Reaction to the lot
# of the other person

EVENTS THAT HAVE THEIR SOURCE in the environment and that affect $p$ in some way have been referred to throughout the book, and their general characteristics were examined in Chapter 6. These environmental effects make up the "lot of $p$." That environmental changes are positive or negative for the other person can also affect $p$. It is in this sense that the lot of $o$ becomes a lot of $p$. However, there may be a real difference between the subjective state of $o$ and what is generally considered the affective connotations of his lot. For instance, $o$ may be very happy in spite of the fact that a misfortune has befallen him.

## Formal Statement of Reactions

If we take into account only the value dimension of an experience, i.e., its positive or negative character, four types of reaction to the lot of the other person may be schematically distinguished: (1) That $o$ has a positive experience is positive for $p$. (2) That $o$ has a negative experience is negative for $p$. (3) That $o$ has a positive experience is negative for $p$. (4) That $o$ has a negative experience is positive for $p$. In the first two types, the relation between $p$ and $o$ is syntonic or concordant. It presupposes a sympathetic "identification"; the first may be called sympathetic enjoyment, the second simply sympathy or compassion. The last two types show a discordance or antagonism

277

between *p* and *o*; the third may be called envy, the fourth malicious joy or *Schadenfreude*.

In naive psychology all these reactions are called feelings or emotions, states that occur within the person and are experienced directly only by him. Yet we do not have to ask a person how he is feeling to know that he is happy or sad, sympathetic or envious. The behavior of the person in the context of the situation in which it takes place often permits us to make valid interpretations about his emotions. We call a person envious when, for instance, he belittles the good fortune of another.

Furthermore, these "feelings" are not merely experiences with a certain quality. They also have a well-defined place in a network of relations in which such psychological processes as cognitions, wishes, sentiments, etc. are involved. We shall try to disentangle some of these relations.

### Sympathy, Congruence of Feelings, and Emotional Contagion

The concept of identification has been used to refer to the fact that the reactions of *p* to the lot of *o* may be concordant or discordant with *o*'s feelings about the event. In their survey of the literature on sympathy, Ley and Wauthier define the term "positive identification" in its commonly understood sense, namely as a

... tendency to feel, and to take part in, the emotions and sentiments of another person. It expresses the disposition to suffer or to rejoice with somebody, and its corollaries are pity, compassion, and commiseration. (Ley and Wauthier, 1946, pp. 115–116.)

Some writers have interpreted the concept of identification as implying identity of feelings or reactions, in kind if not in degree, between *p* and *o*. LaPiere and Farnsworth, for instance, assert that

Positive identification consists of mentally putting oneself into the place of another and reacting more or less intensely to the stimuli that actually impinge upon that other person. Thus, should a person with whom we have closely identified ourselves cut his finger in our presence, we would vicariously "feel" the pain of that hurt. ...

[Negative identification] permits a vicarious reaction that is negative; *i.e.*, stimuli that produce "pain" in the other give pleasure to the negatively identified person, and vice versa. Thus we enjoy the suffering of our enemies, whereas their good fortune hurts and angers us. (LaPiere and Farnsworth, 1949, pp. 225–226.)

Dembo and her associates object to such a position. They even doubt that in the sympathy relation the feelings of the donor (agent) and recipient can be identical:

The donor cannot *see* the situation as the recipient sees it. He cannot know all the emotional ramifications of being injured. And even if he were to understand much of what it means to be injured, he would not feel the suffering in the same way as the injured person does. He does not suffer the actual social deprivation nor the self-devaluative feelings of the recipient. The recipient is distressed over the loss itself, the donor because the recipient suffers. The *content* of their distress is therefore different. . . . (Dembo, Leviton, and Wright, 1956, p. 28.)

What is required is congruence rather than identity of feeling:

The donor need not approach the *mood* of the recipient in intensity, nor is it necessary that his mood be the same qualitatively, as long as it is not incongruous. If someone is depressed, a sympathizer need not also become depressed. There are other manifestations of concern sufficiently in harmony with the mood of the recipient to be considered sympathy. . . . (p. 28.)

Nor would identity of feelings have advantages:

. . . were the donor to feel precisely the same way as the recipient, it is questionable whether any *action* he could take would be effective in diminishing the distress. The anxiety and fearfulness of the recipient, for example, would prevent him from realistically evaluating his situation. A similar anxiety and fearfulness in the donor would also act as a barrier to adjustive effort.

Thus, the donor and recipient *perceive* differently, *feel* differently and *act* differently. Congruence rather than identity is required in each of these instances. (p. 28.)

This point, that the reactions of the sympathizer must be differentiated from those of the person with whom he is sympathizing, has also been stressed by those distinguishing true sympathy from emotional contagion. A good example of emotional contagion is given by Becker:

Thus we find that the merriment at a drinking bout or a dinner party *infects* those later joining the merrimakers—infects persons who perhaps a moment before were sorrowful. They are "carried away" by the general jollification. (Becker, 1931, p. 62.)

In emotional contagion, an emotion in *o* simply produces an emotion in *p*. This does not necessarily mean that cognitive elements must perforce be absent. We may know very well that the causal source of our feeling stems from the affective nature of our surroundings, for instance, the mood of another person. The place of cognition is also shown by the fact that we may join a merry party in order to be cheered up, or avoid depressing sights so as not to be infected with sadness and pain.

True sympathy, according to such writers as Scheler (1913, trans.

1954), Becker (1931), Asch (1952), and Westermarck (1932) is quite different from emotional contagion. Asch reminds us that

> Sympathy requires more than for the ego to experience an emotion similar to the one he sees in another . . . we have seen that the first step in social perception is a knowledge of the situation and the psychological condition of the *other* person. We do not confuse the emotion we perceive in our neighbor with the emotion we would experience if we were in a similar situation. We see *that* our friend is perplexed by the puzzle we have put to him, but we are not perplexed in the least; we can comprehend another's intention without it becoming our intention. . . . It is one thing to see that a person is in pain and quite another to experience the pain in ourselves. . . .
> It is because we become aware of the situation and experience of others that we can feel *with* them. The mere duplication of an observed reaction may in fact be a sign of an inadequate social relation. There are times when the sight of suffering merely reminds a person of his own suffering; when this is so, he has simply lost social contact. (Asch, 1952, pp. 171–172.)

Becker, following Scheler's distinction between true sympathy and emotional contagion, points out that true sympathy has as its object the feeling of sorrow and joy in the other person; i.e., it is directed towards the feelings of the other person. It is not sufficient that it merely takes place in the presence of another's sorrow or joy alone (Becker, 1931, p. 62).

The characteristics of congruent emotional reactions have hardly been investigated. We do know that intensity of emotional expression may make a real difference as to whether the other person will regard the reaction as a sympathetic one. In the Dembo (1956) study, some of the injured subjects expressed resentment of manifestations of sympathy. They felt that it was embarrassing, that it made them feel worse off than they had thought they were, that the added emotionality was difficult to bear, and that it reflected insincerity (p. 30). In the true sympathy relation, *p* often does a good job of gauging the appropriate level of emotional responsiveness by virtue of the fact that the feelings of the other person are his main concern. He is able to sense, therefore, when his sympathetic responses are too strong for *o* to take, or perhaps not sufficiently expressive to convey a feeling of real sympathy. For the most part, the subjects in the Dembo study indicated that a deep positive feeling on the part of the sympathizer can be conveyed without emotional display (p. 30).

The recipient, also, modifies his emotional manifestations, but in this case he is guided by the standards of propriety (though, in some instances, he may also be concerned with the effects of his sorrow or joy on the sympathizer). Pain should not be expressed too openly;

it is childish to abandon oneself in ecstasy. Goldings' (1954) hypothesis—that the expression of happiness and unhappiness is guided by a behavioral norm which leads to a narrower range than that of the underlying feelings—found experimental support. In the preceding chapter it was shown that the level of emotional display on the part of the principal sufferer is less intense than the feelings themselves when the establishment of the objectivity of values requires a consensus.

So it is that both the sympathizer and the recipient modify their emotional behavior. They may still understand each other, though (or perhaps more correctly, because) their feelings are not matched in kind or degree. It is then that two people form an integrated unit with we-feeling. If their feelings are out of step, the two become segregated; the sympathetic relationship does not materialize (cf. Chapter 8, pp. 231–232).

There is yet another difference between true sympathy and emotional contagion, a difference that shows in the kinds of action stimulated in each. If $p$ is acting on the basis of emotional contagion, he will try to join a happy $o$ and avoid an unhappy $o$. In a desire for pleasure, $p$ will seek out the person who is happy and avoid the one who is sorrowful. On the other hand, if $p$ is guided by true sympathy, the direction of his actions may be entirely different. If $o$ is unhappy, $p$ will try to make him less so; he will attempt to help him or comfort him. If $o$ is happy, $p$ will try to see that $o$ remains in this state; he will do his best to protect this happiness. Expressing the two cases in terms of forces in the manner of Lewin (1938), we can say that though the forces propelling action appear in $p$'s life space in either case, their points of application and directions are different. With sympathy, the point of application is the other person; one wants to bring about a change concerning the situation of the other person, the direction of change being toward a better state of $o$. With contagion, the point of application is the own person, the direction of change being toward a better state of $p$; that is, one wants to get away from a situation in which one suffers, or one wants to enter a situation which one enjoys. This point is suggested by Westermarck (1932, p. 97) who specifies that in real sympathy, unlike emotional contagion, there is a conative disposition present to promote the welfare of the object. Dembo *et al.* (1956) speak of a "readiness to help" in this connection; they specify the psychological meaning of sympathic help by describing the nature of passive and active help (pp. 30–31).

Sometimes a potential sympathizer is not willing or ready to help a sufferer and yet his "sympathies" are with him. This means that emotionally he is distressed by the negative lot of $o$, but not sufficiently so to do anything about it. He may avoid a person in difficulty, not because of fear of contagion, but because of this unwillingness. He may be afraid, that if should he meet and speak with the sufferer, he would be carried away by true sympathy, becoming emotionally involved and lending him aid which he may later regret. Or, he may be afraid that in declining requested help, such as a loan, he would be regarded as selfish and hard-hearted. Common-sense psychology is well aware that people often try to avoid the unlucky person, the person who is down and out. It is referred to with bitterness: So long as you are secure you will count many friends; if your life becomes clouded you will be alone (Ovid, trans. 1924, p. 45). And, according to an old proverb, "A friend in need is a friend indeed." Whether the avoidance on the part of $p$ stems from fear of contagion or from potentially true sympathy, the sufferer will feel that $p$, if not unsympathetic, is at least not sympathetic. To be assured of true sympathy, he needs to feel that $p$ wants to help him overcome his suffering.

Though the differences between emotional contagion and sympathy are fundamental, there is at least one significant similarity. It is likely that in both kinds of interpersonal relation, sentiments play a parallel role, because emotional contagion and sympathy are more likely to arise in connection with a liked or admired person than with a person toward whom $p$ has negative feelings.

Thus far we have talked mainly about the induction of feelings in $p$ that are concordant with those of $o$. One can call it assimilation if this term is not restricted to processes of simple spreading or contagion. Besides concordant induction, there exists induction of feelings in $p$ that are discordant with those of $o$. There can occur a kind of contrast or counterinduction. A person may not be able to take part in the merriment of his environment, and he may be made unhappy and sad by it. Again, this may occur on different levels of cognitive differentiation. It may occur on the level of simple induction in the manner of countercontagion, in which case $p$ may not even be aware of the reason for his sadness; or it may occur on a level of greater differentiation, as when $p$ is dismayed at the rejoicing of a thoroughly disliked $o$. One can assume that the factor that primarily decides whether concordant or disconcordant induction takes place is the degree of unity between $p$ and $o$ as given in $p$'s life space. If $p$ feels himself segregated from $o$, or even antagonistic to $o$, counterinduction will take place.

Thus, the balance hypothesis linking unit-forming factors and sentiment relations, so fully discussed in Chapter 7 on sentiments, is seen to contribute to the understanding of some of the reactions to the lot of $o$. We proceed to a fuller discussion of aspects of this problem.

## Balance Tendencies in the Reaction of p to o's Lot

We have spoken of the concept of identification as referring to the fact that *p* is able to share *o*'s feelings. Spinoza emphasizes the sentiment relation, in its positive and negative instances, as being conducive to positive and negative identification.

He who conceives that the object of his love is affected pleasurably or painfully, will himself be affected pleasurably or painfully. . . .
He who conceives, that an object of his hatred is painfully affected, will feel pleasure. Contrariwise, if he thinks that the said object is pleasurably affected, he will feel pain. (Spinoza, 1677, trans. 1936, pp. 145–146.)

Dembo *et al.* (1956) propose that the sympathetic reaction most frequently arises in "we groups" where the ties of friendship are strong, though they also recognize that it may arise "between people who have no lasting relationship with each other, whose relationships are as tenuous as being fellow-Americans in a foreign country or even passers-by" (p. 27).

The point that the personal like or dislike *p* bears toward *o* will influence his reactions to *o*'s lot does not have to be belabored; it is part of the experience of everyday life. Formally speaking, a force on *o* toward a more negative state is connected with a negative sentiment toward *o*. If *o* then actually improves his lot, this change is in conflict with the force derived from the sentiment. Consequently, *p* may be unhappy because his enemy has success, or he may be happy because his enemy has failed. Not every negative reaction to a positive lot of *o*, therefore, can be called envy. When *o* is disliked, *p* may mind *o*'s good fortune very much without wanting it for himself. The essence of the disturbance may be said to reside in the tendency toward a balanced situation. The situation is balanced if a liked *o* experiences something positive and a disliked *o* something negative.

Not only personal liking will influence the reaction to *o*'s lot, but also the relation of the lot to the perceived worth of *o*; *p* may feel great satisfaction that *o* got what he deserved, whether in a positive or negative sense; and he may feel annoyed or disgusted when *o*'s lot does not agree with *o*'s worth as he sees it.

These reactions are closely tied in with the requirements of justice (cf. Chapter 8, p. 235). If *o*, through his own efforts, obtains a good to which he has no right, then he violates the ought force and *p* will think that *o* deserves to be punished. Similarly, if *o* sacrifices a good beyond the call of duty, he will be seen as deserving a reward. Even when the lots which come *o*'s way are chance events, their relation to the worth of *o* is taken into account by *p*. For instance, if *o* receives a positive lot through a stroke of undeserved luck, $p$ will also think that the event should not have happened; he may feel satisfied when $o$ has bad luck next time. Or, if $o$ suffers undeserved bad luck, then one sympathizes with him. His fate is considered unjust or cruel, and again the situation as it exists is opposed to the ought force, though it should be added that the ought force may be adjusted to the reality, in which case $p$ will think that $o$ deserves his fate after all (cf. Chapter 8, pp. 235–236). If $o$ does not deserve his negative lot, he ought to be helped. Events have to be corrected in accordance with the ought force. In short, the situation is balanced if the experiences of another are in accord with what he deserves.

As we have seen, the tendency toward balance works in more than one direction. If a situation to be in balance requires the coexistence of $A$ and $B$, $A$ will tend to be induced by $B$ as well as $B$ by $A$. Translating this to the content at hand, it is not only fitting for a deserving person to have good luck, but conversely, the person who is lucky is considered worthy. Or, not only should a scoundrel suffer misfortune, but also the one who had bad luck may be shunned as one who must be guilty. In other words, the value sentiment toward $o$ is assimilated to the lot of $o$; if $o$ experiences a positive $x$ he himself is seen as a person of value; if he experiences a negative $x$ he is seen as in some way negative.

Not always, however, is such comfortable balance obtained in this way through assimilation of the sentiment to the lot of $o$. On the contrary, sometimes the very fact of $o$'s good luck produces a strong dislike on the part of $p$, or the misfortune of $o$ evokes a positive feeling on the part of $p$ toward $o$. It is as if the sentiment moves in a compensatory or opposite direction to the lot of $o$. Such cases often involve a comparison between the lots of $o$ and of $p$. To reach some understanding of compensatory reactions as well as of such other reactions as envy and devaluating pity, it will be necessary to discuss further the problem of the interaction between the lots of $p$ and $o$.

### Interaction Between the Lots of p *and* o

The interaction between the lots of $p$ and $o$ has already entered the discussion to some extent. For instance, when it was pointed out that $p$'s feelings become congruent with those of $o$ in sympathy, or become infected with $o$'s in emotional contagion, it was also implied that $p$'s lot, as represented by his affective state, was dependent upon $o$'s lot. As the nature of the interaction between the two lots is explored further, we shall see that other reactions to the lot of $o$ are distinguishable and at the same time understandable within this framework.

It should be clear that the lots of $p$ and of $o$ may refer to a variety of matters. It may refer to the general positive or negative state of the persons. Then it is their happiness which is interdependent, as when $p$ is unhappy (or happy) and $o$ is happy. Or it may refer to events that befall them, as when $p$ suffers bad luck and $o$ is fortunate. Then it is that their fates are referred to each other. Or it may refer to a more specific lot, such as money, health, or work.

***General principles of interaction.*** The following is one of the principles describing the nature of the interaction between the lots of $p$ and $o$: In evaluating one's own lot, $o$'s lot plays the role of a background or surrounding, which, through the effects of contrast, can serve either to enhance $p$'s lot or to impair it. This principle is not a new one. Kant referred to it when he said:

> To feel one's well-being stronger when the misfortune of other people is put under our own well-being like a background to set it into brighter light, is founded in nature according to the laws of the imagination, namely that of contrast. (Kant, 1797, p. 273.)

By virtue of the same principles, a person's unhappy state will seem all the more so if he is surrounded by a gay party and for some reason cannot join in the happy mood:

> The presence of the wretched is a burden to the happy;
> And, alas! the happy still more so to the wretched.
> (Goethe, *Stella*, Act 3)

It is also possible that the background provided by $o$'s lot may influence the evaluation of $p$'s lot by a kind of assimilatory or diffusion effect. The satisfaction (or dissatisfaction) of $p$ with his own lot then reflects the background satisfaction of $o$ with his lot. This is seen, for example, when a child becomes pleased with his gift the moment a second child happily receives a similar one. Again it is to be mentioned that such assimilation need not preclude cognitive factors. The joy of the second child may highlight the virtues of the gift to which the first child then responds with new-found pleasure. With assimilation one could also use the thought model of the balanced situation which then consists of the dyad ($o$ is happy), ($p$ is happy) or ($o$ is unhappy), ($p$ is unhappy). Either one of the two terms of the dyad can induce the other term. It is understood that the terms, of course, refer to $p$'s life space.

One can also assume that the own lot influences the perception of $o$'s lot. Where the principle of contrast operates, $o$'s lot is inflated or deflated accordingly. Thus, Goldings (1954) found that extremely happy and extremely unhappy subjects project happiness and unhappi-

ness by contrast: very happy subjects tend to view others as unhappy
and very unhappy subjects tend to view others as happy. Where the
principle of assimilation operates, $o$'s lot is perceived after the manner
of one's own, producing the typical case of projection. Again an illustration of this is found in Goldings' experiment. Within the moderate
levels of happiness and unhappiness, his happy subjects tended to view
others as happy and his unhappy subjects tended to view others as
unhappy. Though it is only indirectly relevant to our topic, we want
to mention that Sears (1943) related the projection of traits to the
amount of insight the person has as to his own possession of them. In
the group of subjects who adequately assessed their own standing with
respect to a particular trait, i.e., those with high insight, he found a
negative correlation between the amount of a trait possessed and the
amount attributed to others. With these subjects, then, contrast influenced their perception of the trait in others. On the other hand, those
who lacked insight as to the possession of a trait tended to project it;
that is, they tended to perceive their own trait in others.

Perhaps one should make the point explicit, that in judging his own
or another's lot, $p$'s attitude is, as a rule, not a purely intellectual one.
At the same time, we should like to point out that comparative judgments of lots show in many ways an important feature of affectless
judgments, namely the dependence of the one item judged on the other
items that are grouped with it. (Cf. the concept of anchoring, for
instance, Woodworth and Schlosberg, 1955, pp. 247 ff.; Helson, 1951,
pp. 379 ff.)

**Interaction in envy and other emotions.** Klages (1928), among
others, has stressed that when the lots of $p$ and $o$ are compared, the
self-concept is directly affected. Simply stated, he points out that
when $p$ has less, he feels that the superior lot of $o$ implies his own
inferiority (p. 207). Dembo *et al.* (1956) believe that though such
self-devaluation may occur, it does not necessarily do so. Theorizing
that self-devaluation will result only when what they have called "comparative values" rather than "asset values" are in question, they conclude that it is possible for $p$ to have less than $o$ without referring this
fact to a personal evaluation (p. 23). When lots are being compared,
however, the effects on the self-concept may be an important basis for
the tendency to consider oneself more happy (Goldings, 1954, p. 36)
and more fortunate (Dembo *et al.*, 1956, p. 19) than the average.

Particularly since the self-concept may be enhanced or undermined
as a result of comparing the lots of $p$ and $o$, it is not hard to see that
one's reaction to the lot of another may be highly influenced by personal needs. If $p$ has a need to insure his good fortune, it is important

to him to be the favored one and he will respond positively to the negative lot of others. Under these circumstances, the effects of contrast operate in his favor. As La Rochefoucauld (1665) has said, "In the adversity of our best friends we always find something that is not displeasing" (p. 96).

In addition to the factors already mentioned which influence the nature of the interaction between the lots of *p* and *o*, the general status relations between the two play a significant role. If *p* considers himself in the same class as *o*, then there is a strong tendency also to consider that their fortunes should be the same. The now familiar balance tendency may again be seen to operate here, a tendency that may produce a wish as well as action to eliminate the inequality, or, where the situation cannot be corrected, uneasiness and tension. It may also alter the sentiment relations between *p* and *o*, the evaluation of *x*, and even the status relations between them. Thus, should *o* have a stroke of luck, then *p* may feel unhappy; he wants to experience the positive *x* also, and if possible he will try to share it with *o*; *p* may think that *o* ought not to have the *x*; he may think that the *x* is not so good after all, that it will not make *o* happy; because this negative experience of *p* may be connected with *o* as its source, a negative sentiment of *p* toward *o* may arise; *p* may decide that he is not in the same class with *o* and that the distribution of their fortunes is fair after all. All these are manifestations of the tendency towards an equalization of the fortunes of *p* and *o* when they are felt to belong together.

This tendency toward equalization of lot will be recognized as the common form and source of envy. As was mentioned above, the tendency occurs where *p* feels bound up with *o* in some way, similar to *o*, in the same class with *o*, in the same group. Consequently this form of envy arises in connection with people who are psychologically near to us. Aristotle (trans. 1939) has said that men "envy those who are near to them in time, place, age, and reputation, whence it was said, 'Kinship knows how to envy also'" (p. 239).

At the same time, envy is not a necessary consequence of the inequality of the fortunes of people who are close. For one thing, the specific *x* which *o* has received may not have the same personal relevance as far as *p* is concerned. The mother may not be envious of her son's military distinction because she has no aspirations in this direction. Furthermore, the sentiment relation may be sufficiently strong to control the reaction. Sympathetic pleasure in a basic "we-group" rather than envy may be evoked. We may sometimes envy those with whom we rejoice, but these emotions are so incompatible that they either occur as an alternating sequence, or one finally gives way to the other.

Also, as will be emphasized still again, the comparison of lots may have little importance for $p$. The situation and relationship may be one in which "you as compared with me" does not enter. This is a point which has been emphasized by Dembo *et al.* (1956). The fact of equality or inequality of lots is then irrelevant; instead one reacts to his own lot or that of the other in terms of its inherent characteristics.

When there is a force toward equality of lots, it may be so strong as to partake the character of an ought force, a requirement that is inviolate. In this connection, we note a quotation from Ley and Wauthier:

Envy derives from a certain sentiment of justice, from the desire for an exact distribution of favors or goods. Their being conferred on another person, while we are deprived of them, hurts certain of our natural sentiments of equality. (Ley and Wauthier, 1946, p. 137.)

Then it is that the force toward equality may operate against $p$'s personal interests: If $o$ is unfortunate, $p$ may feel that he also should be unfortunate. He may even feel guilty about having luck.

Of course, not all envy is a product of the requirements of justice or of the tendency toward equalization of fortunes. A greedy person may be envious even though he already has much more than $o$. Nor is every case in which $p$ desires to obtain what another person possesses one of envy. A child can take something that belongs to $o$ because of revenge, as an expression of aggression, or he may simply need a block for his own building. Or, since the perception of $o$'s lot can influence the expectations of $p$, should fate provide $o$ with a good, $p$ may want to have it too. The fact that $o$ has $x$ makes it seem possible that $p$ can realize it also. (Cf. Chapter 4, p. 111.) On the other hand, he may be resentful that he did not get it. With the reality of $o$'s lot, the possibility of $p$'s lot is given. (In like manner, $o$'s misfortune brings the possibility to $p$'s mind that he also might suffer—"There but for the grace of God go I.") In these instances, the goal in wanting $x$ is either to harm $o$ or to have $x$, whereas in envy, $p$ desires $x$ *because* another person has it. Though in everyday language "envy" is sometimes loosely applied to any case in which $p$ desires something belonging to $o$, as when one openly says, "Oh, how I envy him his trip!", this is quite different from the envy we have been talking about. In the former case the trip in itself is positive and is savored in thought independently of the fact that $o$ is able to take it. One does not so easily confess real envy.

Is it not paradoxical that envy, which is derived from what may be considered an ought tendency toward equalization of lots, is at the same time an emotion of which one is ashamed? The problem is a challenging one, and its solution may partly be found in conflicting norms. We have a right to be treated justly, but we are also reminded "that it is better to give than to receive," that one should smile at the fortune of another. Envy is fraught with conflict, conflict over the fact that these feelings should not be entertained though at the same time one may have just cause for them.

The tendency toward equalizing the fortunes of $p$ and $o$ may or may not be concordant with the sentiment relations between them. It is congruent with a positive sentiment only when $p$ has more than $o$. Then there will be either a force downward on $p$ or upward on $o$, the latter being in accord with a wish to make the liked person happy. The tendency toward equality is congruent with a negative sentiment only when $o$ has more than $p$. Then $p$ envies $o$, and wishes to reduce the discrepancy. Envy goes together with dislike, antagonism, segregation. One is more likely to envy a person whom one dislikes, and to dislike a person whom one envies. This affinity is made use of in propaganda aimed at dividing and conquering, as pointed out by Krech and Crutchfield:

One of the deadliest weapons in the arsenal of psychological warfare is propaganda aimed at convincing some segments of the enemy group that they are suffering more hardships or are gaining fewer benefits than other segments of the group. Thus, the soldier may be brought to believe that he is sacrificing more than the industrial worker, that he gets soldier's pay while the worker gets rich on war wages; those who obey the rationing regulations may come to believe that others are profiting on the black market; the poor may come to feel they are being taxed more than the rich in support of the war. Such beliefs in inequality of sacrifice and gain within the group are among the most divisive forces in group morale. (Krech and Crutchfield, 1948, pp. 411–412.)*

The divisive effect of the lot discrepancy is all the more potent because justice is on the side of equality.

Thus far we have assumed that $p$ considers $o$ more or less on an equal footing with himself. Then the tendency toward equalization of lots is strongest. But it is possible that $p$ regards $o$ as being quite different from himself, not at all to be classed in the same group. He may, for instance, consider him far more worthy, valuable, admirable. Instead of a tendency toward equality, then, there may be a tendency toward adjusting the lost difference to the value difference. The standard by which this is done is given by the equation:

$$\text{lot } p : \text{lot of } o = \text{value } p : \text{value } o.$$

* By permission from *Theory and problems of social psychology* by D. Krech and R. Crutchfield. Copyright 1948 by McGraw-Hill.

Consequently, if *p* and *o* suffer the same negative fate, and if *p* feels that *o* stands above him, then he may think that after all, he cannot complain. He may feel that he is not very unfortunate, for, though deserving less than *o*, there is no difference in their lots:

> When we our betters see bearing our woes,
> We scarcely think our miseries our foes. . . .
> How light and portable my pain seems now,
> When that which makes me bend makes the King bow.
> (*Lear*, Act II, Scene 6)

Or, should *p*, who thinks that he is the more valuable one, actually have worse luck than *o*, then he will feel his fate is all the harder to bear.

Thus far we have emphasized the affective consequences of certain kinds of lot distribution between *p* and *o*. Envy, malicious joy, devaluating pity, guilt, enhancement of one's fortune or misfortune, all were seen to depend upon an interaction between the lots of *p* and *o*. In addition, the person tends to adjust the lot distribution in conformity to what it ought to be both on the cognitive level and in action. For instance, where the lots of *p* and *o* should be equal, there often is a tendency to minimize the lot difference. Then, if *o* is the favored one, *p* may try to convince himself and others that the *x* which *o* has is not very valuable, that *o*'s lot is not so much better than *p*'s. In the reverse case, where *o* is worse off than *p*, *p* may urge that *o*'s misfortune, after all, is not so bad. This idea also has the useful consequence of saving *p* from having to make sacrifices in order to restore the equality of lots. Recognition that lot equalization may serve an ulterior purpose is one reason an unfortunate person accepts advice and consolation more easily from a person who has suffered a similar misfortune:

> . . . . Give me not counsel,
> Nor let no comforter delight mine ear
> But such a one whose wrongs do suit with mine.
> Bring me a father that so lov'd his child,
> Whose joy of her is overwhelm'd like mine,
> And bid him speak of patience.
> (*Much Ado About Nothing*, Act V, Scene 1)

To be sure, the belief that a person who is similarly afflicted will understand more deeply is fundamental, but not to be overlooked is the feeling that when a person who did not experience the misfortunate says to *p*, "Oh, that is not so bad, you will soon get over it," the motivation may be not to ease *p*'s burden, but to protect *o*.

Since the proper lot distribution depends on the status relations between *p* and *o*, it is also possible that a lot discrepancy can be made acceptable by adjusting the status of the parties concerned. Thus, should *p* have more than *o*, he will easily think that after all he is a better person and deserves more. This relieves him of the pressure to share his fortune and of possible guilt feelings. Likewise, *p* will not be disturbed should he have less than *o* if he feels that he deserves less.

In Scheler's (1923) views on envy, many of these points dealing with the reaction to lot differences and modes of coping with them find a place. He discusses the fact that the way envy shows itself is influenced by one's own feeling of power and of value. For Scheler, as for Nietzsche, "*ressentiment*" is an envy combined with a feeling of impotence to attain the value that another person has. A disparagement of the value *o* represents has been mentioned as one way of achieving equalization of lots. It becomes "existential envy," when the existence of another person is a continuous reproach to the envious, a constant reminder of his own inferiority. "This envy whispers: I can forgive you everything, except that you exist, and that you are that being that you are; except that I am not what you are, that 'I' am not 'you' " (Scheler, 1923, p. 66).

If a person is secure in his own power and value, then, according to Scheler, he will feel pleasure when another person also has value or even stands above him. If, on the other hand, he is doubtful of his own value, and if a comparison with other people is a constitutive element in his concept of value, then there are two ways open to him: if he is strong and active he will become a competitive climber; if he is weak, he will be the *ressentiment* type and develop his values in such a way that they justify his weakness. Thus, if *o* scores higher on some value scale than *p*, and *p* is unable to improve his lot, then a reorganization will occur. Either *p* will think that *o* is not really better in this value, or (and this is the more profound reorganization) he will think that to score high in this aspect is not very desirable—that is, the idea of value will be changed. In either case, the lot discrepancy is reduced. When the fox said that the grapes were sour, he did not change the value; he did not deny that sweetness is a value. He only said that these particular grapes do not partake in that accepted value. A more subtle fox, one who follows the strategy of the *ressentiment* type, would have said: I really do not care for sweet things, to like them is sissy. Thus, the value of natural gifts, of intelligence or creativity may be reassessed by the person who lacks them (Scheler, 1923, pp. 70 ff.).

It is necessary to add, however, that such re-evaluation may sometimes lead to higher levels of maturity and greater depths of understanding. In serving the purposes of rationalization, it may also serve the purpose of rationality, so that the more superficial values no longer outrank those of fundamental importance. Then it no longer matters so much whether *o* has more of what now has become a value of little account.

**Comparison of lots as applied to work.** A fundamental lot in community life is one's work. How others will react to it, then, often partly depends on the comparative lots of *p* and *o*. First, a few words as to what is meant by "work."

With the discussion of the meaning of work in interpersonal relations we approach questions of primitive, everyday economics. If one spends energy on goals that are not strictly one's own, it is counted as work, and it is sometimes thought of as a negative experience. Of course, there is a difference between a definition based on the subjective meaning of the activity for the person, and a definition based on objective features of the task. The distinction of whether the activity is fed by one's own needs or whether it is felt to be imposed, is the subjective definition; but activities also exist which in themselves are considered work, regardless of their relation to personal needs. This is particularly true of useful activities by which one earns money. And there are other activities that are considered play, for instance, activities whose usefulness is not directly perceptible. Of course, what is considered work depends also on the culture.

The concepts work, energy, or force, were originally concepts of naive psychology, that is, concepts applied to the behavior of human beings. Then they were appropriated and sharpened by physics. Now, these concepts, after they had lost much of their original connotation, have been transferred back to psychology. In naive psychology, working is opposed to playing or being lazy; but a machine, though it can do work, can neither play nor be lazy. Like many achievement concepts work has psychological importance. We take it into account in evaluating other people and ourselves.

Just as it is felt that there should be an approximately equal distribution of goods among equals, so it is felt that the work should be apportioned equally. If *o* causes an unequal distribution by taking more than his share of the goods or by working less than his share in a team of equals, *p* will be resentful; and if the unequal distribution is caused by an agent other than *o*, then *p* will be envious and will try to re-establish the equilibrium. The one who works bears a resentment against the one who plays. The unequal allotment of work is especially aggravating when it is flaunted, as when one person lies on a sofa while the other one works. Again, the relative status or value of *p* and *o* has a bearing on this reaction. It is often held that the valuable person should get more than an equal share. He deserves more and he ought to do less work. In older times it was assumed that the gentleman should not work, that work was degrading. Therefore, if *o* does not contribute an objectively equal share, it is often interpreted by *p* as: *o* thinks too well of himself, he considers himself too good for work. It is this which arouses *p*'s anger, more than the unequal distribution itself. It implies conceit, egocentrism, and contempt for the others.

These quality considerations can be refined by taking into account the person's available energy. That is to say, the energy expense of the contributors should be subjectively the same. The value of the act is thus weighted by the property of the person; the strong should work more, the weak less. This is comparable to paying income tax, where one pays according to a graduated scale.

Before proceeding further, we should like to mention once more the point that satisfaction or dissatisfaction with one's lot is not always based on comparison with another person's lot, that one can evaluate one's affairs and oneself in terms of the intrinsic nature rather than the comparative score of the values in question (cf. Dembo *et al.*, 1956).

## Control of o's Envy and Compassion

We have shown on several occasions that the naive psychology of interpersonal relations allows *p* not only to grasp the relationship between *p* and *o*, but also to predict and control it to some extent. It is notable that people try to arouse or prevent the envy, sympathy, or pity of other persons in order to produce or avoid the effects of these reactions on themselves. For instance, *p* can incite *o*'s envy by emphasizing the superiority of *p*'s lot. He may brag about it or in subtler ways make certain that *o* becomes aware of his good fortune. He may be interested in impressing *o* because his lot may seem more positive to him when he is envied, when his superiority is socially recognized. Or, to arouse *o* out of a state of inactivity, he may try to stimulate *o*'s competitive spirit. He may want to arouse *o*'s envy of *q* in order to make *o* dislike *q*, etc.

When *p* wants to prevent *o* from envying him, he will disparage his own lot or try not to let his superiority show. He may pretend to be just like *o*, or just like an average person. Again, there may be different reasons for this; for instance, he may want to keep the positive *x*, but fears that if *o* realized how good it was he would try to take it from him; he may want to avoid arousing *o*'s antagonism; he may want to be liked by *o*. In some countries, the code of polite behavior requires extreme disparagement of one's possessions and of one's family. Likewise, *p* may try to arouse sympathy in *o* by complaining and presenting his lot as especially unfortunate. He may do so in order to receive emotional support or other help from *o*, to prevent *o* from engaging in certain activities, to make *o* feel guilty, etc. Or, he may try to prevent *o* from sympathizing or pitying him by pretending that everything is fine and by avoiding discussion of his troubles. He will do so when he does not want *o*'s sympathy, or, if *o* is his enemy, in order to avoid an occasion where *o* might openly or secretly gloat over his misfortune.

### Summary

Four types of reaction to the lot of another person were listed, of which two are concordant, and two discordant.

True sympathy which has as its object the sorrow or joy of another person was distinguished from emotional contagion, and it was pointed out that the difference between these two concordant reactions shows in behavior. A similar distinction can be made in regard to discordant reactions.

The sentiment toward *o* influences the reaction to his lot, and a balanced state exists when *o* and his experiences are both positive or both negative. This balanced state is closely related to requirements of justice.

The own lot of *p* is of great importance in his reaction to the lot of *o*. The evaluation of *p*'s lot and that of *o*'s lot influence each other, and the one often plays the role of a background for the assessment of the other; it is either assimilated to this background, or seen in contrast to it.

There may exist a tendency towards equalization of lots, which plays a role in envy. This tendency towards equality is influenced by sentiments, power, ought forces, and unit formations.

Some comments were added on the everyday conception of work, and on the control of *o*'s envy.

# CHAPTER 12

# Conclusion

IN THIS BOOK some of the phenomena that play a role in interpersonal relations have been discussed. As we said in the beginning, there are doubtless others of equal importance which have been left out or treated only tangentially, like falling in love, or conversation. Also, many have been largely disregarded which cannot be treated without taking into account processes concerning larger groups, though they may also influence the behavior of one person toward one other person.

One of the convictions guiding our approach was that psychology is not yet a fully developed science; it is still in an infantile stage and one must expect it to crawl and not yet to walk like an adult (cf. Köhler, 1929, Chapter 2). It should grow gradually and organically out of the matrix of implicit theory and should not be weaned prematurely from unformulated and intuitive thinking about behavior. This does not imply a rejection of the attempts to define exacting standards for a fully developed science. One can accept those and still be tolerant toward the muddling and vague ambiguities through which a vital growth has to pass. Compliance with these standards does not guarantee value: an approach can be spelled out clearly in operational or mathematical terms and still be sterile—another can commit every possible sin against the canons and still be full of promise. In the early stages of a science it is hard to measure the value of a contribution by explicit standards, perhaps as difficult as it is to measure artistic production.

Thus, we do not claim that the present essay aspires to be a full-grown system. All it attempts is to present some thoughts which may be helpful in the transition from an intuitive level with its implicit theories to the explicitly systematic thinking of a developed science: it contains pretheoretical speculations, hunches, and suggestions. Koch (1956) used for his paper at a recent Nebraska Symposium the subtitle "Work notes toward a pre-theory of phenomena called 'motivational' "; in this sense, this book might be called "work notes towards a pretheory of interpersonal relations."

Especially in discussing interpersonal relations we should avoid losing contact with the level of common-sense thinking—we have tried to give reasons for that in the first chapter. In making use of this thinking and in theorizing about it—and these two aspects may not always have been sharply separated—we found that what Koch says is true, namely, that common sense contains much psychological theory and that "such theory constitutes a most abstract and epistemologically complex ordering of the data of experience and behavior" (p. 60).

We started out with the observation that the person is located in the complicated causal network of the environment. It is useful to distinguish two parts within this network: on the one hand the mediation, the part that is close to the skin of the organism, comprising the proximal stimuli which impinge on the organism, and the immediate influences of the person on the environment; on the other hand the distal environment, made up of the vitally relevant persons and things. The person is separated by the mediation from the contents of the distal environment, though the mediation at the same time allows the establishment of a close functional contact between person and environment, spanning, as it were, the variable manifold of mediating events. Our perceptions and actions are directed to the contents of the distal environment.

Close relations across a distance exist also between the thoughts, wishes, emotions, and sentiments of one person and those of another person. In the perception of other people we are directed towards them and their psychological processes. We try to make sense out of the manifold of proximal stimuli by ordering them in terms of the distal invariants and their relevant dispositional properties.

This ordering and classifying can often be considered a process of attribution. The main features of the environment are given in representation; we find ourselves in a certain situation, and something happens which has to be fitted into the situation—it has to be attributed to one or the other of the contents of the environment. For instance, our subjective environment contains the self and another person and a new event occurs: one of the persons will be held responsible for it.

That is, we interpret the events as being caused by particular parts of the relatively stable environment.

Of special importance for the interpretation of the social world is the separation of the factors located in persons, and those that have their source in the environment of these persons. Many examples of this implicit "factor analysis" were given, for instance, in Chapter 3, visibility of object as the environmental factor vs. perceptual ability as the personal factor; in Chapter 4, difficulty of task vs. ability; in Chapter 5, desirability of object vs. personal desire, and environmental and personal factors in enjoyment; in Chapters 6, 10 and 11, the factors that are responsible for what happens to the person; in Chapter 8, objective requirements and personal wishes; in Chapter 9, the factors making for induced action.

The basis for this analysis is often a series of observations which can give information about the events and dispositional entities and which makes possible the disentanglement of causal belonging-together in a way analogous to experimental methods, and that leads to a veridical assessment of the important features of the environment. However, in many cases the attribution is dictated by personal preferences, habits of thought, or needs, and results in distorted views.

Thus, the proximal event is always interpreted in terms of the relatively invariant contents of the world around us. These contents must be consistent with each other, and that means that we have definite ideas about fittingness, about consonance and dissonance. We assume implications between the parts of the environment, whether in regard to the structure of space, the logic of illumination, or the perceived psychological phenomena in other persons. Thus, the interpretation does not consist merely of arbitrarily connecting meanings to data; that feature which is characteristic of science—namely, that a network of concepts that are systematically defined is fitted to the empirical manifold, and lends the terms in which this manifold is encoded—is already present in naive perception and judgment. One might say we are much more implicit Newtonians than implicit Baconians. As example of these formal connections underlying our naive thinking we can refer to the relations between can, try, and success (Chapter 4): The statement that somebody who can do something and tries to do it will succeed in doing it, is analytic and does not have to be proven by experiment. The relation between desire and enjoyment (Chapter 5) is also of this character. It is likely that the interdependence of belonging and sentiment (Chapter 7) is based on analytic statements.

The general features of the causal network are thus in some way internalized and mastered. They form the content of the cognitive matrix that underlies our interpretations of other people's behavior and our attempts to influence it. We have specific ideas about the possible conditions and effects of the different vitally relevant changes and entities. Our implicit knowledge of the conditions allows us to influence the distal parts of the world in purposeful action; and our knowledge of the effects makes cognition and expectation possible. These considerations were applied to the analysis of our cognitions and actions in regard to the perceptions of another person (Chapter 3), to his success in action (Chapter 4), to his wishes and affects (Chapter 5), to his sentiments (Chapter 7), etc.

We arrived thus at a description of the implicit theoretical models of perception, action, motivation, sentiments, and norms. An explication of these thought models may not only be helpful in understanding interpersonal relations, but also in getting a clearer idea of the pretheories out of which some of the concepts of "scientific" psychology grew.

However, one has to be aware that the picture that evolves in this way shows only a part of what is going on between people, that part which, let us say, inclines toward the side of "intellectualism." To complete the picture one would have to add other facets, for instance, one would have to give an account of the genetic sources of interpersonal behavior.

# A notation for representing interpersonal relations

MANY OF THE EXAMPLES discussed in this book were first analyzed with the help of a notation partly fashioned after that of symbolic logic, though its basic concepts are by no means connected by systematic definitions. Such a notation forces one to explicate the conglomerate terms of everyday language and to restrict oneself to the use of a few concepts. A translation from the vernacular into this notation is an excellent exercise in explication. However, one should keep in mind that it is not completely worked out and is only meant to offer suggestions as to what one can do with a tool of this kind.

The own person, i.e., the person whose life space is being considered, is, as has been done throughout the book, symbolized by $p$, other persons by $o$ and $q$; $r$ stands for an undetermined person (somebody). If material is analyzed in which the persons have proper names, abbreviations for these names can be used. The letters $x$, $y$, and $z$ designate impersonal entities, things, situations, or changes, etc.

Actions, attitudes, etc., can be represented as relational propositions. In agreement with the usage of symbolic logic the terms related will be symbolized by small letters and the relations by capitals. Thus, $a\,\mathrm{R}\,b$ means that a relation R holds between $a$ and $b$. The first term of the relation will often be a person; the second term can be a personal or impersonal entity, or another relation. If the second term is itself a relational proposition, a colon will be inserted between the symbol for the first relation and the expression for the second relation. Thus,

$p$ C:$o$ $S$ —$x$ means $p$ causes $o$ to suffer something negative, or, simply $p$ harms $o$.

A list of the symbols we have used most often in the analysis follows:

| | |
|---|---|
| $p$ Lsp $x$ | $x$ is content of $p$'s life space. |
| $p$ C $x$ | $p$ causes $x$; $p$ Lsp:$o$ C $x$ would mean $p$ thinks $o$ causes $x$. The negative can be symbolized by a "not" written before the relation. $p$ notC $x$ is $p$ does not cause $x$. Past time is represented by a small d after the relation sign. $p$ Cd $x$ is $p$ caused $x$. |
| $p$ CanC $x$ | $p$ can cause $x$. |
| $p$ W $x$ | $p$ wants or wishes for $x$. $p$ W:$o$ C $x$ is $p$ wants $o$ to cause $x$. |
| $p$ TrC $x$ | $p$ tries to cause $x$. |
| $p$ S $x$ | $p$ suffers $x$, or, a change occurs which affects $p$. |
| $p$ oughtC $x$ | $p$ ought to cause $x$. $p$ ought notC $x$ means $p$ ought not to do it, he has an obligation not to do it, which is different from $p$ not oughtC $x$, $p$ has no obligation to do it. $p$ not ought notC $x$ means $p$ may cause $x$. |
| $p$ L $x$ | $p$ likes $x$, he has a positive attitude towards $x$. |
| $p$ U $x$ | $x$ belongs to $p$ in some way. |

We want to add three more symbols which are really cases of causing:

| | |
|---|---|
| $p$ Pres $o$:$x$ | $p$ presents to $o$ the fact $x$, $p$ tells $x$ to $o$, or informs $o$ of $x$. ($x$, of course, does not have to be true.) |
| $p$ B $o$ | $p$ benefits $o$. |
| $p$ H $o$ | $p$ harms $o$. |

## Examples

In the following section we give a few examples in order to show how some of the basic concepts are combined in words of everyday language which we use to describe our social environment. Often, of course, one can represent the meaning of a word only approximately, for instance, the word may have different meanings and these meanings color each other and are united in a global total meaning. Usually it is easier to analyze the content of a connected text; the context then specifies the meanings of the single words.

Let us take first a few examples of the general form $p$ C:$o$ R $x$, that is, $p$ causes that $o$ stands in one of these basic relations to $x$.

$p$ C:$o$ Lsp $x$, means $p$ causes that $x$ becomes part of $o$'s life space. This is equal to $p$ Pres $o$:$x$, $p$ tells $x$ to $o$.

$p$ C:$o$ C $x$, means $p$ causes that $o$ causes $x$. Specific examples: $p$ asks $o$ to do $x$, or he forces, commands, or induces him in some way to do $x$.

$p$ C:$o$ CanC $x$, means $p$ makes it possible for $o$ to do $x$, he helps him.

$p$ C:$o$ W $x$, means $p$ induces a wish for $x$ in $o$. Luring, tempting would be examples.

*p* C:*o* S *x*, means *p* causes something that affects *o*. Examples are *p* B *o* and *p* H *o*.

*p* C:*o* ought C *x*, means *p* puts *o* in a situation in which he ought to cause *x*, *p* obliges *o*. Both of the following: *p* induces a motive in *o*, and *p* induces an ought force in *o*, can be examples of *p* causes *o* to cause *x*; *p*'s real intention will usually be in some way to bring about that *p* causes *x*.

*p* C:*o* L *x*, means *p* causes *o* to like *x*. Any case of influencing an attitude would be represented in this way; it may be by persuasion or convincing.

*p* C:*o* U *x*, means *p* causes *x* to belong to *o*. If the unit relation U is one of possession, then it would mean: *p* gives *x* to *o*.

**Examples of more complex combinations.** This notation also makes the representation of more complex phenomena possible. Such phenomena are frequently encountered in everyday life and we often understand them directly without being able to analyze them into their components.

*p* W:*o* B *q*, means *p* wants that *o* benefit *q*.

*p* Pres *o*:*q* Cd *x*, means *p* tells *o* that *q* caused *x*.

A further variation can be introduced by specifying an entity by a relation. The relation is then put in parentheses after the expression for the entity. For instance, *x*(*p* Cd *x*) means that *x* that *p* caused; *o*(*o* Cd *x*) means the *o* who caused *x*.

*p* Pres *o*:*p* notL *x*(*o* Cd *x*), means *p* tells *o* that he does not like the *x* that *o* caused.

By introducing a new symbol, a circumflex above a letter, one can represent the sum total of all entities for which a relation is true. For instance, $\hat{x}$(*p* canC *x*) means the totality of all *x*'s that *p* can cause; $\hat{x}$(*p* W:*o* not Perc *x*) means all the *x*'s that *p* wants *o* not to perceive. $\hat{x}$(*p* canC:*o* C *x*) are all the *x*'s that *p* can induce *o* to do: one kind of power of *p* over *o*, which can be distinguished from $\hat{x}$(*p* canC:*o* S *x*), all the experiences *p* can inflict on *o*. Of course, this symbol can also be used with persons: $\hat{o}$(*o* L *p*) are all the other persons who like *p*.

# Bibliography

Adams, D. K. 1953. The organs of perception: sentiments. *J. Pers.*, 22, 52–60.

Addison, J., R. Steel, *et al.* 1712. *The spectator.* Everyman's Library. New York: Dutton, 1907, Vol. 4.

Albert, D. K. 1956. Moral judgment of social actions. Unpublished master's thesis. Univ. of Kansas.

Allport, F. H. 1955. *Theories of perception and the concept of structure.* New York: Wiley.

Allport, G. W. 1937. *Personality: a psychological interpretation.* New York: Holt.

——. 1940. Motivation in personality: reply to Mr. Bertocci. *Psychol. Rev.*, 47, 533–554.

——. 1947. Scientific models and human morals. *Psychol. Rev.*, 54, 182–192.

——. 1955. *Becoming: basic considerations for a psychology of personality.* New Haven: Yale Univ. Press.

Angyal, A. 1941. *Foundations for a science of personality.* New York: The Commonwealth Fund and Cambridge: Harvard Univ. Press.

Aristotle. *The Nicomachean ethics.* Cambridge: Harvard Univ. Press, 1945.

——. *Rhetoric.* Cambridge: Harvard Univ. Press, 1939.

Arsenian, J. M. 1943. Young children in an insecure situation. *J. abnorm. soc. Psychol.*, 38, 225–249.

Asch, S. E. 1948. The doctrine of suggestion, prestige and imitation in social psychology. *Psychol. Rev.*, 55, 5.

——. 1952. *Social psychology.* New York: Prentice-Hall.

Attneave, F. 1954. Some informational aspects of visual perception. *Psychol. Rev.*, 61, 183–193.

Bacon, F. 1597. *Essays.* Vol. 3, Harvard Classics. New York: Collier, 1909.

Baldwin, A. L. 1955. *Behavior and development in childhood.* New York: Dryden.

Baldwin, J. M. 1902. *Social and ethical interpretations in mental development.* New York: Macmillan,

Ball, W. W.  1956.  Calculating prodigies.  In: J. R. Newman (ed.).  *The world of mathematics.*  New York: Simon and Schuster.

Barker, R. G., B. A. Wright, L. Meyerson, and M. Gonich.  1953.  *Adjustment to physical handicap and illness: a survey of the social psychology of physique and disability.*  New York: Social Science Research Council, Bulletin 55, Rev.

Barker, R. G., and H. F. Wright.  1955.  *Midwest and its children: the psychological ecology of an American town.*  Evanston, Ill.: Row, Peterson.

Bartlett, F. C.  1932.  *Remembering.*  Cambridge: Cambridge Univ. Press.

Becker, H.  1931.  Some forms of sympathy: a phenomenological analysis.  *J. abnorm. soc. Psychol., 26,* 58–68.

Benchley, R.  1942.  Nothing but the tooth.  Condensed from *Inside Benchley. Reader's Digest,* May, 73–75.

Bertalanffy, L. F.  1950.  An outline of general system theory.  *Brit. J. philos. Sci., 1,* 134–165.

Bieri, J.  1953.  Changes in interpersonal perceptions following social interaction.  *J. abnorm. soc. Psychol., 48,* 61–66.

Boring, E. G.  1952.  Visual perception as invariance.  *Psychol. Rev., 59,* 141–148.

Bovard, E. W.  1951.  The experimental production of interpersonal affect.  *J. abnorm. soc. Psychol., 46,* 521–528.

Bruner, J. S.  1957.  Going beyond the information given.  In: Gruber *et al.* (eds.).  *Contemporary approaches to cognition.*  Cambridge: Harvard Univ. Press.

Bruner, J. S., and R. Tagiuri.  1954.  The perception of people.  In: G. Lindzey (ed.).  *Handbook of social psychology.*  Cambridge: Addison-Wesley, Vol. II.

Brunswik, E.  1934.  *Wahrnehmung und Gegenstandswelt.*  Leipzig and Wien: Deuticke.

———.  1936.  Psychology in terms of objects.  *Proceedings of the 25th Anniversary Celebration of the Inauguration of Graduate Studies at the University of Southern California,* 122–125.

———.  1952.  The conceptual framework of psychology.  In: *International Encyclopedia of Unified Science,* Vol. 1, No. 10.  Chicago: Univ. of Chicago Press.

———.  1955.  Representative design and probabilistic theory.  *Psychol. Rev., 62,* 193–217.

———.  1956.  *Perception and the representative design of psychological experiments.*  Berkeley: Univ. of California Press.

Buehler, K.  1929.  *Die Krise der Psychologie.*  Jena: G. Fischer.

Buijtendijk, F. J. J., and H. Plessner.  1925.  Die Deutung des mimischen Ausdrucks.  *Philosophischer Anzeiger, 1,* I. Halbband, 72–126.

Carnap, R.  1953.  The two concepts of probability.  In: H. Feigl, and M. Brodbeck (eds.).  *Readings in the philosophy of science.*  New York: Appleton-Century-Crofts.

Cartwright, D., and F. Harary.  1956.  Structural balance: a generalization of Heider's theory.  *Psychol. Rev., 63,* 277–293.

Cassirer, E.  1944.  *An essay on man.*  New Haven: Yale Univ. Press.

Chesterfield, Earl of.  1774.  *Letters to his son.*  Ed. by O. H. Leigh.  New York: Tudor.

Cline, M. G.  1956.  The influence of social context on the perception of faces.  *J. Pers., 25,* 142–158.

Cohen, M. R., and E. Nagel.  1934.  *An introduction to logic and scientific method.*

Published for the United States Armed Forces by Harcourt, Brace, Education Manual 621.

Crawley, E. 1927. *The mystic rose: A study of primitive marriage and of primitive thought in its bearing on marriage,* 2d ed. revised by Th. Besterman. New York: Boni and Liveright, Vol. I.

Dembo, T. 1931. Der Aerger als dynamisches Problem. *Psychol. Forschung, 15,* 1–144.

Dembo, T., G. L. Leviton, and B. A. Wright. 1956. Adjustment to misfortune—a problem of social-psychological rehabilitation. *Artificial Limbs, 3, 2,* 4–62.

Deutsch, M. A. 1949. Theory of cooperation and competition. *Human Relations, 2,* 129–152.

Dewey, J. 1929. *The quest for certainty: a study of the relation of knowledge and action.* New York: Minton, Balch.

Dollard, J., L. Doob, N. Miller, O. Mowrer, and R. Sears. 1939. *Frustration and aggression.* New Haven: Yale Univ. Press.

Douglas, C. N. 1940. *Forty thousand quotations.* New York: Halcyon House.

Duncker, K. 1947. Phenomenology and epistemology of consciousness of objects. *Philos. phenomenol. Res., 7,* 505–542.

Ellis, W. D. 1939. *A source book of gestalt psychology.* New York: Harcourt, Brace.

Engel, J. J. 1785. *Ideen zu einer Mimik.* Berlin: A. Mylius.

Epictetus. *The works of Epictetus.* Translated by E. Carter and T. W. Higginson. Boston: Little, Brown, 1865.

Esch, J. 1950. *A study of judgments of social situations.* Unpublished term paper. Univ. of Kansas.

Festinger, L., and H. A. Hutte. 1954. An experimental investigation of the effect of unstable interpersonal relations in a group. *J. abnorm. soc. Psychol., 49,* 513–522.

Festinger, L., S. Schachter, and K. Back. 1950. *Social pressures in informal groups.* New York: Harper.

Fiedler, F. E. 1953. The psychological-distance dimension in interpersonal relations. *J. Pers., 22,* 142–150.

Fiedler, F. E., W. G. Warrington, and F. J. Blaisdell. 1952. Unconscious attitudes as correlates of sociometric choice in a social group. *J. abnorm. soc. Psychol., 47,* 790–96.

Fielding, H. 1749. *The history of Tom Jones,* 2 Vols. Everyman's Library. New York: Dutton, 1908, 1909.

Fite, M. D. 1940. Aggressive behavior in young children and children's attitudes toward aggression. *Genet. Psychol. Monogr., 22,* 151–319.

Frank, J. D. 1944. Experimental studies of personal pressure and resistance: I. Experimental production of resistance. *J. gen. Psychol., 30,* 23–41.

French, J. R. P., Jr. 1956. A formal theory of social power. *Psychol. Rev., 63,* 181–194.

Frenkel-Brunswik, E. 1942. Motivation and behavior. *Genet. Psychol. Monogr., 26,* 121–265.

———. 1948. Dynamic and cognitive categorization of qualitative material: II. Application to interviews with the ethnically prejudiced. *J. Psychol., 25,* 261–277.

Gibson, J. J. 1950. *The perception of the visual world.* New York: Houghton Mifflin.

Gibson, J. J. 1951. Theories of perception. In: W. Dennis (ed.). *Current trends in psychological theory.* Pittsburgh: Univ. of Pittsburgh Press.

Goldings, H. J. 1954. On the avowal and projection of happiness. *J. Pers., 23,* 30–48.

Goldstein, K. 1947. *Human nature in the light of psychopathology.* Cambridge: Harvard Univ. Press.

Graham, F. K., W. A. Charwat, A. S. Honig, and P. C. Weltz. 1951. Aggression as a function of the attack and the attacker. *J. abnorm. soc. Psychol., 46,* 512–520.

Gruber, H. E. 1954. The relation of perceived size to perceived distance. *Amer. J. Psychol., 67,* 411–526.

Hammond, K. R. 1955. Probabilistic functioning and the clinical method. *Psychol. Rev., 62,* 255–262.

Hanfmann, E. 1957. Social perception in Russian displaced persons and an American comparison group. *Psychiatry, 20,* 131–149.

Hayek, F. A. 1952. *The sensory order.* Chicago: Univ. of Chicago Press.

Hebb, D. O. 1946. Emotion in man and animal: an analysis of the intuitive processes of recognition. *Psychol. Rev., 53,* 88–106.

Heider, F. 1926. Ding und Medium. *Symposion, 1,* 109–157.

———. 1930. Die Leistung des Wahrnehmungssystems. *Z. Psychol., 114,* 371–394.

———. 1939. Environmental determinants of psychological theories. *Psychol. Rev., 46,* 383–410.

———. 1944. Social perception and phenomenal causality. *Psychol. Rev., 51,* 358–374.

———. 1946. Attitudes and cognitive organization. *J. Psychol., 21,* 107–112.

Heider, F., and M. Simmel. 1944. An experimental study of apparent behavior. *Amer. J. Psychol., 57,* 243–259.

Hellpach, W. 1913. Vom Ausdruck der Verlegenheit. *Arch. Ges. Psychol., 27,* 1–62.

Helmholtz, H. von. 1867. Concerning the perceptions in general. In: W. Dennis (ed.). *Readings in the history of psychology.* New York: Appleton-Century-Crofts, 1948.

Helson, H. 1951. Perception. In: H. Helson (ed.). *Theoretical foundations of psychology.* New York: Van Nostrand.

Henle, M. 1956. On activity in the goal region. *Psychol. Rev., 63,* 299–302.

Hochberg, J. 1956. Report at the symposium: Psychophysics of form. Chicago: *Meeting of the Amer. Psychol. Assn.*

Hollingworth, H. L. 1949. *Psychology and ethics: a study of the sense of obligation.* New York: Ronald.

Holt, E. B. 1916. *The Freudian wish and its place in ethics.* New York: Moffat, Yard.

Homans, G. C. 1950. *The human group.* New York: Harcourt, Brace.

Horney, K. 1945. *Our inner conflicts.* New York: Norton.

Horowitz, M. W., J. Lyons, and H. V. Perlmutter. 1951. Induction of forces in discussion groups. *Human Relations, 41,* 57–76.

Hovland, C. I., I. L. Janis, and H. H. Kelley. 1953. *Communication and persuasion.* New Haven: Yale Univ. Press.

Hume, D. 1741. *Essays moral, political, and literary.* London: Longmans, Green, 1907, Vol. 2.

Ichheiser, G. 1933. Das Koennen, die Bedingungen des Koennens und das Erlebnis des Koennens. *Z. angew. Psychol.*, *44*, 367–378.

———. 1949. Misunderstandings in human relations. *Amer. J. Sociol.*, *55*, 2, Part 2.

Ihrig, H. 1953. *Literalism and animism in schizophrenia*. Ph.D. thesis. Univ. of Kansas.

Irwin, F. W., and M. E. Gebhard. 1946. Studies in object-preferences: the effect of ownership and other social influences. *Amer. J. Psychol.*, *59*, 633–651.

Isaacs, S. 1933. *Social development in young children*. New York: Harcourt, Brace.

James, W. 1890. *The principles of psychology*. New York: Holt, 1905, Vol. II.

Janet, P. 1929. *L'Évolution psychologique de la personnalité*. Paris: Maloine.

Jennings, H. H. 1943. *Leadership and isolation: a study of personality in interpersonal relations*. New York: Longmans, Green.

Jordan, N. 1953. Behavioral forces that are a function of attitudes and of cognitive organization. *Human Relations*, *6*, 273–287.

Kant, I. 1797. Die Metaphysik der Sitten. *Werke*. Berlin: Cassirer, 1922, Vol. 7.

Kelsen, H. 1946. *Society and nature: a sociological inquiry*. London: Kegan Paul.

Kilpatrick, F. P., and W. H. Ittelson. 1953. The size-distance invariance hypothesis. *Psychol. Rev.*, *60*, 223–232.

Klages, L. 1928. *Die Grundlagen der Charakterkunde*, 5th ed. Leipzig: Barth.

———. 1942. *Grundlegung der Wissenschaft vom Ausdruck*, 6th ed. Leipzig: Barth.

Klein, G. 1951. The personal world through perception. In: R. R. Blake, and G. V. Ramsey (eds.). *Perception: An approach to personality*. New York: Ronald.

Koch, S. 1956. Behavior as "intrinsically" regulated: work notes towards a pre-theory of phenomena called "motivational." In: Jones, M. R. (ed.). *Nebraska symposium on motivation*. Lincoln: Univ. of Nebraska Press.

Koffka, K. 1935. *Principles of gestalt psychology*. New York: Harcourt, Brace.

Kogan, N., and R. Tagiuri. 1958. Interpersonal preference and cognitive organization. *J. abnorm. soc. Psychol.*, *56*, 113–116.

Köhler, W. 1929. *Gestalt Psychology*. New York: Liveright.

———. 1938. *The place of value in a world of facts*. New York: Liveright.

———. 1940. *Dynamics in Psychology*. New York: Liveright.

Krech, D., and R. S. Crutchfield. 1948. *Theory and problems of social psychology*. New York: McGraw-Hill.

Ladieu, G., E. Hanfmann, and T. Dembo. 1947. Studies in adjustment to visible injuries: evaluation of help by the injured. *J. abnorm. soc. Psychol.*, *42*, 169–192.

Lapie, P. 1902. *Logique de la volonté*. Paris: Alcan.

LaPiere, T., and R. Farnsworth. 1949. *Social psychology*, 3d ed. New York: McGraw-Hill.

La Rochefoucauld. 1665. *Réflexions*. Paris: Garnier.

Lecky, P. 1945. *Self-consistency: a theory of personality*. New York: Island Press.

Lewin, K. 1935a. Psycho-sociological problems of a minority group. *Character and Personality*, *3*, 175–187.

———. 1935b. *A dynamic theory of personality*. New York: McGraw-Hill.

Lewin, K. 1936. *Principles of topological psychology.* New York: McGraw-Hill.
———. 1938. The conceptual representation and measurement of psychological forces. *Contr. Psychol. Theor., 1, 4.* Durham, N. C.: Duke Univ. Press.
———. 1939. Field theory and experiment in social psychology: conceptual methods. *Amer. J. Sociol., 44,* 868–896.
———. 1944. Constructs in psychology and psychological ecology. *Univ. Iowa Stud. Child Welf., 20,* 1–29.
———. 1948. *Resolving social conflicts.* New York: Harper.
———. 1954. Behavior and development as a function of the total situation. In: Carmichael, L. (ed.). Manual of child psychology, 2d ed. New York: Wiley.
Ley, A., and M. L. Wauthier. 1946. *Études de psychologie instinctive et affective.* Paris: Presses Univ. de France.
Lippitt, R. 1940. An experimental study of authoritarian and democratic group atmospheres. Studies in topological and vector psychology. Vol. I. *Univ. Iowa Stud. Child Welf., 16,* 44–195.
Lippitt, R., N. Polansky, F. Redl, and S. Rosen. 1952. The dynamics of power. *Human Relations, 5,* 37–64.
Loomis, C. P., and D. M. Davidson, Jr. 1939. Measurement of the dissolution of ingroups in the integration of a rural settlement project. *Sociometry, 2,* 84–94.
Maine de Biran. *Journal intime 1792–1817.* Paris: Plon, 1927.
Malinowski, B. 1923. The problem of meaning in primitive languages. In: C. K. Ogden, and I. A. Richards. *The meaning of meaning.* New York: Harcourt, Brace.
Marston, W. M. 1928. *Emotions of normal people.* New York: Harcourt, Brace.
Maslow, A. H. 1937. The influence of familiarization on preference. *J. exp. Psychol., 21,* 162–180.
———. 1941. Deprivation, threat and frustration. *Psychol. Rev., 48,* 364–366.
McTeer, W. 1953. Observational definitions of emotion. *Psychol. Rev., 60,* 172–181.
Mead, G. H. 1934. *Mind, self and society.* Chicago: Univ. of Chicago Press.
Merleau-Ponty, M. 1945. *Phénoménologie de la perception.* Paris: Gallimard.
Michotte, A. E. 1946. *La perception de la causalité.* Paris: J. Vrin.
———. 1950. The emotions regarded as functional connections. In: M. I. Reymert (ed.). *Feelings and emotions.* New York: McGraw-Hill.
Mills, M. 1953. Power relations in three-person groups. In: D. Cartwright, and A. Zander (eds.). *Group Dynamics.* Evanston, Ill.: Row, Peterson & Co.
Murphy, G. 1947. *Personality.* New York: Harper.
Murray, H. A. 1938. *Explorations in personality.* New York: Oxford Univ. Press.
———. 1951. Toward a classification of interaction. In: T. Parsons, and E. A. Shils (eds.). *Toward a general theory of action.* Cambridge: Harvard Univ. Press.
Murray, H. A., and C. D. Morgan. 1945. A clinical study of sentiments: I. *Genet. Psychol. Monogr., 32,* 3–149.
Newcomb, T. M. 1953a. An approach to the study of communicative acts. *Psychol. Rev., 60,* 393–404.
———. 1953b. Motivation in social behavior. In: *Current theory and research in motivation: a symposium.* Lincoln: Univ. of Nebraska Press.
Nietzsche, F. 1881. Morgenroethe. *Werke.* Leipzig: Kroener, 1922, Vol. 4.

Northrop, F. S. C. 1947. *The logic of the sciences and the humanities.* New York: Macmillan.

Nuttin, J. 1950. Intimacy and shame in the dynamic structure of personality. In: M. I. Reymert (ed.). *Feelings and emotions.* New York: McGraw-Hill.

———. 1955. Consciousness, behavior, and personality. *Psychol. Rev., 62,* 349–355.

Oppenheimer, R. 1956. Analogy in science. *Amer. Psychologist, 11,* 127–136.

Osgood, C. E., and P. H. Tannenbaum. 1955. The principle of congruity in the prediction of attitude change. *Psychol. Rev., 62,* 42–55.

Ovid. *Tristia; ex ponto.* With translation by A. L. Wheeler. New York: Putnam, 1924.

Park, R. E., and E. W. Burgess. 1921. *Introduction to the science of sociology.* Chicago: Univ. of Chicago Press.

Pepitone, A. 1950. Motivational effects in social perception. *Human Relations, 3,* 57–76.

Perlmutter, H. V. 1954. Some characteristics of the xenophilic personality. *J. Psychol., 38,* 291–300.

———. 1956. Correlates of two types of xenophilic organization. *J. abnorm. soc. Psychol., 52,* 130–136.

Piaget, J. 1932. *The moral judgment of the child.* New York: Harcourt, Brace.

———. 1950. *The psychology of intelligence.* New York: Harcourt, Brace.

Precker, J. A. 1952. Similarity of valuings as a factor in selection of peers and near-authority figures. *J. abnorm. soc. Psychol., 47,* 406–414.

Preston, M. G., W. L. Peltz, E. H. Mudd, and H. B. Froscher. 1952. Impressions of personality as a function of marital conflict. *J. abnorm. soc. Psychol., 47,* 326–336.

Proust, M. 1926. *The past recaptured.* New York: Albert and Charles Boni, 1932.

Radiguet, R. 1923. *Le diable au corps.* Paris: Grasset.

Rapaport, D. 1951. *Organization and pathology of thought.* New York: Columbia Univ. Press.

Reardon, J. 1953. *Tragedy and unintended effects of actions.* Unpublished term paper. Univ. of Kansas.

Redl, F. 1949. The phenomenon of contagion and shock effect in group therapy. In: W. Healy, and A. Bronner (eds.). *Searchlights on delinquency.* New York: International Universities Press.

Riecken, H. W., and G. C. Homans. 1954. Psychological aspects of social structure. In: G. Lindzey (ed.). *Handbook of social psychology.* Cambridge: Addison-Wesley.

Russell, B. 1930. *The conquest of happiness.* New York: The New American Library, Signet Book, 1951.

———. 1950. *Unpopular Essays.* New York: Simon and Schuster, Readers' Edition.

Ryle, G. 1949. *The concept of mind.* London: Hutchinson's Univ. Library.

Sartre, J.-P. 1943. *Being and nothingness. An essay on phenomenological ontology.* Translated by H. E. Barnes. New York: Philosophical Library, 1956.

Scheler, M. 1913. *The nature of sympathy.* Translated by P. Heath. London: Routledge & Kegan Paul, 1954.

———. 1923. *Vom Umsturz der Werte,* 2d ed. Leipzig: Der Neue Geist Verlag, Vol. 1.

Scheler, M. 1927. *Der Formalismus in der Ethik und die materiale Wertethik.* Halle: Niemeyer.

Schmidt, W. 1930. Ueber den Drang nach Aehnlichkeit mit der geliebten Person. *Z. Sexualwissenschaft und Sexualpolitik, 17,* 50–53.

Schuetz, A. 1945. On multiple realities. *Philos. phenomenol. Res., 5,* 533–576.

———. 1948. Sartre's theory of the alter ego. *Philos. phenomenol. Res., 9,* 181–199.

Sears, R. R. 1943. Experimental studies of projection: I. Attribution of traits. In: S. S. Tompkins (ed.). *Contemporary psychology.* Cambridge: Harvard Univ. Press.

———. 1946. Frustration and aggression. In: P. L. Harriman (ed.). *Encyclopedia of Psychology.* New York: Philosophical Library.

Seeman, W., and R. Buck. 1952. On a behavioristic approach to the concept of wishfulfillment. *J. abnorm. soc. Psychol., 47,* 17–24.

Shand, A. F. 1920. *The foundations of character,* 2d ed. London: Macmillan.

Sherif, M. 1951. A preliminary experimental study of inter-group relations. In: J. H. Rohrer and M. Sherif (eds.). *Social Psychology at the Crossroads.* New York: Harper.

Shor, R. E. 1957. Effect of preinformation upon human characteristics attributed to animated geometric figures. *J. abnorm. soc. Psychol., 54,* 124–126.

Simmel, G. 1921. Sociology of the senses: visual interaction. In: R. E. Park, and E. W. Burgess. *Introduction to the science of sociology.* Chicago: Univ. of Chicago Press.

———. 1950. *The sociology of Georg Simmel.* Translated, edited, and with an introduction by K. H. Wolff. Glencoe, Ill.: Free Press.

Skinner, B. F. 1938. *The behavior of organisms.* New York: Appleton-Century-Crofts.

———. 1950. Are theories of learning necessary? *Psychol. Rev., 57,* 193–216.

Smith, A. 1759. *The theory of moral sentiments.* London: Bell & Daldy, 1869

Smith, A. J. 1957. Similarity of values and its relation to acceptance and the projection of similarity. *J. Psychol., 43,* 251–260.

Snow, C. P. 1951. *The masters.* London: Macmillan.

Sorokin, P. A. 1947. *Society, culture, and personality.* New York: Harper.

Spencer, H. 1873. The principles of psychology. New York: Appleton, Vol. II.

Spiegel, L. A. 1950. The child's concept of beauty: a study in concept formation. *J. genet. Psychol., 77,* 11–23.

Spinoza. 1677. *Philosophy of B. de Spinoza.* Translated by R. H. M. Elwes. New York: Tudor, 1936.

Stagner, R. 1951. Homeostasis as a unifying concept in personality theory. *Psychol. Rev., 58,* 5–18.

Stern, W. 1923. *Die menschliche Persoenlichkeit.* Leipzig: Barth.

———. 1935. *Allgemeine Psychologie auf personalistischer Grundlage.* Haag: M. Nijhoff.

Thibaut, J. W., and H. W. Riecken. 1955. Some determinants and consequences of the perception of social causality. *J. Pers., 24,* 113–134.

Titchener, E. B. 1909. *A textbook of psychology.* New York: Macmillan.

Titus, H. E., and E. P. Hollander. 1957. The California F scale in psychological research: 1950–1955. *Psychol. Bull., 54,* 47–65.

Tolman, E. C. 1932. *Purposive behavior in animals and men.* New York: Century.

Tolman, E. C., and E. Brunswik. 1935. The organism and the causal texture of the environment. *Psychol. Rev.*, *42*, 43–77.

Wapner, G., and T. G. Alper. 1952. Audience and choice behavior. *J. abnorm. soc. Psychol.*, *47*, 222–229.

Werner, H. 1922. Grundfragen der Intensitätspsychologie. *Z. Psychol.*, Ergänzungsband 10.

———. 1948. *Comparative psychology of mental development*, rev. ed. Chicago: Follett.

Wertheimer, M. 1923. Untersuchungen zur Lehre von der Gestalt. II. *Psychol. Forschung*, *4*, 301–350.

———. 1935. Some problems in the theory of ethics. *Social Research*, *2*, 353–367.

Westermarck, E. 1932. *Ethical relativity*. New York: Harcourt, Brace.

White, R. K., B. A. Wright, and T. Dembo. 1948. Studies in adjustment to visible injuries: evaluation of curiosity by the injured. *J. abnorm. soc. Psychol.*, *43*, 13–28.

Whitehead, A. N. 1929. *The aims of education and other essays*. New York: The New American Library, 1949.

Whyte, W. F. 1943. *Street corner society*. Chicago: Univ. of Chicago Press.

Wiese, L. V. 1932. *Systematic sociology*. Adapted and amplified by H. Becker. New York: Wiley.

Woodworth, R. S., and H. Schlosberg. 1955. *Experimental psychology*. New York: Holt.

Wright, B. A. 1942. Altruism in children and the perceived conduct of others. *J. abnorm. soc. Psychol.*, *37*, 218–233.

Wright, H. F. 1937. The influence of barriers upon strength of motivation. *Contr. Psychol. Theor.*, *1*, 3. Durham, N. C.: Duke Univ. Press.

Young, P. T. 1955. The role of hedonic processes in motivation. M. R. Jones (ed.). *Nebraska symposium on motivation*. Lincoln: Univ. of Nebraska Press.

Zimmer, H. 1956. Motivational factors in dyadic interaction. *J. Pers.*, *24*, 251–262.

Znaniecky, F. 1925. *The laws of social psychology*. Chicago: Univ. of Chicago Press.

# Author Index

*313*

# Subject Index